The Ethics

Treatise on the Emendation of the Intellect

Selected Letters

Translated by
SAMUEL SHIRLEY

Edited, with Introductions, by
SEYMOUR FELDMAN

Hackett Publishing Company
Indianapolis / Cambridge

Baruch Spinoza: 1632–1677

Copyright © 1992 by Hackett Publishing Company, Inc.

Printed in the United States of America

Second edition, first printing

99 98 97 96 95 94 93 92 91   1 2 3 4 5 6 7 8 9 10

Cover design by Listenberger Design & Associates

Interior design by James N. Rogers

For further information, please address
  Hackett Publishing Company, Inc.
  P.O. Box 44937, Indianapolis, Indiana 46244-0937

Library of Congress Cataloging-in-Publication Data

Spinoza, Benedictus de, 1632–1677.
    [Selections. English. 1991]
    The ethics; Treatise on the emendation of the intellect; Selected letters
/ Spinoza; translated by Samuel Shirley; edited with introductions by
Seymour Feldman.—2nd ed.
        p.   cm.
    Includes bibliographical references and index.
    ISBN 0-87220-131-7 (alk. paper):
    ISBN 0-87220-130-9 (pbk.)
    1. Ethics, Modern—17th century.   2. Knowledge, Theory of—Early
works to 1800.   3. Spinoza, Benedictus de, 1632–1677—Correspondence.
4. Philosophers—Netherlands—Correspondence. I. Shirley, Samuel,
1912–   . II. Feldman, Seymour. III. Title: Ethics. IV. Title: Treatise
on the emendation of the intellect. V. Title: Selected letters.
  B3958.E5   1991   91-27212
  199′.492—dc20   CIP

The paper used in this publication meets the minimum requirements of
American National Standard for Information Services—Permanence of
Paper for Printed Library Material, ANSI Z39.48-1984.

∞

CONTENTS

INTRODUCTION

I

If Socrates' execution was the key event in Plato's life that shaped his subsequent career in philosophy, Spinoza's excommunication from the Jewish community of Amsterdam in 1656 at the age of twenty-four was similarly the critical episode in his life and thought. For it affected not only where, how, and with whom he spoke and lived; it also thrust him into an intellectual world that would henceforth be his own and would claim him for its own. From that day on Spinoza was no longer a resident of the Jewish quarter of Amsterdam, but of the Dutch Netherlands and indeed of Western Civilization. How did this come about and what was its significance for his philosophy?

To understand why Spinoza was excommunicated, we must first say something about the Jewish world of seventeenth-century Amsterdam. But to do this is to take us back not only further in time but to a different geographical setting. Spinoza was a Sephardic Jew, i.e. his parents were originally exiles from the Iberian peninsula where Spanish- and Portuguese-speaking Jews had lived for over a thousand years. In 1391, many Spanish Jews had been forcibly converted to Christianity; thereafter, increasing social, economic, and religious pressures led to even more conversions. It became evident to Spanish authorities, however, that many of these new converts—usually referred to as 'conversos,' 'New Christians,' or 'marranos'—were not sincere Christians, and that in some measure and form they still practiced Judaism. In 1478 the notorious Spanish Inquisition was established to deal with this problem, and for the next three centuries the Spanish Empire, both in Europe and in the New World, experienced continued inquisitional trials and executions of those New Christians who were suspected of "Judaizing." In 1492, a further measure was introduced to solve Spain's "Jewish Problem": all practicing Jews were to be expelled unless they chose to convert. Given their strong attachment to their homeland and to their Spanish cultural heritage, as well as their family ties and economic interests, plus the perils of transportation and emigration, a considerable number of Jews converted, thus increasing both the class of New Christians and the work of the Inquisition. The fate of the Portuguese Jewish community, from which Spinoza's family probably originated, was even worse. In 1497 all were converted by force, not having even the option of exile. Obviously, the sincerity of the Portuguese *converso* was even more doubtful. Throughout the late fifteenth, sixteenth, and seventeenth centuries there existed then in both Spain and Portugal, and their new colonies, a group of Christians whose loyalty to the Catholic faith was either tenuous or

1

suspected by the Old Christians as being of doubtful strength. And so the Inquisition persisted in its work. One immediate consequence of this series of events was the continuous and often clandestine flow of refugees from the Iberian peninsula to the few places of relative religious freedom, such as non-Spanish Italy, Germany, the Muslim world, and finally the newly established Republic of the Netherlands, which had achieved its independence from Spain in 1609 after a struggle of almost one hundred years. Eventually Amsterdam became the center of the Spanish-Portuguese Diaspora in the Christian world. And it was to Amsterdam that Spinoza's parents fled after having lived in Portugal as Catholics.

Now the Catholic background of the *converso* who reconverted to Judaism, as did Spinoza's parents when they arrived in Amsterdam around 1622, was of no small significance in shaping the thinking of these old-new Jews. This is especially the case where the individual had been exposed to a university education, which in Spain or Portugal meant a more than liberal dose of Scholastic philosophy and theology. Some *conversos* who reconverted to Judaism did not shake off their Catholic upbringing and culture easily; some never did. The Amsterdam Jewish Community was therefore far from monolithic and reflected a variety of religious and philosophical perspectives, of which some were close to heresy, other not too distant from Christianity. The most notorious example of one old-new Jew who failed in his transition from Christianity to Judaism was Uriel D'Acosta, who committed suicide in 1640 after several excommunications from and re-admissions to the Amsterdam Jewish community. Spinoza was only eight at the time; but *l'affaire d'Acosta* must have been talked about for years afterwards. There were other such cases of difficult intellectual and religious re-adjustments, and one in particular will be important for understanding Spinoza's ultimate break with and excommunication from Judaism.

Before this happened, however, Spinoza had undergone the traditional Jewish educational program of Sephardic Jewry. In contrast to the Ashkenazic, or German-Polish, academies, which focus upon Talmudic studies, Sephardic schools stressed the study of Hebrew language and Bible, subjects that stood Spinoza in good stead when he came to write several of his later works and in which he had an abiding interest. It was common for a Jewish adolescent to continue his studies informally after his completion of the standard curriculum at the age of about fourteen, even while engaged in some trade or commercial pursuit. Spinoza himself worked with his father and brother in the family importing business until his eventual break with the Jewish community. Nevertheless, during this ten-year interim he continued his studies either by informal attendance in the more advanced Jewish school or by his own reading. It was during this period that he began his study of the medieval Jewish philosophers Maimonides (1140–1205), Gersonides (1288–1344), and Hasdai Crescas (1340–1410), in whose writings the whole range of Aristotelian philosophy in its medieval setting was extensively and intensively discussed. It is likely that his study of the classical Jewish thinkers raised for Spinoza doubts which ultimately mushroomed into full-scale philosophical perplexities. Perhaps it was at this time too that he began his study of Latin, a language familiar to many of his coreligionists in Amsterdam and certainly to one of his teachers, Menasseh ben Israel, who wrote several philosophical treatises in that language. However, on this point there is no certainty; a number of Spinoza biographers date Spinoza's entry into the world of Latin letters *after* his excommunication. If he did know Latin prior to that event, he would have been able to read Descartes' writings, and these materials would only have aggravated Spinoza's philosophical perplexities. (Remember that Descartes lived in Holland from 1628 until 1649 and that many of his writings were first published there.)

All these philosophical musings reached maturation under a catalyst which appeared in the form of a certain Dr. Juan de Prado, a recent old-new Jew who arrived in Amsterdam in the 1640s already a man of about thirty and a practicing physician and graduate of Spanish universities. The work of Carl Gebhardt and I.S. Revah has clearly indicated that Juan de Prado gave Spinoza the encouragement, and perhaps some of the ideas that eventually led to trouble with the Jewish religious establishment. [I.S. Revah, *Spinoza et Le Dr. Juan de Prado* (Paris, 1959)] On the basis of a close study of the polemical writings of another such reconverted *converso*, Isaac Orobio de Castro, who came to Amsterdam after Spinoza's death in 1677, Revah has shown that under de Prado's stimulus there existed a "free-thinking" circle within the Sephardic community in Amsterdam. This group no longer accepted the traditional Jewish-Christian dogmas of the divinity of Scripture, the election of Israel, and the popular ideas about the Hereafter. This free-thinking circle began to propound a more philosophical, or naturalistic, conception of God and religion, one that would become more fashionable in the next century in the intellectual circles of London, Paris, and Berlin, but was still too precocious for seventeenth-century Amsterdam. By 1656 these ideas were translated into action, and Prado and Spinoza were no longer fully observant Jews. Since traditional Judaism has always given greater emphasis to action than to dogma, it was this divergence from *orthopraxis* that led the religious authorities to inquire into the matter, resulting in Spinoza's excommunication in 1656. Prado was excommunicated too, but recanted and was readmitted into the community in 1658. Soon thereafter, however, he was excommunicated again. Until 1659 Spinoza was in contact with de Prado and both continued to develop their radical views and on occasion revealed them to others. It was probably the latter activity that caused the Jewish authorities in 1660 to petition the Amsterdam municipal government to expel Spinoza from the city as a menace to "all piety and morals," whether Jewish or Christian. No doubt the Jewish leaders wanted to preserve the residence rights granted to the Jews, rights that stipulated the inner control of heresy and heterodoxy. Spinoza's excommunication and exile from Amsterdam meant a complete social, economic, and religious break with the Jewish community. Henceforth, he was to live as an outcast from the Jews of Holland. What intellectual and social relations he was to have would be found elsewhere.

For the remainder of his life Spinoza resided outside Amsterdam, first in several small villages near the city and finally in The Hague, where he died. It was commonly believed until recently that he supported himself by making lenses for telescopes and other purposes. However, it is more likely that his optical activities were scientifically motivated. If so, we still are not too well-informed as to his means of support. It is possible that he was supported at least in part by his friends, who were devoted to him. These friends were themselves "marginal" members of the Protestant Dutch community; after all, orthodox Christians would find Spinoza equally intolerable as would orthodox Jews. The high and deep regard with which they held Spinoza is reflected in his Correspondence, of which some specimens are included in this edition. Spinoza spent the remainder of his relatively short life thinking, performing scientific experiments in optics, chemistry, and perhaps too in anatomy, writing, and in conversation with his friends. Eventually his reputation grew, and he was offered a professorship at the famous Heidelberg University in Germany. Spinoza rejected the invitation on grounds that such a position might compromise his philosophical principles and freedom. Although he never left the Netherlands, his philosophical correspondence with Henry Oldenburg, the secretary of the London Royal Society, kept him informed of scientific ideas in England, especially of the chemical experiments of Robert Boyle. He was visited by the German thinkers Tschirnhaus and Leibniz, both of whom were close students of the *Ethics* even before it was published. Never too strong physically, Spinoza began to show signs of increasing poor health; perhaps he had inherited a congenital lung disease which caused the deaths of his mother and sister. He died on February 21, 1677. Contemporary accounts of his last days testify to his serenity and moral strength as he died, which is what we should expect of someone who wrote "A free man thinks of nothing less than of death, and his wisdom is not a meditation upon death but upon life." (*Ethics*, Proposition LXVII, IV) Spinoza's friends published his unpublished writings posthumously in 1677, first in Latin and then in Dutch in 1678. It is not without significance that these published editions did not contain Spinoza's full name, but only his initials. His friends were quite aware of the radical and novel features of his philosophy; and the inscription on Spinoza's signet-ring of 'caute,' i.e. 'be careful,' guided them in the publication of his writings. During his lifetime Spinoza himself published only two books: *The Principles of Descartes' Philosophy* and *The Theological-Political Treatise*; the latter bore only Spinoza's initials. Several of Spinoza's letters testify to his realization of the revolutionary character of his ideas and his unwillingness to publish in particular the *Ethics*, for fear of popular and religious opposition. [Letters 43, 44, 68, 73, 75, and 83 reveal Spinoza's reaction to criticisms of his *Theological-Political Treatise*; Letter 6 his worry about the theologians' response to his *Short Treatise on God, Man and his Well-Being*; Letter 13 his reluctance to publish the *Ethics*.] That his fears were justified will be seen when we turn to the *Ethics* itself.

II

One of the outstanding Spinoza scholars of our century, H.A. Wolfson, claimed that Spinoza was the first modern philosopher, a title and dignity usually assigned to Descartes. [H.A. Wolfson, *Philo: Foundations of Religious Philosophy in Judaism, Christianity and Islam* (Cambridge, Mass. 1948), volume II, chapter 14.] By the term 'modern' Wolfson understood not a chronological concept but an adjective that describes a certain style or type of philosophizing. To understand what this adjective connotes we have to contrast it with one of its contraries: 'medieval.' Medieval philosophy for Wolfson emerged in human history when the human wisdom of the Greeks met with the divine wisdom of the Jews in Alexandria in the person of Philo Judaeus (20 B.C.–A.D. 50). Philo was the progenitor of medieval philosophy because he proceeded to philosophize, using Greek materials, about his religious heritage, the Jewish Scriptures. In doing so he set the goals and style of a new kind of philosophizing, unknown for the most part to the Greeks, that has endured to this day. This mode of philosophy begins with certain "Scriptural Assumptions" which it takes over as divinely revealed, and then attempts to understand and prove them philosophically. During the period prior to Descartes the philosophical sources used for this purpose were of course taken from the Greeks; but this is not essential. Someone who sees philosophy as did Philo, yet uses *any* philosophical tradition in his attempt to understand Scripture philosophically, is still a medieval philosopher no matter whether he relies upon Aristotle, Husserl, or Wittgenstein. Medieval philosophy comes to an end or is abandoned when the philosopher cuts his ties to a religious tradition as a source of information, when he relies solely upon natural means for arriving at philosophical truth. According to Wolfson, Spinoza was the first philosopher since Philo who succeeded in making a clean and decisive break with religious tradition, and thus merits the title 'the first modern philosopher.'

Although Descartes' philosophy does exhibit certain novel features, and despite his own claims to originality, Descartes was still concerned to defend many of the fundamental "medieval" theses found in medieval philosophical texts of Augustine, Aquinas, and Scotus. The dedication to the Faculty of the Sorbonne that serves as a preface to the *Meditations* clearly betrays the medieval character of Descartes' philosophical enterprise:

> I have always considered that the two questions respecting God and the Soul were the chief of those that ought to be demonstrated by

philosophical rather than theological arguments . . . it certainly does not seem possible to persuade infidels of any religion, indeed, we may almost say, of any moral virtue, unless, to begin with, we prove these two facts by means of natural reason." [R. Descartes, *Philosophical Works*, trans. E.S. Haldane and G.R.T. Ross (Cambridge U. Press, 1970) volume I, page 133.]

This passage is virtually identical with Aquinas' statement of his goals and procedures in the first book of the *Summa Contra Gentiles*, chapters 2–3. Descartes never emancipated himself from his medieval philosophical education and commitments, a fact that both Spinoza and modern historical research on Descartes have clearly recognized. [See E. Gilson's classic studies on the "medieval Descartes": *Index scolastico-cartésien* (Paris 1913): *Études sur le role de la pensée medievale dans la formation du système cartésien* (Paris 1951)] Indeed, we might say that Spinoza's philosophy is an attempt to show both how medieval Descartes' philosophy is and what has to be done to "modernize" philosophy. The *Ethics* represents a complete and radical rupture with the medieval philosophical legacy that still pervaded the seventeenth-century philosophical world.

The medieval-Cartesian philosophy—and despite the differences between the medievals and Descartes, Spinoza saw them as doing the same thing—was for Spinoza incoherent because it contained several ineliminable contradictions about some of the more fundamental philosophical issues. Consider, for example, the problem of creation. From Philo through the seventeenth century many philosophers were continually attempting to prove the temporal beginning of the universe in order to defend Scripture against the Aristotelian theory of the eternity of the world. Although Descartes himself abandoned this enterprise, he accepted the traditional religious doctrine on faith, realizing, perhaps only unconsciously, that this was a hopeless task. It was hopeless to prove creation, Spinoza was to demonstrate, not because human reason was impotent, as Descartes believed, but because creation of the universe is simply a false hypothesis; indeed, it is for Spinoza utterly incoherent. For how can a being that is *ex hypothesi* incorporeal produce something that is corporeal? [There was a medieval version of Aristotle's eternity theory; however, it was not too subtly disguised by the language of creation. For example, the Muslim philosophers Al-Farabi, Avicenna, and Averroes spoke of "eternal creation," as did the Jewish theologian Hasdai Crescas (S. Feldman, "The Theory of Eternal Creation in Hasdai Crescas and Some of his Predecessors," *Viator* 11 (1980), 289–320). Spinoza was familiar with Crescas, and there is a strong likelihood that he was influenced by him on this and other topics. However, on this particular point, Spinoza went at least one step further than did Crescas: he never speaks in the *Ethics* of the creation of the universe, and he drops the teleological tone of the medieval eternal creation theory.] Or consider the medieval-Cartesian theory of human nature. On this view man is a composite being, comprising both mental and physical substances that somehow not only coexist but interact. Moreover, one of these substances, the mind, is regarded as primary and privileged, having the job of directing and controlling the other, the body, and being capable of surviving the latter's demise and enjoying a supernal and individual immortality. But for Spinoza this concept of man was just as incoherent as the theory of creation, and for the same reason: How could an incorporeal substance be united with and govern a corporeal substance? As Spinoza studied Maimonides, the other medieval thinkers, and Descartes, he concluded that a radically new philosophy was needed, one that would once and for all cut the umbilical cord which tied philosophy to religion and that would provide a coherent and true account of man's place in the world. If this could be achieved, human happiness would be attainable through man's own efforts and devices. The *Ethics* is after all a book designed to teach us how to be happy in the life that we have, which had been the goal of philosophy for the Greeks.

Two stylistic features of the *Ethics* are worthy of our attention before we discuss some of the major themes of the work. First, in the opening to the title-page of the *Ethics* the reader will note that Spinoza tells his reader that this work is written in a geometrical manner ("ordine geometrico demonstrata"): the propositions of Spinoza's philosophy are presented and proved in a quasi-geometrical manner, with the definitions and axioms clearly laid out and the proof itself developed step-by-step. Second, Spinoza's terminology is the familiar Aristotelian-Cartesian vocabulary of 'substance,' 'mode,' 'cause,' 'thought,' 'extension,' and so forth. Concerning Spinoza's geometrical method, a considerable amount of scholarly debate has attempted to determine whether this method is purely stylistic or has some important philosophical significance. The history of philosophy does not lack specimens of this method of philosophical writing: some of the sixteenth- and seventeenth-century Spanish and Dutch theologians and philosophers wrote some of their works in a very formal manner; Descartes too sketched an axiomatic exposition of some of his theses in the second set of replies to the *Meditations*. Nevertheless, Spinoza's *Ethics* is perhaps the first purely philosophical treatise that presents its conclusions consistently and completely in an axiomatic manner. In this respect it is the paradigm of the hypothetical-deductive method suggested by Aristotle in his *Posterior Analytics* as the model for a scientific theory, which until Spinoza was only exemplified by Euclid's geometry. A few decades after Spinoza this method found another advocate and practitioner in Isaac Newton, whose *Mathematical Principles of Natural Philosophy* (1687) is the finest specimen of this genre in the natural sciences.

Wolfson claimed that Spinoza's choice of the formal-axiomatic method was based upon literary and pedagogical reasons. He rightly reminds us that many, if not all, of Spinoza's conclusions were presented in an informal, nonaxiomatic style in his early *Short Treatise*.[1] However, it may be that these very same stylistic reasons express philosophical

1. H. Wolfson, *Philosophy of Spinoza*, vol. I, chapter 1.

motivations as well. If, for example, Spinoza chose the geometrical method because of the clarity and evidence of Euclidean proofs which he wanted to emulate in his own work, this tells us that clarity and evidence are philosophical, and not only literary, virtues and requirements. Unlike Descartes, Spinoza really believed that clear and distinct ideas were true, indeed self-evidently true. Descartes enunciated this belief; but he did not consistently adhere to it throughout, and with some disastrous results for his philosophy, as his critics were quick to point out. This firm and unshakable conviction that truth resides in clear and distinct ideas, which man is not only capable of possessing but actually possesses, and that these ideas are fertile enough to produce a complete system of phi- losophy which, if not the best, is certainly a true system of philosophy— this conviction Spinoza never abandoned. Given these assumptions about the role of clear and distinct ideas, the nature of truth and cer- tainty, and the need to pursue these notions to the end, Spinoza's adop- tion of the formal method is what we would have expected. The personal ruminations of Descartes' *Meditations* or the polished literary style of some of the Italian Renaissance philosophical littérateurs was no sub- stitute for rigorous philosophical proof. In using the geometrical method Spinoza was telling his reader: this is the proper way to do philosophy; for philosophy is a science based upon clear and precise definitions, self- evident axioms, and valid argumentation. Utilizing this method Spinoza expresses and practices his epistemological convictions as he pursues metaphysical, psychological, and moral questions. For Spinoza one should not begin to philosophize by reporting one's own doubts or by in- venting "metaphysical doubts" in order to reach certainty, as did Descartes. This can only lead to a philosophical dead-end: doubts breed doubts. Clear and distinct ideas, however, cannot be doubted; and that is why Spinoza begins his *Ethics* by laying down such ideas as definitions and axioms. Indeed, for Spinoza doubt is impossible. Spinoza's method then is his philosophy.

When we look at Spinoza's vocabulary, it is indeed thoroughly permeated by the medieval-Cartesian semantics. One might then raise the question, why do you say he was the first modern philosopher? If he was so radical, why didn't he create a new philosophical language, as did Aristotle or Hegel? The use of traditional terminology only misleads us into thinking that Spinoza was doing the same thing as did Descartes or Maimonides. A new philosophy should have a new vocabulary.

These queries and objections are quite natural and understandable; and occasionally both beginning and advanced readers of the *Ethics* often wish that Spinoza had completely cut his umbilical cord to his philosophical parents. Yet, the traditional terminology has at least one advantage: it allows Spinoza to debate with his predecessors on common ground and with a common language. Spinoza really wanted to sever his ties with his philosophical past. One very effective way to do this is to come to grips head-on with this burden and all its trappings and to show that it is empty in its own terms. What Spinoza does then is to take the philosophical language of his predecessors and turn it against them, by showing that if these terms are clearly understood and consistently thought through, different conclusions will follow.

Let us take one example. If, as Descartes postulated, a substance is that which needs nothing else in order to exist, then there is, as he himself admits, only one substance, God. However, Descartes goes on to say that it is permissible to speak of substances that are not totally self-sufficient and autonomous: created minds and bodies. (Descartes, *Principles of Philosophy* I:51) To Spinoza this philosophical-linguistic license leads to serious logical and metaphysical sins. In adopting Descartes' definition of substance but by adhering to it consistently, Spinoza produces both an effective argument against Descartes and a new theory of substance and God.

III

God and Nature

Some of the great systematic philosophers of the past proceeded to philosophize from an underlying perception of *the way things are*—an intuition, to use one of Spinoza's key terms, of the way everything hangs together. This fundamental insight gives birth to a system, which represents the unfolding of the ramifications and consequences of that intuition. This is certainly true for Spinoza. The last word in the first prayer he learned in Hebrew stayed with him all his life: "Hear O Israel, the Lord our God the Lord is *one*." (Deuteronomy 6:4; my italics.) Unity is the dominant and pervasive theme in Spinoza's philosophy. Almost obsessed with the perception of the oneness of all things, he could not but be offended or troubled by some of the main assertions or consequences of Aristotelian and Cartesian metaphysics; for these latter philosophies are in essence dualistic. In Aristotle's case we have an immutable and unextended God that exists apart from a mutable and extended world that he did not create; in Descartes' system we have again an immutable and unextended God that creates, however, a mutable and extended universe. Against Aristotle Spinoza asks, if God is totally independent of the universe, what need is there for him? If God does have some role to play, how can he perform this role if he is so unlike the universe? Against Descartes this latter question is even more pertinent; for Descartes stresses the radical difference between unextended, mental substances and extended, bodily substances. But if the difference is so great, Spinoza asks, how does an *unextended* substance create *extended* substances? Moreover, how is it possible for an extended substance to interact with an unextended substance?

Another problem in the philosophical tradition was the plurality of substances posited by both Aristotle and Descartes. The problem arises from the Aristotelian conception of a substance as an independently existing entity. But if this is what a substance is, Spinoza now asks, why would it interact with anything else? After all, if it is independent, then it is self-sufficient. Either there is only one independent thing or if many they do not interact at all. Spinoza opted for the first of these two alternatives; Leibniz chose the second. Thus Spinoza replaces the pluralism of substance of Aristotle and Descartes with his own brand of metaphysical monism, which asserts that there is one and only one substance. The first fifteen Propositions in Book I of the *Ethics* are devoted to proving this claim.

One key feature of Spinoza's monism is that substance, or God, is characterizable by an infinite number of attributes, each one of which expresses God's infinite nature. An attribute was defined by Descartes as "the principle property that constitutes the essence and nature of a substance . . . and on which all the other properties depend." [Descartes, *Principles of Philosophy*, Part I, principle 53] For Descartes mental substances are defined by the attribute of thought, whereas physical substances are constituted by the attribute of extension. Although Spinoza accepts this general account of what attribute is, he diverges from Descartes in his novel claim that God is constituted by the attribute of extension. After all, if God is infinite, then he must have *all* the attributes, of which extension is one. Spinoza's God is then quite different from the unextended being of Aristotle, the medievals, and Descartes. By ascribing extension to God, Spinoza was able to overcome the dualist dilemmas that plagued Aristotelian and Cartesian metaphysics. No longer are we pressed to account for the creation of an extended universe by an unextended creator or to explain how an incorporeal entity can interact with a corporeal entity. For Spinoza there is a fundamental continuity between the ultimate cause of everything, God, or substance, and that which is caused, or the *modes*. This continuity is an expression and consequence of God's causal activity. Spinoza's God is an "effacious" being that is incessantly productive; for, "from the necessity of the divine nature there must follow an infinite number of things in infinite ways" [Prop. 16, Book I]. The absolutely infinite being God is infinitely causative; hence, the world is "maximally rich": it contains everything that can possibly exist. Thus, the universe too is for Spinoza infinite, not only in duration but also in size and content. It would then seem, however, that we have *two* actual infinites, God and the universe, both exemplifying the attribute of extension. How can this be? If two volumes of the same magnitude occupy the same space, they coincide and become one. Is this true too for God and the universe? In some sense, yes. Now we have come to one of the more fundamental yet difficult theses in Spinoza's metaphysics: God and nature are in some sense identical.

The identification of God with Nature, which is reflected in Spinoza's frequent phrase 'God, or Nature,' led many of his first readers to accuse him of atheism. Nor was this accusation restricted to the unwitting only; no less a philosopher than David Hume characterized Spinoza as an "atheist." [D. Hume, *A Treatise of Human Nature,* Book I, section 5, pp. 240–241 in the Selby-Bigge edition.] But as the German poet Novalis remarked, Spinoza was "a God-intoxicated man"; indeed, there are passages in the *Ethics* in which Spinoza speaks of God with almost mystical ardor, especially in Part V. With due respect to Hume, we must say that Spinoza was no atheist. But what about pantheism? By equating nature with God did Spinoza deify nature so that everything is divine? It is clear that for Spinoza no individual mode is itself a 'God'; nor is the total collection of such individual things God. God is no mere aggregate that can be divided up or decomposed; yet, each mode is a particular manifestation of God, and the whole infinite system of modes is collectively the "face" of God, or God expressed concretely. In this sense we cannot sever nature from God or conversely; for God is, as Spinoza stresses, the indwelling, or immanent, cause of the world, just as all the modes, both individually and collectively, are in God. The total dependence of all modes upon God and the intimate and incessant causal activity of God obliterate any real gap between nature and God. Because the term 'pantheism' is vague and misleading, some commentators have suggested instead 'pan-en-theism': "everything is in God." But, as we have indicated, this is only one side of the coin: true, everything is in God; yet God is in everything too. Perhaps it would be better to avoid using both terms; neither label is an appropriate title for Spinoza's system. Better to employ Spinoza's own expression—'God, or Nature.'

But the term 'nature' has in this context a dual connotation. In the Scholium to Prop. 29 of Part I Spinoza distinguishes between two different facets of nature, which he labels *Natura Naturans* and *Natura Naturata.* Unfortunately, there are no suitable English equivalents for these technical terms in philosophical Latin. The Latin 'natura' derives from the verb 'to grow,' 'to be born'; this in turn is derived from the Greek 'phuo' and 'physis,' from which we get the English 'physics,' a *natural* science. Reflected in this classical etymology is the idea of nature as a dynamical system of growth and activity. The phrase 'Natura Naturans' is a Scholastic term, in which the word 'naturans' is the active participle, "nature naturing," which for Spinoza connotes the active aspect of God, or nature. Here God is described as manifesting infinite energy, or power. The phrase 'Natura Naturata,' "nature natured," however, contains the passive participle, 'naturata,' signifying nature as produced and referring to the modes. Nature, then, exhibits two aspects: one productive, the other produced; yet both are different dimensions of one and the same substance, God.

Spinoza has described for us a picture of an infinite but unitary system of interrelated things and events. It is a further consequence of such a conception that all phenomena satisfy fixed laws. Nature is not only an ordered system, a point insisted upon by Aristotle and repeated by many of the medievals, but it is a deterministic system. It is a world wherein not only lawfulness reigns but in which purpose is absent. And here we have another of Spinoza's radical conclusions. His natural determinism not only precludes chance, contingency, and irregularity; it disallows our customary conception of events and things as exemplifying design and goals. Aristotle's "natural teleology" has been completely abandoned in favor of a model according to which nature "obeys" strict mechanistic laws that do not express or manifest any ultimate goals and purpose. The traditional dicta that God or nature does nothing in vain, that God does everything for the best and that there are no gaps in nature—are all reinterpreted by Spinoza in such a way that we get a totally different perspective on the world. True—God does nothing in vain; for God acts according to the laws of his perfect nature, which is true freedom. True—God does everything for the best; for everything that happens happens necessarily according to God's nature, which is infinitely perfect. True—nature manifests no discontinuities; but that is because God acts regularly, consistently, and omnipotently. The common ways of describing natural phenomena as good for some purpose are all "fictions," whereby man imposes his own arbitrary and limited perspective upon nature. Here Spinoza anticipates the dominant tendency in modern biology, which dispenses with teleological notions in favor of the conceptual apparatus of biochemical and biophysical theories. All of nature is for Spinoza too a system in which ultimate purposes have no sense.

Human Nature

Since all of nature constitutes a unitary system, indeed one substance, human nature must be seen as an integrated element within this total complex. The medieval-Cartesian attempt to distinguish man from the rest of nature, to elevate him above the rest of the animal kingdom, was seen by Spinoza as not only an illusory metaphysical extravagance but also as a symptom of a faulty psychology, whose moral consequences are serious, as we shall see. Keep in mind that the title of Spinoza's treatise is 'Ethics,' i.e. it is a book that is concerned with human life and the right way to live. But there is no use in writing about ethics if we have an erroneous conception of nature in general and of human nature in particular. Spinoza has attempted to give us a true account of the former in Part I; he now sets out to achieve the latter in Parts II and III.

Implicit in the medieval-Cartesian legacy is a philosophical theme that goes all the way back to Plato: psychological dualism.[2] From Plato through Descartes man was conceived as a composite entity comprising both mental and physical substances. For Plato, most of the medievals, and Descartes, these two elements were radically distinct in nature and separable, especially after the decay of the body. And thus we have the doctrine of the immortality of the soul. From this psychological dualism a moral dualism was developed: the soul has, by virtue of its superior and immortal nature, the function of governing the body, in particular of ruling over the latter's passions. That reason has the power and duty to exercise this role was virtually an unquestioned assumption in philosophy from Plato through Descartes. Spinoza rejects this whole tradition.

---

2. A microscale replica of the macroscale metaphysical dualism referred to in the previous section.

To see why let us begin with Descartes, whom Spinoza chooses as his philosophical antagonist. Descartes bequeathed to philosophy a very strong form of psychological dualism that asserts the following:

1. Man consists of two radically different substances, mind and body.

2. Although distinct in nature these two substances are united into one individual.

3. Again, despite their dissimilarities, mind and body interact.

4. Reason has the unlimited capacity to control and direct passion.

Spinoza believes that all of these claims are false.

Consider Thesis I, which is the cornerstone of the Cartesian theory of human nature. Even prior to Spinoza several of Descartes' more acute readers realized that his psychological dualism was difficult sledding. The Princess Elizabeth of Bohemia quickly perceived that if two things are as unlike as Descartes claimed the soul and the body are, how can they be said to be united and to interact? After all, if oil and water don't mix, why should we expect the mind and the body to get together and get along with each other? It just doesn't seem plausible. Descartes' replies to the Princess were perfunctory or feeble, and many of Descartes' contemporaries and immediate successors attempted to develop alternative accounts of human nature that would avoid the difficulties of Descartes' version of psychological dualism.

One alternative was to eliminate entirely the mind from philosophical discourse. This was the route chosen by Hobbes and the materialists, who reduced man to a set of physical particles in motion. Another alternative was to define man solely as a mind, or a perceiver with all its perceptions. This was the route taken by Berkeley and the later Leibniz. Spinoza took neither road. Man is a finite mode of an infinitely various substance, two of whose attributes are thought and extension. This means that man too is both thinking and extended; but unlike Descartes' man, Spinoza's human mode is not a composite substance, whose elements—mind and body—are mysteriously united. Rather, each and every human being can be considered as a physical organism capable of performing a variety of physical functions and activities; it can also be viewed as a mental agent engaging in all sorts of intellectual and psychical operations. The former set of functions falls under the attribute of extension, the latter under the attribute of thought, both attributes being exemplified in man since he is a mode of God, who is constituted by at least these two attributes. These two basic kinds of activities are not the expressions of two radically different constituents in human nature that are either causally related, as in Descartes, or totally independent, as in Malebranche. Rather, there is *one* series of events or processes that can be described either as extended or as mental modes. Indeed, since substance, God, or nature is infinite, there is an infinite number of ways in which one could in principle explain human nature. But Spinoza speaks only of two: the way of extension and the way of thought. To elucidate this notion let us refer to Spinoza himself.

In Letter 9 Spinoza tries to explain to his correspondent, by means of a biblical illustration, how the indivisible one substance God can have many distinct attributes. Of the three Patriarchs the last was called by the names 'Jacob' and 'Israel.' Now the first name signifies to a Hebrew speaker the connotation of clinging to the heel (Genesis 25:24–26), whereas the second connotes victory over the angel (Gen. 32:23–32). But it is the same person who both seized the heel of his brother and who fought with the angel. Spinoza uses this example to make the general point that substance can have many attributes without itself being many. The example can also serve to explain how one mode can exhibit two very different kinds of activities without being divisible into two radically different kinds of elements. For just as the names 'Jacob' and 'Israel' have different connotations but denote the same person, so too the attributes of thought and extension have different connotations although they are manifested in one and the same individual. But they are exemplified not as two radically distinct constituent elements within the same person, as Descartes believed. Nor is it the case that when we describe someone as thinking we really are referring to movements in his nervous system, as Hobbes claimed; or that when we describe someone as eating an apple we are referring to his sensations of eating the apple, as Berkeley believed. Reducing mind to matter or matter to mind is just as wrong as marrying mind to matter without explaining how this union can be consummated. For Spinoza, there is just the human being, who can be conceived either as a mode of extension, a body, or as a mode of thought, a mind. In describing man under each of these attributes we commit ourselves to a distinct method of explanation and analysis that if consistently and correctly employed will yield adequate knowledge of man. Each explanatory model is autonomous and legitimate; both are needed to account for the richness of human nature. So long as we do not mix attributes and we refrain from asserting causal connections between modes under different attributes, we are in no danger (Propositions 6 and 7, Part II). Spinoza's monistic metaphysics permits, therefore, multiple possibilities for the description and explanation of human nature.

The Emotions

Once we appreciate how Spinoza solved the Cartesian mind-body riddle, we need not be puzzled any longer by queries concerning the mechanism of mind-body interaction and union. Yet, one serious problem does remain: if human reason is not a semi-independent, superior substance whose job it is to govern bodily passions, as Descartes believed, how are our emotions to be controlled? Indeed, can they be controlled? Actually, it is not clear how this classic question can be formulated within Spinoza's psychology, since he doesn't assert a mind-body dualism at all. If mind and body are just two different ways of looking at the same thing, what sense does it make to ask whether one can control the other? Yet, Spinoza is quite aware of the underlying motivation of the question. He knows that man as a mode is a creature of passion and he firmly believes that man's route to happiness is only by way of moderating and directing these passions. Accordingly, although Spinoza has produced a new psychology, he concerns himself with the traditional ethical problems. It is this new psychology, however, that will provide, he believes, a genuine solution of these problems.

Spinoza's fundamental assumption is that a new method is needed in order to achieve the goal of the classical philosophers, human happiness. The older method—whether in its Greek, medieval, or Cartesian version —proceeded from a moralistic condemnation of human emotion to a list of prescriptions on how to avoid, temper, suppress, or repress passion. Few if any of these thinkers provided a detailed, objective analysis of human emotion. Descartes attempted it in his *Treatise on the Passions;* but to Spinoza, Descartes' efforts were not successful. Spinoza believed that his predecessors failed because either they did not study emotion scientifically, or if they did they used the wrong science or did not complete the project. Having laid down and developed in detail the requisite metaphysical and psychological foundations in Parts I and II Spinoza now proceeds to apply these insights to the question of human emotion and how man is to deal with it. These preliminary truths furnish Spinoza with the tools for an objective, neutral analysis of human passion. Psychology is, then, a natural science, subject to the same methods, norms, and goals as the other sciences. And it is from and upon this naturalistic psychology that Spinoza establishes his moral philosophy.

Beginning with this methodological assumption Spinoza claims that man is capable of having both actions and passions, which Spinoza calls affects, or, in our language, emotions. Stated in this way this thesis seems banal. But by the terms 'action' and 'passion' Spinoza intends something not so trivial. First, we must take the word 'passion' literally as connoting a process or event whereby the individual undergoes an experience that causes him to suffer. The individual is affected by some stimulus that produces in him an affect. The crucial notion here is that of passivity. Second, the basic difference between actions and passions is not, as some of Spinoza's predecessors (e.g. Descartes) insisted, one between a mental state and a physical condition, but a difference between two levels of one and the same emotion. If an affect is understood clearly and distinctly, or in Spinoza's terminology, if we have an "adequate idea" of this emotion, then it is an *action,* i.e. we are the cause of it. Thus, knowledge results in activity. An emotion not adequately understood is a *passion,* because in this situation we do not act but suffer, or in common parlance we are on the "receiving end." Here we are not properly agents, but reagents, i.e. we *react,* not act. Thus, on Spinoza's view, what makes a person an agent is self-knowledge; lacking such knowledge, an individual is merely a passive recipient of external and internal stimuli to which he responds either blindly or inadequately. Self-knowledge, however, means realizing that we are elements within a complicated and diverse system of modes. Again, psychology is part of natural science; and ethics must be grounded in these sciences. Earlier philosophers, Spinoza claims, tried to "supernaturalize" man, and by doing so they made it impossible for us to understand ourselves and to achieve human happiness.

For Spinoza, knowledge is freedom. In Part I Spinoza argues that only God is strictly speaking free; for only God acts consistently according to His nature, which is Spinoza's definition of freedom (Definition 7, Propositions 17, 26, Part I). However, even though a finite mode, and hence capable of only limited action according to his own nature, man by virtue of knowledge can become "relatively free." To the extent that he acquires adequate ideas of himself and his place within nature, man acts, which is to say he responds creatively to his environment and acts upon it. To be free is then to be active, to cause things to happen according to our understanding of the way things are and ought to be. True, we shall never be free as God is; after all, we are but finite modes. Yet, we are capable of knowledge, and to that extent we can be free (Definitions 1, 2, Propositions 1, 3, Part III).

Spinoza's conception of freedom is one version of a theory currently referred to by such terms as 'compatibilism,' 'reconciliationism,' or 'soft-determinism.' This kind of theory attempts to hold on both to a deterministic account of human behavior and to the notion of a free action. Spinoza himself clearly states in the opening list of definitions that 'free' is not opposed to 'necessary' but to 'compelled' (Definition 7, Part I). It is only when we are compelled to do something that we are not free. In such a situation we merely react to the external force; we don't act upon it, since our hands are, so to speak, tied. Another way of looking at Spinoza's concept of freedom is to consider it as a form of self-determinism. A thing is free if and only if it acts according to its *own* nature. But to act is to be a cause of things and not to be a mere recipient and reagent to stimuli. And we act to the extent that we have adequate ideas, especially of ourselves and our place within nature. Spinoza's freedom is then a kind of Socratic self-knowledge that makes its possessor capable of acting, i.e. to behave with knowledge and control. And just as Socrates viewed knowledge as a kind of power, so Spinoza sees freedom as power, the capacity to act with understanding on and in the world. Indeed, Spinoza conceives of man as an organism constantly striving to maximize his power to act, to be free. All emotions that contribute to this *conatus,* or endeavor, increase his freedom; those that decrease it subject man to external and internal forces (Propositions 6, 7, 11, Part III). The freeman is, therefore, the man of power, a person who determines himself.

We are now prepared for the final phase in Spinoza's search for salvation. Armed with the proper understanding of human emotion and human freedom we can confidently confront the most serious obstacle to human happiness, the bondage of the emotions. Spinoza fully appreciates the force of emotion; unlike many of his predecessors, he is neither blind to nor does he underestimate their power. Indeed, for

Spinoza most people live in "servitude to passion." They are slaves to emotion precisely because they are ignorant. It is not that they do not know what is right, as Socrates and the Stoics believed; it is because they do not know what the world and man are like. Virtue, the fundamental concept in Greek and Roman moral philosophy, is for Spinoza power, the capacity to act, which, as we have seen, implies knowledge. The bondage of passion can be loosened through virtue understood as the power to act with understanding. Spinozistic self-knowledge leads to an understanding of one's nature as an organism necessarily subject to emotions; but by the same token it teaches us how this subjection can be weakened.

In Part V Spinoza sketches for us a kind of moral psychotherapy by virtue of which we can liberate ourselves from the bondage of passion. This therapy comprises two levels of cognition: first, knowledge of how our emotions are related to external factors; second, knowledge of how we can attain a certain kind of insight that is, to use religious terminology, redemptive. With respect to the initial level Spinoza prescribes for us a psychological regimen whose general purpose is to detach us from emotion. [The compatibility of these prescriptions with Spinoza's determinism is not evident. After all, if I am suffering from a passion over whose origin in me I had no control, how am I free to eliminate it? Indeed, if I am convinced of Spinoza's advice, this is too determined! So what is the point of Spinoza's moral therapy? Spinoza attempts to answer these objections in Letters 56, 58, and 78.] This is achieved primarily by understanding the nature of the particular emotions, their etiology, and how and to what extent they dominate us. Having acquired this knowledge we are well on the way toward becoming free of emotional bondage. For example, most people become fixated upon some one thing, person, or activity that holds them under its sway. The most obvious example of such a fixation is sexual passion. However, the power and pain of this emotional bond can be enervated and perhaps broken once we realize that this emotion is very likely to cause frustration and perhaps grief. With this knowledge we can redirect the energy we might be tempted to put into such a relationship. Moreover, we come to realize that the particular relationship is not the *only* one that can satisfy our emotional needs. Emotions are transferable. Indeed, we may attain the more important insight that these emotions can be transformed into other emotions that can be satisfied by objects, activities, or persons that are more stable or advantageous. Here Spinoza has anticipated the Freudian notions of obsession and sublimation. Like his twentieth-century counterpart Spinoza did not advocate asceticism, but moderation. He as well as Freud realized that emotions had to be understood and effectively controlled or channeled into profitable directions; otherwise, we suffer.

The second level of knowledge requisite for our happiness has to do with our place within the whole of nature, or, in religious terms, with our relationship to God. Indeed, Spinoza claims that adequate self-knowledge is the first step toward a manifestation of our love of God (Propositions 14, 15, Part V). Remember that to understand oneself is to see oneself as a particular mode within Nature, or God. Self-knowledge is then knowledge of God. But love for Spinoza is an affect, or emotion, that involves knowledge; for love is "joy accompanied by an idea of its cause" (Definitions of the Emotions, Definition 6, Part III). All knowledge, especially in so far as it is defined as adequate ideas, can be related to the idea of the whole system of nature, or God. To know is then to love God, and the more we know the more we love God (Propositions 15, 24, Part V). It is this love of God that constitutes for Spinoza the *summum bonum*, that which makes for human happiness. Because of the essential role of this kind of knowledge in Spinoza's philosophy a special term is used by Spinoza to characterize it: *scientia intuitiva*, or "intuitive knowledge." From an epistemological vantage-point this kind of knowledge is superior to both sense-perception and inference. It is complete and systematic, unlike the fragmentary and partial character of sense-experience; it is synthetic and categorical, unlike the discursive and hypothetical nature of inference. Intuitive cognition enables us to perceive the whole of reality in a comprehensive grasp, wherein everything is "clear and distinct." From this insight we are then able to "descend" to the individual elements of nature and see their mutual relationships in a way that was only dimly, partially, or sequentially perceived heretofore. With intuitive knowledge everything becomes systematically intelligible (Proposition 40, Scholium 2, Part II; Proposition 25, Part V).

From the ethical perspective intuitive cognition results in an understanding of man and his place in the universe such that life becomes not only intelligible but livable. For the *scientia intuitiva* gives us the "highest possible peace of mind" (Proposition 27, Part V). Why is this so? Happiness or, if we prefer, salvation, is the attainment of such knowledge because intuitive knowledge shows us why things happen in the ways they do happen, that they cannot be otherwise, that man is not some extraterrestrial visitor who temporally inhabits this planet and then returns to some foreign domain, and that as an integral element of this one and only world he must learn to live in it. This knowledge can be characterized, Spinoza claims, as an insight of and into eternity, whereby the whole universe and everything within it are perceived "under a form of eternity."

Now we have reached one of the more famous Spinozistic notions, but at the same time a difficult one. For what does Spinoza mean by 'eternity'? He tells us explicitly that he does *not* mean thereby infinite duration, which is how Aristotle and some of his medieval disciples construed this idea (Proposition 29, Part V). For Spinoza, to say that God, or Nature, is eternal is not to imply merely that God exists for infinite time. Rather, there is a sense in which, according to Spinoza, God, or Nature, is *timeless*. This latter notion is also, admittedly, not without its problems. But Spinoza tells in his initial list of definitions in Part I that eternity implies the kind of existence that characterizes a being that is totally self-sufficient and necessary. Indeed, given his definition of freedom, it turns out that for Spinoza the being that is free is also eternal, and conversely; for both of these attributes are features of a being whose existence and activity follow necessarily and only from its own nature. The key term here is 'necessity': that which exists and acts necessarily in complete conformity to its own nature is both free and eternal. For Spinoza only God, or Nature, satisfies totally this condition. In this sense then God is not subject to time; for a being that falls within time is one that is not self-sufficient and perfect. Such entities are truly changeable, whereas God is immutable.

The perception of the universe "under a form of eternity" is the true and most precise insight about God. For we recognize the inevitable and constant character of reality as it is, and with this knowledge we attain happiness. [At this juncture another problem in Spinoza emerges: human immortality. In Propositions 21-31, Part V, Spinoza elusively alludes to a kind of immortality of the mind, which the commentators have found quite difficult to make precise. For some recent discussion of this topic see A. Donagan "Spinoza's Proof of Immortality," in *Spinoza: A Collection of Critical Essays* edited by Marjorie Grene (N.Y. 1973), 241-258; C.L. Hardin, "Spinoza on Immortality and Time," in *Spinoza: New Perspectives*, edited by R. Shahan and J. Biro (Norman, Oklahoma 1978), 129-138.] In one sense this is not a new idea. The ancient Stoics too emphasized the importance of accepting and living according to nature and her inevitable laws. And the medieval philosophers spoke of a stage of intellectual perception that results in a kind of mystic union with its object, in this case, God. In fact, probably the first philosopher Spinoza read, Maimonides, ends his famous *Guide of The Perplexed* with a description of this kind of vision, which he characterizes as love of God through knowledge, a love that unites the lover with the beloved. [Maimonides, *Guide of The Perplexed*, Part III, chapters 51-54.] Another Jewish philosopher, Leone Ebreo, or Judah Abravanel,[3] whose book was owned by Spinoza, referred to this type of intellectual mysticism as "the intellectual love of God," the precise term used by Spinoza in the concluding pages of the *Ethics*. Nevertheless, although the general idea and perhaps even the term may not be new, Spinoza's "intellectual love of God" *(amor intellectualis Dei)* is different from both the Stoic and Maimonidean notions. Spinoza is not a Stoic because he does not believe, as Stoics did, that man is capable of complete self-mastery, that our emotions and behavior are totally under the sway of our will and reason. We have already seen that because man is but a mode of and within nature, his power, and hence freedom, is limited. The Stoic and Cartesian vision of man exercising complete control over his emotional life is for Spinoza just false; it rests upon a totally

---

3. Leone Ebreo, *The Philosophy of Love* (Dialoghi d'Amore), trans. F. Friedeberg-Sealey and J.H. Barnes (London, Soncino, 1937).

inadequate psychology, which in turn is based upon a faulty meta-physics. Moreover, Spinoza rejects the Stoic notions of passivity, with-drawal, and asceticism. For Spinoza, let us recall, freedom, to the extent that we have it, consists in activity, power, and joy. Spinoza's free spirit, to use Nietzsche's term, is a person who says 'Yes' to life, not 'No.' Hap-piness consists not in suppressing or repressing one's emotions but in transforming them into adequate ideas so one can be free and joyful. In Spinoza's own life we can see the difference between the Stoics and himself in his pursuit and cultivation of friendship; for the Stoics, however, friendship was a neutral, or indifferent, activity.

Nor is Spinoza's intellectual love of God identical with the medieval doctrine of union with God through knowledge. To Spinoza this notion of literal union with God is obscure (Definitions of the Emotions, Defini-tion 6, Part III). It rests upon the dualistic metaphysics wherein God and man are conceived as radically distinct, such that the desired union with God has to come about through some supernatural mediation, either through prophecy or incarnation. Spinoza's monistic metaphysics makes prophecy and incarnation both unnecessary and incoherent. True, the in-tuitive cognition that is required for and results in human happiness is "difficult and rare"; but it is attainable by man with the capacities that *he* possesses. The fact that most people have not achieved human hap-piness is, for Spinoza, not to be attributed to some irremediable taint that they have inherited from Adam, but to ignorance and superstition. It was to the defeat and removal of the latter enemies of mankind that Spinoza dedicated his life and his *Ethics*.

TRANSLATOR'S PREFACE

Spinoza's *Ethics*, composed in the Latin of late medieval scholasticism, presents to the reader a formidable and intellectually challenging task. My purpose in this Foreword is merely to help the reader to acclimatize himself to a terminology that is at first bound to appear obscure and forbidding. It need hardly be said that this will not in itself provide a magic key to unlock the meaning of a philosopher who has been variously interpreted by outstanding scholars. But I hope it will assist in the study of a profound thinker who speaks to us today no less cogently than he spoke to his seventeenth-century contemporaries.

My debt to previous translators is obvious, but I would not offer this new version if I did not think that it makes some contribution to the problem of translating Spinoza. I have attempted to elucidate meaning without interposing between Spinoza and the reader, and to this end I occasionally insert in brackets the Latin word I am translating.

The text used is Gebhardt (Heidelberg, 1925).

The Letters of Spinoza are rightly regarded as throwing valuable light on his thinking. A selection from these letters follows the TIE.

Abbreviations Pr. = Proposition.
Cor. = Corollary.
Sch. = Scholium. (An explanatory note which enables Spinoza to escape occasionally from the restrictions imposed by his 'geometrical method.')
Post. = Postulate.
Def. = Definition.
Ax. = Axiom.

The five Parts of the Ethics are indicated by Roman numerals. For example, Cor.2, Pr.17, I = the second Corollary of Proposition 17 of Part I.

Terminology

1. Essence (*Essentia*) and Existence (*Existentia*)

These two concepts have a vital role to play in Spinoza's system, and we can do no better than to quote Spinoza's own words at the end of Chapter 2 of his *Cogitata Metaphysica:* "If any philosopher still doubts whether essence is distinct from existence in created things, there is no need for him to toil away at definitions of essence and existence to

21

remove that doubt. For if he merely approaches a sculptor or wood-carver, they will show him how they conceive in fixed order a non-existent statue, and afterwards bring it into existence.''

A thing's essence is 'what' a thing is. Spinoza often uses the word 'natura,' the nature of the thing, as its equivalent. When the essence of a thing—what the thing essentially is—is expressed in words, we have the definition (definitio) of the thing. Spinoza sharply distinguishes between the essence of a thing and its properties, the latter being what can be deduced from the essence.

The existence of a thing is the fact that it is, without regard to what it is. So the existence of finite things is always temporary; they come into being and pass away. But the essence of a thing is independent of time, and is, in Spinoza's language, an eternal truth. Of something that has ceased to exist it remains eternally true that it was the sort of thing that it was. Its 'whatness' is unimpaired by consideration of time.

Traditionally, the scholastics regarded 'existentia' as corresponding to the question 'An sit?'—does it exist?, and 'essentia' as corresponding to the question 'Quid sit?'—what is it?.

It will be seen as soon as Spinoza unfolds his definitions that it is only in the case of the all-inclusive reality—God or Nature or Substance—that essence and existence are the same, or, in Spinoza's language, essence involves existence.

2. *In*

Nothing would appear simpler than this word, but the reader will find that, in addition to its normal spatial sense, Spinoza uses it in the sense of logically dependent on, logically contained in. The concepts of 'in se esse' and 'in alio esse'—to be in oneself and to be in something else—are basic to his thinking. That which is in itself is completely dependent on itself alone, completely independent both in its being and in its conception, and therefore 'causa sui'—self-caused. It will become clear that for Spinoza there is only one thing that is completely and absolutely in itself, the all-inclusive reality that is God.

Closely connected is the logical use of 'per'—through. When B is conceived 'through' A, A is logically prior to B, and B cannot be conceived unless A is first conceived. So B is in something else, in this case, A. But that which can be conceived only through itself must be in itself.

3. Substance (*substantia*)

This word must be divested of many of its common or scientific connotations. Spinoza's definition is rooted in a long philosophical tradition in which the term 'substance' played a very important role. For Aristotle the word had several connotations, of which one signified independent and primary existence: a substance was the basic metaphysical individual that could exist by itself (Aristotle, *Categories*, 2–5). Descartes applied this notion of primary and independent existence to God and claimed that God alone was the only entity that was really independent of every-thing else. Nevertheless, he went on to permit the use of the term 'substance' to refer to created entities as well (Descartes, *Principles of Philosophy* I: 51-53). It is the Cartesian theory that furnishes the framework within which Spinoza develops his own definition and theory of substance. Spinoza adopts Descartes' proposal to apply this term to God alone, but he strictly adheres to this usage. The main theme of the first book of the *Ethics* is the demonstration that there is one and only one substance, God-or-Nature.

4. Attribute (*Attributum*)

In its common meaning, this word indicates that which is attributed to, or predicated of, a subject; a quality of that subject. But in the *Ethics* Spinoza uses it almost exclusively in a special sense, defining it as that which the intellect perceives as constituting the essence of substance. Now since substance is by definition infinite, it must have infinite at-tributes; but of these the human intellect perceives only two, extension and thought. That is to say, whatever we perceive as real must come under one of these two headings, extension and thought.

5. God (*Deus*)

Although Spinoza gives repeated warnings that his 'Deus' is far from the anthropomorphic conception of God prevalent in the theology of his time, the reader will find it difficult to bear this constantly in mind. It is not until *Ethics*, Pr.14,I, that God, by definition, is shown to be identical with the infinite, all-inclusive, unique substance, and thereafter it is all too easy to lose sight of this, as the religious overtones of the word 'God' keep asserting themselves. So Spinoza's frequent use of the phrase 'Deus sive Natura'—God, or Nature—is intended as a salutary corrective. For Spinoza God is all Being, all Reality, in all its aspects and in all its infinite richness.

6. Mode (*modus*)

This common Latin noun means what it seems to mean—mode, way, or manner—and is frequently used by Spinoza with this unremarkable meaning. But, deriving from this, there is also a more specialized sense. God, who is pure power, expresses himself in infinite 'modes' or 'ways.' So God is prior to all his modes, and a mode is defined as that which is 'in' something else and is conceived 'through' something else. All ex-istence is summed up in God and his modes. There is nothing else.

7. Affection (*affectio*) and the verb 'to affect' (*afficere*)

This poses a problem for the translator, who can do no better than to translate as 'affection' and 'to affect,' having first given due warning of the special use of these terms in Spinoza. 'Affection' *never* means love, liking, regard, and so forth. It is the form 'taken on' by some thing, a state of that thing, and therefore logically posterior to that of which it is an affection. Perhaps there is a hint of this usage in such English expressions as 'he affects an air of unconcern,' except that there is no implication of pretence in 'affection.' So in Def.5,I, mode is defined as the 'affections of substance.' Mode and affection are similar, but do not cover the same ground. Mode is restricted to the 'way' in which substance, or an attribute of God, finds expression, whereas 'affection' is of much wider application, extending to finite things. But the reader should beware of assuming that an affection is a mere appearance: Spinoza is no phenomenalist.

Special warning should be given regarding the passive voice of the verb 'to affect.' In Spinoza, this is not really passive in force. When he says that 'God is affected by a modification. . . ' he does not mean that there is something external to God by which God is affected, for there is nothing external to God. Similarly, with 'God is modified by a modification. . . ' (Pr.28,I), where he uses 'modificatus est' as synonymous with 'affectus est,' he means quite simply that God 'takes on'—expresses himself in—a particular form or state.

8. Sive or Seu

The orthodox translation of these Latin words is 'or.' Spinoza nearly always uses them to indicate an alternative expression for what he is trying to say, and this in fact gives us a valuable insight into the interlocking of concepts that characterises his system. But the English 'or' is frequently disjunctive; e.g. you can travel by this road or by that. So the unvarying translation of sive (seu) by 'or' can be quite misleading.

I have therefore usually translated it by 'that is' when it implies equivalence. When Spinoza uses 'hoc est,' which he frequently does, I also translate as 'that is.'

9. Thing

This is the regular translation of 'res,' but the reader should be warned that Spinoza gives it a much more extensive meaning than is normal in English. He uses it to cover not only inanimate objects, but man, God, and sometimes occurrences.

10. Follow (*sequi*)

A very hard-worked term in Spinoza, who uses it mainly with its non-spatial, non-temporal, purely logical meaning. For example, it 'follows' from the nature of a triangle that its three angles are equal to two right angles.

11. Nature (*Natura*)

This word is used in two senses, Firstly, it is the equivalent of 'essence,' the sort of thing that a thing is, and is frequently coupled with 'essence' (essentia sive natura). Secondly, it can mean the whole of reality, as in 'Deus, sive Natura.' One should beware of restricting it to the physical aspect of reality.

When it is used in this second sense, I give it a capital letter, although Spinoza—or his printers—were not always consistent in this.

12.   Cause (*causa*)

The reader will find that Spinoza's 'cause' is not quite what he is used to. It need not imply temporal succession; indeed, for Spinoza a cause is more the logical ground from which a consequent follows, in the logical sense of 'follow' noted in item 10. Hence, Spinoza occasionally couples the word 'cause' with the term 'reason' ('ratio').

By the phrase 'efficient cause' Spinoza means primarily the cause that produces the effect in question and is quite close to the notion of a sufficient condition. His theory of causality excludes the Aristotelian final cause, the goal or purpose of a thing or event. In his Appendix to Part I Spinoza explicitly claims that final causes are human fictions.

The phrases 'immanent cause' (causa immanens) and 'transitive cause' (causa transiens) appear in Pr. 18, I. A transitive cause is one in which causation "passes over" from the cause to the effect, while cause and effect remain really distinct. Mechanical causation would be an example of transitive causation; e.g. one billiard ball hitting another into the pocket. An immanent cause, however, is an "indwelling cause," one that is inseparable from its effect. For example, the numbers 1 and 2 are immanent causes of the number 4 insofar as they are factors of it. Although 1 and 2 can be separated out of 4 by analysis, they are nevertheless always "in" it. It is Spinoza's thesis that God is the immanent, not the transitive, cause of all things. This is the denial of the traditional idea of God as the creative, transcendent cause of the world. Insofar as God is the unique substance of which everything else is a mode, all modes will be in God and God will be their indwelling cause.

13.   Idea (*idea*)

This is an extremely important term in Spinoza's philosophy. It is not usually equivalent to the English 'idea,' when the latter is synonymous with 'notion' or 'image.' In fact, Spinoza warns us not to construe 'idea' as signifying a pictorial representation of a thing, a "dumb picture on a tablet." An idea, for Spinoza is an act of thought; it is almost a transitive verb having an object, its ideate ('ideatum'), i.e. 'that which is idea-ed.'' Spinoza does in fact use '*objectum*' ('object') and '*ideatum*' ('ideate') as alternative expressions.

In many contexts the term 'idea' has the meaning of judgment, or assertion (Pr. 48–49, II). Accordingly, 'idea' is for Spinoza closer in signification to the term 'proposition' than to such terms as 'concept' or 'notion.' Ideas then will be true or false.

14.   Determine (*Determinare*)

This is never used in the sense of to decide, resolve, and so forth. It is always used in the sense that gives rise to the philosophical term 'determinism.' Spinoza's declaration of determinism in Pr. 28, I, asserts that every finite thing is determined to exist and to act by another finite cause, which itself is determined by another finite cause, and so ad infinitum. It is noteworthy that there is no appropriate Latin verb with the transitive force of 'to cause,' and 'determinare' does duty for this.

The adjective 'determinate' (determinatus) should occasion no difficulty, having the normal English meaning of 'limited, having fixed bounds.' It appears frequently in the phrase 'certo et determinato modo'—'in a definite and determinate way,' where the two adjectives do no more than reinforce each other.

There is a close connection between 'necessary' (necessarius) and the concept of determinism. Def. 7, I—'A thing is called necessary if it is determined to exist and to act in a definite and determinate way.'

15. Explication (*explicatio*) and to explicate (*explicare*)

These Latin words are usually translated as 'explanation' and 'to explain,' and this is sometimes a satisfactory rendering when the intended meaning is to elucidate that which is obscure. But this is not always the case. There are perfectly good English words, 'explication' and 'to explicate,' not in frequent use today, but much closer to the Latin. The dictionary gives 'explicate' as 'unfold the meaning of, give further development to an idea.' I shall use these words when 'explain' and 'explanation' are ill-suited to the context.

16. In so far as (*quatenus*), often paired with *eatenus*—to that extent.

This word, scattered in profusion throughout the *Ethics*, indicates a restriction in the way a thing is considered, the seeing of a thing in a certain perspective. It could be said to be integral to Spinoza's thinking. The rich concreteness of the real can be approached only by isolating some one of its infinite aspects, while never losing sight of its concrete unity.

Such expressions as 'in so far as,' 'in respect of' were commonplace in the philosophical language of the time, and Shakespeare makes fun of them in *As You Like It*, when Touchstone is asked by Corin how he likes a shepherd's life. "Truly, shepherd, in respect of itself, it is a good life, but in respect that it is a shepherd's life, it is naught. In respect that it is solitary, I like it well; but in respect that it is private, it is a very vile life. Now in respect that it is in the fields, it pleaseth me well; but in respect that it is not in the court, it is tedious."

17. Formal and Objective Essence (*essentia formalis, essentia obiectiva*)

These are difficult terms not only to translate but to understand. Here Spinoza takes over a Cartesian distinction, which in turn is rooted in Scholastic philosophy. Consider some existing thing, say the planet Saturn. As an existing thing revolving around the sun Saturn has formal essence or reality *(essentia formalis, esse formale)*. The formal essence, or being, of something is its very existence. But in considering this planet we have made it an object of our thought. As such it has objective essence or reality *(essentia obiectiva, esse obiectivum)*. Clearly, Saturn in the sky and Saturn in our mind are different things, although the latter is supposed to represent to us the former.

What makes this terminology confusing is that in current usage the term 'subjective' is often employed to express what the Scholastics meant by 'objective.' But the reader of Descartes and Spinoza should realize that when these philosophers use the term 'objective' they are talking about a mental representation of a thing, the thing as an object of thought.

18.   Reality (*realitas*) and Perfection (*perfectio*)

In Spinoza, as in Descartes, there are degrees of reality, a concept that Hobbes found difficult. However, for both Descartes and Spinoza being was a question of degree: one thing can have more "thinghood" than another. Spinoza equates 'perfection' with 'reality'; by 'perfection,' he explains, he means completeness of being. The moral or aesthetic connotations of the word 'perfection' are secondary.

19.   Virtue (*virtus*)

Spinoza equates this word with 'power' (*potentia*). This usage is reflected in the phrase 'by virtue of.' Spinoza often uses the term 'virtue' in a moral sense, whereby the more we are endowed with virtue the more we act according to reason, and hence attain happiness.

20.   Imagine (*imaginari*)

Spinoza employs the term 'imaginari' as the verb of 'imago,' which refers, strictly speaking, to a physical representation of a thing. To imagine is to contemplate a thing as present in sense-perception or to represent it in memory or other kinds of fantasy. The *imago*, or image, is an affection of the body, a state of the body resulting from sense-perception, when an external body has in some way affected our body. The repeated impressions made by an external body upon our body may cause more or less permanent traces (*vestigia*) in our body—although Spinoza is quick to point out that these images are not in themselves miniature physical reproductions of external bodies (Sch. Pr. 17, II). When these images, whose mental counterparts are ideas, are activated, we are said to imagine (*imaginari*), and the process is called "imagination" (*imaginatio*). Imagination is opposed to intellect, just as image is opposed to idea. It is because the common conception of God is through imagination rather than through intellect that the multitude is prone to think of God in an anthropomorphic way.

There is a wider, though closely allied, meaning that Spinoza gives to "imaginatio." In Sch. 2, Pr. 40, II "imaginatio' is defined as covering the entire field of "knowledge of the first kind," which he elsewhere equates with opinion, a level of cognition similar to Plato's belief (*doxa*). It is contrasted with knowledge of the second kind, reason (ratio), and with knowledge of the third kind, intuition (*scientia intuitiva*), and is intended to cover all uncritical belief into which systematic reasoning does not enter.

Consequently, the translator finds himself much challenged by this group of Latin words. According to context, I sometimes translate 'imaginari' as 'to imagine,' sometimes 'to think' or 'to believe,' when it is quite clear that the thinking and believing are casual and uncritical. As for 'imaginatio' there are some passages where I can do no better than to translate it as 'imagination,' or 'imagining.'

21.   Emotion (*affectus*)

This is the usual translation of 'affectus,' and the translator had best retain it in default of a more accurate term. It certainly seems odd to speak of 'the emotion of desire,' and this is a sufficient indication that 'affectus' is not quite the equivalent of our 'emotion.' Its definition in Def. 3, III makes it clear that 'affectus' is equally a bodily state (*affectio*) and its mental counterpart as idea, but it is inevitable that Spinoza should be more concerned with the latter than the former.

The names assigned to the particular emotions in Parts III and IV will sometimes appear strange to the reader. But Spinoza emphasises on more than one occasion that he is not analysing the way that words are used in common parlance. He claims to deduce emotions by strict scientific reasoning from his basic philosophic position, and he assigns to these emotions such names from common usage as come nearest to expressing his meaning. Indeed, some of the emotions thus deduced, he says, have no names in common language. This is in keeping with his nominalism. Words are not vitally important; they are merely our way of getting to the 'real.'

22.   To Act and To Suffer (*agere and pati*)

These verbs, usually meaning to do and to suffer, are employed by Spinoza in a special sense which is clearly explained in the Definitions of Part III. They are fundamental to Spinoza's ethical position, for they are involved in the most important of all questions, the power of the mind over the emotions. Insofar as the mind alone—and for Spinoza the essence of mind is our capacity to reason—is the cause of our affective states, we are said to be active (*agere*), and we are passive (*pati*) insofar as our emotions have their causes outside ourselves and are therefore beyond our control. No human being, Spinoza asserts, is entirely active or entirely passive, but the degree of our activity and passivity determines our moral status.

The corresponding nouns, 'actio' and 'passio,' are difficult to render. I cannot reconcile myself to translating 'passio' as 'passion,' which is too violent a word and is grotesquely inappropriate to many of the 'passiones' of Parts III and IV. I translate it, with reservations, as 'passive emotions,' emotions whereby we are subject to that which is outside our control. The term 'actiones' I translate as 'activity' or 'active emotions,' according to context. However, it should be noted that Spinoza is not always consistent in his specialised use of 'actiones,' and sometimes employs it in the familiar neutral sense of 'actions.'

23. Pleasure and Pain (*Laetitia and Tristitia*)

I have had recourse to these traditionally acceptable English terms in default of any more accurate. But the reader is urged to attend carefully to their definitions in Part III, where he will find that they signify the felt transition to a state of greater or less power. As a consequence, many of the usual associations of these terms must be discarded.

24. Thought (*Cogitatio*)

It would be well to remind the reader at the outset—though Spinoza makes it abundantly clear—that this term includes not only intellect but all that is 'mental'—will, love, and all the emotions. Thought and Extension (*Extensio*) are nearly, but not quite, correlated with our 'mental' and 'physical.'

THE ETHICS

PART I

CONCERNING GOD

DEFINITIONS

1. By that which is self-caused I mean that whose essence involves existence; or that whose nature can be conceived only as existing.

2. A thing is said to be finite in its own kind (in suo genere finita) when it can be limited by another thing of the same nature. For example, a body is said to be finite because we can always conceive of another body greater than it. So, too, a thought is limited by another thought. But body is not limited by thought, nor thought by body.

3. By substance I mean that which is in itself and is conceived through itself; that is, that the conception of which does not require the conception of another thing from which it has to be formed.

4. By attribute I mean that which the intellect perceives of substance as constituting its essence.

5. By mode I mean the affections of substance; that is, that which is in something else and is conceived through something else.

6. By God I mean an absolutely infinite being; that is, substance consisting of infinite attributes, each of which expresses eternal and infinite essence.

Explication

I say 'absolutely infinite,' not 'infinite in its kind.' For if a thing is only infinite in its kind, one may deny that it has infinite attributes. But if a thing is absolutely infinite, whatever expresses essence and does not involve any negation belongs to its essence.

7. That thing is said to be free (liber) which exists solely from the necessity of its own nature, and is determined to action by itself alone. A thing is said to be necessary (necessarius) or rather, constrained (coactus), if it is determined by another thing to exist and to act in a definite and determinate way.

8. By eternity I mean existence itself insofar as it is conceived as necessarily following solely from the definition of an eternal thing.

31

Explication

For such existence is conceived as an eternal truth, just as is the essence of the thing, and therefore cannot be explicated through duration or time, even if duration be conceived as without beginning and end.

AXIOMS

1. All things that are, are either in themselves or in something else.

2. That which cannot be conceived through another thing must be conceived through itself.

3. From a given determinate cause there necessarily follows an effect; on the other hand, if there be no determinate cause it is impossible that an effect should follow.

 4. The knowledge of an effect depends on, and involves, the knowledge of the cause. how we conceive

5. Things which have nothing in common with each other cannot be understood through each other; that is, the conception of the one does not involve the conception of the other.

 6. A true idea must agree with that of which it is the idea *(ideatum)*.

7. If a thing can be conceived as not existing, its essence does not involve existence.

PROPOSITION 1

Substance is by nature prior to its affections.

Proof

This is evident from Defs. 3 and 5.

PROPOSITION 2

Two substances having different attributes have nothing in common.

Proof

This too is evident from Def. 3; for each substance must be in itself and be conceived through itself; that is, the conception of the one does not involve the conception of the other.

PROPOSITION 3

When things have nothing in common, one cannot be the cause of the other.

Proof

If things have nothing in common, then (Ax.5) they cannot be understood through one another, and so (Ax.4) one cannot be the cause of the other.

PROPOSITION 4

Two or more distinct things are distinguished from one another either by the difference of the attributes of the substances or by the difference of the affections of the substances.

Proof

All things that are, are either in themselves or in something else (Ax.1); that is, (Defs.3 and 5), nothing exists external to the intellect except substances and their affections. Therefore there can be nothing external to the intellect through which several things can be distinguished from one another except substances or (which is the same thing) (Def.4) the attributes and the affections of substances.

PROPOSITION 5

In the universe there cannot be two or more substances of the same nature or attribute.

Proof

If there were several such distinct substances, they would have to be distinguished from one another either by a difference of attributes or by a difference of affections (Pr.4). If they are distinguished only by a difference of attributes, then it will be granted that there cannot be more than one substance of the same attribute. But if they are distinguished by a difference of affections, then, since substance is by nature prior to its affections (Pr.1), disregarding therefore its affections and considering substance in itself, that is (Def.3 and Ax.6) considering it truly, it cannot be conceived as distinguishable from another substance. That is (Pr.4), there cannot be several such substances but only one.

PROPOSITION 6

One substance cannot be produced by another substance.

Proof

In the universe there cannot be two substances of the same attribute (Pr.5), that is (Pr.2) two substances having something in common. And so (Pr.3) one cannot be the cause of the other; that is, one cannot be produced by the other.

Corollary

Hence it follows that substance cannot be produced by anything else. For in the universe there exists nothing but substances and their affections, as is evident from Ax.1 and Defs.3 and 5. But, by Pr.6, it cannot be produced by another substance. Therefore substance cannot be produced by anything else whatsoever.

Another Proof

This can be proved even more readily by the absurdity of the contradictory. For if substance could be produced by something else, the knowledge of substance would have to depend on the knowledge of its cause (Ax.4), and so (Def.3) it would not be substance.

PROPOSITION 7

Existence belongs to the nature of substance.

Proof

Substance cannot be produced by anything else (Cor.Pr.6) and is therefore self-caused (causa sui); that is (Def.1), its essence necessarily involves existence; that is, existence belongs to its nature.

PROPOSITION 8

Every substance is necessarily infinite.

Proof

There cannot be more than one substance having the same attribute (Pr.5), and existence belongs to the nature of substance (Pr.7). It must therefore exist either as finite or as infinite. But it cannot exist as finite, for (Def.2) it would have to be limited by another substance of the same nature, and that substance also would have to exist (Pr.7). And so there would exist two substances of the same attribute, which is absurd (Pr.5). Therefore it exists as infinite.

Scholium 1

Since in fact to be finite is in part a negation and to be infinite is the unqualified affirmation of the existence of some nature, it follows from Proposition 7 alone that every substance must be infinite.

Scholium 2

I do not doubt that for those who judge things confusedly and are not accustomed to know things through their primary causes it is difficult to grasp the proof of Proposition 7. Surely, this is because they neither distinguish between the modifications of substances and substances themselves, nor do they know how things are produced. And so it comes about that they ascribe to substances a beginning which they see natural things as having; for those who do not know the true causes of things confuse everything. Without any hesitation they imagine trees as well as men talking and men being formed from stones as well as from seed; indeed, any forms whatsoever are imagined to change into any other forms. So too, those who confuse the divine nature with human nature easily ascribe to God human emotions, especially so long as they are ignorant of how the latter are produced in the mind. But if men were to attend to the nature of substance, they would not doubt at all the truth of Proposition 7; indeed, this Proposition would be an axiom to all and would be ranked among universally accepted truisms. For by substance they would understand that which is in itself and is conceived through itself; that is, that the knowledge of which does not require the knowledge of any other thing. By modifications they would understand that which is another thing, and whose conception is formed from the conception of the thing in which they are. Therefore in the case of non-existent modifications we can have true ideas of them since their essence is included in something else, with the result that they can be conceived through that something else, although they do not exist in actuality externally to the intellect. However, in the case of substances, because they are conceived only through themselves, their truth external to the intellect is only in themselves. So if someone were to say that he has a clear and distinct—that is, a true—idea of substance and that he nevertheless doubts whether such a substance exists, this would surely be just the same as if he were to declare that he has a true idea but nevertheless suspects that it may be false (as is obvious to anyone who gives his mind to it). Or if anyone asserts that substance is created, he at the same time asserts that a false idea has become true, than which nothing more absurd can be conceived. So it must necessarily be admitted that the existence of substance is as much an eternal truth as it is essence.

Hence we can derive in another way that there cannot be more than one substance of the same nature, and I think it worthwhile to set out the proof here. Now to do this in an orderly fashion I ask you to note:

1. The true definition of each thing involves and expresses nothing beyond the nature of the thing defined. Hence it follows that—

2. No definition involves or expresses a fixed number of individuals, since it expresses nothing but the nature of the thing defined. For example, the definition of a triangle expresses nothing other than simply the nature of a triangle, and not a fixed number of triangles.

3. For each single existent thing there must necessarily be a definite cause for its existence.

4. The cause for the existence of a thing must either be contained in the very nature and definition of the existent thing (in effect, existence belongs to its nature) or must have its being independently of the thing itself.

From these premises it follows that if a fixed number of individuals exist in Nature, there must necessarily be a cause why those individuals and not more or fewer, exist. If, for example, in Nature twenty men were to exist (for the sake of greater clarity I suppose that they exist simultaneously and that no others existed in Nature before them), in order to account for the existence of these twenty men it will not be enough for us to demonstrate the cause of human nature in general; it will furthermore be necessary to demonstrate the cause why not more or fewer than twenty men exist, since (Note 3) there must necessarily be a cause for the existence of each one. But this cause (Notes 2 and 3) cannot be contained in the nature of man, since the true definition of man does not involve the number twenty. So (Note 4) the cause of the existence of these twenty men, and consequently of each one, must necessarily be external to each one, and therefore we can reach the unqualified conclusion that whenever several individuals of a kind exist, there must necessarily be an external cause for their existence. Now since existence belongs to the nature of substance (as has already been shown in this Scholium) the definition of substance must involve necessary existence, and consequently the existence of substance must be concluded solely from its definition. But the existence of several substances cannot follow from the definition of substance (as I have already shown in Notes 2 and 3). Therefore, from the definition of substance it follows necessarily that there exists only one substance of the same nature, as was proposed.

PROPOSITION 9

The more reality or being a thing has, the more attributes it has.

Proof

This is evident from Definition 4.

PROPOSITION 10

Each attribute of one substance must be conceived through itself.

Proof

For an attribute is that which intellect perceives of substance as constituting its essence (Def.4), and so (Def.3) it must be conceived through itself.

Scholium

From this it is clear that although two attributes be conceived as really distinct, that is, one without the help of the other, still we cannot deduce therefrom that they constitute two entities, or two different substances. For it is in the nature of substance that each of its attributes be conceived through itself, since all the attributes it possesses have always been in it simultaneously, and one could not have been produced by another; but each expresses the reality or being of substance. So it is by no means absurd to ascribe more than one attribute to one substance. Indeed, nothing in Nature is clearer than that each entity must be conceived under some attribute, and the more reality or being it has, the more are its attributes which express necessity, or eternity, and infinity. Consequently nothing can be clearer than this, too, that an absolutely infinite entity must necessarily be defined (Def.6) as an entity consisting of infinite attributes, each of which expresses a definite essence, eternal and infinite. Now if anyone asks by what mark can we distinguish between different substances, let him read the following Propositions, which show that in Nature there exists only one substance, absolutely infinite.

So this distinguishing mark would be sought in vain.

premis I.   PROPOSITION 11

God, or substance consisting of infinite attributes, each of which expresses eternal and infinite essence, necessarily exists.

Proof

If you deny this, conceive, if you can, that God does not exist. Therefore (Ax.7) his essence does not involve existence. But this is absurd (Pr.7). Therefore God necessarily exists.

Second Proof

For every thing a cause or reason must be assigned either for its existence or for its non-existence. For example, if a triangle exists, there must be a reason, or cause, for its existence. If it does not exist, there must be a reason or cause which prevents it from existing, or which annuls its existence. Now this reason or cause must either be contained in the nature of the thing or be external to it. For example, the reason why a square circle does not exist is indicated by its very nature, in that it involves a contradiction. On the other hand, the reason for the existence of substance also follows from its nature alone, in that it involves existence (Pr.7). But the reason for the existence or non-existence of a circle or a triangle does not follow from their nature, but from the order of universal corporeal Nature. For it is from this latter that it necessarily follows that either the triangle necessarily exists at this moment or that its present existence is impossible. This is self-evident, and therefrom it follows that a thing necessarily exists if there is no reason or cause which prevents its existence. Therefore if there can be no reason or cause which prevents God from existing or which annuls his existence, we are bound to conclude that he necessarily exists. But if there were such a reason or cause, it would have to be either within God's nature or external to it; that is, it would have to be in another substance of another nature. For if it were of the same nature, by that very fact it would be granted that God exists. But a substance of another nature would have nothing in common with God (Pr.2), and so could neither posit nor annul his existence. Since therefore there cannot be external to God's nature a reason or cause that would annul God's existence, then if indeed he does not exist, the reason or cause must necessarily be in God's nature, which would therefore involve a contradiction. But to affirm this of a Being absolutely infinite and in the highest degree perfect is absurd. Therefore neither in God nor external to God is there any cause or reason which would annul his existence. Therefore God necessarily exists.

A Third Proof

To be able to not exist is weakness; on the other hand, to be able to exist is power, as is self-evident. So if what now necessarily exists is nothing but finite entities, then finite entities are more potent than an absolutely infinite Entity—which is absurd, (as is self-evident). Therefore either nothing exists, or an absolutely infinite Entity necessarily exists, too. But we do exist, either in ourselves or in something else which necessarily exists (Ax.1 and Pr.7). Therefore an absolutely infinite Entity—that is (Def.6), God—necessarily exists.

Scholium

In this last proof I decided to prove God's existence a posteriori so that the proof may be more easily perceived, and not because God's existence does not follow a priori from this same basis. For since the ability to exist is power, it follows that the greater the degree of reality that belongs to the nature of a thing, the greater amount of energy it has from itself for existence. So an absolutely infinite Entity, or God, will have from himself absolutely infinite power to exist, and therefore exists absolutely.

But perhaps many will not readily find this proof convincing because they are used to consider only such things as derive from external causes. Of these things they observe that those which come quickly into being—that is, which readily exist—likewise readily perish, while things which they conceive as more complex they regard as more difficult to bring into being—that is, not so ready to exist. However, to free them from these misconceptions I do not need at this point to show what measure of truth there is in the saying; "Quickly come, quickly go," neither need I raise the question whether or not everything is equally easy in respect of Nature as a whole. It is enough to note simply this, that I am not here speaking of things that come into being through external causes, but only of substances, which (Pr.6) cannot be produced by any external cause. For whether they consist of many parts or few, things that are brought about by external causes owe whatever degree of perfection or reality they possess entirely to the power of the external cause, and so their existence has its origin solely in the perfection of the external cause, and not in their own perfection. On the other hand, whatever perfection substance possesses is due to no external cause; therefore its existence, too, must follow solely from its own nature, and is therefore nothing else but its essence. So perfection does not annul a thing's existence: on the contrary, it posits it; whereas imperfection annuls a thing's existence. So there is nothing of which we can be more certain than the existence of an absolutely infinite or perfect Entity; that is, God. For since his essence excludes all imperfection and involves absolute perfection, it thereby removes all reason for doubting his existence and affords the utmost certainty of it. This, I think, must be quite clear to all who give a modicum of attention to the matter.

PROPOSITION 12

No attribute of substance can be truly conceived from which it would follow that substance can be divided.

Proof

The parts into which substance thus conceived would be divided will either retain the nature of substance or they will not. In the first case each part will have to be infinite (Pr.8) and self-caused (Pr.6) and consist of a different attribute (Pr.5); and so several substances could be formed from one substance, which is absurd (Pr.6). Furthermore, the parts would have nothing in common with the whole (Pr.2), and the whole could exist and be conceived without its parts (Def.4 and Pr.10), the absurdity of which none can doubt. But in the latter case where the parts will not retain the nature of substance, then when the whole substance would have been divided into equal parts it would lose the nature of substance and would cease to be. This is absurd (Pr.7).

PROPOSITION 13

Absolutely infinite substance is indivisible.

Proof

If it were divisible, the parts into which it would be divided will either retain the nature of absolutely infinite substance, or not. In the first case, there would therefore be several substances of the same nature, which is absurd (Pr.5). In the second case, absolutely infinite substance can cease to be, which is also absurd (Pr.11).

Corollary

From this it follows that no substance, and consequently no corporeal substance, insofar as it is substance, is divisible.

Scholium

The indivisibility of substance can be more easily understood merely from the fact that the nature of substance can be conceived only as infinite, and that a part of substance can mean only finite substance, which involves an obvious contradiction (Pr.8).

PROPOSITION 14

There can be, or be conceived, no other substance but God.

Proof

Since God is an absolutely infinite being of whom no attribute expressing the essence of substance can be denied (Def.6) and since he necessarily exists (Pr.11), if there were any other substance but God, it would have to be explicated through some attribute of God, and so there would exist two substances with the same attribute, which is absurd (Pr.5). So there can be no substance external to God, and consequently no such substance can be conceived. For if it could be conceived, it would have to be conceived necessarily as existing; but this is absurd (by the first part of this proof). Therefore no substance can be or be conceived external to God.

Corollary 1

Hence it follows quite clearly that God is one: that is, (Def.6), in the universe there is only one substance, and this is absolutely infinite, as I have already indicated in Scholium Pr.10.

Corollary 2

It follows that the thing extended and the thing thinking are either attributes of God or (Ax.1) affections of the attributes of God.

PROPOSITION 15

Whatever is, is in God, and nothing can be or be conceived without God.

Proof

Apart from God no substance can be or be conceived (Pr.14), that is, (Def.3), something which is in itself and is conceived through itself. Now modes (Def.5) cannot be or be conceived without substance; therefore they can be only in the divine nature and can be conceived only through the divine nature. But nothing exists except substance and modes (Ax.1). Therefore nothing can be or be conceived without God.

Scholium

Some imagine God in the likeness of man, consisting of mind and body, and subject to passions. But it is clear from what has already been proved how far they stray from the true knowledge of God. These I dismiss, for all who have given any consideration to the divine nature deny that God is corporeal. They find convincing proof of this in the fact that by body we understand some quantity having length, breadth and depth, bounded by a definite shape; and nothing more absurd than this can be attributed to God, a being absolutely infinite.

At the same time, however, in other arguments whereby which they try to prove this point they show clearly that in their thinking corporeal or extended substance is set completely apart from the divine nature, and they assert that it is created by God. But they have no idea from what divine power it could have been created, which clearly shows that they don't know what they are saying. Now I have clearly proved—at any rate, in my judgment (Cor.Pr.6 and Sch.2 Pr.8)—that no substance can be produced or created by anything else. Furthermore, in Proposition 14 we showed that apart from God no substance can be or be conceived, and hence we deduced that extended substance is one of God's infinite attributes.

However, for a fuller explanation I will refute my opponents' arguments, which all come down to this. Firstly, they think that corporeal substance, insofar as it is substance, is made up of parts, and so they deny that it can be infinite, and consequently that it can pertain to God. This they illustrate with many examples, of which I will take one or two. They say that if corporeal substance is infinite, suppose it to be

divided into two parts. Each of these parts will be either finite or infinite.
If the former, then the infinite is made up of two finite parts, which is absurd. If the latter, then there is an infinite which is twice as great as
another infinite, which is also absurd.

Again, if an infinite length is measured in feet, it will have to consist
of an infinite number of feet; and if it is measured in inches, it will
consist of an infinite number of inches. So one infinite number will be
twelve times greater than another infinite number.

Lastly, if from one point in an infinite quantity two lines, AB and

AC, be drawn of fixed and determinate length,
and thereafter be produced to infinity, it is clear
that the distance between B and C continues to
increase and finally changes from a determinate
distance to an indeterminate distance.

As these absurdities follow, they think, from supposing quantity to
be infinite, they conclude that corporeal substance must be finite and
consequently cannot pertain to God's essence.

The second argument is also drawn from God's consummate perfection. Since God, they say, is a supremely perfect being, he cannot be that
which is acted upon. But corporeal substance, being divisible, can be
acted upon. It therefore follows that corporeal substance does not pertain to God's essence.

These are the arguments I find put forward by writers who thereby
seek to prove that corporeal substance is unworthy of the divine essence
and cannot pertain to it. However, the student who looks carefully into
these arguments will find that I have already replied to them, since they
are all founded on the same supposition that material substance is composed of parts, and this I have already shown to be absurd (Pr.12 and
Cor. Pr.13). Again, careful reflection will show that all those alleged absurdities (if indeed they are absurdities, which is not now under discussion) from which they seek to prove that extended substance is finite do
not at all follow from the supposition that quantity is infinite, but that
infinite quantity is measurable and is made up of finite parts. Therefore
from the resultant absurdities no other conclusion can be reached but
that infinite quantity is not measurable and cannot be made up of finite
parts. And this is exactly what we have already proved (Pr.12). So the
weapon they aim at us is in fact turned against themselves. If therefore
from this 'reductio ad absurdum' argument of theirs they still seek to
deduce that extended substance must be finite, they are surely just like
one who, having made the supposition that a circle has the properties of
a square, deduces therefrom that a circle does not have a centre from
which all lines drawn to the circumference are equal. For corporeal
substance, which can be conceived only as infinite, one, and indivisible
(Prs. 8,5 and 12) they conceive as made up of finite parts, multiplex, and
divisible, so as to deduce that it is finite. In the same way others, too,
having supposed that a line is composed of points, can find many
arguments to prove that a line cannot be infinitely divided. Indeed, it is
just as absurd to assert that corporeal substance is composed of bodies or

parts as that a body is composed of surfaces, surfaces of lines, and lines of points. This must be admitted by all who know clear reason to be infallible, and particularly those who say that a vacuum cannot exist. For if corporeal substance could be so divided that its parts were distinct in reality, why could one part not be annihilated while the others remain joined together as before? And why should all the parts be so fitted together as to leave no vacuum? Surely, in the case of things which are in reality distinct from one another, one can exist without the other and remain in its original state. Since therefore there is no vacuum in Nature (which is discussed elsewhere[1]) and all its parts must so harmonise that there is no vacuum, it also follows that the parts cannot be distinct in reality; that is, corporeal substance, in so far as it is substance, cannot be divided.

If I am now asked why we have this natural inclination to divide quantity, I reply that we conceive quantity in two ways, to wit, abstractly, or superficially—in other words, as represented in the imagination—or as substance, which we do only through the intellect. If therefore we consider quantity as it is presented in the imagination—and this is what we more frequently and readily do—we find it to be finite, divisible, and made up of parts. But if we consider it intellectually and conceive it in so far as it is substance—and this is very difficult—then it will be found to be infinite, one, and indivisible, as we have already sufficiently proved. This will be quite clear to those who can distinguish between the imagination and the intellect, especially if this point also is stressed, that matter is everywhere the same, and there are no distinct parts in it except in so far as we conceive matter as modified in various ways. Then its parts are distinct, not really but only modally.[2] For example, we conceive water to be divisible and to have separate parts in so far as it is water, but not in so far as it is corporeal substance. In this latter respect it is not capable of separation or division. Furthermore, water, qua water, comes into existence and goes out of existence; but qua substance it does not come into existence nor go out of existence [corrumpitur].

I consider that in the above I have also replied to the second argument, since this too is based on the supposition that matter, in so far as it is substance, is divisible and made up of parts. And even though this

---

1. If this refers to anything in Spinoza's extant works, it must be to his early *Descartes' Principles of Philosophy* II. 2–3. For an inter-relating of the two passages, see Jonathan Bennett, 'Spinoza's Vacuum Argument'; *Midwest Studies in Philosophy* V (1980), pp. 391–399.

2. In this passage Spinoza makes use of a distinction that was frequently employed by philosophers in the middle ages and by Descartes as well. Indeed, it is probably the Cartesian version of the distinction that is relevant in this context. According to Descartes, a real distinction obtains between two or more substances or attributes, each one of which being clearly and distinctly conceivable without the other. Because of this clear and distinct conception of each substance one can exist without the other. For Descartes, the mind can be clearly and distinctly conceived without the body; hence, it can exist without the latter. A modal distinction, however, is a distinction either between a mode and the substance of which it is a mode or between the various modes of a substance. There is, for example, a modal distinction between the movement of a body and the body itself; there is also a modal distinction between one movement and another movement of the same body.

were not so, I do not know why matter should be unworthy of the divine nature, since (Pr.14) there can be no substance external to God by which it can be acted upon. All things, I repeat, are in God, and all things that come to pass do so only through the laws of God's infinite nature and follow from the necessity of his essence (as I shall later show). Therefore by no manner of reasoning can it be said that God is acted upon by anything else or that extended substance is unworthy of the divine nature, even though it be supposed divisible, as long as it is granted to be eternal and infinite.

But enough of this subject for the present.

PROPOSITION 16

From the necessity of the divine nature there must follow infinite things in infinite ways (modis), (that is, everything that can come within the scope of infinite intellect).

Proof

This proposition should be obvious to everyone who will but consider this point, that from the given definition of any one thing the intellect infers a number of properties which necessarily follow in fact from the definition (that is, from the very essence of the thing), and the more reality the definition of the thing expresses (that is, the more reality the essence of the thing defined involves) the greater the number of its properties. Now since divine nature possesses absolutely infinite attributes (Def.6), of which each one also expresses infinite essence in its own kind, then there must necessarily follow from the necessity of the divine nature an infinity of things in infinite ways (that is, everything that can come within the scope of infinite intellect).

Corollary 1

Hence it follows that God is the efficient cause of all things that can come within the scope of infinite intellect.

Corollary 2

Secondly, it follows that God is the cause through himself, not per accidens.

[Descartes, *Principles of Philosophy* I, sections 60—61]

Spinoza uses this philosophical terminology to express the difference between matter as divided up into individual corporeal parts and matter as pure homogeneous extension. In the former case, we have, for example, different portions of water, each one of which being capable of dissolution into hydrogen and oxygen. Such parts are modes of extension, and hence only *modally distinct* from substance and from each other. In the latter case, we have substance as extended, i.e., substance conceived under the attribute of extension, and in this sense it is neither divisible nor dissoluble. For substance and its attributes are not divisible, nor separable from each other such that either one attribute of substance could be separated from another attribute in reality or all the attributes could be separated from substance itself. (Propositions 12 and 13). By means of this distinction Spinoza believes he is able to preserve our ordinary way of talking about matter being divisible into bodily parts and to retain nevertheless his philosophical thesis about the indivisibility of substance and its attributes. Whether he succeeds is a subject of controversy. [Spinoza, *Thoughts on Metaphysics*, II, chapter 5]

Corollary 3

Thirdly, it follows that God is absolutely the first cause.

PROPOSITION 17

God acts solely from the laws of his own nature, constrained by none.

Proof

We have just shown that an infinity of things follow, absolutely, solely from the necessity of divine nature, or—which is the same thing—solely from the laws of that same nature (Pr.16); and we have proved (Pr.15) that nothing can be or be conceived without God, but that everything is in God. Therefore there can be nothing external to God by which he can be determined or constrained to act. Thus God acts solely from the laws of his own nature and is constrained by none.

Corollary 1

Hence it follows, firstly, that there is no cause, except the perfection of his nature, which either extrinsically or intrinsically moves God to act.

Corollary 2

It follows, secondly, that God alone is a free cause. For God alone exists solely from the necessity of his own nature (Pr.11 and Cor.1 Pr.14) and acts solely from the necessity of his own nature (Pr.17). So he alone is a free cause (Def.7).

Scholium

Others take the view that God is a free cause because—so they think—he can bring it about that those things which we have said follow from his nature—that is, which are within his power—should not come about, that is, they should not be produced by him. But this is as much as to say that God can bring it about that it should not follow from the nature of a triangle that its three angles are equal to two right angles, or that from a given cause the effect should not follow, which is absurd.

Furthermore, I shall show later on without the help of this proposition that neither intellect nor will pertain to the nature of God. I know indeed that there are many who think they can prove that intellect in the highest degree and free-will belong to the nature of God; for they say they know of nothing more perfect which they may attribute to God than that which is the highest perfection in us. Again, although they conceive of God as having in actuality intellect in the highest degree, they yet do not believe he can bring about the existence of everything which in actuality he understands, for they think they would thereby be nullifying God's power. If, they say, he had created everything that is within his intellect, then he would not have been able to create anything more; and this they regard as inconsistent with God's omnipotence. So they have preferred to regard God as indifferent to everything and as creating nothing but what he has decided, by some absolute exercise of will, to create. However, I think I have shown quite clearly (Pr.16) that from God's supreme power or infinite nature an infinity of things in infinite ways—that is, everything—have necessarily flowed or are always following from that same necessity, just as from the nature of a triangle it follows from eternity to eternity that its three angles are equal to two right angles. Therefore God's omnipotence has from eternity been actual and will remain for eternity in the same actuality. In this way, I submit, God's omnipotence is established as being far more perfect. Indeed my opponents—let us speak frankly—seem to be denying God's omnipotence. For they are obliged to admit that God understands an infinite number of creatable things which nevertheless he can never create. If this were not so, that is, if he were to create all the things that he understands, he would exhaust his omnipotence, according to them, and render himself imperfect. Thus, to affirm God as perfect they are reduced to having to affirm at the same time that he cannot bring about everything that is within the bounds of his power. I cannot imagine anything more absurd than this, or more inconsistent with God's omnipotence.

Furthermore, I have something here to say about the intellect and will that is usually attributed to God. If intellect and will do indeed pertain to the eternal essence of God, one must understand in the case of both these attributes something very different from the meaning widely entertained. For the intellect and will that would constitute the essence of God would have to be vastly different from human intellect and will, and could have no point of agreement except the name. They could be no more alike than the celestial constellation of the Dog and the dog that barks. This I will prove as follows. If intellect does pertain to the divine nature, it cannot, like man's intellect, be posterior to (as most thinkers hold) or simultaneous with the objects of understanding, since God is prior in causality to all things. (Cor.1 Pr.16). On the contrary, the truth and formal essence of things is what it is because it exists as such in the intellect of God as an object of thought. Therefore God's intellect, in so far as it is conceived as constituting God's essence, is in actual fact the cause of things, in respect both of their essence and their existence. This seems to have been recognised also by those who have asserted that God's intellect, will and power are one and the same. Since therefore God's intellect is the one and only cause of things, both of their essence and their existence, as we have shown, it must necessarily be different from them both in respect of essence and existence. For that which is caused differs from its cause precisely in what it has from its cause. For example, a man is the cause of the existence of another man, but not of the other's essence; for the essence is an eternal truth. So with regard to their essence the two men can be in full agreement, but they must differ with regard to existence; and for that reason if the existence of the one should cease, the existence of the other would not thereby cease. But if the essence of the one could be destroyed and rendered false, so too would the essence of the other. Therefore a thing which is the cause of the essence and existence of some effect must differ from that effect both in respect of essence and existence. But God's intellect is the cause of the essence and existence of man's intellect. Therefore God's intellect, in so far as it is conceived as constituting the divine essence, differs from man's intellect both in respect of essence and existence, and cannot agree with it in any respect other than name—which is what I sought to prove. In the matter of will, the proof is the same, as anyone can readily see.

PROPOSITION 18

God is the immanent, not the transitive, cause of all things.[3]

Proof

All things that are, are in God, and must be conceived through God (Pr.15), and so (Cor.1 Pr.16) God is the cause of the things that are in him, which is the first point. Further, there can be no substance external to God (Pr.14); that is (Def.3), a thing which is in itself external to God—which is the second point. Therefore God is the immanent, not the transitive, cause of all things.

PROPOSITION 19

God, that is, all the attributes of God, are eternal.

Proof

God is substance (Def.6) which necessarily exists (Pr.11); that is, (Pr.7) a thing to whose nature it pertains to exist, or—and this is the same thing—a thing from whose definition existence follows; and so (Def.8) God is eternal. Further, by the attributes of God must be understood that which expresses the essence of the Divine substance (Def.4), that is, that which pertains to substance. It is this, I say, which the attributes themselves must involve. But eternity pertains to the nature of substance (as I have shown in Pr.7). Therefore each of the attributes must involve eternity, and so they are all eternal.

Scholium

This proposition is also perfectly clear from the manner in which I proved the existence of God (Pr.11). From this proof, I repeat, it is obvious that God's existence is, like his essence, an eternal truth. Again, I have also proved God's eternity in another way in Proposition 19 of my *Principles of the Philosophy of Descartes,* and there is no need here to go over that ground again.

PROPOSITION 20

God's existence and his essence are one and the same.

3. See Translator's Foreword, Item No. 12.

Proof

God and all his attributes are eternal (Pr.19); that is, each one of his attributes expresses existence (Def.8). Therefore the same attributes of God that explicate his eternal essence (Def.4) at the same time explicate his eternal existence; that is, that which constitutes the essence of God at the same time constitutes his existence, and so his existence and his essence are one and the same.

Corollary 1

From this it follows, firstly, that God's existence, like his essence, is an eternal truth.

Corollary 2

It follows, secondly, that God is immutable; that is, all the attributes of God are immutable. For if they were to change in respect of existence, they would also have to change in respect of essence (Pr.20); that is—and this is self-evident—they would have to become false instead of true, which is absurd.

PROPOSITION 21

All things that follow from the absolute nature of any attribute of God must have existed always, and as infinite; that is, through the said attribute they are eternal and infinite.

Proof

Suppose this proposition be denied and conceive, if you can, that something in some attribute of God, following from its absolute nature, is finite and has a determinate existence or duration; for example, the idea of God in Thought.[4] Now Thought, being assumed to be an attribute of God, is necessarily infinite by its own nature (Pr.11). However, in so far as it has the idea of God, it is being supposed as finite. Now (Def.2) it cannot be conceived as finite unless it is determined through Thought itself. But it cannot be determined through Thought itself in so far as Thought constitutes the idea of God, for it is in that respect that Thought is supposed to be finite. Therefore it is determined through Thought in so far as Thought does not constitute the idea of God, which Thought must nevertheless necessarily exist (Pr.11). Therefore there must be Thought which does not constitute the idea of God, and so the idea of God does not follow necessarily from its nature in so far as it is absolute Thought. (For it is conceived as constituting and as not con-

4. The term 'idea of God' (idea Dei) is one of the more difficult phrases in Spinoza's philosophical vocabulary, and it has occasioned a variety of interpretations amongst Spinoza's commentators. One point is agreed upon by all: the term does *not* in this context signify a concept of God that any human may have, e.g. the Jewish-Muslim concept of God as distinct from the Christian concept. Rather, the 'idea of God' represents an idea that God has, in particular the idea that God has of himself, or of his essence. (cf. Pr.4,II)

stituting the idea of God). This is contrary to our hypothesis. Therefore if the idea of God in Thought, or anything in some attribute of God (it does not matter what is selected, since the proof is universal), follows from the necessity of the absolute nature of the attribute, it must necessarily be infinite. That was our first point.

Furthermore, that which thus follows from the necessity of the nature of some attribute cannot have a determinate existence, or duration. If this be denied, suppose that there is in some attribute of God a thing following from the necessity of the nature of the attribute, for example, the idea of God in Thought, and suppose that this thing either did not exist at some time, or will cease to exist in the future. Now since Thought is assumed as an attribute of God, it must necessarily exist, and as immutable (Pr.11 and Cor.2 Pr.20). Therefore outside the bounds of the duration of the idea of God (for this idea is supposed at some time not to have existed, or will at some point cease to exist) Thought will have to exist without the idea of God. But this is contrary to the hypothesis, for it is supposed that when Thought is granted the idea of God necessarily follows. Therefore the idea of God in Thought, or anything that necessarily follows from the absolute nature of some attribute of God, cannot have a determinate existence, but is eternal through that same attribute. That was our second point. Note that the same holds for anything in an attribute of God which necessarily follows from the absolute nature of God.

PROPOSITION 22

Whatever follows from some attribute of God in so far as the attribute is modified by a modification that exists necessarily and as infinite through that same attribute, must also exist both necessarily and as infinite.

Proof

This proposition is proved in the same way as the preceding one.

PROPOSITION 23

Every mode which exists necessarily and as infinite must have necessarily followed either from the absolute nature of some attribute of God or from some attribute modified by a modification which exists necessarily and as infinite.

Proof

A mode is in something else through which it must be conceived (Def.5); that is, (Pr.15), it is in God alone and can be conceived only through God. Therefore if a mode is conceived to exist necessarily and to be infinite, both these characteristics must necessarily be inferred or perceived through some attribute of God in so far as that attribute is conceived to express infinity and necessity of existence, or (and by Def.8 this is the same) eternity; that is (Def.6 and Pr.19), in so far as it is considered absolutely. Therefore a mode which exists necessarily and as infinite must have followed from the absolute nature of some attribute of God, either directly (Pr.21) or through the mediation of some modification which follows from the absolute nature of the attribute; that is (Pr.22), which exists necessarily and as infinite.

PROPOSITION 24

The essence of things produced by God does not involve existence.

Proof

This is evident from Def. 1. For that whose nature (considered in itself) involves existence is self-caused and exists solely from the necessity of its own nature.

Corollary

Hence it follows that God is the cause not only of the coming into existence of things but also of their continuing in existence, or, to use a scholastic term, God is the cause of the being of things (essendi rerum). For whether things exist or do not exist, in reflecting on their essence we realise that this essence involves neither existence nor duration. So it is not their essence which can be the cause of either their existence or their duration, but only God, to whose nature alone existence pertains (Cor.1 Pr.14).

PROPOSITION 25

God is the efficient cause not only of the existence of things but also of their essence.

Proof

If this be denied, then God is not the cause of the essence of things, and so (Ax.4) the essence of things can be conceived without God. But this is absurd (Pr.15). Therefore God is also the cause of the essence of things.

Scholium

This proposition follows more clearly from Pr.16; for from that proposition it follows that from the given divine nature both the essence and the existence of things must be inferred. In a word, in the same sense that God is said to be self-caused he must also be said to be the cause of all things. This will be even clearer from the following Corollary.

Corollary

Particular things are nothing but affections of the attributes of God; that is, modes wherein the attributes of God find expression in a definite and determinate way. The proof is obvious from Pr.15 and Def.5.

PROPOSITION 26

A thing which has been determined to act in a particular way has necessarily been so determined by God; and a thing which has not been determined by God cannot determine itself to act.

Proof

That by which things are said to be determined to act in a particular way must necessarily be something positive (as is self-evident). So God, from the necessity of his nature, is the efficient cause both of its essence and its existence (Prs. 25 and 16)—which was the first point. From this the second point quite clearly follows as well. For if a thing which has not been determined by God could determine itself, the first part of this proposition would be false, which, as I have shown, is absurd.

PROPOSITION 27

A thing which has been determined by God to act in a particular way cannot render itself undetermined.

Proof

This proposition is evident from Axiom 3.

PROPOSITION 28

Every individual thing, i.e. anything whatever which is finite and has a determinate existence, cannot exist or be determined to act unless it be determined to exist and to act by another cause which is also finite and has a determinate existence, and this cause again cannot exist or be determined to act unless it be determined to exist and to act by another cause which is also finite and has a determinate existence, and so ad infinitum.

Proof

Whatever is determined to exist and to act has been so determined by God (Pr. 26 and Cor.Pr.24). But that which is finite and has a determinate existence cannot have been produced by the absolute nature of one of God's attributes, for whatever follows from the absolute nature of one of God's attributes is infinite and eternal (Pr.21). It must therefore have followed from God or one of his attributes in so far as that is considered as affected by some mode; for nothing exists but substance and its modes (Ax.1 and Defs. 3 and 5), and modes (Cor.Pr.25) are nothing but affections of God's attributes. But neither could a finite and determined thing have followed from God or one of his attributes in so far as that is affected by a modification which is eternal and infinite (Pr.22). Therefore, it must have followed, or been determined to exist and to act, by God or one of his attributes in so far as it was modified by a modification which is finite and has a determinate existence. That was the first point. Then again this cause or this mode (the reasoning is the same as in the first part of this proof) must also have been determined by another cause, which is also finite and has a determinate existence, and again this last (the reasoning is the same) by another, and so *ad infinitum.*

Scholium

Since some things must have been produced directly by God (those things, in fact, which necessarily follow from his absolute nature) and others through the medium of these primary things (which other things nevertheless cannot be or be conceived without God) it follows, firstly, that God is absolutely the proximate cause of things directly produced by him. I say 'absolutely' (absoluté), and not 'in his own kind' (suo genere), as some say. For the effects of God can neither be nor be conceived without their cause (Pr.15 and Cor.Pr.24). It follows, secondly, that God cannot properly be said to be the remote cause of individual things, unless perchance for the purpose of distinguishing these things from things which he has produced directly, or rather, things which follow from his absolute nature. For by 'remote cause' we understand a cause which is in no way conjoined with its effect. But all things that are, are in God, and depend on God in such a way that they can neither be nor be conceived without him.

PROPOSITION 29   *Determinism*

Nothing in nature is contingent, but all things are from the necessity of the divine nature determined to exist and to act in a definite way.

Proof

Whatever is, is in God (Pr.15). But God cannot be termed a contingent thing, for (Prop.11) he exists necessarily, not contingently. Again, the modes of the divine nature have also followed from it necessarily, not contingently (Pr.16), and that, too, whether in so far as the divine nature is considered absolutely (Pr.21) or in so far as it is considered as determined to act in a definite way (Pr.27). Furthermore, God is the cause of these modes not only in so far as they simply exist (Cor.Pr.24), but also in so far as they are considered as determined to a particular action (Pr.26). Now if they are not determined by God (Pr.26), it is an impossibility, not a contingency, that they should determine themselves. On the other hand (Pr.27), if they are determined by God, it is an impossibility, not a contingency, that they should render themselves undetermined. Therefore, all things are determined from the necessity of the divine nature not only to exist but also to exist and to act in a definite way. Thus, there is no contingency.

Scholium

Before I go any further, I wish to explain at this point what we must understand by 'Natura naturans' and 'Natura naturata.'[5] I should perhaps say not 'explain,' but 'remind the reader,' for I consider that it is

5. See Editor's Introduction, p.11.

already clear from what has gone before that by 'Natura naturans' we must understand that which is in itself and is conceived through itself; that is, the attributes of substance that express eternal and infinite essence; or (Cor.1 Pr.14 and Cor.2 Pr.17), God in so far as he is considered a free cause. By 'Natura naturata' I understand all that follows from the necessity of God's nature, that is, from the necessity of each one of God's attributes; or all the modes of God's attributes in so far as they are considered as things which are in God and can neither be nor be conceived without God.

PROPOSITION 30

The finite intellect in act or the infinite intellect in act must comprehend the attributes of God and the affections of God, and nothing else. [6]

Proof

A true idea must agree with its ideate (Ax.6); that is (as is self-evident), that which is contained in the intellect as an object of thought must necessarily exist in Nature.[7] But in Nature (Cor.1 Pr.14) there is but one substance—God—and no other affections (Pr.15) than those which are in God and that can neither be nor be conceived (Pr.15) without God. Therefore, the finite intellect in act or the infinite intellect in act must comprehend the attributes of God and the affections of God, and nothing else.

PROPOSITION 31

The intellect in act, whether it be finite or infinite, as also will, desire, love etc., must be related to Natura naturata, not to Natura naturans.

Proof

By intellect (as is self-evident) we do not understand absolute thought, but only a definite mode of thinking which differs from other modes such as desire, love, etc., and so (Def.5) must be conceived through absolute Thought—that is (Pr.15 and Def.6), an attribute of God which expresses the eternal and infinite essence of Thought—in such a way that without this attribute it can neither be nor be conceived; and therefore (Sch.Pr.29) it must be related to Natura naturata, not to Natura naturans, just like the other modes of thinking.

6. In Propositions 30 and 31 Spinoza makes use of several terms that were widely employed in medieval psychology and metaphysics. Aristotle originally suggested that human thinking is such that we need to distinguish three phases in its development. First, there is the mere capacity for thinking, say for doing mathematics. All humans, except those who are unfortunately diseased or mutilated, have this capacity. This kind of intellect was called by the medieval Aristotelians the material, or the potential, intellect (intellectus in potentia). Second, when this capacity is exercised and brought into play, it is called the intellect in act (intellectus in actu), since now the intrinsic capacity for thinking possessed by all humans is "actualized." Another expression then for this aspect of intellection is the

7. See Translator's Foreword, Item No. 13

Scholium

The reason for my here speaking of the intellect in act is not that I grant there can be any intellect in potentiality, but that, wishing to avoid any confusion, I wanted to confine myself to what we perceive with the utmost clarity, to wit, the very act of understanding, than which nothing is more clearly apprehended by us. For we can understand nothing that does not lead to a more perfect cognition of the understanding.

PROPOSITION 32

Will cannot be called a free cause, but only a necessary cause.

Proof

Will, like intellect, is only a definite mode of thinking, and so (Pr.28) no single volition can exist or be determined to act unless it is determined by another cause, and this cause again by another, and so ad infinitum. Now if will be supposed infinite, it must also be determined to exist and to act by God, not in so far as he is absolutely infinite substance, but in so far as he possesses an attribute which expresses the infinite and eternal essence of Thought (Pr.23). Therefore in whatever way will is conceived, whether finite or infinite, it requires a cause by which it is determined to exist and to act; and so (Def.7) it cannot be said to be a free cause, but only a necessary or constrained cause.

Corollary 1

Hence it follows, firstly, that God does not act from freedom of will.

Corollary 2

It follows, secondly, that will and intellect bear the same relationship to God's nature as motion-and-rest and, absolutely, as all natural phenomena that must be determined by God (Pr.29) to exist and to act in a definite way. For will, like all the rest, stands in need of a cause by which it may be determined to exist and to act in a definite manner. And although from a given will or intellect infinite things may follow, God cannot on that account be said to act from freedom of will any more than he can be said to act from freedom of motion-and-rest because of what follows from motion-and-rest (for from this, too, infinite things follow).

---

actual intellect. Finally, the medievals, influenced by Aristotle, introduced a third character into this story to account for the stimulation, or energizing, of the potential intellect so that it actually thinks, i.e. the agent, or active, intellect (*intellectus agens*). This latter entity was identified by some philosophers as a suprahuman, supranatural power akin to or identical with God, or by others as a distinct power in the human intellect that acts upon the mere capacity for thought, or the potential intellect. In any case, the agent, or active, intellect is *always actual,* whereas the human intellect is only *actual at times.* As Spinoza himself confesses in the Scholium to Proposition 31, he isn't really committed to this whole way of talking about thought; for he holds that intellect is always in act. If this is so, there is nothing to contrast it with, so this entire conceptual apparatus and its vocabulary become idle.

Therefore will pertains to God's nature no more than do other natural phenomena. It bears the same relationship to God's nature as does motion-and-rest and everything else that we have shown to follow from the necessity of the divine nature and to be determined by that divine nature to exist and to act in a definite way.

PROPOSITION 33

Things could not have been produced by God in any other way or in any other order than is the case.

Proof

All things have necessarily followed from the nature of God (Pr.16) and have been determined to exist and to act in a definite way from the necessity of God's nature (Pr.29). Therefore if things could have been of a different nature or been determined to act in a different way so that the order of Nature would have been different, then God's nature, too, could have been other than it now is, and therefore (Pr.11) this different nature, too, would have had to exist, and consequently there would have been two or more Gods, which (Cor.1, Pr.14) is absurd. Therefore things could not have been produced by God in any other way or in any other order than is the case.

Scholium 1

Since I have here shown more clearly than the midday sun that in things there is absolutely nothing by virtue of which they can be said to be 'contingent,' I now wish to explain briefly what we should understand by 'contingent'; but I must first deal with 'necessary' and 'impossible.' A thing is termed 'necessary' either by reason of its essence or by reason of its cause. For a thing's existence necessarily follows either from its essence and definition or from a given efficient cause. Again, it is for these same reasons that a thing is termed 'impossible'—that is, either because its essence or definition involves a contradiction or because there is no external cause determined to bring it into existence. But a thing is termed 'contingent' for no other reason than the deficiency of our knowledge. For if we do not know whether the essence of a thing involves a contradiction, or if, knowing full well that its essence does not involve a contradiction, we still cannot make any certain judgment as to its existence because the chain of causes is hidden from us, then that thing cannot ever appear to us either as necessary or as impossible. So we term it either 'contingent' or 'possible.'

Scholium 2

It clearly follows from the above that things have been brought into being by God with supreme perfection, since they have necessarily followed from a most perfect nature. Nor does this imply any imperfection in God, for it is his perfection that has constrained us to make this affirmation. Indeed, from its contrary it would clearly follow (as I have just shown) that God is not supremely perfect, because if things had been brought into being in a different way by God, we should have to attribute to God another nature different from that which consideration of a most perfect Being has made us attribute to him.

However, I doubt not that many will ridicule this view as absurd and will not give their minds to its examination, and for this reason alone, that they are in the habit of attributing to God another kind of freedom very different from that which we (Def.7) have assigned to him; that is, an absolute will. Yet I do not doubt that if they were willing to think the matter over and carefully reflect on our chain of proofs they would in the end reject the kind of freedom which they now attribute to God not only as nonsensical but as a serious obstacle to science. It is needless for me here to repeat what was said in the Scholium to Proposition 17. Yet for their sake I shall proceed to show that, even if it were to be granted that will pertains to the essence of God, it would nevertheless follow from his perfection that things could not have been created by God in any other way or in any other order. This will readily be shown if we first con- sider—as they themselves grant—that on God's decree and will alone does it depend that each thing is what it is. For otherwise God would not be the cause of all things. Further, there is the fact that all God's decrees have been sanctioned by God from eternity, for otherwise he could be accused of imperfection and inconstancy. But since the eternal does not admit of 'when' or 'before' or 'after,' it follows merely from God's perfection that God can never decree otherwise nor ever could have de- creed otherwise; in other words, God could not have been prior to his decrees nor can he be without them. "But," they will say, "granted the supposition that God had made a different universe, or that from eternity he had made a different decree concerning Nature and her order, no imperfection in God would follow therefrom." But if they say this, they will be granting at the same time that God can change his decrees. For if God's decrees had been different from what in fact he has decreed regarding Nature and her order—that is, if he had willed and conceived differently concerning Nature—he would necessarily have had a differ- ent intellect and a different will from that which he now has. And if it is permissible to attribute to God a different intellect and a different will without any change in his essence and perfection, why should he not now be able to change his decrees concerning created things, and nevertheless remain equally perfect? For his intellect and will regarding created things and their order have the same relation to his essence and perfection, in whatever manner it be conceived.

Then again, all philosophers whom I have read grant that in God there is no intellect in potentiality but only intellect in act. Now since all of them also grant that his intellect and will are not distinct from his essence, it therefore follows from this, too, that if God had had a differ- ent intellect in act and a different will, his essence too would necessarily have been different. Therefore—as I deduced from the beginning—if things had been brought into being by God so as to be different from what they now are, God's intellect and will—that is (as is granted), God's essence—must have been different, which is absurd. Therefore since things could not have been brought into being by God in any other way or order—and it follows from God's supreme perfection that this is true—surely we can have no sound reason for believing that God did not wish to create all the things that are in his intellect through that very same perfection whereby he understands them.

"But," they will say, "there is in things no perfection or imperfection; that which is in them whereby they are perfect or imperfect, and are called good or bad, depends only on the will of God. Accordingly, if God had so willed it he could have brought it about that that which is now perfection should be utmost imperfection, and vice versa." But what else is this but an open assertion that God, who necessarily understands that which he wills, can by his will bring it about that he should understand things in a way different from the way he understands them—and this, as I have just shown, is utterly absurd. So I can turn their own argument against them, as follows. All things depend on the power of God. For things to be able to be otherwise than as they are, God's will, too, would necessarily have to be different. But God's will cannot be different (as we have just shown most clearly from the consideration of God's perfection). Therefore neither can things be different.

I admit that this view which subjects everything to some kind of indifferent will of God and asserts that everything depends on his pleasure, diverges less from the truth than the view of those who hold that God does everything with the good in mind. For these people seem to posit something external to God that does not depend upon him, to which in acting God looks as if it were a model, or to which he aims, as if it were a fixed target. This is surely to subject God to fate; and no more absurd assertion can be made about God, whom we have shown to be the first and the only free cause of both the essence and the existence of things. So I need not spend any more time in refuting this absurdity.

PROPOSITION 34

God's power is his very essence.

Proof

From the sole necessity of God's essence it follows that God is self-caused (Pr.11) and the cause of all things (Pr.16 and Cor.). Therefore God's power whereby he and all things are and act, is his very essence.

PROPOSITION 35

Whatever we conceive to be within God's power necessarily exists.

Proof

Whatever is within God's power must be so comprehended in his essence (Pr.34) that it follows necessarily from it, and thus necessarily exists.

PROPOSITION 36

Nothing exists from whose nature an effect does not follow.

Proof

Whatever exists expresses God's nature or essence in a definite and determinate way (Cor. Pr.25); that is, (Pr.34), whatever exists expresses God's power, which is the cause of all things, in a definite and determinate way, and so (Pr.16) some effect must follow from it.

APPENDIX

I have now explained the nature and properties of God: that he necessarily exists, that he is one alone, that he is and acts solely from the necessity of his own nature, that he is the free cause of all things and how so, that all things are in God and are so dependent on him that they can neither be nor be conceived without him, and lastly, that all things have been predetermined by God, not from his free will or absolute pleasure, but from the absolute nature of God, his infinite power. Furthermore, whenever the opportunity arose I have striven to remove prejudices that might hinder the apprehension of my proofs. But since there still remain a considerable number of prejudices, which have been, and still are, an obstacle—indeed, a very great obstacle—to the acceptance of the concatenation of things in the manner which I have expounded, I have thought it proper at this point to bring these prejudices before the bar of reason.

Now all the prejudices which I intend to mention here turn on this one point, the widespread belief among men that all things in Nature are like themselves in acting with an end in view. Indeed, they hold it as certain that God himself directs everything to a fixed end; for they say that God has made everything for man's sake and has made man so that he should worship God. So this is the first point I shall consider, seeking the reason why most people are victims of this prejudice and why all are so naturally disposed to accept it. Secondly, I shall demonstrate its falsity; and lastly I shall show how it has been the source of misconceptions about good and bad, right and wrong, praise and blame, order and confusion, beauty and ugliness, and the like.

However, it is not appropriate here to demonstrate the origin of these misconceptions from the nature of the human mind. It will suffice at this point if I take as my basis what must be universally admitted, that all men are born ignorant of the causes of things, that they all have a desire to seek their own advantage, a desire of which they are conscious. From this it follows, firstly, that men believe that they are free, precisely because they are conscious of their volitions and desires; yet concerning the causes that have determined them to desire and will they have not the faintest idea, because they are ignorant of them. Secondly, men act always with an end in view, to wit, the advantage that they seek. Hence it happens that they are always looking only for the final causes of things done, and are satisfied when they find them, having, of course, no reason for further doubt. But if they fail to discover them from some external source, they have no recourse but to turn to themselves, and to reflect on what ends would normally determine them to similar actions, and so they necessarily judge other minds by their own. Further, since they find within themselves and outside themselves a considerable number of means very convenient for the pursuit of their own advantage—as, for instance, eyes for seeing, teeth for chewing, cereals and living creatures for food, the sun for giving light, the sea for breeding fish—the result is that they look on all the things of Nature as means to their own advantage. And realising that these were found, not produced by them, they came to believe that there is someone else who produced these means for their use. For looking on things as means, they could not believe them to be self-created, but on the analogy of the means which they are accustomed to produce for themselves, they were bound to conclude that there was some governor or governors of Nature, endowed with human freedom, who have attended to all their needs and made everything for their use. And having no information on the subject, they also had to estimate the character of these rulers by their own, and so they asserted that the gods direct everything for man's use so that they may bind men to them and be held in the highest honour by them. So it came about that every individual devised different methods of worshipping God as he thought fit in order that God should love him beyond others and direct the whole of Nature so as to serve his blind cupidity and insatiable greed. Thus it was that this misconception developed into superstition and became deep-rooted in the minds of men, and it was for this reason that every man strove most earnestly to understand and to explain the final causes of all things. But in seeking to show that Nature does nothing in vain—that is, nothing that is not to man's advantage—they seem to have shown only this, that Nature and the gods are as crazy as mankind.

Consider, I pray, what has been the upshot. Among so many of Nature's blessings they were bound to discover quite a number of disasters, such as storms, earthquakes, diseases and so forth, and they maintained that these occurred because the gods were angry at the wrongs done to them by men, or the faults committed in the course of their worship. And although daily experience cried out against this and showed by any number of examples that blessings and disasters befall the godly and the ungodly alike without discrimination, they did not on that account abandon their ingrained prejudice. For they found it easier to regard this fact as one among other mysteries they could not understand and thus maintain their present and innate condition of ignorance rather than to demolish in its entirety the theory they had constructed and devise a new one. Hence they made it axiomatic that the judgment of the gods is far beyond man's understanding. Indeed, it is for this reason, and this reason only, that truth might have evaded mankind forever had not Mathematics, which is concerned not with ends but only with the essences and properties of figures, revealed to men a different standard of truth. And there are other causes too—there is no need to mention them here—which could have made men aware of these widespread misconceptions and brought them to a true knowledge of things.

I have thus sufficiently dealt with my first point. There is no need to spend time in going on to show that Nature has no fixed goal and that all final causes are but figments of the human imagination. For I think that this is now quite evident, both from the basic causes from which I have traced the origin of this misconception and from Proposition 16 and the Corollaries to Proposition 32, and in addition from the whole set of proofs I have adduced to show that all things in Nature proceed from an eternal necessity and with supreme perfection. But I will make this additional point, that this doctrine of Final Causes turns Nature completely upside down, for it regards as an effect that which is in fact a cause, and vice versa. Again, it makes that which is by nature first to be last; and finally, that which is highest and most perfect is held to be the most imperfect. Omitting the first two points as self-evident, Propositions 21, 22 and 23 make it clear that that effect is most perfect which is directly produced by God, and an effect is the less perfect in proportion to the number of intermediary causes required for its production. But if the things produced directly by God were brought about to enable him to attain an end, then of necessity the last things for the sake of which the earlier things were brought about would excel all others. Again, this doctrine negates God's perfection; for if God acts with an end in view, he must necessarily be seeking something that he lacks. And although theologians and metaphysicians may draw a distinction between a purpose arising from want and an assimilative purpose[8], they still admit that God has acted in all things for the sake of himself, and not for the sake of the things to be created. For prior to creation they are not able to point to anything but God as a purpose for God's action. Thus they have to admit that God lacked and desired those things for the procurement of which he willed to create the means—as is self-evident.

I must not fail to mention here that the advocates of this doctrine, eager to display their talent in assigning purpose to things, have introduced a new style of argument to prove their doctrine, i.e. a reduction, not to the impossible, but to ignorance, thus revealing the lack of any other argument in its favour. For example, if a stone falls from the roof on somebody's head and kills him, by this method of arguing they will prove that the stone fell in order to kill the man; for if it had not fallen for this purpose by the will of God, how could so many circumstances (and there are often many coinciding circumstances) have chanced to

8. Spinoza alludes here to a late scholastic distinction between two kinds of purposes, or goals: (1) a purpose that satisfies some internal need or lack (fines indigentiae); and (2) a purpose that aims to share what one already has with others who lack it (fines assimilationis). In the present case, this distinction implies that when God does something purposively, He acts not to fulfill a need He has, but to benefit creatures. [In their commentaries on the *Ethics* both Lewis Robinson and Harry Wolfson refer to the seventeenth-century Dutch theologian A. Heereboord as Spinoza's source for this distinction. (L. Robinson, *Kommentar zu Spinoza's Ethik* (Leipzig 1928), 234-235. H. Wolfson, *The Philosophy of Spinoza* (N.Y. 1969), vol. I, 432)]

The theologians derided by Spinoza hoped to avoid by means of this distinction the suggestion that if God acts purposively, He does so because of a need on His part.

concur? Perhaps you will reply that the event occurred because the wind was blowing and the man was walking that way. But they will persist in asking why the wind blew at that time and why the man was walking that way at that very time. If you again reply that the wind sprang up at that time because on the previous day the sea had begun to toss after a period of calm and that the man had been invited by a friend, they will again persist—for there is no end to questions—"But why did the sea toss, and why was the man invited for that time?" And so they will go on and on asking the causes of causes, until you take refuge in the will of God—that is, the sanctuary of ignorance. Similarly, when they consider the structure of the human body, they are astonished, and being ignorant of the causes of such skilful work they conclude that it is fashioned not by mechanical art but by divine or supernatural art, and is so arranged that no one part shall injure another.

As a result, he who seeks the true causes of miracles and is eager to understand the works of Nature as a scholar, and not just to gape at them like a fool, is universally considered an impious heretic and denounced by those to whom the common people bow down as interpreters of Nature and the gods. For these people know that the dispelling of ignorance would entail the disappearance of that sense of awe which is the one and only support for their argument and for the safeguarding of their authority. But I will leave this subject and proceed to the third point that I proposed to deal with.

When men became convinced that everything that is created is created on their behalf, they were bound to consider as the most important quality in every individual thing that which was most useful to them, and to regard as of the highest excellence all those things by which they were most benefited. Hence they came to form these abstract notions to explain the natures of things:—Good, Bad, Order, Confusion, Hot, Cold, Beauty, Ugliness; and since they believe that they are free, the following abstract notions came into being:—Praise, Blame, Right, Wrong. The latter I shall deal with later on after I have treated of human nature; at this point I shall briefly explain the former.

All that conduces to well-being and to the worship of God they call Good, and the contrary, Bad. And since those who do not understand the nature of things, but only imagine things, make no affirmative judgments about things themselves and mistake their imagination for intellect,[9] they are firmly convinced that there is order in things, ignorant as they are of things and of their own nature. For when things are in such arrangement that, being presented to us through our senses, we can readily

9. One of the more fundamental doctrines in Spinoza's theory of knowledge is the radical distinction between imagination and understanding, a point that will be developed in detail in Book II, Propositions 40–49. A corollary of this distinction is the important difference for Spinoza between images and ideas. The former are virtually identical with pictures, which the etymology of the word 'imagine' indicates. The capacity of imagination, or better the act of imagining, is for Spinoza the ability we have to represent to ourselves things, which may or may not exist, without regard to truth. In this sense the imagination is always "free" and "spontaneous": reality doesn't tie it down. Understanding, or intellect, however, is not so "fancy free." It is concerned with reality and truth. Ideas, for Spinoza, are the products of the intellect, or understanding: they are not pictures of

picture them and thus readily remember them, we say that they are well arranged; if the contrary, we say that they are ill-arranged, or confused. And since those things we can readily picture we find pleasing compared with other things, men prefer order to confusion, as though order were something in Nature other than what is relative to our imagination. And they say that God has created all things in an orderly way, without realising that they are thus attributing human imagination to God—unless perchance they mean that God, out of consideration for the human imagination, arranged all things in the way that men could most easily imagine. And perhaps they will find no obstacle in the fact that there are any number of things that far surpass our imagination, and a considerable number that confuse the imagination because of its weakness.

But I have devoted enough time to this. The other notions, too, are nothing but modes of imagining whereby the imagination is affected in various ways, and yet the ignorant consider them as important attributes of things because they believe—as I have said—that all things were made on their behalf, and they call a thing's nature good or bad, healthy or rotten and corrupt, according to its effect on them. For instance, if the motion communicated to our nervous system by objects presented through our eyes is conducive to our feeling of well-being, the objects which are its cause are said to be beautiful, while the objects which provoke a contrary motion are called ugly. Those things that we sense through the nose are called fragrant or fetid, through the tongue sweet or bitter, tasty or tasteless, those that we sense by touch are called hard or soft, rough or smooth, and so on. Finally, those that we sense through our ears are said to give forth noise, sound, or harmony, the last of which has driven men to such madness that they used to believe that even God delights in harmony. There are philosophers who have convinced themselves that the motions of the heavens give rise to harmony. All this goes to show that everyone's judgment is a function of the disposition of his brain, or rather, that he mistakes for reality the way his imagination is affected. Hence it is no wonder—as we should note in passing—that we find so many controversies arising among men, resulting finally in scepticism. For although human bodies agree in many respects, there are very many differences, and so one man thinks good what another thinks bad; what to one man is well-ordered, to another is confused; what to one is pleasing, to another is displeasing, and so forth. I say no more here because this is not the place to treat at length of this subject, and also because all are well acquainted with it from experience. Everybody

---

things but judgments about them, and hence are true or false. (Book II, Proposition 43, Scholium)

In this passage Spinoza is contrasting those who merely have images about things, and accordingly picture them as being good or bad, beautiful or ugly, with those who, concerned with truth, make rational judgments about reality based upon some understanding of nature. Such people may be wrong, but at least they have ventured a judgment about the world, which can be in principle verified. Spinoza maintains here that those who employ ideas, i.e. understanding, recognize that in reality things are neither good nor bad; they just are and must be the way they are. Moralizing about nature is for him idle and empty, since it is based upon imagination, not the intellect.

knows those sayings:—"So many heads, so many opinions," "everyone is wise in his own sight," "brains differ as much as palates," all of which show clearly that men's judgment is a function of the disposition of the brain, and they are guided by imagination rather than intellect. For if men understood things, all that I have put forward would be found, if not attractive, at any rate convincing, as Mathematics attests.

We see therefore that all the notions whereby the common people are wont to explain Nature are merely modes of imagining, and denote not the nature of any thing but only the constitution of the imagination. And because these notions have names as if they were the names of entities existing independently of the imagination I call them 'entities of imagination' (entia imaginationis) rather than 'entities of reason' (entia rationis). So all arguments drawn from such notions against me can be easily refuted. For many are wont to argue on the following lines: if everything has followed from the necessity of God's most perfect nature, why does Nature display so many imperfections, such as rottenness to the point of putridity, nauseating ugliness, confusion, evil, sin, and so on? But, as I have just pointed out, they are easily refuted. For the perfection of things should be measured solely from their own nature and power; nor are things more or less perfect to the extent that they please or offend human senses, serve or oppose human interests. As to those who ask why God did not create all men in such a way that they should be governed solely by reason, I make only this reply, that he lacked not material for creating all things from the highest to the lowest degree of perfection; or, to speak more accurately, the laws of his nature were so comprehensive as to suffice for the production of everything that can be conceived by an infinite intellect, as I proved in Proposition 16.

These are the misconceptions which I undertook to deal with at this point. Any other misconception of this kind can be corrected by everyone with a little reflection.

PART II

OF THE NATURE AND ORIGIN OF THE MIND

I now pass on to the explication of those things that must necessarily have followed from the essence of God, the eternal and infinite Being; not indeed all of them—for we proved in Proposition 16 Part I that from his essence there must follow infinite things in infinite ways—but only those things that can lead us as it were by the hand to the knowledge of the human mind and its utmost blessedness.

DEFINITIONS

1. By 'body' I understand a mode that expresses in a definite and determinate way God's essence in so far as he is considered as an extended thing. (See Cor. Pr.25, I)

2. I say that there pertains to the essence of a thing that which, when granted, the thing is necessarily posited, and by the annulling of which the thing is necessarily annulled; or that without which the thing can neither be nor be conceived, and, vice versa, that which cannot be or be conceived without the thing.

3. By idea I understand a conception of the Mind which the Mind forms because it is a thinking thing.

Explication

I say 'conception' rather than 'perception' because the term perception seems to indicate that the Mind is passive to its object, whereas conception seems to express an activity of the Mind.

4. By an adequate idea I mean an idea which, in so far as it is considered in itself without relation to its object, has all the properties— that is, intrinsic characteristics—of a true idea.

Explication

I say 'intrinsic' so as to exclude the extrinsic characteristic—to wit, the agreement of the idea with that of which it is an idea (ideatum).

5. Duration is the indefinite continuance of existing.

Explication

I say 'indefinite' because it can in no wise be determined through the nature of the existing thing, nor again by the thing's efficient cause, which necessarily posits, but does not annul, the existence of the thing.

6. By reality and perfection I mean the same thing.

7. By individual things (res singulares) I mean things that are finite and have a determinate existence. If several individual things concur in one

act in such a way as to be all together the simultaneous cause of one effect, I consider them all, in that respect, as one individual.

AXIOMS

1. The essence of man does not involve necessary existence; that is, from the order of Nature it is equally possible that a certain man exists or does not exist.

2. Man thinks.

3. Modes of thinking such as love, desire, or whatever emotions are designated by name, do not occur unless there is in the same individual the idea of the thing loved, desired, etc. But the idea can be without any other mode of thinking.

4. We feel a certain body to be affected in many ways.

5. We do not feel or perceive any individual things except bodies and modes of thinking. [N.B.: For Postulates, see after Proposition 13.]

PROPOSITION 1

Thought is an attribute of God; i.e. God is a thinking thing.

Proof

Individual thoughts, or this and that thought, are modes expressing the nature of God in a definite and determinate way (Cor.Pr.25,I). Therefore there belongs to God (Def.5,I) an attribute the conception of which is involved in all individual thoughts, and through which they are conceived. Thought, therefore, is one of God's infinite attributes, expressing the eternal and infinite essence of God (Def.6,I); that is, God is a thinking thing.

Scholium

This Proposition is also evident from the fact that we can conceive of an infinite thinking being. For the more things a thinking being can think, the more reality or perfection we conceive it to have. Therefore a being that can think infinite things in infinite ways is by virtue of its thinking necessarily infinite. Since therefore by merely considering Thought we conceive an infinite being, Thought is necessarily one of the infinite attributes of God (Defs. 4 and 6,I), as we set out to prove.

PROPOSITION 2

Extension is an attribute of God; i.e. God is an extended thing.

Proof

This Proposition is proved in the same way as the preceding proposition.

PROPOSITION 3

In God there is necessarily the idea both of his essence and of every-

thing that necessarily follows from his essence.

Proof

For God can (Pr.1,II) think infinite things in infinite ways, or (what is the same thing, by Pr.16,I) can form the idea of his own essence and of everything that necessarily follows from it. But all that is in God's power necessarily exists (Pr.35,I). Therefore such an idea necessarily exists, and only in God (Pr.15,I).

Scholium

By God's power the common people understand free-will and God's right over all things that are, which things are therefore commonly considered as contingent. They say that God has power to destroy everything and bring it to nothing. Furthermore, they frequently compare God's power with that of kings. But this doctrine we have refuted in Cors. 1 and 2, Pr.32,I; and in Pr.16,I we proved that God acts by the same necessity whereby he understands himself; that is, just as it follows from the necessity of the divine nature (as is universally agreed) that God understands himself, by that same necessity it also follows that God acts infinitely in infinite ways. Again, we showed in Pr.34,I that God's power is nothing but God's essence in action, and so it is as impossible for us to conceive that God does not act as that God does not exist. Furthermore, if one wished to pursue the matter, I could easily show here that the power that common people assign to God is not only a human power (which shows that they conceive God as a man or like a man) but also involves negation of power. But I am reluctant to hold forth so often on the same subject. I merely request the reader most earnestly to reflect again and again on what we said on this subject in Part I from Proposition 16 to the end. For nobody will rightly apprehend what I am trying to say unless he takes great care not to confuse God's power with a king's human power or right.

PROPOSITION 4

The idea of God, from which infinite things follow in infinite ways, must be one, and one only.

Proof

Infinite intellect comprehends nothing but the attributes of God and his affections (Pr.30,I). But God is one, and one only (Cor.1,Pr.14,I). Therefore the idea of God, from which infinite things follow in infinite ways, must be one, and one only.

PROPOSITION 5

The formal being[1] of ideas recognizes God as its cause only in so far as he is considered as a thinking thing, and not in so far as he is explicated by any other attribute; that is, the ideas both of God's attributes and of individual things recognize as their efficient cause not the things

---

1. See Translator's Foreword, Item No. 17.

of which they are ideas,—that is, the things perceived,—but God himself in so far as he is a thinking thing.

Proof

This is evident from Pr.3,II. For there our conclusion that God can form the idea of his own essence and of everything that necessarily follows therefrom was inferred solely from God's being a thinking thing, and not from his being the object of his own idea. Therefore the formal being of ideas recognizes God as its cause in so far as he is a thinking thing. But there is another proof, as follows. The formal being of ideas is a mode of thinking (as is self-evident); that is, (Cor.Pr.25,I) a mode which expresses in a definite manner the nature of God in so far as he is a thinking thing, and so does not involve (Pr.10,I) the conception of any other attribute of God. Consequently (Ax.4,I), it is the effect of no other attribute but Thought; and so the formal being of ideas recognizes God as its cause only in so far as he is considered as a thinking thing.

PROPOSITION 6

The modes of any attribute have God for their cause only in so far as he is considered under that attribute, and not in so far as he is considered under any other attribute.

Proof

Each attribute is conceived through itself independently of any other (Pr.10,I). Therefore the modes of any attribute involve the conception of their own attribute, and not that of any other. Therefore they have God for their cause only in so far as he is considered under the attribute of which they are modes, and not in so far as he is considered under any other attribute (Ax.4,I).

Corollary

Hence it follows that the formal being of things that are not modes of thinking does not follow from the nature of God by reason of his first having known them; rather, the objects of ideas follow and are inferred from their own attributes in the same way and by the same necessity as we have shown ideas to follow from the attribute of Thought.

PROPOSITION 7

The order and connection of ideas is the same as the order and connection of things.

Proof

This is evident from Ax.4,I; for the idea of what is caused depends on the knowledge of the cause of which it is the effect.

Corollary

Hence it follows that God's power of thinking is coextensive with his actualized power of acting. That is, whatever follows formally from the infinite nature of God, all this follows from the idea of God with the same order and the same connection, as an object of thought in God.

Scholium

At this point, before proceeding further, we should recall to mind what I have demonstrated above—that whatever can be perceived by infinite intellect as constituting the essence of substance pertains entirely to the one sole substance. Consequently, thinking substance and extended substance are one and the same substance, comprehended now under this attribute, now under that. So, too, a mode of Extension and the idea of that mode are one and the same thing, expressed in two ways. This truth seems to have been glimpsed by some of the Hebrews,[2] who hold that God, God's intellect and the things understood by God are one and the same. For example, a circle existing in Nature and the idea of the existing circle—which is also in God—are one and the same thing, explicated through different attributes. And so, whether we conceive Nature under the attribute of Extension or under the attribute of Thought or under any other attribute, we find one and the same order, or one and the same connection of causes—that is, the same things following one another. When I said that God is the cause—e.g.—of the idea of a circle only in so far as he is a thinking thing, and of a circle only in so far as he is an extended thing, my reason was simply this, that the formal being of the idea of a circle can be perceived only through another mode of thinking as its proximate cause, and that mode through another, and so ad infinitum, with the result that as long as things are considered as modes of thought, we must explicate the order of the whole of Nature, or the connection of causes, through the attribute of Thought alone; and in so far as things are considered as modes of Extension, again the order of the whole of Nature must be explicated through the attribute of Extension only. The same applies to other attributes. Therefore God, in so far as he consists of infinite attributes, is in fact the cause of things as they are in themselves. For the present, I cannot give a clearer explanation.

PROPOSITION 8

The ideas of non-existing individual things or modes must be comprehended in the infinite idea of God in the same way as the formal essences of individual things or modes are contained in the attributes of God.

Proof

This proposition is obvious from the preceding one, but may be understood more clearly from the preceding Scholium.

Corollary

Hence it follows that as long as individual things do not exist except in so far as they are comprehended in the attributes of God, their being

2. The reference is most likely to Moses Maimonides, *The Guide of The Perplexed,* Part 1, Chapter 68.

as objects of thought—that is, their ideas—do not exist except in so far as the infinite idea of God exists; and when individual things are said to exist not only in so far as they are comprehended in the attributes of God but also in so far as they are said to have duration, their ideas also will involve the existence through which they are said to have duration.

Scholium

Should anyone want an example for a clearer understanding of this matter, I can think of none at all that would adequately explicate the point with which I am here dealing, for it has no parallel. Still, I shall try to illustrate it as best I can. The nature of a circle is such that the rectangles formed from the segments of its intersecting chords are equal. Hence an infinite number of equal rectangles are contained in a circle,

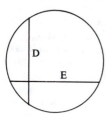

but none of them can be said to exist except in so far as the circle exists, nor again can the idea of any one of these rectangles be said to exist except in so far as it is comprehended in the idea of the circle. Now of this infinite number of intersecting chords let two, E and D, exist. Now indeed their ideas also exist not only in so far as they are merely comprehended in the idea of the circle but also in so far as they involve the existence of those rectangles, with the result that they are distinguished from the other ideas of the other rectangles.

PROPOSITION 9

The idea of an individual thing existing in actuality has God for its cause not in so far as he is infinite but in so far as he is considered as affected by another idea of a thing existing in actuality, of which God is the cause in so far as he is affected by a third idea, and so ad infinitum.

Proof

The idea of an individual actually existing thing is an individual mode of thinking distinct from other modes (Cor. and Sch.Pr.8,II), and so (Pr.6,II) it has God as its cause only in so far as he is a thinking thing. But not (Pr.28,I) in so far as he is a thinking thing absolutely, but in so far as he is considered as affected by another definite mode of thinking. And of this latter God is also the cause in so far as he is affected by another definite mode of thinking, and so ad infinitum. But the order and connection of ideas is the same as the order and connection of causes (Pr.7,II). Therefore an individual idea is caused by another idea; i.e. God in so far as he is considered as affected by another idea. And this last idea is caused by God, in so far as he is affected by yet another idea, and so ad infinitum.

Corollary

Whatsoever happens in the individual object of any idea, knowledge of it is in God only in so far as he has the idea of that object.

Proof

Whatsoever happens in the object of any idea, the idea of it is in God (Pr.3,II) not in so far as he is infinite, but in so far as he is considered as affected by another idea of an individual thing (preceding Pr.). But the order and connection of ideas is the same as the order and connection of things (Pr.7,II). Therefore the knowledge of what happens in an individual object is in God only in so far as he has the idea of that object.

PROPOSITION 10

The being of substance does not pertain to the essence of man; i.e. substance does not constitute the form (forma) of man.

Proof

The being of substance involves necessary existence (Pr.7,I). So if the being of substance pertained to the essence of man, man would necessarily be granted together with the granting of substance (Def.2,II), and consequently man would necessarily exist, which is absurd (Ax.1,II). Therefore . . . etc.

Scholium

This Proposition is also proved from Pr.5,I, which states that there cannot be two substances of the same nature. Now since many men can exist, that which constitutes the form of man is not the being of substance. This Proposition is furthermore evident from the other properties of substance—that substance is by its own nature infinite, immutable, indivisible, etc., as everyone can easily see.

Corollary

Hence it follows that the essence of man is constituted by definite modifications of the attributes of God.

Proof

For the being of substance does not pertain to the essence of man (preceding Pr.), which must therefore (Pr.15,I) be something that is in God, and which can neither be nor be conceived without God; i.e. an affection or mode (Cor.Pr.25,I) which expresses the nature of God in a definite and determinate way.

Scholium

All must surely admit that nothing can be or be conceived without God. For all are agreed that God is the sole cause of all things, both of their essence and their existence; that is, God is the cause of things not only in respect of their coming into being (secundum fieri), as they say, but also in respect of their being. But at the same time many assert that that without which a thing can neither be nor be conceived pertains to the essence of the thing, and so they believe that either the nature of God pertains to the essence of created things or that created things can either be or be conceived without God; or else, more probably, they hold no consistent opinion. I think that the reason for this is their failure to observe the proper order of philosophical enquiry. For the divine nature, which they should have considered before all else—it being prior both in cognition and in Nature—they have taken to be last in the order of cognition, and the things that are called objects of sense they have taken as prior to everything. Hence it has come about that in considering natural phenomena, they have completely disregarded the divine nature. And when thereafter they turned to the contemplation of the divine nature, they could find no place in their thinking for those fictions on which they had built their natural science, since these fictions were of no avail in attaining knowledge of the divine nature. So it is little wonder that they have contradicted themselves on all sides.

But I pass over these points, for my present purpose is restricted to explaining why I have not said that that without which a thing can neither be nor be perceived pertains to the essence of the thing. My reason is that individual things can neither be nor be conceived without God, and yet God does not pertain to their essence. But I did say that that necessarily constitutes the essence of a thing which, when posited, posits the thing, and by the annulling of which the thing is annulled; i.e. that without which the thing can neither be nor be conceived, and vice versa, that which can neither be nor be conceived without the thing.

PROPOSITION 11

That which constitutes the actual being of the human mind is basically nothing else but the idea of an individual actually existing thing.

Proof

The essence of man (Cor.Pr.10,II) is constituted by definite modes of the attributes of God, to wit (Ax.2,II), modes of thinking. Of all these modes the idea is prior in nature (Ax.3,II), and when the idea is granted, the other modes—modes to which the idea is prior by nature—must be in the same individual (Ax.3,II). And so the idea is that which basically constitutes the being of the human mind. But not the idea of a nonexisting thing; for then (Cor.Pr.8,II) the idea itself could not be said to exist. Therefore it is the idea of an actually existing thing. But not the idea of an infinite thing, for an infinite thing (Prs.21 and 22,I) must always necessarily exist, and this is absurd (Ax.1,II). Therefore that which first constitutes the actual being of the human mind is the idea of an individual actually existing thing.

Corollary

Hence it follows that the human mind is part of the infinite intellect of God; and therefore when we say that the human mind perceives this or that, we are saying nothing else but this: that God—not in so far as he is infinite but in so far as he is explicated through the nature of the human mind, that is, in so far as he constitutes the essence of the human mind—has this or that idea. And when we say that God has this or that idea not only in so far as he constitutes the essence of the human mind but also in so far as he has the idea of another thing simultaneously with the human mind, then we are saying that the human mind perceives a thing partially or inadequately.

Scholium

At this point our readers will no doubt find themselves in some difficulty and will think of many things that will give them pause. So I ask them to proceed slowly step by step with me, and to postpone judgment until they have read to the end.

PROPOSITION 12

Whatever happens in the object of the idea constituting the human mind is bound to be perceived by the human mind; i.e. the idea of that thing will necessarily be in the human mind. That is to say, if the object of the idea constituting the human mind is a body, nothing can happen in that body without its being perceived by the mind.

Proof

Whatever happens in the object of any idea, knowledge thereof is necessarily in God (Cor.Pr.9,II) in so far as he is considered as affected by the idea of that object; that is, (Pr.11,II) in so far as he constitutes the mind of some thing. So whatever happens in the object of the idea constituting the human mind, knowledge thereof is necessarily in God in so far as he constitutes the nature of the human mind; that is (Cor.Pr.11, II), knowledge of that thing is necessarily in the mind; i.e. the mind perceives it.

Scholium

This Proposition is also obvious, and is more clearly understood, from Sch.Pr.7,II,q.v.

PROPOSITION 13

The object of the idea constituting the human mind is the body—i.e. a definite mode of extension actually existing, and nothing else.

Proof

If the body were not the object of the human mind, the ideas of the affections of the body would not be in God (Cor.Pr.9,II) in so far as he constitutes our mind, but in so far as he constitutes the mind of another thing; that is, (Cor.Pr.11,II) the ideas of the affections of the body would not be in our mind. But (Ax.4,II) we do have ideas of the affections of a body. Therefore the object of the idea constituting the human mind is a body, a body actually existing (Pr.11,II). Again, if there were another object of the mind apart from the body, since nothing exists from which some effect does not follow (Pr.36,I), there would necessarily have to be in our mind the idea of some effect of it (Pr.12,II). But (Ax.5,II) there is no such idea. Therefore the object of our mind is an existing body, and nothing else.

Corollary

Hence it follows that man consists of mind and body, and the human body exists according as we sense it.

Scholium

From the above we understand not only that the human Mind is united to the Body but also what is to be understood by the union of Mind and Body. But nobody can understand this union adequately or distinctly unless he first gains adequate knowledge of the nature of our body. For what we have so far demonstrated is of quite general application, and applies to men no more than to other individuals, which are all animate, albeit in different degrees. For there is necessarily in God an idea of each thing whatever, of which idea God is the cause in the same way as he is the cause of the idea of the human body. And so whatever we have asserted of the idea of the human body must necessarily be asserted of the idea of each thing. Yet we cannot deny, too, that ideas differ among themselves as do their objects, and that one is more excellent and contains more reality than another, just as the object of one idea is more excellent than that of another and contains more reality. Therefore in order to determine the difference between the human mind and others and in what way it excels them, we have to know the nature of its object (as we have said); that is, the nature of the human body. Now I cannot here explain this nature, nor is it essential for the points that I intend to demonstrate. But I will make this general assertion, that in proportion as a body is more apt than other bodies to act or be acted upon simultaneously in many ways, so is its mind more apt than other minds to perceive many things simultaneously; and in proportion as the actions of one body depend on itself alone and the less that other bodies concur with it in its actions, the more apt is its mind to understand distinctly. From this we can realise the superiority of one mind over others, and we can furthermore see why we have only a very confused knowledge of our body, and many other facts which I shall deduce from this basis in what follows. Therefore I have thought it worthwhile to explicate and demonstrate these things more carefully. To this end there must be a brief preface concerning the nature of bodies.

Axiom 1

All bodies are either in motion or at rest.

Axiom 2

Each single body can move at varying speeds.

Lemma 1

Bodies are distinguished from one another in respect of motion and rest, quickness and slowness, and not in respect of substance.

Proof

The first part of this Lemma I take to be self-evident. As to bodies not being distinguished in respect of substance, this is evident from both Pr.5 and Pr.8, Part 1, and still more clearly from Sch. Pr.15, Part 1.

Lemma 2

All bodies agree in certain respects.

Proof

All bodies agree in this, that they involve the conception of one and the same attribute (Def.1,II), and also in that they may move at varying speeds, and may be absolutely in motion or absolutely at rest.

Lemma 3

A body in motion or at rest must have been determined to motion or rest by another body, which likewise has been determined to motion or rest by another body, and that body by another, and so ad infinitum.

Proof

Bodies are individual things (Def.1,II) which are distinguished from one another in respect of motion and rest (Lemma 1), and so (Pr.28,I) each body must have been determined to motion or rest by another individual thing, namely, another body (Pr.6,II), which is also in motion or at rest (Ax.1). But this body again—by the same reasoning—could not have been in motion or at rest unless it had been determined to motion or rest by another body, and this body again—by the same reasoning—by another body, and so on, ad infinitum.

Corollary

Hence it follows that a body in motion will continue to move until it is determined to rest by another body, and a body at rest continues to be at rest until it is determined to move by another body. This, too, is self-evident; for when I suppose for example, that a body A is at rest and I give no consideration to other moving bodies, I can assert nothing about body A but that it is at rest. Now if it should thereafter happen that body A is in motion, this surely could not have resulted from the fact that it was at rest; for from that fact nothing else could have followed than that body A should be at rest. If on the other hand A were supposed to be in motion, as long as we consider only A, we can affirm nothing of it but that it is in motion. If it should thereafter happen that A should be at rest, this surely could not have resulted from its previous motion; for from its motion nothing else could have followed but that A was in motion. So this comes about from a thing that was not in A, namely, an external cause by which the moving body A was determined to rest.

Axiom 1

All the ways in which a body is affected by another body follow from the nature of the affected body together with the nature of the body affecting it, so that one and the same body may move in various ways in accordance with the various natures of the bodies causing its motion; and, on the other hand, different bodies may be caused to move in different ways by one and the same body.

Axiom 2

When a moving body collides with a body at rest and is unable to cause it to move, it is reflected so as to continue its motion, and the angle between the line of motion of the reflection and the plane of the body at rest with which it has collided is equal to the angle between the line of incidence of motion and the said plane.

So far we have been discussing the simplest bodies, those which are distinguished from one another solely by motion and rest, quickness and slowness. Now let us advance to composite bodies.

Definition

When a number of bodies of the same or different magnitude form close contact with one another through the pressure of other bodies upon them, or if they are moving at the same or different rates of speed so as to preserve an unvarying relation of movement among themselves, these bodies are said to be united with one another and all together to form one body or individual thing, which is distinguished from other things through this union of bodies.

Axiom 3

The degree of difficulty with which the parts of an individual thing or composite body can be made to change their position and consequently the degree of difficulty with which the individual takes on different shapes, is proportional to the extent of the surface areas along which they are in close contact. Hence bodies whose parts maintain close contact along large areas of their surfaces I term hard; those whose parts maintain contact along small surface areas I term soft; while those whose parts are in a state of motion among themselves I term liquid.

Lemma 4

If from a body, or an individual thing composed of a number of bodies, certain bodies are separated, and at the same time a like number of other bodies of the same nature take their place, the individual thing will retain its nature as before, without any change in its form (forma).

Proof

Bodies are not distinguished in respect of substance (Lemma 1). That which constitutes the form of the individual thing consists in a union of bodies (preceding definition). But this union, by hypothesis, is retained in spite of the continuous change of component bodies.

Therefore the individual thing will retain its own nature as before, both in respect of substance and of mode.

Lemma 5

If the parts of an individual thing become greater or smaller, but so proportionately that they all preserve the same mutual relation of motion-and-rest as before, the individual thing will likewise retain its own nature as before without any change in its form.

Proof

The reasoning is the same as in the preceding Lemma.

Lemma 6

If certain bodies composing an individual thing are made to change the existing direction of their motion, but in such a way that they can continue their motion and keep the same mutual relation as before, the individual thing will likewise preserve its own nature without any change of form.

Proof

This is self-evident; for, by hypothesis, the individual thing retains all that we, in defining it, asserted as constituting its form.

Lemma 7

Furthermore, the individual thing so composed retains its own nature, whether as a whole it is moving or at rest, and in whatever direction it moves, provided that each constituent part retains its own motion and continues to communicate this motion to the other parts.

Proof

This is evident from its definition, which you will find preceding Lemma 4.

Scholium

We thus see how a composite individual can be affected in many ways and yet preserve its nature. Now hitherto we have conceived an individual thing composed solely of bodies distinguished from one another only by motion-and-rest and speed of movement; that is, an individual thing composed of the simplest bodies. If we now conceive another individual thing composed of several individual things of different natures, we shall find that this can be affected in many other ways while still preserving its nature. For since each one of its parts is composed of several bodies, each single part can therefore (preceding Lemma), without any change in its nature, move with varying degrees of speed and consequently communicate its own motion to other parts with varying degrees of speed. Now if we go on to conceive a third kind of individual things composed of this second kind, we shall find that it can be affected in many other ways without any change in its form. If we thus continue to infinity, we shall readily conceive the whole of Nature as one individual whose parts—that is, all the constituent bodies—vary in infinite ways without any change in the individual as a whole.

If my intention had been to write a full treatise on body, I should have had to expand my explications and demonstrations. But I have already declared a different intention, and the only reason for my dealing with this subject is that I may readily deduce therefrom what I have set out to prove.

POSTULATES

1. The human body is composed of very many individual parts of different natures, each of which is extremely complex.

2. Of the individual components of the human body, some are liquid, some are soft, and some are hard.

3. The individual components of the human body, and consequently the human body itself, are affected by external bodies in a great many ways.

4. The human body needs for its preservation a great many other bodies, by which, as it were (quasi), it is continually regenerated.

5. When a liquid part of the human body is determined by an external body to impinge frequently on another part which is soft, it changes the surface of that part and impresses on it certain traces of the external body acting upon it.

6. The human body can move external bodies and dispose them in a great many ways.

PROPOSITION 14

The human mind is capable of perceiving a great many things, and this capacity will vary in proportion to the variety of states which its body can assume.

Proof

The human body (Posts.3 and 6) is affected by external bodies in a great many ways and is so structured that it can affect external bodies in a great many ways. But the human mind must perceive all that happens in the human body (Pr.12,II). Therefore the human mind is capable of perceiving very many things, and . . . etc.

PROPOSITION 15

The idea which constitutes the formal being of the human mind is not simple, but composed of very many ideas.

Proof

The idea which constitutes the formal being of the human mind is the idea of the body (Pr.13,II), which is composed of a great number of very composite individual parts (Postulate 1). But in God there is necessarily the idea of every individual component part (Cor.Pr.8,II). Therefore (Pr.7,II) the idea of the human body is composed of these many ideas of the component parts.

PROPOSITION 16

The idea of any mode wherein the human body is affected by external bodies must involve the nature of the human body together with the nature of the external body.

Proof

All the modes wherein a body is affected follow from the nature of the body affected together with the nature of the affecting body (Ax.1 after Cor.Lemma 3). Therefore the idea of these modes will necessarily involve the nature of both bodies (Ax.4,I). So the idea of any mode wherein the human body is affected by an external body involves the nature of the human body and the external body.

Corollary 1

Hence it follows that the human mind perceives the nature of very many bodies along with the nature of its own body.

Corollary 2

Secondly, the ideas that we have of external bodies indicate the constitution of our own body more than the nature of external bodies. This I have explained with many examples in Appendix, Part I.

PROPOSITION 17

If the human body is affected in a way (modo) that involves the nature of some external body, the human mind will regard that same external body as actually existing, or as present to itself, until the human body undergoes a further modification which excludes the existence or presence of the said body.

Proof

This is evident; for as long as the human body is thus affected, so long will the human mind (Pr.12,II) regard this affection of the body; that is (by the preceding Proposition), so long will it have the idea of a mode existing in actuality, an idea involving the nature of an external body; that is, an idea which does not exclude but posits the existence or presence of the nature of the external body. So the mind (Cor.1 of the preceding proposition) will regard the external body as actually existing, or as present, until . . . etc.

Corollary

The mind is able to regard as present external bodies by which the human body has been once affected, even if they do not exist and are not present.

Proof

When external bodies so determine the fluid parts of the human body that these frequently impinge on the softer parts, they change the surfaces of these softer parts (Post.5). Hence it comes about (Ax.2 after Cor. Lemma 3) that the fluid parts are reflected therefrom in a manner different from what was previously the case; and thereafter, again coming into contact with the said changed surfaces in the course of their own spontaneous motion, they are reflected in the same way as when they were impelled towards those surfaces by external bodies. Consequently, in continuing this reflected motion they affect the human body in the same manner, which manner will again be the object of thought in the mind (Pr.12,II); that is (Pr.17,II), the mind will again regard the external body as present. This will be repeated whenever the fluid parts of the human body come into contact with those same surfaces in the course of their own spontaneous motion. Therefore, although the external bodies by which the human body has once been affected may no longer exist, the mind will regard them as present whenever this activity of the body is repeated.

Scholium

So we see how it can come about that we regard as present things which are not so, as often happens. Now it is possible that there are other causes for this fact, but it is enough for me at this point to have indicated one cause through which I can explicate the matter just as if I had demonstrated it through its true cause. Yet I do not think that I am far from the truth, since all the postulates that I have assumed contain scarcely anything inconsistent with experience; and after demonstrating that the human body exists just as we sense it (Cor.Pr.13,II), we may not doubt experience.

In addition (preceding Cor. and Cor.2 Pr.16,II), this gives a clear understanding of the difference between the idea, e.g. of Peter which constitutes the essence of Peter's mind, and on the other hand the idea of Peter which is in another man, say Paul. The former directly explicates the essence of Peter's body, and does not involve existence except as long as Peter exists. The latter indicates the constitution of Paul's body rather than the nature of Peter; and so, while that constitution of Paul's body continues to be, Paul's mind will regard Peter as present to him although Peter may not be in existence. Further, to retain the usual terminology, we will assign the word 'images' (imagines) to those affections of the human body the ideas of which set forth external bodies as if they were present to us, although they do not represent shapes. And when the mind regards bodies in this way, we shall say that it 'imagines' (imaginari).

At this point, to begin my analysis of error, I should like you to note that the imaginations of the mind, looked at in themselves, contain no error; i.e. the mind does not err from the fact that it imagines, but only in so far as it is considered to lack the idea which excludes the existence of those things which it imagines to be present to itself. For if the mind, in imagining non-existing things to be present to it, knew at the same time that those things did not exist in fact, it would surely impute this power of imagining not to the defect but to the strength of its own nature, especially if this faculty of imagining were to depend solely on its own nature; that is, (Def.7,I) if this faculty of imagining were free.

PROPOSITION 18

If the human body has once been affected by two or more bodies at the same time, when the mind afterwards imagines one of them, it will straightway remember the others too.

Proof

The mind imagines (preceding Cor.) any given body for the following reason, that the human body is affected and conditioned by the impressions of an external body in the same way as it was affected when certain of its parts were acted upon by the external body. But, by hypothesis, the human mind was at that time conditioned in such a way that the mind imagined two bodies at the same time. Therefore it will now also imagine two bodies at the same time, and the mind, in imagining one of them, will straightway remember the other as well.

Scholium

Hence we clearly understand what memory is. It is simply a linking of ideas involving the nature of things outside the human body, a linking which occurs in the mind parallel to the order and linking of the affections of the human body. I say, firstly, that it is only the linking of those ideas that involve the nature of things outside the human body, not of those ideas that explicate the nature of the said things. For they are in fact (Pr. 16,II) ideas of the affections of the human body which involve the nature both of the human body and of external bodies. Secondly, my purpose in saying that this linking occurs in accordance with the order and linking of the affections of the human body is to distinguish it from the linking of ideas in accordance with the order of the intellect whereby the mind perceives things through their first causes, and which is the same in all men.

Furthermore, from this we clearly understand why the mind, from thinking of one thing, should straightway pass on to thinking of another thing which has no likeness to the first. For example, from thinking of the word 'pomum' (apple) a Roman will straightway fall to thinking of the fruit, which has no likeness to that articulated sound nor anything in common with it other than that the man's body has often been affected by them both; that is, the man has often heard the word 'pomum' while seeing the fruit. So everyone will pass on from one thought to another according as habit in each case has arranged the images in his body. A soldier, for example, seeing the tracks of a horse in the sand will straightway pass on from thinking of the horse to thinking of the rider, and then thinking of war, and so on. But a peasant, from thinking of a horse, will pass on to thinking of a plough, and of a field, and so on. So every person will pass on from thinking of one thing to thinking of another according as he is in the habit of joining together and linking the images of things in various ways.

PROPOSITION 19

The human mind has no knowledge of the body, nor does it know it to exist, except through ideas of the affections by which the body is affected.

Proof

The human mind is the very idea or knowledge of the human body (Pr.13,II), and this idea is in God (Pr.9,II) in so far as he is considered as affected by another idea of a particular thing; or, since (Post.4) the human body needs very many other bodies by which it is continually regenerated, and the order and connection of ideas is the same (Pr.7,II) as the order and connection of causes, this idea is in God in so far as he is considered as affected by the ideas of numerous particular things. Therefore God has the idea of the human body, or knows the human body, in so far as he is affected by numerous other ideas, and not in so far as he constitutes the nature of the human mind; that is, (Cor.Pr.11, II), the human mind does not know the human body. But the ideas of the affections of the body are in God in so far as he does constitute the nature of human mind; i.e. the human mind perceives these affections (Pr.12,II) and consequently perceives the human body (Pr.16,II), and perceives it as actually existing (Pr.17,II). Therefore it is only to that extent that the human mind perceives the human body.

PROPOSITION 20

There is also in God the idea or knowledge of the human mind, and this follows in God and is related to God in the same way as the idea or knowledge of the human body.

Proof

Thought is an attribute of God (Pr.1,II), and so (Pr.3,II) the idea of both Thought and all its affections—and consequently (Pr.11,II) of the human mind as well—must necessarily be in God. Now this idea or knowledge of the mind does not follow in God in so far as he is infinite, but in so far as he is affected by another idea of a particular thing (Pr.9,II). But the order and connection of ideas is the same as the order and connection of causes (Pr.7,II). Therefore this idea or knowledge of the mind follows in God and is related to God in the same way as the idea or knowledge of the body.

PROPOSITION 21

This idea of the mind is united to the mind in the same way as the mind is united to the body.

Proof

That the mind is united to the body we have shown from the fact that the body is the object of the mind (Prs.12 and 13,II), and so by the same reasoning the idea of the mind must be united to its object—that is, to the mind itself—in the same way as the mind is united to the body.

Scholium

This proposition is understood far more clearly from Sch.Pr.7,II. There we showed that the idea of the body and the body itself—that is, (Pr.13,II) mind and body—are one and the same individual thing, conceived now under the attribute of Thought and now under the attribute of Extension. Therefore the idea of the mind and the mind itself are one and the same thing, conceived under one and the same attribute, namely, Thought. The idea of the mind, I repeat, and the mind itself follow in God by the same necessity and from the same power of thought. For in fact the idea of the mind—that is, the idea of an idea—is nothing other than the form (forma) of the idea in so far as the idea is considered as a mode of thinking without relation to its object. For as soon as anyone knows something, by that very fact he knows that he knows, and at the same time he knows that he knows that he knows, and so on ad infinitum. But I will deal with this subject later.

PROPOSITION 22

The human mind perceives not only the affections of the body but also the ideas of these affections.

Proof

The ideas of ideas of affections follow in God and are related to God in the same way as ideas of affections, which can be proved in the same manner as Pr.20,II. But the ideas of affections of the body are in the human mind (Pr.12,II); that is (Cor.Pr.11,II), in God in so far as he constitutes the essence of the human mind. Therefore the ideas of these ideas will be in God in so far as he has knowledge or the idea of the human mind; that is (Pr.21,II), they will be in the human mind itself, which therefore perceives not only the affections of the body but also the ideas of these affections.

PROPOSITION 23

The mind does not know itself except in so far as it perceives ideas of affections of the body.

Proof

The idea or knowledge of the mind (Pr.20,II) follows in God and is related to God in the same way as the idea or knowledge of the body. But since (Pr.19,II) the human mind does not know the human body—that is, (Cor.Pr.11,II) since the knowledge of the human body is not related to God in so far as he constitutes the nature of the human mind—therefore neither is knowledge of the mind related to God in so far as he constitutes the essence of the human mind. And so (Cor.Pr.11,II) the human mind to that extent does not know itself. Again, the ideas of the affections by which the body is affected involve the nature of the human body (Pr.16,II); that is, (Pr.13,II) they are in agreement (conveniunt) with the nature of the mind. Therefore the knowledge of these ideas will necessarily involve knowledge of the mind. But (preceding Pr.) the knowledge of these ideas is in the human mind. Therefore the human mind knows itself only to that extent.

PROPOSITION 24

The human mind does not involve an adequate knowledge of the component parts of the human body.

Proof

The component parts of the human body do not pertain to the essence of the body itself save in so far as they preserve an unvarying relation of motion with one another (Def. after Cor.Lemma 3), and not in so far as they can be considered as individual things apart from their relation to the human body. For the parts of the human body (Post.1) are very composite individual things, whose parts can be separated from the human body (Lemma 4) without impairing in any way its nature and specific reality (forma), and can establish a quite different relation of motion with other bodies (Ax.1 after Lemma 3). Therefore (Pr.3,II) the idea or knowledge of any component part will be in God, and will be so (Pr.9,II) in so far as he is considered as affected by another idea of a particular thing, a particular thing which is prior in Nature's order to the part itself (Pr.7,II). Further, the same holds good of any part of an individual component part of the human body, and so of any component part of the human body there is knowledge in God in so far as he is affected by very many ideas of things, and not in so far as he has the idea only of the human body, that is (Pr.13,II) the idea that constitutes the nature of the human mind. So (Cor.Pr.11,II) the human mind does not involve adequate knowledge of the component parts of the human body.

PROPOSITION 25

The idea of any affection of the human body does not involve an adequate knowledge of an external body.

Proof

We have shown that the idea of an affection of the human body involves the nature of an external body in so far as the external body determines the human body in some definite way (Pr.16,II). But in so far as the external body is an individual thing that is not related to the human body, the idea or knowledge of it is in God (Pr.9,II) in so far as God is considered as affected by the idea of another thing which is (Pr.7,II) prior in nature to the said external body. Therefore an adequate knowledge of the external body is not in God in so far as he has the idea of an affection of the human body; i.e. the idea of an affection of the human body does not involve an adequate knowledge of an external body.

PROPOSITION 26

The human mind does not perceive any external body as actually existing except through the ideas of affections of its own body.

Proof

If the human body is not affected in any way by an external body, then (Pr.7,II) neither is the idea of the human body—that is (Pr.13,II), the human mind—affected in any way by the idea of the existence of that body; i.e. it does not in any way perceive the existence of that external body. But in so far as the human body is affected in some way by an external body, to that extent it perceives the external body (Pr.16,II, with Cor.1).

Corollary

In so far as the human mind imagines[3] (imaginatur) an external body, to that extent it does not have an adequate knowledge of it.

Proof

When the human mind regards external bodies through the ideas of affections of its own body, we say that it imagines (imaginatur) (see Sch.Pr.17,II), and in no other way can the mind imagine external bodies as actually existing (preceding Pr.). Therefore, in so far as the mind imagines external bodies (Pr.25,II), it does not have adequate knowledge of them.

PROPOSITION 27

The idea of any affection of the human body does not involve adequate knowledge of the human body.

Proof

Any idea whatsoever of any affection of the human body involves the nature of the human body only to the extent that the human body is considered to be affected in some definite way (Pr.16,II). But in so far as the human body is an individual thing that can be affected in many other ways, the idea . . . etc. (See Proof Pr.25,II).

PROPOSITION 28

The ideas of the affections of the human body, in so far as they are related only to the human mind, are not clear and distinct, but confused.

Proof

The ideas of the affections of the human body involve the nature both of external bodies and of the human body itself (Pr.16,II), and must involve the nature not only of the human body but also of its parts. For affections are modes in which parts of the human body (Post.3), and consequently the body as a whole, is affected. But (Prs.24 and 25,II) an adequate knowledge of external bodies, as also of the component parts of the human body, is not in God in so far as he is considered as affected

---

3. See Translator's Foreword, Item No. 20.

by the human mind, but in so far as he is considered as affected by other ideas. Therefore these ideas of affections, in so far as they are related only to the human mind, are like conclusions without premisses; that is, as is self-evident, confused ideas.

Scholium

The idea that constitutes the nature of the human mind is likewise shown, when considered solely in itself, not to be clear and distinct, as is also the idea of the human mind and the ideas of ideas of affections of the human body in so far as they are related only to the human mind, as everyone can easily see.

PROPOSITION 29

The idea of the idea of any affection of the human body does not involve adequate knowledge of the human mind.

Proof

The idea of an affection of the human body (Pr.27,II) does not involve adequate knowledge of the body itself; in other words, it does not adequately express the nature of the body; that is (Pr.13,II), it does not adequately agree (convenit) with the nature of the mind. So (Ax.6,I) the idea of this idea does not adequately express the nature of the human mind; i.e. it does not involve an adequate knowledge of it.

Corollary

Hence it follows that whenever the human mind perceives things after the common order of nature, it does not have an adequate knowledge of itself, nor of its body, nor of external bodies, but only a confused and fragmentary knowledge. For the mind does not know itself save in so far as it perceives ideas of the affections of the body (Pr.23,II). Now it does not perceive its own body (Pr.19,II) except through ideas of affections of the body, and also it is only through these affections that it perceives external bodies (Pr.26,II). So in so far as it has these ideas, it has adequate knowledge neither of itself (Pr.29,II) nor of its own body (Pr.27,II) nor of external bodies (Pr.25,II), but only a fragmentary (mutilatam) and confused knowledge (Pr.28,II and Sch.).

Scholium

I say expressly that the mind does not have an adequate knowledge, but only a confused and fragmentary knowledge, of itself, its own body, and external bodies whenever it perceives things from the common order of nature, that is, whenever it is determined externally—namely, by the fortuitous run of circumstance—to regard this or that, and not when it is determined internally, through its regarding several things at the same time, to understand their agreement, their differences, and their opposition. For whenever it is conditioned internally in this or in another way, then it sees things clearly and distinctly, as I shall later show.

PROPOSITION 30

We can have only a very inadequate knowledge of the duration of our body.

Proof

The duration of our body does not depend on its essence (Ax.1,II), nor again on the absolute nature of God (Pr.21,I), but (Pr.28,I) it is determined to exist and to act by causes which are also determined by other causes to exist and to act in a definite and determinate way, and these again by other causes, and so ad infinitum. Therefore the duration of our body depends on the common order of nature and the structure of the universe. Now there is in God adequate knowledge of the structure of the universe in so far as he has ideas of all the things in the universe, and not in so far as he has only the idea of the human body (Cor.Pr.9,II). Therefore knowledge of the duration of our body is very inadequate in God in so far as he is considered only to constitute the nature of the human mind. That is (Cor.Pr.11,II), this knowledge is very inadequate in the human mind.

PROPOSITION 31

We can have only a very inadequate knowledge of the duration of particular things external to us.

Proof

Each particular thing, just like the human body, must be determined by another particular thing to exist and to act in a definite and determinate way, and this latter thing again by another, and so on ad infinitum (Pr.28,I). Now since we have shown in the preceding Proposition that from this common property of particular things we can have only a very inadequate knowledge of the duration of the human body, in the case of the duration of particular things we have to come to the same conclusion: that we can have only a very inadequate knowledge thereof.

Corollary

Hence it follows that all particular things are contingent and perishable. For we can have no adequate knowledge of their duration (preceding Pr.), and that is what is to be understood by contingency and perishability (Sch.I,Pr.33,I). For apart from this there is no other kind of contingency (Pr.29,I).

PROPOSITION 32

All ideas are true in so far as they are related to God.

Proof

All ideas, which are in God, agree completely with the objects of which they are ideas (Cor.Pr.7,II), and so they are all true. (Ax. 6,I)

PROPOSITION 33

There is nothing positive in ideas whereby they can be said to be false.

Proof

If this be denied, conceive, if possible, a positive mode of thinking which constitutes the form (forma) of error or falsity. This mode of thinking cannot be in God (preceding Pr.), but neither can it be or be conceived externally to God (Pr.15,I). Thus there can be nothing positive in ideas whereby they can be called false.

PROPOSITION 34

Every idea which in us is absolute, that is, adequate and perfect, is true.

Proof

When we say that there is in us an adequate and perfect idea, we are saying only this (Cor.Pr.11,II), that there is an adequate and perfect idea in God in so far as he constitutes the essence of our mind. Consequently we are saying only this, that such an idea is true (Pr.32,II).

PROPOSITION 35

Falsity consists in the privation of knowledge which inadequate ideas, that is, fragmentary and confused ideas, involve.

Proof

There is nothing positive in ideas which constitutes the form (forma) of falsity (Pr.33,II). But falsity cannot consist in absolute privation (for minds, not bodies, are said to err and be deceived), nor again in absolute ignorance, for to be ignorant and to err are different. Therefore it consists in that privation of knowledge which inadequate knowledge, that is, inadequate and confused ideas, involves.

Scholium

In Sch. Pr.17,II I explained how error consists in the privation of knowledge, but I will give an example to enlarge on this explanation. Men are deceived in thinking themselves free, a belief that consists only in this, that they are conscious of their actions and ignorant of the causes by which they are determined. Therefore the idea of their freedom is simply the ignorance of the cause of their actions. As to their saying that human actions depend on the will, these are mere words without any corresponding idea. For none of them knows what the will is and how it moves the body, and those who boast otherwise and make up stories of dwelling-places and habitations of the soul provoke either ridicule or disgust.

As another example, when we gaze at the sun, we see it as some two hundred feet distant from us. The error does not consist in simply seeing the sun in this way but in the fact that while we do so we are not aware of the true distance and the cause of our seeing it so. For although we may later become aware that the sun is more than six hundred times the diameter of the earth distant from us, we shall nevertheless continue to see it as close at hand. For it is not our ignorance of its true distance that causes us to see the sun to be so near; it is that the affection of our body involves the essence of the sun only to the extent that the body is affected by it.

PROPOSITION 36

Inadequate and confused ideas follow by the same necessity as adequate, or clear and distinct, ideas.

Proof

All ideas are in God (Pr.15,I), and in so far as they are related to God, they are true (Pr.32,II) and adequate (Cor.Pr.7,II). So there are no inadequate or confused ideas except in so far as they are related to the particular mind of someone (see Prs.24 and 28,II). So all ideas, both adequate and inadequate, follow by the same necessity (Cor.Pr.6,II).

PROPOSITION 37

That which is common to all things (see Lemma 2 above) and is equally in the part as in the whole, does not constitute the essence of any one particular thing.

Proof

If this be denied, conceive, if possible, that it does constitute the essence of one particular thing, B. Therefore it can neither be nor be conceived without B (Def.2,II). But this is contrary to our hypothesis. Therefore it does not pertain to B's essence, nor does it constitute the essence of any other particular thing.

PROPOSITION 38

Those things that are common to all things and are equally in the part as in the whole, can be conceived only adequately.

Proof

Let A be something common to all bodies, and equally in the part of any body as in the whole. I say that A can be conceived only adequately. For its idea (Cor.Pr.7,II) will necessarily be in God both in so far as he has the idea of the human body and in so far as he has the ideas of affections of the human body, affections which partly involve the natures of both the human body and external bodies (Prs.16,25 and 27,II). That is, (Prs.12 and 13,II), this idea will necessarily be adequate in God in so far as he constitutes the human mind; that is, in so far as he has the ideas which are in the human mind. Therefore the mind (Cor.Pr.11,II) necessarily perceives A adequately, and does so both in so far as it perceives itself and in so far as it perceives its own body or any external body; nor can A be perceived in any other way.

Corollary

Hence it follows that there are certain ideas or notions common to all men. For (by Lemma 2) all bodies agree in certain respects, which must be (preceding Pr.) conceived by all adequately, or clearly and distinctly.

PROPOSITION 39

Of that which is common and proper to the human body and to some external bodies by which the human body is customarily affected, and which is equally in the part as well as in the whole of any of these bodies, the idea also in the mind will be adequate.

Proof

Let A be that which is common and proper to the human body and to some external bodies, and is equally in the human body as in those same external bodies, and, finally, is equally in a part of any external body as in the whole. There will be in God an adequate idea of A (Cor.Pr.7,II) both in so far as he has the idea of the human body and in so far as he has ideas of those posited external bodies. Let it now be supposed that the human body is affected by an external body through that which is common to them both, that is, A. The idea of this affection will involve the property A (Pr.16,II), and so (Cor.Pr.7,II) the idea of this affection, in so far as it involves the property A, will be adequate in God in so far as he is affected by the idea of the human body; that is, (Pr.13,II) in so far as he constitutes the nature of the human mind. So this idea will also be adequate in the human mind (Cor.Pr.11,II).

Corollary

Hence it follows that the mind is more capable of perceiving more things adequately in proportion as its body has more things in common with other bodies.

PROPOSITION 40

Whatever ideas follow in the mind from ideas that are adequate in it are also adequate.

Proof

This is evident. For when we say that an idea follows in the human mind from ideas that are adequate in it, we are saying no more (Cor.Pr.11,II) than that there is in the divine intellect an idea of which God is the cause, not in so far as he is infinite nor in so far as he is affected by ideas of numerous particular things, but only in so far as he constitutes the essence of the human mind.

Scholium 1

I have here set forth the cause of those notions that are called 'common,' and which are the basis of our reasoning processes. Now certain axioms or notions have other causes which it would be relevant to set forth by this method of ours; for thus we could establish which notions are more useful compared with others, and which are of scarcely any value. And again, we could establish which notions are more common to all, which ones are clear and distinct only to those not labouring under prejudices (praejudiciis) and which ones are ill-founded. Furthermore, this would clarify the origin of those notions called 'secondary'—and consequently the axioms which are based on them—as well as other related questions to which I have at times given thought. But I have decided not to embark on these questions at this point because I have set them aside for another treatise,[4] and also to avoid wearying the reader with too lengthy a discussion of this subject. Nevertheless, to omit nothing that it is essential to know, I shall briefly deal with the question of the origin of the so-called 'transcendental terms,' such as 'entity,' 'thing,' 'something' (ens, res, aliquid).

These terms originate in the following way. The human body, being limited, is capable of forming simultaneously in itself only a certain number of distinct images. (I have explained in Sch.Pr.17,II what an image is.) If this number be exceeded, these images begin to be confused, and if the number of distinct images which the body is capable of forming simultaneously in itself be far exceeded, all the images will be utterly confused with one another. This being so, it is evident from Cor.Pr.17 and Pr.18,II that the human mind is able to imagine simultaneously and distinctly as many bodies as there are images that can be formed simultaneously in its body. But when the images in the body are utterly confused, the mind will also imagine all the bodies confusedly without any distinction, and will comprehend them, as it were, under one attribute, namely, that of entity, thing, etc. This conclusion can also be reached from the fact that images are not always equally vivid, and also from other causes analogous to these, which I need not here explicate. To consider only one cause will suffice for our purpose, for they all reduce to this, that these terms signify ideas confused in the highest degree.

Again, from similar causes have arisen those notions called 'universal,' such as 'man,' 'horse,' 'dog,' etc; that is to say, so many images are formed in the human body simultaneously (e.g. of man) that our capacity to imagine them is surpassed, not indeed completely, but to the extent that the mind is unable to imagine the unimportant differences of individuals (such as the complexion and stature of each) and their exact number, and imagines distinctly only their common characteristic in so far as the body is affected by them. For it was by this that the body was affected most repeatedly, by each single individual. The mind expresses this by the word 'man,' and predicates this word of an infinite number of individuals. For, as we said, it is unable to imagine the determinate number of individuals.

4. This is Spinoza's incomplete essay, *On The Improvement of the Understanding.*

But it should be noted that not all men form these notions in the same way; in the case of each person the notions vary according as that thing varies whereby the body has more frequently been affected, and which the mind more readily imagines or calls to mind. For example, those who have more often regarded with admiration the stature of men will understand by the word 'man' an animal of upright stature, while those who are wont to regard a different aspect will form a different common image of man, such as that man is a laughing animal, a feather-less biped, or a rational animal. Similarly, in other cases, each will form universal images according to the conditioning of his body. Therefore it is not surprising that so many controversies have arisen among philosophers who have sought to explain natural phenomena through merely the images of these phenomena.

Scholium 2

From all that has already been said it is quite clear that we perceive many things and form universal notions:

1. Firstly, from individual objects presented to us through the senses in a fragmentary (mutilate) and confused manner without any intellectual order (see Cor.Pr.29,II); and therefore I call such perceptions 'knowl-edge from casual experience.'

2. Secondly, from symbols. For example, from having heard or read certain words we call things to mind and we form certain ideas of them similar to those through which we imagine things (Sch.Pr.18,II).

Both these ways of regarding things I shall in future refer to as 'knowledge of the first kind,' 'opinion' or 'imagination.'

3. Thirdly, from the fact that we have common notions and adequate ideas of the properties of things (see Cor.Pr.38 and 39 with its Cor., and Pr.40,II). I shall refer to this as 'reason' and 'knowledge of the second kind.'

Apart from these two kinds of knowledge there is, as I shall later show, a third kind of knowledge, which I shall refer to as 'intuition.' This kind of knowledge proceeds from an adequate idea of the formal essence of certain attributes of God to an adequate knowledge of the essence of things. I shall illustrate all these kinds of knowledge by one single example. Three numbers are given; it is required to find a fourth which is related to the third as the second to the first. Tradesmen have no hesitation in multiplying the second by the third and dividing the product by the first, either because they have not yet forgotten the rule they learnt without proof from their teachers, or because they have in fact found this correct in the case of very simple numbers, or else from the force of the proof of Proposition 19 of the Seventh Book of Euclid, to wit, the common property of proportionals. But in the case of very simple numbers, none of this is necessary. For example, in the case of the given numbers 1, 2, 3, everybody can see that the fourth pro-portional is 6, and all the more clearly because we infer in one single intuition the fourth number from the ratio we see the first number bears to the second.

PROPOSITION 41

Knowledge of the first kind is the only cause of falsity; knowledge of the second and third kind is necessarily true.

Proof

In the preceding Scholium we asserted that all those ideas which are inadequate and confused belong to the first kind of knowledge; and thus (Pr.35,II) this knowledge is the only cause of falsity. Further, we asserted that to knowledge of the second and third kind there belong those ideas which are adequate. Therefore (Pr.34,II) this knowledge is necessarily true.

PROPOSITION 42

Knowledge of the second and third kind, and not knowledge of the first kind, teaches us to distinguish true from false.

Proof

This Proposition is self-evident. For he who can distinguish the true from the false must have an adequate idea of the true and the false; that is (Sch.2 Pr.40,II) he must know the true and the false by the second or third kind of knowledge.

PROPOSITION 43

He who has a true idea knows at the same time that he has a true idea, and cannot doubt its truth.

Proof

A true idea in us is one which is adequate in God in so far as he is explicated through the nature of the human mind (Cor.Pr.11,II). Let us suppose, then, that there is in God, in so far as he is explicated through the nature of the human mind, an adequate idea, A. The idea of this idea must also necessarily be in God, and is related to God in the same way as the idea A (Pr.20,II, the proof being of general application). But by our supposition the idea A is related to God in so far as he is explicated through the nature of the human mind. Therefore the idea of the idea A must be related to God in the same way; that is (Cor.Pr.11,II), this adequate idea of the idea A will be in the mind which has the adequate idea A. So he who has an adequate idea, that is, he who knows a thing truly (Pr.34,II) must at the same time have an adequate idea—that is, a true knowledge—of his knowledge; that is, (as is self-evident) he is bound at the same time to be certain.

Scholium

I have explained in the Scholium to Pr.21,II what is an idea of an idea; but it should be noted that the preceding proposition is sufficiently self-evident. For nobody who has a true idea is unaware that a true idea involves absolute certainty. To have a true idea means only to know a thing perfectly, that is, to the utmost degree. Indeed, nobody can doubt this, unless he thinks that an idea is some dumb thing like a picture on a tablet, and not a mode of thinking, to wit, the very act of understanding. And who, pray, can know that he understands some thing unless he first understands it? That is, who can know that he is certain of something unless he is first certain of it? Again, what standard of truth can there be that is clearer and more certain than a true idea? Indeed, just as light makes manifest both itself and darkness, so truth is the standard both of itself and falsity.

I think I have thus given an answer to those questions which can be stated as follows: if a true idea is distinguished from a false one only inasmuch as it is said to correspond with that of which it is an idea, then a true idea has no more reality or perfection than a false one (since they are distinguished only by an extrinsic characteristic) and consequently neither is a man who has true ideas superior to one who has only false ideas. Secondly, how do we come to have false ideas? And finally, how can one know for certain that one has ideas which correspond with that of which they are ideas? I have now given an answer, I repeat, to these problems. As regards the difference between a true and a false idea, it is clear from Pr.35,II that the former is to the latter as being to non-being. The causes of falsity I have quite clearly shown from Propositions 19 to 35 with the latter's Scholium, from which it is likewise obvious what is the difference between a man who has true ideas and one who has only false ideas. As to the last question, how can a man know that he has an idea which corresponds to that of which it is an idea, I have just shown, with abundant clarity, that this arises from the fact that he does have an idea that corresponds to that of which it is an idea; that is, truth is its own standard. Furthermore, the human mind, in so far as it perceives things truly, is part of the infinite intellect of God (Cor.Pr.11,II), and thus it is as inevitable that the clear and distinct ideas of the mind are true as that God's ideas are true.

PROPOSITION 44

It is not in the nature of reason to regard things as contingent, but as necessary.

Proof

It is in the nature of reason to perceive things truly (Pr.41,II), to wit, (Ax.6,I) as they are in themselves; that is (Pr.29,I), not as contingent, but as necessary.

Corollary 1

Hence it follows that it solely results from imagination (imaginatio) that we regard things, both in respect of the past and of the future, as contingent.

Scholium

I shall explain briefly how this comes about. We have shown above (Pr.17,II and Cor.) that although things may not exist, the mind nevertheless always imagines them as present unless causes arise which exclude their present existence. Further, we have shown (Pr.18,II) that if the human body has once been affected by two external bodies at the same time, when the mind later imagines one of them, it will straightway call the other to mind as well; that is, it will regard both as present to it unless other causes arise which exclude their present existence. Furthermore, nobody doubts that time, too, is a product of the imagination, and arises from the fact that we see some bodies move more slowly than others, or more quickly, or with equal speed. Let us therefore suppose that yesterday a boy saw Peter first of all in the morning, Paul at noon, and Simon in the evening, and that today he again sees Peter in the morning. From Pr.18,II it is clear that as soon as he sees the morning light, forthwith he will imagine the sun as traversing the same tract of sky as on the previous day, that is, he will imagine a whole day, and he will imagine Peter together with morning, Paul with midday, and Simon with evening; that is, he will imagine the existence of Paul and Simon with reference to future time. On the other hand, on seeing Simon in the evening he will refer Paul and Peter to time past by imagining them along with time past. This train of events will be the more consistent the more frequently he sees them in that order. If it should at some time befall that on another evening he sees James instead of Simon, then the following morning he will imagine along with evening now Simon, now James, but not both together. For we are supposing that he has seen only one of them in the evening, not both at the same time. Therefore his imagination will waver, and he will imagine, along with a future evening, now one, now the other; that is, he will regard neither of them as going to be there for certain, but both of them contingently. This wavering of the imagination occurs in the same way if the imagination be of things which we likewise regard with relation to past or present time, and consequently we shall imagine things, as related both to present and past or future time, as contingent.

Corollary 2

It is in the nature of reason to perceive things in the light of eternity (sub quadam specie aeternitatis).

Proof

It is in the nature of reason to regard things as necessary, not as contingent (previous Pr.). Now it perceives this necessity truly (Pr.41,II); that is, as it is in itself (Ax.6,I). But (Pr.16,I) this necessity is the very necessity of God's eternal nature. Therefore it is in the nature of reason to regard things in this light of eternity. Furthermore, the basic principles of reason are those notions (Pr.38,II) which explicate what is common to all things, and do not explicate (Pr.37,II) the essence of any particular thing, and therefore must be conceived without any relation to time, but in the light of eternity.

PROPOSITION 45

Every idea of any body or particular thing existing in actuality necessarily involves the eternal and infinite essence of God.

Proof

The idea of a particular thing actually existing necessarily involves both the essence and the existence of the thing (Cor.Pr.8,II). But particular things cannot be conceived without God (Pr.15,I). Now since they have God for their cause (Pr.6,II) in so far as he is considered under that attribute of which the things themselves are modes, their ideas (Ax.4,I) must necessarily involve the conception of their attribute; that is, (Def.6,I) the eternal and infinite essence of God.

Scholium

Here by existence I do not mean duration, that is, existence in so far as it is considered in the abstract as a kind of quantity. I am speaking of the very nature of existence, which is attributed to particular things because they follow in infinite numbers in infinite ways from the eternal necessity of God's nature (Pr.16,I). I am speaking, I repeat, of the very existence of particular things in so far as they are in God. For although each particular thing is determined by another particular thing to exist in a certain manner, the force by which each persists in existing follows from the eternal necessity of God's nature. See Cor.Pr.24,I.

PROPOSITION 46

The knowledge of the eternal and infinite essence of God which each idea involves is adequate and perfect.

Proof

The proof of the preceding proposition is universally valid, and whether a thing be considered as a part or a whole, its idea, whether of whole or part, involves the eternal and infinite essence of God (preceding Pr.). Therefore that which gives knowledge of the eternal and infinite essence of God is common to all things, and equally in the part as in the whole. And so this knowledge will be adequate (Pr.38,II).

PROPOSITION 47

The human mind has an adequate knowledge of the eternal and infinite essence of God.

Proof

The human mind has ideas (Pr.22,II) from which (Pr.23,II) it perceives itself, its own body (Pr.19,II) and external bodies (Cor.1,Pr.16 and Pr.17,II) as actually existing, and so it has an adequate knowledge of the eternal and infinite essence of God (Prs. 45 and 46,II).

Scholium

Hence we see that God's infinite essence and his eternity are known to all. Now since all things are in God and are conceived through God, it follows that from this knowledge we can deduce a great many things so as to know them adequately and thus to form that third kind of knowledge I mentioned in Sch.2 Pr.40,II, of the superiority and usefulness of which we shall have occasion to speak in Part Five. That men do not have as clear a knowledge of God as they do of common notions arises from the fact that they are unable to imagine God as they do bodies, and that they have connected the word God with the images of things which they commonly see; and this they can scarcely avoid, being affected continually by external bodies. Indeed, most errors result solely from the incorrect application of words to things. When somebody says that the lines joining the centre of a circle to its circumference are unequal, he surely understands by circle, at least at that time, something different from what mathematicians understand. Likewise, when men make mistakes in arithmetic, they have different figures in mind from those on paper. So if you look only to their minds, they indeed are not mistaken; but they seem to be wrong because we think that they have in mind the figures on the page. If this were not the case, we would not think them to be wrong, just as I did not think that person to be wrong whom I recently heard shouting that his hall had flown into his neighbour's hen, for I could see clearly what he had in mind. Most controversies arise from this, that men do not correctly express what is in their mind, or they misunderstand another's mind. For, in reality, while they are hotly contradicting one another, they are either in agreement or have different things in mind, so that the apparent errors and absurdities of their opponents are not really so.

PROPOSITION 48

In the mind there is no absolute, or free, will. The mind is determined to this or that volition by a cause, which is likewise determined by another cause, and this again by another, and so ad infinitum.

Proof

The mind is a definite and determinate mode of thinking (Pr.11,II), and thus (Cor.2,Pr.17,I) it cannot be the free cause of its actions: that is, it cannot possess an absolute faculty of willing and non-willing. It must be determined to will this or that (Pr.28,I) by a cause, which likewise is determined by another cause, and this again by another, etc.

Scholium

In the same way it is proved that in the mind there is no absolute faculty of understanding, desiring, loving, etc. Hence it follows that these and similar faculties are either entirely fictitious or nothing more than metaphysical entities or universals which we are wont to form from particulars. So intellect and will bear the same relation to this or that idea, this or that volition, as stoniness to this or that stone, or man to Peter and Paul. As to the reason why men think they are free, we explained that in the Appendix to Part One.

But before proceeding further, it should here be noted that by the will I mean the faculty of affirming and denying, and not desire. I mean, I repeat, the faculty whereby the mind affirms or denies what is true or what is false, not the desire whereby the mind seeks things or shuns them. But now that we have proved that these faculties are universal notions which are not distinct from the particulars from which we form them, we must inquire whether volitions themselves are anything more than ideas of things. We must inquire, I say, whether there is in the mind any other affirmation and denial apart from that which the idea, in so far as it is an idea, involves. On this subject see the following proposition and also Def.3,II, lest thought becomes confused with pictures. For by ideas I do not mean images such as are formed at the back of the eye—or, if you like, in the middle of the brain—but conceptions of thought.

PROPOSITION 49

There is in the mind no volition, that is, affirmation and negation, except that which an idea, in so far as it is an idea, involves.

Proof

There is in the mind (preceding Pr.) no absolute faculty of willing and non-willing, but only particular volitions, namely, this or that affirmation, and this or that negation. Let us therefore conceive a particular volition, namely, a mode of thinking whereby the mind affirms that the three angles of a triangle are equal to two right angles. This affirmation involves the conception, or idea, of a triangle; that is, it cannot be conceived without the idea of a triangle. For to say that A must involve the conception of B is the same as to say that A cannot be conceived without B. Again, this affirmation (Ax.3,II) cannot even be without the idea of a triangle. Therefore this idea can neither be nor be conceived without the idea of a triangle. Furthermore, this idea of a triangle must involve this same affirmation, namely, that its three angles are equal to two right angles. Therefore, vice versa, this idea of a triangle can neither be nor be conceived without this affirmation, and so (Def.2,II) this affirmation belongs to the essence of the idea of a triangle, and is nothing more than the essence itself. And what I have said of this volition (for it was arbitrarily selected) must also be said of every volition, namely, that it is nothing but an idea.

Corollary

Will and intellect are one and the same thing.

Proof

Will and intellect are nothing but the particular volitions and ideas (Pr.48,II and Sch.). But a particular volition and idea are one and the same thing (preceding Pr.). Therefore will and intellect are one and the same thing.

Scholium

By this means we have removed the cause to which error is commonly attributed. We have previously shown that falsity consists only in the privation that fragmentary and confused ideas involve. Therefore a false idea, in so far as it is false, does not involve certainty. So when we say that a man acquiesces in what is false and has no doubt thereof, we are not thereby saying that he is certain, but only that he does not doubt, or that he acquiesces in what is false because there is nothing to cause his imagination to waver. On this point see Sch.Pr.44,II. So however much we suppose a man to adhere to what is false, we shall never say that he is certain. For by certainty we mean something positive (Pr.43,II and Sch.), not privation of doubt. But by privation of certainty we mean falsity.

But for a fuller explanation of the preceding proposition some things remain to be said. Then, again, there is the further task of replying to objections that may be raised against this doctrine of ours. Finally, to remove every shred of doubt, I have thought it worthwhile to point out certain advantages of this doctrine. I say certain advantages, for the most important of them will be better understood from what we have to say in Part Five.

I begin, then, with the first point, and I urge my readers to make a careful distinction between an idea—i.e. a conception of the mind—and the images of things that we imagine. Again, it is essential to distinguish between ideas and the words we use to signify things. For since these three—images, words, and ideas—have been utterly confused by many, or else they fail to distinguish between them through lack of accuracy, or, finally, through lack of caution, our doctrine of the will, which it is essential to know both for theory and for the wise ordering of life, has never entered their minds. For those who think that ideas consist in images formed in us from the contact of external bodies are convinced that those ideas of things whereof we can form no like image are not ideas, but mere fictions fashioned arbitrarily at will. So they look on ideas as dumb pictures on a tablet, and misled by this preconception they fail to see that an idea, in so far as it is an idea, involves affirmation or negation. Again, those who confuse words with idea, or with the affirmation which an idea involves, think that when they affirm or deny something merely by words contrary to what they feel, they are able to will contrary to what they feel. Now one can easily dispel these misconceptions if one attends to the nature of thought, which is quite removed from the concept of extension. Then one will clearly understand that an idea, being a mode of thinking, consists neither in the image of a thing nor in words. For the essence of words and images is constituted solely by corporeal motions, far removed from the concept of thought. With these few words of warning, I turn to the aforementioned objections.

The first of these rests on the confident claim that the will extends more widely than the intellect, and therefore is different from it. The reason for their belief that the will extends more widely than the intellect is that they find—so they say—that they do not need a greater faculty of assent, that is, of affirming and denying, than they already possess, in order to assent to an infinite number of other things that we do not perceive, but that we do need an increased faculty of understanding. Therefore will is distinct from intellect, the latter being finite and the former infinite.

Second, it may be objected against us that experience appears to tell us most indisputably that we are able to suspend judgment so as not to assent to things that we perceive, and this is also confirmed by the fact that nobody is said to be deceived in so far as he perceives something, but only in so far as he assents or dissents. For instance, he who imagines a winged horse does not thereby grant that there is a winged horse; that is, he is not thereby deceived unless at the same time he grants that there is a winged horse. So experience appears to tell us most indisputably that the will, that is, the faculty of assenting, is free, and different from the faculty of understanding.

Third, it may be objected that one affirmation does not seem to contain more reality than another; that is, we do not seem to need greater power in order to affirm that what is true is true than to affirm that what is false is true. On the other hand, we do perceive that one idea has more reality or perfection than another. For some ideas are more perfect than others in proportion as some objects are superior to others. This, again, is a clear indication that there is a difference between will and intellect.

Fourthly, it may be objected that if man does not act from freedom of will, what would happen if he should be in a state of equilibrium like Buridan's ass? Will he perish of hunger and thirst? If I were to grant this, I would appear to be thinking of an ass or a statue, not of a man. If I deny it, then the man will be determining himself, and consequently will possess the faculty of going and doing whatever he wants.

Besides these objections there may possibly be others. But since I am not obliged to stress every objection that can be dreamed up, I shall make it my task to reply to these objections only, and as briefly as possible.

To the first objection I reply that, if by the intellect is meant clear and distinct ideas only, I grant that the will extends more widely than the intellect, but I deny that the will extends more widely than perceptions, that is, the faculty of conceiving. Nor indeed do I see why the faculty of willing should be termed infinite any more than the faculty of sensing. For just as by the same faculty of willing we can affirm an infinite number of things (but in succession, for we cannot affirm an infinite number of things simultaneously), so also we can sense or perceive an infinite number of bodies (in succession) by the same faculty of sensing. If my objectors should say that there are an infinite number of things that we cannot perceive, I retort that we cannot grasp them by any amount of thought, and consequently by any amount of willing. But, they say, if God wanted to bring it about that we should perceive these too, he would have had to give us a greater faculty of perceiving, but not a greater faculty of willing than he has already given us. This is the same as saying that if God wishes to bring it about that we should understand an infinite number of other entities, he would have to give us a greater intellect than he already has, so as to encompass these same infinite entities, but not a more universal idea of entity. For we have shown that the will is a universal entity, or the idea whereby we explicate all particular volitions; that is, that which is common to all particular volitions. So if they believe that this common or universal idea of volitions is a faculty, it is not at all surprising that they declare this faculty to extend beyond the limits of the intellect to infinity. For the term 'universal' is applied equally to one, to many, and to an infinite number of individuals.

To the second objection I reply by denying that we have free power to suspend judgment. For when we say that someone suspends judgment, we are saying only that he sees that he is not adequately perceiving the thing. So suspension of judgment is really a perception, not free will. To understand this more clearly, let us conceive a boy imagining a winged horse and having no other perception. Since this imagining involves the existence of a horse (Cor.Pr.17,II), and the boy perceives nothing to annul the existence of the horse, he will necessarily regard the horse as present and he will not be able to doubt its existence, although he is not certain of it. We experience this quite commonly in dreams, nor do I believe there is anyone who thinks that while dreaming he has free power to suspend judgment regarding the contents of his dream, and of bringing it about that he should not dream what he dreams that he sees. Nevertheless, it does happen that even in dreams we suspend judgment, to wit, when we dream that we are dreaming. Furthermore, I grant that nobody is deceived in so far as he has a perception; that is, I grant that the imaginings of the mind, considered in themselves, involve no error (see Sch.Pr.17,II). But I deny that a man makes no affirmation in so far as he has a perception. For what else is perceiving a winged horse than affirming wings of a horse? For if the mind were to perceive nothing apart from the winged horse, it would regard the horse as present to it, and would have no cause to doubt the existence of the horse nor would it have any faculty of dissenting, unless the imagining of the winged horse were joined to an idea which annuls the existence of the said horse, or unless the mind perceives that the idea which it has of the winged horse is inadequate. Then it will either necessarily deny the existence of the said horse or it will necessarily doubt it.

In the above I think I have also answered the third objection by my assertion that the will is a universal term predicated of all ideas and signifying only what is common to all ideas, namely, affirmation, the adequate essence of which, in so far as it is thus conceived as an abstract term, must be in every single idea, and the same in all in this respect only. But not in so far as it is considered as constituting the essence of the idea, for in that respect particular affirmations differ among themselves as much as do ideas. For example, the affirmation which the idea of a circle involves differs from the affirmation which the idea of a triangle involves as much as the idea of a circle differs from the idea of a triangle. Again, I absolutely deny that we need an equal power of thinking to affirm that what is true is true as to affirm that what is false is true. For these two affirmations, if you look to their meaning and not to the words alone, are related to one another as being to non-being. For there is nothing positive in ideas that constitutes the form of falsity (see Pr.35,II with Sch. and Sch.Pr.47,II). Therefore it is important to note here how easily we are deceived when we confuse universals with particulars, and mental constructs (entia rationis) and abstract terms with the real.

As to the fourth objection, I readily grant that a man placed in such a state of equilibrium (namely, where he feels nothing else but hunger and thirst and perceives nothing but such-and-such food and drink at equal distances from him) will die of hunger and thirst. If they ask me whether such a man is not to be reckoned an ass rather than a man, I reply that I do not know, just as I do not know how one should reckon a man who hangs himself, or how one should reckon babies, fools, and madmen.

My final task is to show what practical advantages accrue from knowledge of this doctrine, and this we shall readily gather from the following points:

1. It teaches that we act only by God's will, and that we share in the divine nature, and all the more as our actions become more perfect and as we understand God more and more. Therefore this doctrine, apart from giving us complete tranquility of mind, has the further advantage of teaching us wherein lies our greatest happiness or blessedness, namely, in the knowledge of God alone, as a result of which we are induced only to such actions as are urged on us by love and piety. Hence we clearly understand how far astray from the true estimation of virtue are those who, failing to understand that virtue itself and the service of God is happiness itself and utmost freedom, expect God to bestow on them the highest rewards in return for their virtue and meritorious actions as if in return for the basest slavery.

2. It teaches us what attitude we should adopt regarding fortune, or the things that are not in our power, that is, the things that do not follow from our nature; namely, to expect and to endure with patience both faces of fortune. For all things follow from God's eternal decree by the same necessity as it follows from the essence of a triangle that its three angles are equal to two right angles.

3. This doctrine assists us in our social relations, in that it teaches us to hate no one, despise no one, ridicule no one, be angry with no one, envy no one. Then again, it teaches us that each should be content with what he has and should help his neighbour, not from womanish pity, or favour, or superstition, but solely from the guidance of reason as occasion and circumstance require. This I shall demonstrate in Part Four.

4. Finally, this doctrine is also of no small advantage to the commonwealth, in that it teaches the manner in which citizens should be governed and led; namely, not so as to be slaves, but so as to do freely what is best.

And thus I have completed the task I undertook in this Scholium, and thereby I bring to an end Part Two, in which I think I have explained the nature of the human mind and its properties at sufficient length and as clearly as the difficult subject matter permits, and that from my account can be drawn many excellent lessons, most useful and necessary to know, as will partly be disclosed in what is to follow.

PART III

CONCERNING THE ORIGIN AND
NATURE OF THE EMOTIONS

PREFACE

Most of those who have written about the emotions (affectibus) and human conduct seem to be dealing not with natural phenomena that follow the common laws of Nature but with phenomena outside Nature. They appear to go so far as to conceive man in Nature as a kingdom within a kingdom. They believe that he disturbs rather than follows Nature's order, and has absolute power over his actions, and is determined by no other source than himself. Again, they assign the cause of human weakness and frailty not to the power of Nature in general, but to some defect in human nature, which they therefore bemoan, ridicule, despise, or, as is most frequently the case, abuse. He who can criticise the weakness of the human mind more eloquently or more shrilly is regarded as almost divinely inspired. Yet there have not been lacking outstanding figures who have written much that is excellent regarding the right conduct of life and have given to mankind very sage counsel; and we confess we owe much to their toil and industry. However, as far as I know, no one has defined the nature and strength of the emotions, and the power of the mind in controlling them. I know, indeed, that the renowned Descartes, though he too believed that the mind has absolute power over its actions, does explain human emotions through their first causes, and has also zealously striven to show how the mind can have absolute control over the emotions. But in my opinion he has shown nothing else but the brilliance of his own genius, as I shall demonstrate in due course; for I want now to return to those who prefer to abuse or deride the emotions and actions of men rather than to understand them. They will doubtless find it surprising that I should attempt to treat of the faults and follies of mankind in the geometric manner, and that I should propose to bring logical reasoning to bear on what they proclaim is opposed to reason, and is vain, absurd and horrifying. But my argument is this: in Nature nothing happens which can be attributed to its defectiveness, for Nature is always the same, and its force and power of acting is everywhere one and the same; that is, the laws and rules of Nature according to which all things happen and change from one form to another are everywhere and always the same. So our approach to the understanding of the nature of things of every kind should likewise be one and the same; namely, through the universal laws and rules of

Nature. Therefore the emotions of hatred, anger, envy, etc., considered in themselves, follow from the same necessity and force of Nature as all other particular things. So these emotions are assignable to definite causes through which they can be understood, and have definite properties, equally deserving of our investigation as the properties of any other thing, whose mere contemplation affords us pleasure. I shall, then, treat of the nature and strength of the emotions, and the mind's power over them, by the same method as I have used in treating of God and the mind, and I shall consider human actions and appetites just as if it were an investigation into lines, planes, or bodies.

DEFINITIONS

1. I call that an adequate cause whose effect can be clearly and distinctly perceived through the said cause. I call that an inadequate or partial cause whose effect cannot be understood through the said cause alone.

2. I say that we are active when something takes place, in us or externally to us, of which we are the adequate cause; that is, (by preceding Def.), when from our nature there follows in us or externally to us something which can be clearly and distinctly understood through our nature alone. On the other hand, I say that we are passive when something takes place in us, or follows from our nature, of which we are only the partial cause.

3. By emotion (affectus) I understand the affections of the body by which the body's power of activity is increased or diminished, assisted or checked, together with the ideas of these affections.

Thus, if we can be the adequate cause of one of these affections, then by emotion I understand activity, otherwise passivity.

POSTULATES

1. The human body can be affected in many ways by which its power of activity is increased or diminished; and also in many other ways which neither increase nor diminish its power of activity.

This postulate or axiom rests on Postulate 1 and Lemmata 5 and 7, following Pr.13,II.

2. The human body can undergo many changes and nevertheless retain impressions or traces of objects (see Post.5,II) and consequently the same images of things;—for the definition of which see Sch.Pr.17,II.

PROPOSITION 1

Our mind is in some instances active and in other instances passive. In so far as it has adequate ideas, it is necessarily active; and in so far as it has inadequate ideas, it is necessarily passive.

Proof

In every human mind, some of its ideas are adequate, others are fragmentary and confused (Sch.Pr.40,II). Now ideas that are adequate in someone's mind are adequate in God in so far as he constitutes the essence of that mind (Cor.Pr.11,II); and furthermore those ideas that are inadequate in the mind are also adequate in God (same Cor.), not in so far as he contains in himself the essence of that mind only, but in so far as he contains the minds of other things as well. Again, from any given idea some effect must necessarily follow (Pr.36,I), of which God is the adequate cause (Def.1,III) not in so far as he is infinite but in so far as he is considered as affected by the given idea (Pr.9,II). But in the case of an effect of which God is the cause in so far as he is affected by an idea which is adequate in someone's mind, that same mind is its adequate cause (Cor.Pr.11,II). Therefore our mind (Def.2,III), in so far as it has adequate ideas, is necessarily active—which is the first point. Again, whatever necessarily follows from an idea that is adequate in God not in so far as he has in himself the mind of one man only, but in so far as he has the minds of other things simultaneously with the mind of the said man, the mind of that man is not the adequate cause of it, but the partial cause (Cor.Pr.11,II), and therefore (Def.2,III) in so far as the mind has inadequate ideas, it is necessarily passive;—which was the second point. Therefore our mind etc.

Corollary

Hence it follows that the more the mind has inadequate ideas, the more it is subject to passive states (passionibus); and, on the other hand, it is the more active in proportion as it has a greater number of adequate ideas.

PROPOSITION 2

The body cannot determine the mind to think, nor can the mind determine the body to motion or rest, or to anything else (if there is anything else).

Proof

All modes of thinking have God for their cause in so far as he is a thinking thing, and not in so far as he is explicated by any other attribute (Pr.6,II). So that which determines the mind to think is a mode of Thinking, and not of Extension; that is (Def.1,II), it is not the body. That was our first point. Now the motion-and-rest of a body must arise from another body, which again has been determined to motion or rest by another body, and without exception whatever arises in a body must have arisen from God in so far as he is considered as affected by a mode of Extension, and not in so far as he is considered as affected by a mode of Thinking (Pr.6,II); that is, it cannot arise from mind, which (Pr.11,II) is a mode of Thinking. That was our second point. Therefore the body cannot . . . etc.

Scholium

This is more clearly understood from Sch.Pr.7,II, which tells us that mind and body are one and the same thing, conceived now under the attribute of Thought, now under the attribute of Extension. Hence it comes about that the order or linking of things is one, whether Nature be conceived under this or that attribute, and consequently the order of the active and passive states of our body is simultaneous in Nature with the order of active and passive states of the mind. This is also evident from the manner of our proof of Pr.12,II.

Yet, although the matter admits of no shadow of doubt, I can scarcely believe, without the confirmation of experience, that men can be induced to examine this view without prejudice, so strongly are they convinced that at the mere bidding of the mind the body can now be set in motion, now be brought to rest, and can perform any number of actions which depend solely on the will of the mind and the exercise of thought. However, nobody as yet has determined the limits of the body's capabilities: that is, nobody as yet has learned from experience what the body can and cannot do, without being determined by mind, solely from the laws of its nature in so far as it is considered as corporeal. For nobody as yet knows the structure of the body so accurately as to explain all its functions, not to mention that in the animal world we find much that far surpasses human sagacity, and that sleepwalkers do many things in their sleep that they would not dare when awake;—clear evidence that the body, solely from the laws of its own nature, can do many things at which its mind is amazed.

Again, no one knows in what way and by what means mind can move body, or how many degrees of motion it can impart to body and with what speed it can cause it to move. Hence it follows that when men say that this or that action of the body arises from the mind which has command over the body, they do not know what they are saying, and are merely admitting, under a plausible cover of words, that they are ignorant of the true cause of that action and are not concerned to discover it.

"But," they will say, "whether or not we know by what means the mind moves the body, experience tells us that unless the mind is in a fit state to exercise thought, the body remains inert. And again, experience tells us that it is solely within the power of the mind both to speak and to keep silent, and to do many other things which we therefore believe to depend on mental decision." Now as to the first point, I ask, does not experience also tell them that if, on the other hand, the body is inert, the mind likewise is not capable of thinking? When the body is at rest in sleep, the mind remains asleep with it and does not have that power of entertaining thoughts which it has when awake. Again, I think that all have experienced the fact that the mind is not always equally apt for concentrating on the same object; the mind is more apt to regard this or that object according as the body is more apt to have arising in it the image of this or that object.

"But," they will say, "it is impossible that the causes of buildings, pictures, and other things of this kind, which are made by human skill alone, should be deduced solely from the laws of Nature considered only as corporeal, nor is the human body capable of building a temple unless it be determined and guided by mind." However, I have already pointed out that they do not know what the body can do, or what can be deduced solely from a consideration of its nature, and that experience abundantly shows that solely from the laws of its nature many things occur which they would never have believed possible except from the direction of mind:—for instance, the actions of sleepwalkers, which they wonder at when they are awake. A further consideration is the very structure of the human body, which far surpasses in ingenuity all the constructions of human skill; not to mention the point I made earlier, that from Nature, considered under any attribute whatsoever, infinite things follow.

As to the second point, the human condition would indeed be far happier if it were equally in the power of men to keep silent as to talk. But experience teaches us with abundant examples that nothing is less within men's power than to hold their tongues or control their appetites. From this derives the commonly held view that we act freely only in cases where our desires are moderate, because our appetites can then be easily held in check by the remembrance of another thing that frequently comes to mind; but when we seek something with a strong emotion that cannot be allayed by the remembrance of some other thing, we cannot check our desires. But indeed, had they not found by experience that we do many things of which we later repent, and that frequently, when we are at the mercy of conflicting emotions, we 'see the better and do the worse,' there would be nothing to prevent them from believing that all our actions are free. A baby thinks that it freely seeks milk, an angry child that it freely seeks revenge, and a timid man that he freely seeks flight. Again, the drunken man believes that it is from the free decision of the mind that he says what he later, when sober, wishes he had not said. So, too, the delirious man, the gossiping woman, the child, and many more of this sort think that they speak from free mental decision, when in fact they are unable to restrain their torrent of words. So experience tells us no less clearly than reason that it is on this account only that men believe themselves to be free, that they are conscious of their actions and ignorant of the causes by which they are determined; and it tells us too that mental decisions are nothing more than the appetites themselves, varying therefore according to the varying disposition of the body. For each man's actions are shaped by his emotion; and those who furthermore are a prey to conflicting emotions know not what they want, while those who are free from emotion are driven on to this or that course by a slight impulse.

Now surely all these considerations go to show clearly that mental decision on the one hand, and the appetite and physical state of the body on the other hand, are simultaneous in nature; or rather, they are one and the same thing which, when considered under the attribute of Thought and explicated through Thought, we call decision, and when considered under the attribute of Extension and deduced from the laws of motion-and-rest, we call a physical state. This will become clearer from later discussion, for there is now another point which I should like you to note as very important. We can take no action from mental decision unless the memory comes into play; for example, we cannot utter a word unless we call the word to mind. Now it is not within the free power of the mind to remember or to forget any thing. Hence comes the belief that the power of the mind whereby we can keep silent or speak solely from mental decision is restricted to the case of a remembered thing. However, when we dream that we are speaking, we think that we do so from free mental decision; yet we are not speaking, or if we are, it is the result of spontaneous movement of the body. Again, we dream that we are keeping something secret, and that we are doing so by the same mental decision that comes into play in our waking hours when we keep silent about what we know. Finally, we dream that from a mental decision we act as we dare not act when awake. So I would very much like to know whether in the mind there are two sorts of decisions, dreamland decisions and free decisions. If we don't want to carry madness so far we must necessarily grant that the mental decision that is believed to be free is not distinct from imagination and memory, and is nothing but the affirmation which an idea, in so far as it is an idea, necessarily involves (Pr.49,II). So these mental decisions arise in the mind from the same necessity as the ideas of things existing in actuality, and those who believe that they speak, or keep silent, or do anything from free mental decision are dreaming with their eyes open.

PROPOSITION 3

The active states (actiones) of the mind arise only from adequate ideas; its passive states depend solely on inadequate ideas.

Proof

The first thing that constitutes the essence of the mind is nothing else but the idea of a body actually existing (Prs.11 and 13,II), which idea is composed of many other ideas (Pr.15,II), of which some are adequate (Cor.Pr.38,II) while others are inadequate (Cor.Pr.29,II). Therefore whatever follows from the nature of the mind and must be understood through the mind as its proximate cause must necessarily follow from an adequate idea or an inadequate idea. But in so far as the mind has inadequate ideas, it is necessarily passive (Prop.1,III). Therefore the active states of mind follow solely from adequate ideas, and thus the mind is passive only by reason of having inadequate ideas.

Scholium

We therefore see that passive states are related to the mind only in so far as the mind has something involving negation: that is, in so far as the mind is considered as part of Nature, which cannot be clearly and distinctly perceived through itself independently of other parts. By the same reasoning I could demonstrate that passive states are a characteristic of particular things just as they are of the mind, and cannot be perceived in any other way; but my purpose is to deal only with the human mind.

PROPOSITION 4

No thing can be destroyed except by an external cause.

Proof

This proposition is self-evident, for the definition of anything affirms, and does not negate, the thing's essence: that is, it posits, and does not annul, the thing's essence. So as long as we are attending only to the thing itself, and not to external causes, we can find nothing in it which can destroy it.

PROPOSITION 5

Things are of a contrary nature, that is, unable to subsist in the same subject, to the extent that one can destroy the other.

Proof

If they were able to be in agreement with one other, or to co-exist in the same subject, there could be something in the said subject which could destroy it, which is absurd (preceding Pr.). Therefore . . . etc.

PROPOSITION 6

Each thing, in so far as it is in itself, endeavors to persist in its own being.

Proof

Particular things are modes whereby the attributes of God are expressed in a definite and determinate way (Cor.Pr.25,I), that is (Pr.34,I), they are things which express in a definite and determinate way the power of God whereby he is and acts, and no thing can have in itself anything by which it can be destroyed, that is, which can annul its existence (Pr.4,III). On the contrary, it opposes everything that can annul its existence (preceding Pr.); and thus, as far as it can and as far as it is in itself, it endeavors to persist in its own being.

PROPOSITION 7

The conatus[1] with which each thing endeavors to persist in its own being is nothing but the actual essence of the thing itself.

Proof

From the given essence of a thing certain things necessarily follow (Pr.36,I), nor do things effect anything other than that which necessarily follows from their determinate nature (Pr.29,I). Therefore, the power of

1. The term 'conatus' plays an important role in Spinoza's psychology. It expresses Spinoza's view that each thing exemplifies an inherent tendency towards self-preservation and activity. This term has a long history, going back to Cicero, who used it to express Aristotle's and the Stoics' notion of impulse (horme). It was later used by medieval and early modern philosophers, such as Hobbes, to connote the natural tendency of an organism to preserve itself. For a history of this term consult H. Wolfson, *The Philosophy of Spinoza* (New York 1969), volume 2, pp. 195–199.)

any thing, or the conatus with which it acts or endeavors to act, alone or in conjunction with other things, that is (Pr.6,III), the power or conatus by which it endeavors to persist in its own being, is nothing but the given, or actual, essence of the thing.

PROPOSITION 8

The conatus with which each single thing endeavors to persist in its own being does not involve finite time, but indefinite time.

Proof

If it involved a limited period of time which would determine the duration of the thing, then solely from the power by which the thing exists it would follow that it could not exist after that limited period of time, but is bound to be destroyed. But (Pr.4,III), this is absurd. Therefore the conatus with which a thing exists does not involve any definite period of time. On the contrary (by the same Pr.4,III), if it is not destroyed by an external cause, it will always continue to exist by that same power by which it now exists. Therefore this conatus involves an indefinite time.

PROPOSITION 9

The mind, both in so far as it has clear and distinct ideas and in so far as it has confused ideas, endeavors to persist in its own being over an indefinite period of time, and is conscious of this conatus.

Proof

The essence of the mind is constituted by adequate and inadequate ideas (as we showed in Pr.3,III), and so (Pr.7,III) it endeavors to persist in its own being in so far as it has both these kinds of ideas, and does so (Pr.8,III) over an indefinite period of time. Now since the mind (Pr.23,II) is necessarily conscious of itself through the ideas of the affections of the body, therefore the mind is conscious of its conatus (Pr.7,III).

Scholium

When this conatus is related to the mind alone, it is called Will (voluntas); when it is related to mind and body together, it is called Appetite (appetitus), which is therefore nothing else but man's essence, from the nature of which there necessarily follow those things that tend to his preservation, and which man is thus determined to perform. Further, there is no difference between appetite and Desire (cupiditas) except that desire is usually related to men in so far as they are conscious of their appetite. Therefore it can be defined as follows: desire is 'appetite accompanied by the consciousness thereof.'

It is clear from the above considerations that we do not endeavor, will, seek after or desire because we judge a thing to be good. On the contrary, we judge a thing to be good because we endeavor, will, seek after and desire it.

PROPOSITION 10

An idea that excludes the existence of our body cannot be in our mind, but is contrary to it.

Proof

Whatsoever can destroy our body cannot be therein (Pr.5,III), and so neither can its idea be in God in so far as he has the idea of our body (Cor.Pr.9,II); that is (Prs.11 and 13,II), the idea of such a thing cannot be in our mind. On the contrary, since (Prs.11 and 13,II) the first thing that constitutes the essence of the mind is the idea of an actually existing body, the basic and most important element of our mind is the conatus (Pr.7,III) to affirm the existence of our body. Therefore the idea that negates the existence of our body is contrary to our mind.

PROPOSITION 11

Whatsoever increases or diminishes, assists or checks, the power of activity of our body, the idea of the said thing increases or diminishes, assists or checks the power of thought of our mind.

Proof

This proposition is evident from Pr.7,II, or again from Pr.14,II.

Scholium

We see then that the mind can undergo considerable changes, and can pass now to a state of greater perfection, now to one of less perfection, and it is these passive transitions (passiones) that explicate for us the emotions of Pleasure (laetitia) and Pain (tristitia). So in what follows I shall understand by pleasure 'the passive transition of the mind to a state of greater perfection,' and by pain 'the passive transition of the mind to state of less perfection.' The emotion of pleasure when it is simultaneously related to mind and body I call Titillation (titillatio) or Cheerfulness (hilaritas); the emotion of pain when it is similarly related I call Anguish (dolor) or Melancholy (melancholia). But be it noted that titillation and anguish are related to man when one part of him is affected more than others, cheerfulness and melancholy when all parts are equally affected. As to Desire (cupiditas), I have explained what it is in Sch.Pr.9,III, and I acknowledge no primary emotion other than these three [i.e. pleasure, pain and desire]; for I shall subsequently show that the others arise from these three. But before going further, I should like to explain Pr.10,III at greater length, so that there may be a clearer understanding of the way in which an idea may be contrary to an idea.

In Sch.Pr.17,II we demonstrated that the idea which constitutes the essence of the mind involves the existence of the body for as long as the body exists. Then from what we proved in Cor.Pr.8,II and its Sch., it follows that the present existence of our mind depends solely on this, that the mind involves the actual existence of the body. Finally we proved that the power of the mind whereby it imagines (imaginatur) and remembers things depends also on this (Prs.17 and 18,II, and Sch.), that it involves the actual existence of the body. From this it follows that the present existence of the mind and its capacity to perceive through the senses are annulled as soon as the mind ceases to affirm the present existence of the body. But the cause of the mind's ceasing to affirm this existence of the body cannot be the mind itself (Pr.4,III), nor again that the body ceases to be. For (Pr.6,II) the cause of the mind's affirming the existence of the body is not that the body began to exist; therefore, by the same reasoning, it does not cease to affirm the existence of the body on account of the body's ceasing to be. This results from another idea, which excludes the present existence of our body and consequently that of our mind, and which is therefore contrary to the idea that constitutes the essence of our mind (Pr.8,II).

PROPOSITION 12

The mind, as far as it can, endeavors to think of those things that increase or assist the body's power of activity.

Proof

As long as the human body is affected in a manner that involves the nature of an external body, so long will the human mind regard that latter body as present (Pr.17,II). Consequently, (Pr.7,II) as long as the human mind regards some external body as present, that is (Sch.Pr.17,II), thinks of it, so long is the human body affected in a manner that involves the nature of that external body. Accordingly, as long as the mind thinks of those things that increase or assist our body's power of activity, so long is the body affected in ways that increase or assist its power of activity (Post.1,III); and, consequently, so long is the mind's power of thinking increased or assisted (Pr.11,III). Therefore, (Pr.6 or 9,III) the mind, as far as it can, endeavors to think of those things.

PROPOSITION 13

When the mind thinks of those things that diminish or check the body's power of activity, it endeavors, as far as it can, to call to mind those things that exclude the existence of the former.

Proof

As long as the mind thinks of something of this kind, so long is the power of mind and body diminished or checked (as we have proved in the preceding proposition). Nevertheless the mind will continue to think of it until it thinks of another thing that excludes the present existence of the former (Pr.17,II); that is, (as we have just demonstrated), the power of mind and body is diminished or checked until the mind thinks of something else that excludes the thing's existence, something which the mind therefore (Pr.9,III) endeavors, as far as it can, to think of or call to mind.

Corollary

Hence it follows that the mind is averse to thinking of things that diminish or check its power and the body's power.

Scholium

From what has been said we clearly understand what are Love, (amor) and Hatred (odium). Love is merely 'pleasure accompanied by the idea of an external cause,' and hatred is merely 'pain accompanied by the idea of an external cause.' Again, we see that he who loves necessarily endeavors to have present and to preserve the thing that he loves; on the other hand, he who hates endeavors to remove and destroy the thing that he hates. But we shall deal with these matters more fully in due course.

PROPOSITION 14

If the mind has once been affected by two emotions at the same time, when it is later affected by the one it will also be affected by the other.

Proof

If the human body has once been affected by two bodies at the same time, when the mind later thinks of the one it will straightway recall the other too (Pr.18,II). Now the images formed by the mind reflect the affective states of our body more than the nature of external bodies (Cor.2,Pr.16,II). Therefore if the body, and consequently the mind (Def.3,III), has once been affected by two emotions, when it is later affected by the one, it will also be affected by the other.

PROPOSITION 15

Anything can indirectly (per accidens) be the cause of Pleasure, Pain, or Desire.

Proof

Let it be supposed that the mind is affected by two emotions simultaneously, of which one neither increases nor diminishes its power of activity, and the other either increases it or diminishes it (Post.1,III). From the preceding proposition it is clear that when the mind is later affected by the former as its true cause—which, by hypothesis, of itself neither increases nor diminishes the mind's power of thinking—it will straightway be affected by the other, which does increase or diminish its power of thinking; that is (Sch.Pr.11,III), it will be affected by pleasure or pain. So the former will be the cause of pleasure or pain, not through itself, but indirectly. In this same way it can readily be demonstrated that the former thing can indirectly be the cause of desire.

Corollary

From the mere fact that we have regarded a thing with the emotion of pleasure or pain of which it is not itself the efficient cause, we may love or hate that thing.

Proof

From this mere fact it comes about (Pr.14,III) that the mind, when later thinking of this thing, is affected by the emotion of pleasure or pain; that is (Sch.Pr.11,III), the power of the mind and body is increased or diminished, etc. Consequently, (Pr.12,III), the mind desires to think of the said thing, or is averse to it (Cor.Pr.13,III); that is (Sch.Pr.13,III), it loves or hates the said thing.

Scholium

Hence we understand how it can come about that we love or hate some things without any cause known to us, but merely from Sympathy and Antipathy, as they are called. We should also classify in this category those objects that affect us with pleasure or pain from the mere fact that they have some resemblance to objects that are wont to affect us with the same emotions, as I shall demonstrate in the next Proposition.

I realise that the writers who first introduced the terms 'sympathy' and 'antipathy' intended them to mean certain occult qualities. Nevertheless, I think it is permissible for us to denote by them qualities that are also familiar or manifest.

PROPOSITION 16

From the mere fact that we imagine a thing to have something similar to an object that is wont to affect the mind with pleasure or pain, we shall love it or hate it, although the point of similarity is not the efficient cause of these emotions.

Proof

By hypothesis, the point of similarity has been regarded by us in the object with the emotion of pleasure or pain; and so (Pr.14,III) when the mind is affected by its image, it will also straightway be affected by the one or other emotion. Consequently the thing which we perceive to have this said point of similarity will indirectly be the cause of pleasure or pain (Pr.15,III); and thus (preceding Corollary), we shall love or hate the thing even though the point of similarity is not the efficient cause of these emotions.

PROPOSITION 17

If we imagine that a thing which is wont to affect us with an emotion of pain, has something similar to another thing which is wont to affect us with an equally great emotion of pleasure, we shall hate it and love it at the same time.

Proof

By hypothesis, this thing is in itself a cause of pain, and (Sch.Pr.13,III) in so far as we imagine it with this emotion, we hate it.

But, in addition, in so far as we imagine it to have something similar to another thing which is wont to affect us with an equally great emotion of pleasure, we shall love it with an equally strong emotion of pleasure (preceding Pr.). So we shall hate it and love it at the same time.

Scholium

This condition of the mind arising from two conflicting emotions is called 'vacillation,' which is therefore related to emotion as doubt is related to imagination (Sch.Pr.44,II), and there is no difference between vacillation and doubt except in respect of intensity. But it should be observed that in the preceding Proposition I deduced these vacillations from causes which are, in the case of one emotion, a direct cause, and in the case of the other an indirect cause. This I did because they could in this way be more readily deduced from what had preceded, and not because I deny that vacillations generally arise from an object which is the efficient cause of both emotions. For the human body is composed (Post.1,II) of very many individual bodies of different nature, and so (Ax.1 after Lemma 3, q.v. after Pr.13,II) it can be affected by one and the same body in many different ways; on the other hand, since one and the same thing can be affected in many ways, it can likewise affect one and the same part of the body in different ways. From this we can readily conceive that one and the same object can be the cause of many conflicting emotions.

PROPOSITION 18

From the image of a thing past or future man is affected by the same emotion of pleasure or pain as from the image of a thing present.

Proof

As long as a man is affected by the image of a thing, he will regard the thing as present even though it may not exist (Pr.17,II and Cor.), and he does not think of it as past or future except in so far as its image is joined to the image of past or future time (Sch.Pr.44,II). Therefore the image of a thing, considered solely in itself, is the same whether it be related to future, past or present; that is (Cor.2,Pr.16,II), the state of the body, or the emotion, is the same whether the image be of a thing past or future or present. So the emotion of pleasure, and of pain, is the same whether the image be of a thing past or future or present.

Scholium 1

Here I call a thing past or future in so far as we have been, or shall be, affected by it; for example, in so far as we have seen or shall see it, it has refreshed or will refresh us, it has injured or will injure us, etc. For in so far as we imagine it in this way, to that extent we affirm its existence; that is, the body is not affected by any emotion that excludes the existence of the thing, and so (Pr.17,II) the body is affected by the image of the thing in the same way as if the thing itself were present. However, since it is generally the case that those who have had much experience vacillate when they are regarding a thing as future or past and are generally in doubt as to its outcome (Sch.Pr.44,II), the result is that emotions that arise from similar images of things are not so constant, but are generally disturbed by images of other things until men become more assured of the outcome.

Scholium 2

From what has just been said we understand what is Hope (spes), Fear (metus), Confidence (securitas), Despair (desperatio), Joy (gaudium) and Disappointment (conscientiae morsus). Hope is 'inconstant pleasure, arising from the image of a thing future or past, of whose outcome we are in doubt.' Fear is 'inconstant pain, likewise arising from the image of a thing in doubt.' Now if the element of doubt be removed from these emotions, hope becomes confidence and fear becomes despair, that is 'pleasure or pain arising from a thing which we have feared or have hoped.' Joy is 'pleasure arising from the image of a past thing of whose outcome we have been in doubt.' Finally, disappointment is 'the pain opposite to joy.'

PROPOSITION 19

He who imagines that what he loves is being destroyed will feel pain. If, however, he imagines that it is being preserved, he will feel pleasure.

Proof

The mind, as far as it can, endeavors to imagine whatever increases or assists the body's power of activity (Pr.12,III), that is (Sch.Pr.13,III), those things it loves. But the imagination is assisted by whatever posits the existence of the thing, and, on the other hand, is checked by whatever excludes the existence of the thing (Pr.17,II). Therefore, the images of things that posit the existence of the loved object assist the mind's conatus wherewith it endeavors to imagine the loved object, that is (Sch.Pr.11,III), they affect the mind with pleasure. On the other hand, those things that exclude the existence of the loved object check that same conatus of the mind, that is (by the same Scholium), they affect the mind with pain. Therefore, he who imagines that what he loves is being destroyed will feel pain, . . . etc.

PROPOSITION 20

He who imagines that a thing that he hates is being destroyed will feel pleasure.

Proof

The mind (Pr.13,III) endeavors to imagine whatever excludes the existence of things whereby the body's power of activity is diminished or checked; that is (Sch.Pr.13,III), it endeavors to imagine whatever excludes the existence of things that it hates. So the image of a thing that excludes the existence of what the mind hates assists this conatus of the mind; that is (Sch.Pr.11,III), it affects the mind with pleasure. Therefore he who thinks that that which he hates is being destroyed will feel pleasure.

PROPOSITION 21

He who imagines that what he loves is affected with pleasure or pain will likewise be affected with pleasure or pain, the intensity of which will vary with the intensity of the emotion in the object loved.

Proof

As we have shown in Proposition 19,III, the images of things which posit the existence of the object loved assist the mind's conatus whereby it endeavors to think of the object loved. But pleasure posits the existence of that which feels pleasure, and the more so as the emotion of pleasure is stronger; for pleasure (Sch.Pr.11,III) is a transition to a state of greater perfection. Therefore the image, which is in the lover, of the pleasure of the object loved, assists his mind's conatus; that is (Sch.Pr.11,III), it affects the lover with pleasure, and all the more to the extent that this emotion is in the object loved. That was the first point. Again, in so far as a thing is affected with some pain, to that extent it is being destroyed, and the more so according to the extent to which it is affected with pain (same Sch.Pr.11,III). Thus (Pr.19,III), he who imagines that what he loves is affected with pain will likewise be affected with pain, the intensity of which will vary with the intensity of this emotion in the object loved.

PROPOSITION 22

If we imagine that someone is affecting with pleasure the object of our love, we shall be affected with love towards him. If on the other hand we think that he is affecting with pain the object of our love, we shall likewise be affected with hatred towards him.

Proof

He who affects with pleasure or pain the object of our love affects us also with pleasure or pain, assuming that we think of the object of our love as affected with that pleasure or pain (preceding Pr.). But it is supposed that this pleasure or pain is in us accompanied by the idea of an external cause. Therefore (Sch.Pr.13,III) if we think that someone is affecting with pleasure or pain the object of our love, we shall be affected with love or hatred towards him.

Scholium

Proposition 21 explains to us what is Pity (commiseratio), which we may define as 'pain arising from another's hurt.' As for pleasure arising from another's good, I know not what to call it. Furthermore, love towards one who has benefited another we shall call Approval (favor), and on the other hand hatred towards one who has injured another we shall call Indignation (indignatio). Finally, it should be observed that we pity not only the thing which we have loved (as we have demonstrated in Pr.21), but also a thing for which we have previously felt no emotion, provided that we judge it similar to ourselves (as I shall show in due course). Likewise, we approve of one who has benefited someone like ourselves; and on the other hand, we are indignant with one who has injured someone like ourselves.

PROPOSITION 23

He who imagines that what he hates is affected with pain will feel pleasure; if, on the other hand, he thinks of it as affected with pleasure, he will feel pain. Both of these emotions will vary in intensity inversely with the variation of the contrary emotion in that which he hates.

Proof

In so far as the thing hated is affected with pain, it is being destroyed, and the more so according to the degree of pain (Sch.Pr.11,III). So (Pr.20,III) he who imagines the object hated to be affected with pain will, on the contrary, be affected with pleasure, and the more so as he imagines the object hated to be affected with more pain. That was the first point. Again, pleasure posits the existence of that which feels pleasure (same Sch.Pr.11,III), and the more so as the pleasure is conceived to be greater. If anyone imagines him whom he hates to be affected with pleasure, this thought will check his conatus (Pr.13,III): that is, (Sch.Pr.11,III), he who hates will be affected with pain, etc.

Scholium

This pleasure can scarcely be unalloyed and devoid of conflict of feeling. For (as I shall forthwith demonstrate in Proposition 27) in so far as he imagines a thing similar to himself to be affected with an emotion of pain, to that extent he is bound to feel pain, and contrariwise if he imagines it to be affected with pleasure. But here it is only his hate that we are considering.

PROPOSITION 24

If we imagine someone to be affecting with pleasure a thing that we hate, we shall be affected with hate towards him too. If on the other hand we think of him as affecting with pain the said thing, we shall be affected with love towards him.

Proof

The proof follows the same lines as Pr.22,III.

Scholium

These and similar emotions of hatred are related to Envy (invidia), which can therefore be defined as 'hatred in so far as it is considered to dispose a man to rejoice in another's hurt and to feel pain at another's good.'

PROPOSITION 25

We endeavor to affirm of ourselves and of an object loved whatever we imagine affects us or the loved object with pleasure, and, on the other hand, to negate whatever we imagine affects us or the loved object with pain.

Proof

What we imagine affects the object loved with pleasure or pain affects us with pleasure or pain (Pr.21,III). Now the mind (Pr.12,III) endeavors, as far as it can, to think of things that affect us with pleasure; that is (Pr.17,II and Cor.), to regard them as present; and, on the other hand, (Pr.13,III) to exclude the existence of things that affect us with pain. Therefore we endeavor to affirm of ourselves and the loved object whatever we imagine affects us or the object loved with pleasure, and vice versa.

PROPOSITION 26

We endeavor to affirm of that which we hate whatever we imagine affects it with pain, and on the other hand to deny what we imagine affects it with pleasure.

Proof

This proposition follows from Proposition 23,III, as does the preceding proposition from Proposition 21,III.

Scholium

Thus we see that it easily happens that a man may have too high an opinion of himself and of the object loved, and on the other hand too mean an opinion of the object of his hatred. This way of thinking, when it concerns the man who has too high an opinion of himself, is called Pride (superbia), and is a kind of madness, in that a man dreams with his eyes open that he can do all those things that his imagination encompasses, which he therefore regards as real, exulting in them, as long as he is incapable of thinking of those things that exclude their existence and limit his power of activity. Therefore pride is 'pleasure arising from the fact that a man has too high an opinion of himself.' Again, 'pleasure that arises from the fact that a man has too high an opinion of another' is called Over-esteem (existimatio). Finally, 'pleasure arising from the fact that a man has too mean an opinion of another' is called Disparagement (despectus).

PROPOSITION 27

From the fact that we imagine a thing like ourselves, towards which we have felt no emotion, to be affected by an emotion, we are thereby affected by a similar emotion.

Proof

Images of things are affections of the human body, the ideas of which set before us external bodies as present (Sch.Pr.17,II); that is (Pr.16,II), the ideas of these affections involve the nature of our own body and simultaneously the nature of the external body as present. If therefore the nature of the external body is similar to the nature of our own body, then the idea of the external body in our thinking will involve an affection of our own body similar to the affection of the external body. Consequently, if we imagine someone like ourselves to be affected by an emotion, this thought will express an affection of our own body similar to that emotion. So from the fact that we imagine a thing like ourselves to be affected by an emotion, we are affected by a similar emotion along with it. But if we hate a thing similar to ourselves, to that extent (Pr.23,III) we shall be affected by a contrary, not similar, emotion along with it.

Scholium

This imitation of emotions, when it is related to pain, is called Pity (see Sch.Pr.22,III), but when it is related to desire it is called Emulation (aemulatio), which is therefore 'nothing else but the desire of some thing which has been engendered in us from the belief that others similar to ourselves have this same desire.'

Corollary 1

If we believe that someone, for whom we have felt no emotion, affects with pleasure a thing similar to ourselves, we shall be affected by love towards him. If, on the other hand, we believe that he affects the said object with pain, we shall be affected with hatred towards him.

Proof

This is proved from the preceding Proposition in the same way as Proposition 22 from Proposition 21,III.

Corollary 2

The fact that its distress affects us with pain cannot cause us to hate a thing that we pity.

Proof

If we could hate it on that account, then (Pr.23,III) we should be pleased at its pain, which is contrary to our hypothesis.

Corollary 3

As far as we can, we endeavor to free from distress the thing that we pity.

Proof

That which affects with pain a thing that we pity affects us too with similar pain (preceding Pr.), and so we shall endeavor to devise whatever annuls the existence of the former or destroys it (Pr.13,III): that is (Sch.Pr.9,III), we shall seek to destroy it; i.e. we shall be determined to destroy it. So we shall endeavor to free from its distress the thing we pity.

Scholium

This will or appetite to do good which arises from our pitying the thing to which we wish to do good is called Benevolence (benevolentia), which is therefore 'nothing else but desire arising from pity.' As to love and hatred towards one who has done good or ill to a thing that we think to be like ourselves, see Sch.Pr.22,III.

PROPOSITION 28

We endeavor to bring about whatever we imagine to be conducive to pleasure; but we endeavor to remove or destroy whatever we imagine to be opposed to pleasure and conducive to pain.

Proof

As far as we can, we endeavor to imagine whatever we think to be conducive to pleasure (Pr.12,III): that is (Pr.17,II), we endeavor, as far as we can, to regard it as present, that is, existing in actuality. But the conatus of the mind, that is, its power to think, is equal to and simultaneous in nature with the conatus of the body, that is, its power to act (as clearly follows from Cor.Pr.7 and Cor.Pr.11,II). Therefore in an absolute sense we endeavor, that is, we seek and purpose (which is the same thing by Sch.Pr.9,III), to bring about its existence. That was our first point. Further, if we imagine that which we believe to be the cause of pain, that is (Sch.Pr.13,III), that which we hate, as being destroyed, we shall feel pleasure (Pr.20,III), and so (by the first part of this proposition) we shall endeavor to destroy it, or (Pr.13,III) to remove it from us so as not to regard it as present. That was our second point. Therefore we endeavor to bring about . . . etc.

PROPOSITION 29

We also endeavor to do whatever we imagine men² to regard with pleasure, and on the other hand we shun doing whatever we imagine men to regard with aversion.

Proof

From the fact that we imagine men love or hate something, we shall love or hate the same thing (Pr.27,III); that is (Sch.Pr.13,III) from that very fact we shall feel pleasure or pain at the presence of the thing. So

2. Here, and in what follows, by 'men' I understand men for whom we have felt no emotion. [Spinoza]

(preceding Pr.) we shall endeavor to do whatever we imagine men love or regard with pleasure . . . etc.

Scholium

This conatus to do, and also to avoid doing, something simply in order to please men is called Ambition (ambitio), especially when we endeavor so earnestly to please the multitude that we do, or avoid doing, things to our own hurt or another's hurt; otherwise, it is called Kindliness (humanitas). Again, the pleasure with which we think of another's action whereby he has endeavored to please us I call Praise (laus), and the pain with which, on the other hand, we dislike his action I call Blame (vituperium).

PROPOSITION 30

If anyone has done something which he imagines affects others with pleasure, he will be affected with pleasure accompanied by the idea of himself as cause; that is, he will regard himself with pleasure. If, on the other hand, he imagines he has done something which affects others with pain, he will regard himself with pain.

Proof

He who imagines he affects others with pleasure or pain will by that very fact be affected with pleasure or pain (Pr.27,III). Now since man (Prs.19 and 23,II) is conscious of himself through the affections by which he is determined to act, he who has done something which he thinks affects others with pleasure will be affected with pleasure along with the consciousness of himself as cause; that is, he will regard himself with pleasure. The contrary likewise follows.

Scholium

Since love (Sch.Pr.13,III) is pleasure accompanied by the idea of an external cause, and hate is pain also accompanied by the idea of an external cause, this pleasure and this pain are species of love and hatred. But as love and hatred have reference to external objects, we shall assign different names to these emotions. The pleasure that is accompanied by an external cause we shall call Honour (gloria), and the pain that is its opposite we shall call Shame (pudor); but be it understood that this is when the pleasure or pain arises from a man's belief that he is praised or blamed. Otherwise, the pleasure that is accompanied by the idea of an internal cause I shall call Self-contentment (Acquiescentia in se ipso), and the pain that is its opposite I shall call Repentance (paenitentia). Again, since it is possible (Cor.Pr.17,II) that the pleasure with which a man imagines he affects others is only imaginary, and (Pr.25,III) everyone endeavors to imagine of himself whatever he thinks affects himself with pleasure, it can easily happen that a vain man may be proud and imagine that he is popular with everybody, when he in fact is obnoxious.

PROPOSITION 31

If we think that someone loves, desires, or hates something that we love, desire, or hate, that very fact will cause us to love, desire or hate the thing more steadfastly. But if we think he dislikes what we love, or vice versa, then our feelings will fluctuate.

Proof

From the mere fact that we imagine someone loves something, we shall love that same thing (Pr.27,III). But even apart from this consideration we are supposing that we love that same thing. Therefore to the existing love there is added a further cause whereby it is nurtured, and by that very fact we shall love more steadfastly the object of our love. Again, from the fact that we think someone dislikes something, we shall dislike the same thing (by the same proposition). But if we suppose that at the same time we love the thing, we shall therefore at the same time love and dislike that thing; that is, (see Sch.Pr.17,III) our feelings will fluctuate.

Corollary

From this and from Pr. 28,III it follows that everyone endeavors, as far as he can, that what he loves should be loved by everyone, and what he hates should be hated by everyone. Hence that saying of the poet:

"As lovers, let our hopes and fears be alike,
Insensitive is he who loves what another leaves."[3]

Scholium

This conatus to bring it about that everyone should approve of one's loves and hates is in reality ambition (see Sch.Pr.29,III). So we see that it is in everyone's nature to strive to bring it about that others should adopt his attitude to life; and while all strive equally to this end they equally hinder one another, and in all seeking the praise or love of all, they provoke mutual dislike.

PROPOSITION 32

If we think that someone enjoys something that only one person can possess, we shall endeavor to bring it about that he should not possess that thing.

Proof

From the mere fact that we imagine somebody to enjoy something (Pr.27,III and Cor.1) we shall love that thing and desire to enjoy it. But by hypothesis we think that this pleasure is impeded by the fact that that person is enjoying the thing in question. Therefore (Pr.28,III) we shall endeavor to bring it about that he should not possess it.

3. Ovid, *Amores*, II, 19.

Scholium

We therefore see that human nature is in general so constituted that men pity the unfortunate and envy the fortunate, in the latter case with a hatred proportionate to their love of what they think another possesses (by the preceding Proposition). Furthermore, we see that from the same property of human nature from which it follows that men are compassionate, it likewise follows that they are prone to envy and ambition. Finally, we shall find that common experience confirms all these points, especially if we turn our attention to childhood. For we find that children, their bodies being, as it were, continually in a state of equilibrium, laugh or weep merely from seeing others laugh or weep, and whatever else they see others do they immediately want to imitate. In short, they want for themselves whatever they see others take pleasure in because, as we have said, the images of things are the very affections of the human body, that is, the ways in which the human body is affected by external causes and disposed to this or that action.

PROPOSITION 33

If we love something similar to ourselves, we endeavor, as far as we can, to bring it about that it should love us in return.

Proof

We endeavor, as far as we can, to think of something we love in preference to other things (Pr.12,III). So if the thing be like ourselves, we shall endeavor to affect it with pleasure in preference to other things (Pr.29,III); that is, we shall endeavor, as far as we can, to bring it about that the object of our love should be affected with pleasure accompanied by the idea of ourselves, that is (Sch.Pr.13,III), that it should love us in return.

PROPOSITION 34

The greater the emotion with which we imagine the object of our love is affected towards us, the greater will be our vanity.

Proof

By the preceding proposition, we endeavor to bring it about, as far as we can, that the object of our love should love us in return; that is (Sch.Pr.13,III), that the object of our love should be affected with pleasure accompanied by the idea of ourselves. So the greater the pleasure with which we think that the object of our love is affected because of us, the more is this endeavor assisted; that is (Pr.11,III and Sch.), the greater the pleasure with which we are affected. Now since our pleasure is due to our having affected with pleasure another person like ourselves, we regard ourselves with pleasure (Pr.30,III). Therefore, the greater the emotion with which we think the object loved is affected towards us, with that much greater pleasure shall we regard ourselves; that is (Sch.Pr.30,III), the greater will be our vanity.

PROPOSITION 35

If anyone thinks that there is between the object of his love and another person the same or a more intimate bond of friendship than there was between them when he alone used to possess the object loved, he will be affected with hatred towards the object loved and will envy his rival.

Proof

The greater the love wherewith one thinks the object of his love is affected towards him, the greater will be his vanity (by the preceding proposition); that is (Sch.Pr.30,III), the more he will be pleased. So (Pr.28,III) he will endeavor, as far as he can, to imagine the object loved as bound to him as intimately as possible, and this conatus, or appetite, is fostered if he imagines someone else desires the same thing for himself (Pr.31,III). But we are supposing that this conatus, or appetite, is checked by the image of the object loved accompanied by the image of him with whom the object loved is associating. Therefore (Sch.Pr.11,III) this will cause him to be affected with pain accompanied by the idea of the object loved as cause and simultaneously by the image of his rival; that is (Sch.Pr.13,III), he will be affected with hatred towards the object loved and at the same time towards his rival (Cor.Pr.15,III), whom he will envy because (Pr.23,III) he enjoys the object loved.

Scholium

This hatred towards the object of one's love, joined with envy, is called Jealousy (zelotypia), which is therefore nothing else but 'vacillation arising from simultaneous love and hatred accompanied by the idea of a rival who is envied.' Furthermore, this hatred towards the object of his love will be greater in proportion to the pleasure wherewith the jealous man was wont to be affected as a result of the returning of his love by the object of his love, and also in proportion to the emotion wherewith he was affected towards him whom he thinks of as being intimately associated with the object of his love. For if he used to hate him, that very fact will make him hate the object of his love (Pr.24,III) because he thinks of it as affecting with pleasure that which he hates, and also (Cor.Pr.15,III) because he is compelled to associate the image of the object of his love with the image of one whom he hates. This is generally the case with love towards a woman; for he who thinks of a woman whom he loves as giving herself to another will not only feel pain by reason of his own appetite being checked but also, being compelled to associate the image of the object of his love with the sexual parts of his rival, he feels disgust for her. Then there is in addition the fact that the jealous man will not receive the same warm welcome as he was wont to receive from the object of his love, and this is a further reason for the lover's pain, as I shall now demonstrate.

PROPOSITION 36

He who recalls a thing which once afforded him pleasure desires to possess the same thing in the same circumstances as when he first took pleasure therein.

Proof

Whatever a man has seen together with the object that has afforded him pleasure will be indirectly a cause of pleasure (Pr.15,III), and so (Pr.28,III) he will desire to possess all this together with the object that afforded him pleasure, that is, he will desire to possess the object along with all the same attendant circumstances as when he first took pleasure in the object.

Corollary

If therefore he finds one of those attendant circumstances missing, the lover will feel pain.

Proof

In so far as he finds some attendant circumstance missing, to that extent he imagines something that excludes its existence. Now since he desires that thing or circumstance (preceding proposition) by reason of his love, then (Pr.19,III) in so far as he thinks it to be lacking he will feel pain.

Scholium

This pain, in so far as it regards the absence of that which we love, is called Longing (desiderium).

PROPOSITION 37

The desire arising from pain or pleasure, hatred or love, is proportionately greater as the emotion is greater.

Proof

Pain diminishes or checks man's power of activity (Sch.Pr.11,III), that is, (Pr.7,III) it diminishes or checks the conatus wherewith a man endeavors to persist in his own being; and therefore it is contrary to this conatus (Pr.5,III), and the conatus of a man affected by pain is entirely directed to removing the pain. But, by the definition of pain, the greater the pain, the greater the extent to which it must be opposed to man's power of activity. Therefore the greater the pain, with that much greater power of activity will a man endeavor to remove the pain; that is (Sch.Pr.9,III), with that much greater desire, or appetite, will he endeavor to remove the pain. Again, since pleasure (Sch.Pr.11,III) increases or assists man's power of activity, it can readily be demonstrated in the same way that a man affected with pleasure desires nothing other than to preserve it, and with all the greater desire as the pleasure is greater. Finally, since hatred and love are emotions of pain or pleasure, it follows in the same way that the conatus, appetite or desire arising through hatred or love is greater in proportion to the hatred and love.

PROPOSITION 38

If anyone has begun to hate the object of his love to the extent that his love is completely extinguished, he will, other things being equal, bear greater hatred towards it than if he had never loved it, and his hatred will be proportionate to the strength of his former love.

Proof

If anyone begins to hate the object of his love, more of his appetites are checked than if he had never loved it. For love is pleasure (Sch.Pr.13,III), which a man endeavors to preserve as far as he can (Pr.28,III), and this he does (same Sch.) by regarding the object loved as present and affecting it with pleasure (Pr.21,III), as far as he can. This conatus (preceding Pr.) is the greater as the love is greater, as also is the conatus that the object loved should return his love (Pr.33,III). But these conatus are checked by hatred towards the object loved (Cor.Pr.13 and Pr.23,III). Therefore for this reason, too, the lover will be affected with pain (Sch.Pr.11,III) which will be proportionate to his previous love; that is, in addition to the pain that was the cause of his hatred, a further pain arises from the fact that he has loved the object. Consequently, he will regard the loved object with a greater emotion of pain, that is (Sch.Pr.13,III), he will bear greater hatred towards it than if he had not loved it, and his hatred will be proportionate to the strength of his former love.

PROPOSITION 39

He who hates someone will endeavor to injure him unless he fears that he will suffer a greater injury in return. On the other hand, he who loves someone will by that same law endeavor to benefit him.

Proof

To hate someone is (Sch.Pr.13,III) to imagine someone to be the cause of one's pain. So (Pr.28,III) he who hates someone will endeavor to remove or destroy him. But if he fears from him something more painful, or (which is the same thing), a greater injury, which he thinks he can avoid by not inflicting the harm he was intending on him whom he hates, he will desire to refrain from so doing (same Pr.28,III), and this conatus (Pr.37,III) will be greater than that which was directed toward inflicting harm. This latter conatus will therefore prevail, as we have said. The second part of this proof proceeds on the same lines. Therefore he who hates someone . . . etc.

Scholium

By 'good' I understand here every kind of pleasure and furthermore whatever is conducive thereto, and especially whatever satisfies a longing of any sort. By 'bad' I understand every kind of pain, and especially that which frustrates a longing. For I have demonstrated above (Sch.Pr.9,III) that we do not desire a thing because we judge it to be good; on the contrary, we call the object of our desire good, and consequently the object of our aversion bad. Therefore it is according to his emotion that everyone judges or deems what is good, bad, better, worse, best or worst. Thus the miser judges wealth the best thing, and its lack the worst thing. The ambitious man desires nothing so much as public acclaim, and dreads nothing so much as disgrace. To the envious man nothing is more pleasant than another's unhappiness, and nothing more obnoxious than another's happiness. Thus every man judges a thing good or bad, advantageous or disadvantageous, according to his own emotion.

Now the emotion whereby a man is so disposed as to refrain from what he wants to do or to choose to do what he does not want is called Timidity (timor), which is merely fear in so far as a man is thereby disposed to avoid by a lesser evil what he judges to be a future evil (see Pr.28,III). But if the evil that he fears is disgrace, then timidity is called Bashfulness (verecundia). Finally, if the desire to avoid a future evil is checked by the apprehension of another evil, so that he does not know what preference to make, then fear is called Consternation (consternatio), especially if both the feared evils are of the greatest.

PROPOSITION 40

He who imagines he is hated by someone to whom he believes he has given no cause for hatred will hate him in return.

Proof

He who imagines someone to be affected with hatred will by that very fact himself be affected with hatred (Pr.27,III), that is (Sch.Pr.13, III), pain accompanied by the idea of an external cause. But, by hypothesis, he himself thinks that there is no other cause of this pain than he who hates him. Therefore from the fact that he imagines that he is hated by someone, he will be affected by pain accompanied by the idea of him who hates him; that is (by the same Sch.), he will hate that person.

Scholium

But if he thinks that he has provided just cause for hatred, then (Pr.30,III and Sch.) he will be affected with shame. But this (Pr.25,III) is rarely the case. Furthermore, this reciprocation of hatred can also arise from the fact that hatred is followed by a conatus to injure him who is hated (Pr.39,III). So he who imagines he is hated by someone will imagine him to be the cause of some evil or pain, and so he will be affected with pain, or fear, accompanied by the idea of him who hates him as being the cause; that is, he will be affected with hatred in return, as we said above.

Corollary 1

He who imagines that one he loves is affected with hatred towards him, will suffer the conflicting emotions of hatred and love. For in so far as he imagines he is hated by him, he is determined to hate him in return (preceding Pr.). But, by hypothesis, he nevertheless loves him. Therefore he will suffer the conflicting emotions of hatred and love.

Corollary 2

If anyone imagines that he has suffered some injury through hatred at the hands of one towards whom he has previously felt no emotion, he will immediately endeavor to return the said injury.

Proof

He who imagines that someone is affected with hatred towards him will hate him in return (preceding Pr.), and he will endeavor to devise anything that can affect that person with pain (Pr.26,III), and will seek to inflict it on him (Pr.39,III). But, by hypothesis, the first thing of that kind that comes to his mind is the injury that has been inflicted on himself. Therefore he will immediately endeavor to inflict that same injury on that person.

Scholium

The conatus to inflict injury on one whom we hate is called Anger (ira). The conatus to return an injury which we have suffered is called Revenge (vindicta).

PROPOSITION 41

If anyone thinks that he is loved by someone and believes that he has given no cause for this (which is possible through Cor.Pr.15 and Pr.16,III), he will love him in return.

Proof

This is proved in the same way as the preceding proposition. See also its Scholium.

Scholium

If he believes that he has given just cause for this love, he will exult in it (Pr.30,III and Sch.), which is more often the case (Pr.25,III); and we have said that the contrary occurs when someone thinks that he is hated by someone (see Sch. preceding Pr.). Now this reciprocal love, and consequently (Pr.39,III) the conatus to benefit one who loves us and who (same Pr.39,III) endeavors to benefit us, is called Gratitude (gratia seu gratitudo). So it is evident that men are far more inclined to revenge than to repay a benefit.

Corollary

He who imagines that he is loved by one whom he hates will feel conflicting emotions of hate and love. This is proved in the same way as the first corollary of the preceding proposition.

Scholium

If hatred prevails, he will endeavor to injure him by whom he is loved, and this emotion is called Cruelty (crudelitas), especially if it is believed that he who loves has not given any cause for hatred between them.

PROPOSITION 42

He who, moved by love or hope of honour, has conferred a benefit on someone, will feel pain if he sees that the benefit is ungratefully received.

Proof

He who loves a thing similar to himself endeavors, as far as he can, to bring it about that he is loved in return (Pr.33,III). So he who through love confers a benefit upon someone does so through his longing to be loved in return; that is (Pr.34,III), through hope of honour, or (Sch.Pr.30,III) pleasure. Thus (Pr.12,III) he will endeavor as far as he can to imagine this cause of honour, i.e. to regard it as actually existing. But, by hypothesis, he thinks of something else that excludes the existence of the said cause. Therefore (Pr.19,III) by that very fact he will feel pain.

PROPOSITION 43

Hatred is increased by reciprocal hatred, and may on the other hand be destroyed by love.

Proof

If someone thinks that one whom he hates is affected with hatred towards him, a new source of hatred thereby arises (Pr.40,III), while the old hatred, by hypothesis, still continues. But if, on the other hand, he thinks that the said person is affected with love towards him, in so far as he thinks this, he regards himself with pleasure (Pr.30,III), and to that extent (Pr.29,III) he will endeavor to please him; that is (Pr.41,III) to that extent he endeavors not to hate him nor affect him with any pain. This conatus (Pr.37,III) will vary proportionately to the strength of the emotion from which it arises, and so if it should be greater than the emotion which arises from hatred whereby he endeavors to affect the object of his hatred with pain (Pr.26,III), it will prevail over it and will eradicate the feeling of hatred.

PROPOSITION 44

Hatred that is fully overcome by love passes into love, and the love will therefore be greater than if it had not been preceded by hatred.

Proof

The proof proceeds along the same lines as that of Pr.38,III. For he who begins to love the object that he hated, that is, used to regard with pain, will feel pleasure by the very fact that he loves, and to this pleasure which love involves (see its Def. in Sch.Pr.13,III) is added the further pleasure arising from the fact that the conatus to remove the pain which hatred involves (as we demonstrated in Pr.37,III) is very much assisted, accompanied by the idea of the one whom he hated as being the cause.

Scholium

Although this is so, nobody will endeavor to hate an object or be affected with pain in order to enjoy this greater feeling of pleasure; that is, nobody will desire to suffer hurt in the hope of recovering from the hurt, or will want to be ill in the hope of recovering his health. For everyone will endeavor always to preserve his own being and to remove pain, as far as he can. If it were possible to conceive the contrary, that a man should want to hate someone so that he might later feel greater love for him, he will always want to be hating him. For the greater was the hatred, the greater will be the love; so he will always want his hatred to go on growing. And for the same reason a man will endeavor to be more and more ill so as later to enjoy greater pleasure from the restoration of health. So he will always endeavor to be ill, which is absurd (Pr.6,III).

PROPOSITION 45

If anyone imagines that someone similar to himself is affected with hatred towards a thing similar to himself, which he loves, he will hate him.

Proof

The object loved returns the hatred of him who hates it (Pr.40,III), and so the lover who thinks that someone hates the object loved is thereby made to think of the object of his love as affected by hatred, that is (Sch.Pr.13,III), as affected by pain. Consequently he feels pain (Pr.21,III), a pain that is accompanied by the idea of him who hates the object of his love as being the cause; that is, (Sch.Pr.13,III), he will hate him.

PROPOSITION 46

If anyone is affected with pleasure or pain by someone of a class or nation different from his own and the pleasure or pain is accompanied by the idea of that person as its cause, under the general category of that class or nation, he will love or hate not only him but all of that same class or nation.

Proof

This is evident from Pr.16,III.

PROPOSITION 47

The pleasure that arises from our imagining that the object of our hatred is being destroyed or is suffering some other harm is not devoid of some feeling of pain.

Proof

This is evident from Pr.27,III. For in so far as we imagine a thing similar to ourselves to be affected with pain, to that extent we feel pain.

Scholium

This Proposition can also be proved from Cor.Pr.17,II. For whenever we call a thing to mind, although it may not actually exist, we regard it as present, and the body is affected in the same way. Therefore in so far as his remembrance of the thing is strong, to that extent the man is determined to regard it with pain. And whereas this determination, the image of the thing still persisting, is checked by the remembrance of those things that exclude its existence, it is not completely annulled, and so the man feels pleasure only in so far as this determination is checked. Hence it comes about that the pleasure that arises from the harm suffered by the object of our hatred is revived whenever we call to mind the said thing. For, as we have said, when the image of the said thing is activated, since it involves the existence of the thing it determines one to regard the thing with the same pain as when one was wont to regard it when it did exist. But since one has associated with the image of the said thing other images which exclude its existence, this determination to pain is immediately checked, and one feels a renewed pleasure, and this is so whenever the series of events is repeated.

It is this same cause that makes men feel pleasure whenever they recall some past ill and makes them enjoy talking about perils from which they have been saved. For when they imagine some peril they regard it as though it were still to come and are determined to fear it, a determination which is again checked by the idea of their escape which they associated with the idea of this peril when they did in fact escape it. This idea makes them feel safe once more, and so their pleasure is renewed.

PROPOSITION 48

Love and hatred towards, say, Peter are destroyed if the pain involved in the latter and the pleasure involved in the former are associated with the idea of a different cause; and both emotions are diminished to the extent that we think Peter not to have been the only cause of either emotion.

Proof

This is evident merely from the definitions of love and hatred, for which see Sch.Pr.13,III. For pleasure is called love for Peter, and pain, hatred for Peter, for this reason alone, that Peter is considered the cause of the one or other emotion. When this consideration is completely or partly removed, the emotion towards Peter disappears or is diminished.

PROPOSITION 49

Love and hatred towards a thing that we think of as free must both

*be greater, other conditions being equal, than towards a thing subject to
necessity.*

Proof

A thing that we think of as free has to be perceived through itself independently of other things (Def.7,I). If therefore we think it to be the
cause of pleasure or pain, by that very fact we shall love or hate it
(Sch.Pr.13,III), and with the utmost love or hatred that can arise from
the postulated emotion (preceding Pr.). But if we think of the thing
which is the cause of the said emotion as subject to necessity, then we
shall think of it not as the sole cause of the said emotion but together
with other causes (same Def.7,I), and so (preceding Pr.) love and hatred
towards it will be less.

Scholium

Hence it follows that, deeming themselves to be free, men feel more
love and hatred towards one another than towards other things. Then
there is the additional factor of imitation of emotions, for which see
Prs.27, 34, 40, and 43,III.

PROPOSITION 50
Any thing can be the indirect cause of hope or fear.

Proof

This proposition is proved in the same way as Pr.15,III, q.v.,
together with Sch.2,Pr.18,III.

Scholium

Things that are indirectly causes of hope or fear are called good or
bad omens. Again, in so far as these same omens are the cause of hope or
fear, to that extent they are the cause of pleasure or pain (by Defs. of
hope and fear, q.v., Sch.2,Pr.18,III), and consequently (Cor.Pr.15,III)
to that extent we love or hate them and (Pr.28,III) we endeavor to procure
them as means to fulfil our hopes or to remove them as obstacles or
causes of fear. Furthermore, it follows from Pr.25,III that we are so constituted by nature that we are ready to believe what we hope and reluctant to believe what we fear, and that we over-estimate and underestimate in such cases. This is the origin of Superstition (superstitiones),
to which men are everywhere a prey.

I do not think it worthwhile to demonstrate here the vacillations that
arise from hope and fear, since it follows merely from the definition of
these emotions that there is no hope without fear and no fear without
hope (as I shall explain at greater length in due course). Furthermore, in
so far as we hope or fear something, to that extent we love or hate it, and
so everyone can easily apply to hope and fear what we have said concerning love and hatred.

PROPOSITION 51

Different men can be affected in different ways by one and the same object, and one and the same man can be affected by one and the same object in different ways at different times.

Proof

The human body (Post.3,II) is affected by external bodies in a great many ways. So two men may be affected at the same time in different ways, and so (Ax.1 after Lemma 3, q.v., after Pr.13,II) they can be affected by one and the same object in different ways. Again (same Post.) the human body can be affected now in one way, now in another, and consequently (same Ax.) it can be affected in different ways at different times by one and the same object.

Scholium

We therefore see that it is possible that what one man loves, another hates, what one man fears, another fears not, and that one and the same man may now love what he previously hated and may now dare what he previously feared, and so on. Again, since everyone according to his emotions judges what is good, what is bad, what is better and what is worse (Sch.Pr.39,III), it follows that men vary as much in judgment as in emotion.[4] So it comes about that in comparing different men we distinguish between them solely by difference of emotion, and call some fearless, others timid, and others by other epithets. For example, I shall call fearless one who despises an evil that I am wont to fear, and if furthermore I have regard to the fact that his desire to inflict injury on one he hates and to benefit one whom he loves is not checked by apprehension of an evil which is wont to restrain me, I shall call him daring. Again, he who fears an evil which I am wont to despise will appear to me timid, and if furthermore I have regard to the fact that his desire is checked by apprehension of an evil which cannot restrain me, I shall say he is cowardly. And this is how everyone judges. Finally, as a result of this characteristic of man and the variability of his judgment—such as the fact that man's judgment is often governed solely by emotion, and that things which he believes to make for pleasure or pain and which he therefore (Pr.28,III) endeavors to promote or remove are often merely imaginary, not to mention other points mentioned in Part II concerning the uncertainty of things—we readily conceive that a man may often be responsible for the pain and pleasure that he feels; that is, for being affected both with pain and pleasure, accompanied by the idea of himself as its cause. Thus we readily understand what repentance (paenitentia) and self-contentment are. Repentance is pain accompanied by the idea of oneself as its cause, and self-contentment is pleasure accompanied by the idea of oneself as its cause, and these emotions are extremely intense since men believe themselves to be free (see Pr.49,III).

4. We have shown in Sch.Pr.13,II that this can be so although the human mind is part of the divine intellect. [Spinoza]

PROPOSITION 52

To an object that we have previously seen in conjunction with others or that we imagine to have nothing but what is common to many other objects, we shall not give as much regard as to that which we imagine to have something singular.

Proof

As soon as we think of an object that we have seen in conjunction with others, we immediately recall the others as well (Pr.18,II and Sch.) and thus from regarding the one we immediately pass on to regarding another. The same holds good of an object which we think to have nothing but what is common to many others. For by that very fact we suppose that we are regarding in it nothing that we have not previously seen in other objects. But in supposing that we perceive in some object something special that we have never seen before we are saying only this, that the mind, while regarding that object, contains nothing in itself to the contemplation of which it can pass on from contemplation of that object. Therefore the mind is determined to regard only that object. Therefore . . . etc.

Scholium

This affection of the mind, or thought of a special thing, in so far as it alone engages the mind is called Wonder (admiratio), which, if evoked by an object that we fear, is called Consternation, because wonder at an evil keeps a man so paralysed in regarding it alone that he is incapable of thinking of other things whereby he might avoid the evil. But if that which we wonder at be a man's prudence, industry, or something of that sort, since by that very fact we regard the man as far surpassing us, then wonder is called Veneration (veneratio); otherwise, if we are wondering at a man's anger, envy, and so on, we call it Horror (horror). Again, if we wonder at the prudence, industry etc. of a person we love, our love will thereby be the greater (Pr.12,III), and this love joined with wonder or veneration we call Devotion (devotio). We may also in the same manner conceive hatred, hope, confidence and other emotions as joined with wonder, and thus we can deduce more emotions than can be signified by accepted terms. Hence it is clear that the names for emotions have been taken from common usage rather than from detailed knowledge of them.

The opposite of wonder is Contempt (contemptus), whose cause, however, is generally as follows. From seeing someone wondering at, loving, fearing etc. some thing, or because some thing at first sight seems similar to things that we wonder at, love, fear, etc. (by Pr.15 and Cor. and Pr.27,III), we are determined to wonder at, love, fear, etc. the same thing. But if from the presence of the thing or from closer contemplation we are compelled to deny of it all that can be the cause of wonder, love, fear, etc., then the mind from the very presence of the thing remains determined to reflect on what is lacking in the object rather than what is in it, whereas from the presence of an object it is customary for the mind to reflect especially on what is in the object. Further, just as devotion arises from wonder at a thing that we love, so does Derision (irrisio) from contempt for a thing we hate or have feared, and Scorn (dedignatio) from contempt of folly, just as veneration from wonder at prudence. Finally, we can conceive of love, hope, honour and other emotions as joined with contempt, and therefrom we can deduce yet other emotions, which again we are not wont to distinguish from others by special names.

PROPOSITION 53

When the mind regards its own self and its power of activity, it feels pleasure, and the more so the more distinctly it imagines itself and its power of activity.

Proof

Man knows himself only through the affections of his body and their ideas (Prs.19 and 23,II). When therefore it happens that the mind can regard its own self, by that very fact it is assumed to pass to a state of greater perfection, that is, (Sch.Pr.11,III), to be affected with pleasure, and the more so the more distinctly it is able to imagine itself and its power of activity.

Corollary

The more a man imagines he is praised by others, the more this pleasure is fostered. For the more he thinks he is praised by others, the more he thinks that others are affected with pleasure by him, and this accompanied by the idea of himself (Sch.Pr.29,III). So (Pr.27,III) he is affected with greater pleasure, accompanied by the idea of himself.

PROPOSITION 54

The mind endeavors to think only of the things that affirm its power of activity.

Proof

The mind's conatus, or power, is the very essence of the mind (Pr.7,III). But the essence of the mind affirms only what the mind is and can do (as is self-evident), and not what the mind is not and cannot do. So the mind endeavors to think only of what affirms, or posits, its power of activity.

PROPOSITION 55

When the mind thinks of its own impotence, by that very fact it feels pain.

Proof

The essence of the mind affirms only what the mind is and can do;

that is, it is of the nature of the mind to think only of those things that affirm its power of activity (preceding Pr.). Therefore, when we say that the mind, in regarding itself, thinks of its own impotence, we are simply saying that while the mind is endeavoring to think of something that affirms its power of activity, this conatus is checked; that is, it feels pain (Sch.Pr.11,III).

Corollary
This pain is fostered all the more if one thinks he is blamed by others. The proof is on the same lines as Cor.Pr.53,III.

Scholium
This pain, accompanied by the idea of our own impotence, is called Humility (humilitas). The pleasure that arises from regarding ourselves is called Self-love (philautia) or Self-contentment (acquiescentia in se ipso). And since this pleasure is repeated whenever a man regards his own capabilities, that is, his power of activity, the result is again that everyone is eager to tell of his exploits and to boast of his strength both of body and mind, and for this reason men bore one another. From this it again follows that men are by nature envious (see Sch.Pr.24, and Sch.Pr.32, III), that is, they rejoice at the weakness of their fellows and are pained at their accomplishments. For whenever a man imagines his own actions he is affected with pleasure (Pr.53,III), and the more so as his actions express greater perfection and he imagines them more distinctly; that is (by what was said in Sch.1,Pr.40,II), the more he can distinguish them from the actions of others and regard them as something special. Therefore everybody will most enjoy regarding himself when he regards in himself something that he denies of others. But if what he affirms of himself belongs to the universal idea of man or animal, he will derive no such great joy therefrom, and he will on the other hand feel pain if he thinks of his actions as inferior, compared with the actions of others. This pain (Pr.28,III) he will endeavor to remove by wrongly interpreting the actions of his fellows or by embellishing his own as much as he can. It is therefore clear that men are prone to hatred and envy, and this is accentuated by their upbringing. For parents are wont to incite their children to excellence solely by the spur of honour and envy. But perhaps there remains a shadow of doubt on the grounds that we not infrequently admire the virtues of men and venerate them. To remove this shadow of doubt I shall add the following Corollary.

Corollary
Nobody envies another's virtue unless he is his peer.

Proof
Envy is hatred itself (Sch.Pr.24,III) or pain (Sch.Pr.13,III); that is (Sch.Pr.11,III), an affection whereby a man's power of activity, that is, his conatus, is checked. Now man (Sch.Pr.9,III) endeavors or desires to do nothing save what can follow from his given nature. Therefore, a man will not desire to be attributed to himself any power of activity, or (which

is the same thing) virtue, which is proper to the nature of another and foreign to his own. So his desire cannot be checked, that is (Sch.Pr.11, III), he cannot be pained, by reason of his regarding some virtue in somebody unlike himself; consequently he cannot envy him. But he would envy his peer, who is assumed to be of the same nature as himself.

Scholium

So when we said in Sch.Pr.52,III that we venerate a man as a result of wondering at his prudence, strength of mind, and so on, this comes about (as is obvious from the proposition) because we think these virtues are special to him and not common to our nature, and so we do not envy him them any more than we envy trees their height, lions their strength, etc.

PROPOSITION 56

There are as many kinds of pleasure, pain, desire and consequently of every emotion that is compounded of these (such as vacillation) or of every emotion that is derived from these (love, hatred, hope, fear, etc), as there are kinds of objects by which we are affected.

Proof

Pleasure, pain, and consequently the emotions that are compounded of these or derived from them are passive emotions (Sch.Pr.11,III). Now we are necessarily passive (Pr.1,III) in so far as we have inadequate ideas, and only in so far as we have inadequate ideas are we passive (Pr.3,III). That is to say (Sch.Pr.40,II), we are necessarily passive only to the extent that we form mental images (imaginamur), i.e. (Pr.17,II and Sch.) to the extent that we are affected in a way that involves both the nature of our own body and the nature of an external body. Therefore the explication of the nature of every passive emotion must necessarily include an expression of the nature of the object by which we are affected. The pleasure arising from object A involves the nature of object A and the pleasure arising from object B involves the nature of object B, and so these two emotions of pleasure are different in nature because they arise from causes of different natures. So too the emotion of pain that arises from one object is different in nature from the pain that arises from a different cause, and this must also be understood of love, hatred, hope, fear, and vacillation. Therefore there are necessarily as many kinds of pleasure, pain, love, hatred, etc. as there are kinds of objects by which we are affected. Now desire is the very essence, or nature, of each individual in so far as that is conceived as determined by some given state of its constitution to do something (Sch.Pr.9,III). Therefore according as each individual is affected from external causes with various kinds of pleasure, pain, love, hate, etc., that is, according as his nature is conditioned in various ways, so must his desire be of different kinds; and the nature of one desire must differ from the nature of another to the same extent as the emotions, from which each single desire arises, differ amongst themselves. Therefore, there are as many kinds of desire as there are kinds of pleasure, pain, love, etc., and consequently (by what has been proved) as there are kinds of objects by which we are affected.

Scholium

Among the kinds of emotional states which (by the preceding proposition) must be very numerous, most noteworthy are Dissipation (luxuria), Drunkenness (ebrietas), Lust (libido), Avarice (avaritia) and Ambition (ambitio), which are only concepts springing from love or desire, and which explicate the nature of both these emotions through the objects to which they are related. For by dissipation, drunkenness, lust, avarice and ambition we mean quite simply uncontrolled love or desire for feasting, drinking, sex, riches and popular acclaim. Furthermore, these emotions have no opposites in so far as we distinguish them from other emotions solely through the objects to which they are related. For Self-control (temperantia), Sobriety (sobrietas) and Chastity (castitas), which we are wont to oppose to dissipation, drunkenness and lust, are not emotions or passive states, but indicate the power of the mind that controls these emotions.

However, I cannot here give an account of the remaining kinds of emotion, for they are as many as there are kinds of objects; nor, if I could, is it necessary. For it suffices for our purpose, which is to determine the strength of the emotions and the power of the mind over them, to have a general definition of all the individual emotions. It is sufficient, I repeat, to understand the common properties of the emotions and the mind so as to determine the nature and the extent of the mind's power in controlling and checking the emotions. So although there is a great difference between this and that emotion of love, hatred or desire, e.g. between the love towards one's children and love towards one's wife, there is no need for us to investigate these differences and to trace any further the nature and origin of the emotions.

PROPOSITION 57

Any emotion of one individual differs from the emotion of another to the extent that the essence of the one individual differs from the essence of the other.

Proof

This proposition is obvious from Ax.1, q.v., after Lemma 3 Sch.Pr.13,II. But we shall nevertheless prove it from the definitions of the three primary emotions.

All emotions are related to desire, pleasure or pain, as is made clear by the definitions we have given of them. Now desire is the very nature or essence of every single individual (see its definition in Sch.Pr.9,III). Therefore the desire of each individual differs from the desire of another to the extent that the nature or essence of the one differs from the essence of the other. Again, pleasure and pain are passive emotions whereby each individual's power, that is, his conatus to persist in his own being, is increased or diminished, assisted or checked (Pr.11,III and Sch.). But by the conatus to persist in one's own being, in so far as it is related to mind and body together, we understand appetite and desire (Sch.Pr.9,III). Therefore pleasure and pain is desire or appetite, in so far as it is increased or diminished, assisted or checked, by external causes; that is, (by the same Sch.), it is each individual's very nature. So each individual's pleasure or pain differs from the pleasure or pain of another to the extent that the nature or essence of the one also differs from that of the other. Consequently, any emotion . . . etc.

Scholium

Hence it follows that the emotions of animals that are called irrational (for now that we know the origin of mind we can by no means doubt that beasts have feelings) differ from the emotions of men as much as their nature differs from human nature. Horse and man are indeed carried away by lust to procreate, but the former by equine lust, the latter by human lust. So too the lusts and appetites of insects, fishes and birds are bound to be of various different kinds. So although each individual lives content with the nature wherewith he is endowed and rejoices in it, that life wherewith each is content and that joy are nothing other than the idea or soul (anima) of the said individual, and so the joy of the one differs from the joy of another as much as the essence of the one differs from the essence of the other. Finally, it follows from the preceding proposition that there is also no small difference between the joy which guides the drunkard and the joy possessed by the philosopher, a point to which I wish to draw attention in passing.

So much for emotions that are related to man in so far as he is passive. It remains for me to add a few words concerning emotions that are related to man in so far as he is active.

PROPOSITION 58

Besides the pleasure and desire that are passive emotions, there are other emotions of pleasure and desire that are related to us in so far as we are active.

Proof

When the mind conceives itself and its power to act, it feels pleasure (Pr.53,III). Now the mind necessarily regards itself when it conceives a true, that is, adequate, idea (Pr.43,II). But the mind does conceive adequate ideas (Sch.2,Pr.40,II). Therefore it feels pleasure, too, in so far as it conceives adequate ideas, that is (Pr.1,III), in so far as it is active. Again, it is both in so far as it has clear and distinct ideas and in so far as it has confused ideas that the mind endeavors to persist in its own being (Pr.9,III). But by conatus we understand desire (Sch.Pr.9,III). Therefore desire is also related to us in so far as we understand, i.e. in so far as we act (Pr.1,III).

PROPOSITION 59

Among all the emotions that are related to the mind in so far as it is active, there are none that are not related to pleasure or desire.

Proof

All emotions are related to desire, pleasure or pain, as is shown by the definitions we have given of them. Now by pain we understand that which diminishes or checks the mind's power of thinking (Pr.11,III, and Sch.). So in so far as the mind feels pain, to that extent its power of understanding, that is, its power of activity, is diminished or checked (Pr.1,III). So no emotions of pain can be related to the mind in so far as it is active, but only emotions of pleasure and desire, which (preceding Pr.) are to that extent also related to the mind.

Scholium

All the activities which follow from emotions that are related to the mind in so far as it exercises understanding I refer to Strength of mind (fortitudo), which I subdivide into Courage (animositas) and Nobility (generositas). By courage I understand 'the desire whereby every individual endeavors to preserve his own being according to the dictates of reason alone.' By nobility I understand 'the desire whereby every individual, according to the dictates of reason alone, endeavors to assist others and make friends of them.' So I classify under courage those activities that are directed solely to the advantage of the agent, and those that are directed to the advantage of another I classify under nobility. So self-control, sobriety, and resourcefulness in danger, etc. are kinds of courage; Courtesy (modestia) and Mercy (clementia) are kinds of nobility.

And now I think I have explained the principal emotions and vacillations that arise from the combination of the three basic emotions—desire, pleasure and pain—and have clarified them through their first causes. From this it is clear that we are in many respects at the mercy of external causes and are tossed about like the waves of the sea when driven by contrary winds, unsure of the outcome and of our fate. But I have said that I have clarified only the principal conflicts of feeling, not all that can be. For by proceeding in the same manner as above we can readily demonstrate that love is joined with repentance, scorn, shame, and so on. Indeed, from what has been said I think everyone is quite convinced that emotions can be combined with one another in so many ways and give rise to so many variations that they cannot be numbered. But it suffices for my purpose to have enumerated only the principal emotions; for those I have passed over would be a matter of curiosity rather than utility.

However, one further point should be observed concerning love. It frequently happens, while we are enjoying what we were seeking, that from that very enjoyment the body changes to a new condition, as a result of which it is differently determined and different images are activated in it, and at the same time the mind begins to think of and desire other things. For example, when we think of something that is wont to delight us with its taste, we desire to enjoy it, to eat it. But while we are thus enjoying it the stomach is being filled and the body is changing its condition. If therefore, with the body now in a different condition, the image of the said food is fostered by its being set before us, and consequently also the conatus or desire to eat the food, this conatus, or desire, will be opposed by the new condition of the body, and consequently the presence of the food which we used to want will be hateful, and this is what we call Satiety (fastidium) and Weariness (taedium).

I have passed by those external affections of the body which can be observed in the case of emotions, such as trembling, pallor, sobbing, laughter and so on, because they are related to the body without any relation to the mind. Finally, with regard to the definitions of emotions there are certain points to be noted, and I shall therefore repeat those definitions here in proper order, accompanied by such observations as I think necessary in each case.

DEFINITIONS OF THE EMOTIONS

1. Desire is the very essence of man in so far as his essence is conceived as determined to any action from any given affection of itself.

Explication

We said above in Sch.Pr.9,III that desire is appetite accompanied by consciousness of itself, and that appetite is the very essence of man in so far as his essence is determined to such actions as contribute to his preservation. But in the same Scholium I also noted that in fact I acknowledge no difference between human appetite and desire. For whether or not a man is conscious of his appetite, the appetite remains one and the same. So to avoid appearing to be guilty of tautology, I declined to explicate desire through appetite; my object was so to define it as to include all the endeavors of human nature that we term appetite, will, desire, or urge. I could merely have said: 'Desire is the very essence of man in so far as his essence is conceived as determined to some action'; but then it would not follow from this definition (Pr.23,II) that the mind can be conscious of its own desire or appetite. Thus, in order to involve the cause of this consciousness it was necessary (by the same Pr.) to add 'from any given affection of itself.' For by 'any affection of the human essence' we understand 'any condition (constitutio) of the said essence,' whether it be innate, whether it be conceived solely through the attribute of Thought or solely through the attribute of Extension, or whether it be related to both attributes together. So here I mean by the word 'desire' any of man's endeavors, urges, appetites and volitions, which vary with man's various states, and are not infrequently so opposed to one another that a man may be drawn in different directions and know not where to turn.

2. Pleasure is man's transition from a state of less perfection to a state of greater perfection.

3. Pain is man's transition from a state of greater perfection to a state of less perfection.

Explication

I say 'transition,' for pleasure is not perfection itself. If a man were to be born with the perfection to which he passes, he would be in possession of it without the emotion of pleasure. This is clearer in the case of pain, the contrary emotion. For nobody can deny that pain consists in the transition to a state of less perfection, not in the less perfection itself, since man cannot feel pain in so far as he participates in any degree of perfection. Nor can we say that pain consists in the privation of greater perfection, for privation is nothing, whereas the emotion of pain is an actuality, which therefore can be nothing other than the actuality of the transition to a state of less perfection; that is, the actuality whereby a man's power of activity is diminished or checked (Sch.Pr.11,III).

As to the definitions of Cheerfulness, Titillation, Melancholy and Anguish, I omit them because they are related chiefly to the body, and are only species of pleasure and pain.

4. Wonder is the thought of any thing on which the mind stays fixed because this particular thought has no connection with any others. See Proposition 52 and its Scholium.

Explication

In Sch.Pr.18,II we demonstrated the reason why the mind, from thinking of one thing, passes immediately on to the thought of another, and that is that in such cases the images are bound together and so ordered that one follows another. This concept cannot cover the case when the image is a strange one. The mind will be kept in contemplation of the said thing until it is determined by other causes to think of other things. So the thought of an unusual thing, considered in itself, is of the same nature as other thoughts, and for this reason I do not count wonder among the emotions; nor do I see why I should do so, since this distraction of the mind arises from no positive cause that distracts it from other things, but only from the lack of a cause for determining the mind, from the contemplation of one thing, to think of other things.

Therefore, as I noted in Sch.Pr.11,III, I acknowledge only three basic or primary emotions, pleasure, pain, and desire; and I have made mention of wonder only because it is customary for certain emotions derived from the three basic emotions to be signified by different terms when they are related to objects that evoke our wonder. There is an equally valid reason for my adding here a definition of contempt.

5. Contempt is the imagining (imaginatio) of some thing that makes so little impact on the mind that the presence of the thing motivates the mind to think of what is not in the thing rather than of what is in the thing. See Sch.Pr.52,III.

I here pass over the definitions of Veneration and Scorn because, as far as I know, there are no emotions that take their name from them.

6. Love is pleasure accompanied by the idea of an external cause.

Explication

This definition explains quite clearly the essence of love. The definition given by writers who define love as 'the lover's wish to be united with the object of his love' express not the essence of love, but a property of it; and since these writers have not sufficiently grasped the essence of love, neither have they succeeded in forming any clear conception of its property. This has led to the universal verdict that their definition is very obscure. However, be it noted that when I say that in the case of a lover it is a property to wish to be united with the object of his love, by 'wish' I do not mean consent or deliberate intention, that is, free decision, (for in Pr.48,II we proved this to be fictitious), nor again desire to be united with the loved object when it is absent or to continue in its presence when it is there; for love can be conceived without any one particular desire. By 'wish' I mean the contentment that is in the lover by reason of the presence of the object of his love, by which the lover's pleasure is strengthened, or at least fostered.

7.   Hatred is pain accompanied by the idea of an external cause.

Explication

The points here to be noted can be easily perceived from the Explication of the preceding Proposition. See also Sch.Pr.13,III.

8.   Inclination (propensio) is pleasure accompanied by the idea of a thing which is indirectly the cause of the pleasure.

9.   Aversion (aversio) is pain accompanied by the idea of a thing which is indirectly the cause of the pain. (For these see Sch.Pr.15,III).

10.   Devotion is love towards one at whom we wonder.

Explication

We demonstrated in Pr.52,III that Wonder (admiratio) arises from the strangeness of a thing. So if it happens that we often think about the object of our wonder, we shall cease to wonder at it. So we see that the emotion of devotion can easily degenerate into mere love.

11.   Derision is pleasure arising from our imagining that there is in the object of our hate something that we despise.

Explication

In so far as we despise a thing that we hate, to that extent we deny existence regarding it (Sch.Pr.52,III) and to that extent we feel pleasure (Pr.20,III). But since we are supposing that what a man derides he nevertheless hates, it follows that this pleasure is not unalloyed (Sch. Pr.47,III).

12.   Hope is inconstant pleasure arising from the idea of a thing future or past, of whose outcome we are in some doubt.

13.   Fear is inconstant pain arising from the idea of a thing future or past, of whose outcome we are in some doubt.
    For these see Sch.2,Pr.18,III.

Explication

From these definitions it follows that there is no hope without fear and no fear without hope. For he who is in hopeful suspense and has doubts as to the outcome of a thing is assumed to be imagining something that excludes the existence of the hoped-for thing, and so to that extent he feels pain (Pr.19,III). Consequently, as long as he is in hopeful suspense, he fears as to the outcome. On the other hand, he who is in a state of fear, that is, is unsure of the occurrence of a thing that he hates, is also imagining something that excludes the existence of the said thing, and so (Pr.20,III) he feels pleasure, and to that extent he entertains hope of its not happening.

14.   Confidence is pleasure arising from the idea of a thing future or past, concerning which reason for doubt has been removed.

15.   Despair is pain arising from the idea of a thing future or past concerning which reason for doubt has been removed.

Explication

Therefore confidence arises from hope and despair from fear when reason for uncertainty as to the outcome of a thing has been removed. This comes about either because man imagines a thing past or future as being at hand and regards it as present, or because he thinks of other things that exclude the existence of those things that were causing his uncertainty. For although we can never be certain as to the outcome of particular things (Cor.Pr.31,II), it is possible for us not to be doubtful as to their outcome. For we have demonstrated (Sch.Pr.49,II) that not having doubts concerning a thing is different from being certain of the thing. So it is possible for us to be affected by the same emotion of pleasure or pain from the image of a thing past or future as from the image of a thing present, as we proved in Proposition 18,III, q.v., with Sch.

16.   Joy is pleasure accompanied by the idea of a past thing whose outcome was contrary to our fear.

17.   Disappointment (conscientiae morsus) is pain accompanied by the idea of a past thing whose outcome was contrary to our hope.

18.   Pity is pain accompanied by the idea of ill that has happened to another whom we think of as like ourselves. See Sch.Pr.22 and Sch.Pr.27,III.

Explication

There seems to be no difference between pity and compassion (misericordia), unless perhaps pity has reference to a particular occurrence of emotion, while compassion has regard to a set disposition to that emotion.

19.   Approbation is love towards one who has benefited another.

20.   Indignation is hatred towards one who has injured another.

Explication

I know that these words are commonly used with a different meaning. But my purpose is to explain not the meaning of words but the nature of things, and to assign to things terms whose common meaning is not very far away from the meaning I decide to give them. Let this one reminder suffice. As to the cause of these emotions, see Cor.1,Pr.27 and Sch.Pr.22,III.

21. Over-esteem is to think too highly of someone by reason of love.

22. Disparagement (despectus) is to think too meanly of someone by reason of hatred.

Explication

Over-esteem is therefore a result, or a property, of love, and disparagement of hatred. So over-esteem can also be defined as 'love, in so far as it so affects a man that he thinks too highly of the object of his love'; and disparagement as 'hatred, in so far as it so affects a man that he thinks too meanly of the object of his hatred.' For these see Sch.Pr.26,III.

23. Envy is hatred, in so far as it so affects a man that he is pained at another's good fortune and rejoices at another's ill-fortune.

Explication

The opposite of envy is commonly said to be compassion which therefore, with some distortion of its usual meaning, can be defined thus:

24. Compassion is love, in so far as it so affects a man that he rejoices at another's good and feels pain at another's hurt.

Explication

As to envy, see Sch.Pr.24,III and Sch.Pr.32,III.

Such are the emotions of pleasure and pain which are accompanied by the idea of an external thing as direct (per se) or indirect (per accidens) cause. From these I pass on to other emotions which are accompanied by the idea of an internal thing as cause.

25. Self-contentment is pleasure arising from a man's contemplation of himself and his power of activity.

26. Humility is pain arising from a man's contemplation of his own impotence, or weakness.

Explication

Self-contentment is the opposite of humility in so far as by the former we understand pleasure that arises from our regarding our power of activity. But in so far as we also understand by it pleasure accompanied by the idea of some deed which we think we have done from free decision of the mind, then its opposite is repentance, which we define thus:

27. Repentance is pain accompanied by the idea of some deed which we believe we have done from free decision of the mind.

Explication

We have demonstrated the causes of these emotions in Sch.Pr.51,III and Prs.53,54,55,III and its Sch. As for free decision of the mind, see Sch.Pr.35,II. But here we should also note that it is not surprising that all our actions that are customarily called wrong are followed by pain, and those which are said to be right, by pleasure. For we readily understand from what has been said that our upbringing is chiefly responsible for this. By disapproving of wrong actions and frequently rebuking their children when they commit them, and contrariwise by approving and praising right actions, parents have caused the former to be associated with painful feelings and the latter with pleasurable feelings. This is further confirmed by experience. For not all people have the same customs and religion. What some hold as sacred, others regard as profane; what some hold as honourable, others regard as disgraceful. So each individual repents of a deed or exults in it according to his upbringing.

28.   Pride is thinking too highly of oneself by reason of self-love.

Explication

So pride differs from over-esteem, for the latter is related to an external object, while pride is related to a subject who thinks too highly of himself. However, as over-esteem is an effect or property of love, so is pride of self-love, and so it can also be defined as 'love of self, or self-contentment, in so far as it so affects a man that he thinks too highly of himself' (see Sch.Pr.26,III). This emotion has no opposite, for nobody thinks too meanly of himself by reason of self-hatred. Indeed, nobody thinks too meanly of himself in so far as he thinks this or that is beyond his capability. For whenever a man thinks something is beyond his capability, he necessarily thinks so, and by this belief he is so conditioned that he really cannot do what he thinks he cannot do. For while thinking that he cannot do this or that, he is not determined to do it, and consequently it is impossible that he should do it.

However, if we direct our attention solely to the way that others see him, we can conceive it as possible that a man may think too meanly of himself. For it can happen that a man, regarding with pain his own weakness, should think that everyone despises him, and this while the rest of the world is very far from despising him. Furthermore, a man may think too meanly of himself if he denies of himself in present time something related to future time of which he is not sure, as that he may say that he cannot achieve any certainty, or that he can desire or do nothing that is not wrong or disgraceful, and so on. Again, we can say that a man thinks too meanly of himself when we see that from excessive fear of disgrace he does not dare what others who are his peers dare. So we can take this emotion, which I shall call Self-abasement (abjectio), to be the opposite of pride. For as pride arises from self-contentment, so self-abasement arises from humility. Therefore we shall define it as follows:

29.   Self-abasement is thinking too meanly of oneself by reason of pain.

Explication

We usually oppose humility to pride, but then we are having regard to the effects of the two emotions rather than their nature. For we usually apply the term 'proud' to one who exults over-much (Sch.Pr.30,III), who talks only of his own virtues and the faults of others, who expects to take precedence over all, and who goes about with the pomp and style usually affected by those far above him in station. On the other hand, we apply the term 'humble' to one who blushes frequently, who confesses his faults and talks of the virtues of others, who gives way to all, and who goes about downcast and careless of his appearance.

Now these emotions, humility and self-abasement, are very rare; for human nature, considered in itself, strives against them as far as it can (Prs.13 and 54,III). So those who are believed to be most self-abased and humble are generally the most ambitious and envious.

30.   Honour is pleasure accompanied by the idea of some action of ours which we think that others praise.

31.   Shame is pain accompanied by the idea of some action of ours that we think that others censure.

Explication

For these, see Sch.Pr.30,III. But one should here observe the difference between shame and bashfulness. Shame is the pain that follows on a deed of which we are ashamed. Bashfulness is the fear or apprehension of shame, whereby a man is restrained from some disgraceful act. The opposite of bashfulness is usually Impudence (impudentia), which is not really an emotion, as I shall demonstrate in due course. But the names of emotions, as I have noted, have regard more to usage than to their nature.

Herewith I have completed my proposed task of explicating the emotions of pleasure and pain. I now pass on to those emotions that are related to desire.

32.   Longing is desire or appetite for possessing something, a desire fostered by remembrance of the said thing and at the same time checked by remembrance of other things that exclude the existence of the said object of appetite.

Explication

As I have often said, when we recall something we are thereby conditioned to regard it with the same emotion as if the thing were actually present. But in our waking hours, this disposition or conatus is generally restrained by the images of things that exclude the existence of that which we recall. So when we remember a thing that affected us with some kind of pleasure, by that very fact we endeavor to regard it as present along with that same emotion of pleasure; but this conatus is straightway checked by the remembrance of things that exclude the existence of the said thing. Therefore longing is really the opposite pain to the pleasure that arises from the absence of a thing that we hate, concerning which see Sch.Pr.47,III. But as the word 'longing' seems to have regard to desire, I classify this emotion under emotions of desire.

33.   Emulation is the desire for some thing, engendered in us from the fact that we think others to have the same desire.

Explication

When someone flees because he sees others fleeing, or fears because he sees others fearing, or again, on seeing that someone has burnt his hand, draws his hand back and makes a movement of the body as if his own hand were burnt, we say that he is imitating another's emotion, not that he is emulating him. This is not because we realise that the causes of imitation and emulation are different, but because it is the usual practice to call only him emulous who imitates what we judge to be honourable, useful or pleasant. As to the cause of emulation, see Pr.27,III and Sch. As to the reason why envy is generally associated with this emotion, see Pr.32,III and Sch.

34.   Gratitude is the desire, or eagerness of love (amoris studium), whereby we endeavor to benefit one who, from a like emotion of love, has bestowed a benefit on us. See Pr.39, and Sch.Pr.41,III.

35.   Benevolence is the desire to benefit one whom we pity. See Sch.Pr.27,III.

36.   Anger is the desire whereby we are urged from hatred to inflict injury on one whom we hate. See Pr.39,III.

37.   Revenge is the desire whereby we are urged from mutual hatred to inflict injury on one who, from like emotion, has injured us. See Cor.2,Pr.40,III and Sch.

38.   Cruelty, or savageness (saevitia), is the desire whereby someone is urged to inflict injury on one whom we love or whom we pity.

Explication

The opposite of cruelty is mercy, which is not a passive emotion but the power of the mind whereby a man controls anger and revenge.

39.   Timidity is the desire to avoid a greater evil, which we fear, by a lesser evil. See Sch.Pr.39,III.

40.   Boldness is the desire whereby someone is urged to some dangerous action which his fellows fear to undertake.

41.   Cowardice is a term applied to one whose desire is checked by apprehension of a danger which his fellows dare to face.

Explication

So cowardice is simply the fear of some evil which most people are not wont to fear. So I do not classify it as an emotion of desire. Still, I have decided to explain it here because it is the opposite of boldness in so far as we attend to desire.

42. Consternation is a term applied to one whose desire to avoid evil is checked by a feeling of wonder at the evil that he fears.

Explication

So consternation is a kind of cowardice. But since consternation arises from a two-fold timorousness, it can therefore be more fittingly be defined as 'fear that holds a man in such a state of stupefaction and hesitation that he is not able to remove the evil.' I say 'stupefaction' in as much as we mean that his desire to remove the evil is checked by a feeling of wonder. I say 'hesitation' in so far as we conceive the said desire to be checked by apprehension of another evil by which he is equally tormented, with the result that he knows not which of the two to avert. For this see Sch.Pr.39 and Sch.Pr.52,III. With regard to cowardice and boldness, see Sch.Pr.51,III.

43. Courtesy (humanitas) or Politeness (modestia) is desire to do things that please men and avoid things that displease them.

44. Ambition is the immoderate desire for honour.

Explication

Ambition is the desire whereby all emotions (Prs.27 and 31,III) are encouraged and strengthened; and thus this emotion can scarcely be overcome. For as long as a man is subject to any desire, he is necessarily subject to this one. "The best men," said Cicero, "are particularly led by the hope of renown. Even philosophers, in the books that they write in condemnation of fame, add their names thereto . . . " and so on.[5]

45. Dissipation is the immoderate desire, or also love, of sumptuous living.

46. Drunkenness is the immoderate desire and love of drinking.

47. Avarice is the immoderate desire and love of riches.

48. Lust is also the desire and love of sexual intercourse.

Explication

Whether this desire for sex is moderate or not, it is usually called lust.

These five emotions (as I noted in Sch.Pr.56,III), have no opposites. For politeness is a species of ambition (concerning which see Sch.Pr.29, III); and self-control, sobriety and chastity, too, I have already noted as indicating the power of the mind, not its passivity. And although it is possible that a miser, an ambitious or a timid man may abstain from excessive food, drinking and sex, yet avarice, ambition and timidity are not the opposites of dissipation, drunkenness and lust. For the miser gen-

5. Cicero, *Pro Archia,* II

erally longs to gorge himself on other people's food and drink. The ambitious man will not exercise any kind of self-control if secrecy is assured; and if he should live in the company of drunkards and libertines, he will be more prone to these vices because he is ambitious. The timid man does what he wants not to do. Although the miser may cast his riches into the sea to avoid death, he nevertheless remains a miser. If a libertine is pained at not being able to indulge himself, he does not on that account cease to be a libertine. Fundamentally, these emotions do not have regard so much to the activities of sumptuous living, drinking, and so on, as to appetite and love. Therefore these emotions have no opposites except for courage and nobility, with which I shall deal hereafter.

I pass over the definitions of jealousy and other vacillations, both because they arise from the combination of emotions which we have already defined and because the majority have no names, which shows that for practical purposes it suffices to know them in a general way. Now it is clear from the definitions of the emotions we have dealt with that they all spring from desire, pleasure or pain, or rather that they are nothing apart from these three emotions, each of which is wont to appear under various names according to their various contexts and extrinsic characteristics. If now we direct our attention to these basic emotions and to the explanation we have already given of the nature of the mind, we can define emotions, in so far as they are related only to the mind, as follows:

GENERAL DEFINITION OF EMOTIONS

The emotion called a passive experience is a confused idea whereby the mind affirms a greater or less force of existence of its body, or part of its body, than was previously the case, and by the occurrence of which the mind is determined to think of one thing rather than another.

Explication

I say in the first place that an emotion, or passivity of the mind, is a 'confused idea.' For we have demonstrated (Pr.3,III) that the mind is passive only to the extent that it has inadequate or confused ideas. Next, I say 'whereby the mind affirms a greater or less force of existence of its body or part of its body than was previously the case.' For all ideas that we have of bodies indicate the actual physical state of our own body rather than the nature of the external body (Cor.2,Pr.16,II). Now the idea that constitutes the specific reality of emotion must indicate or express the state of the body or some part of it, which the body or some part of it possesses from the fact that its power of activity or force of existence (vis existendi) is increased or diminished, assisted or checked. But it should be noted that when I say 'a greater or less force of existence than was previously the case,' I do not mean that the mind compares the body's present state with its past state, but that the idea that constitutes the specific reality of emotion affirms of the body something that in fact involves more or less reality than was previously the case. And since the essence of the mind consists in this (Prs.11 and

13, II), that it affirms the actual existence of its body, and by perfection we mean the very essence of a thing, it therefore follows that the mind passes to a state of greater or less perfection when it comes about that it affirms of its body, or some part of it, something that involves more or less reality than was previously the case. So when I said above that the mind's power of thinking increases or diminishes, I meant merely this, that the mind has formed an idea of its body or some part of it that expresses more or less reality than it had been affirming of it. For the excellence of ideas and the actual power of thinking are measured by the excellence of the object. Lastly, I added 'by the occurrence of which the mind is determined to think of one thing rather than another' in order to express the nature of desire in addition to the nature of pleasure and pain as explicated in the first part of the definition.

Part IV

OF HUMAN BONDAGE, OR THE STRENGTH OF THE EMOTIONS

PREFACE

I assign the term 'bondage' to man's lack of power to control and check the emotions. For a man at the mercy of his emotions is not his own master but is subject to fortune, in whose power he so lies that he is often compelled, although he sees the better course, to pursue the worse. In this Part I have set myself the task of demonstrating why this is so, and also what is good and what is bad in emotions. But before I begin, I should like to make a few preliminary observations on perfection and imperfection, and on good and bad.

He who has undertaken something and has brought it to completion[1] will say that the thing is completed (perfectus = completed,-Tr.); and not only he but everyone who rightly knew, or thought he knew, the intention and aim of the author of that work. For example, if anyone sees a work (which I assume is not yet finished) and knows that the aim of the author is to build a house, he will say that the house is imperfect. On the other hand, as soon as he sees that the work has been brought to the conclusion that its author had intended to give it, he will say that it is perfect. But if anyone sees a work whose like he had never seen before, and he does not know the artificer's intention, he cannot possibly know whether the work is perfect or imperfect.

This appears to have been the original meaning of these terms. But when men began to form general ideas and to devise ideal types of houses, buildings, towers and so on, and to prefer some models to others, it came about that each called 'perfect' what he saw to be in agreement with the general idea he had formed of the said thing, and 'imperfect' that which he saw at variance with his own preconceived ideal, although in the artificer's opinion it had been fully completed. There seems to be no other reason why even natural phenomena (those not made by human hand) should commonly be called perfect or imperfect. For men are wont to form general ideas both of natural phenomena and of artifacts, and these ideas they regard as models, and they believe that Nature (which they consider does nothing without an end in view) looks to these ideas and holds them before herself as models. So when they see something occurring in Nature at variance with their preconceived ideal of the thing in question, they believe that Nature has then

---

1. The Latin term 'perfectus,' which is crucial in this Preface, can mean both 'perfect' and 'completed.' For Spinoza the emphasis here is upon completion: that which has been finished or accomplished is perfect; contrarily, that which is not yet completed is imperfect. Spinoza will go on to say that we eventually learn to make evaluative judgments on the basis of what we have come to take as completed specimens of things. The latter now become normative models for further comparison and valuation.

failed or blundered and has left that thing imperfect. So we see that men are in the habit of calling natural phenomena perfect or imperfect from their own preconceptions rather than from true knowledge. For we have demonstrated in Appendix, Part I that Nature does not act with an end in view; that the eternal and infinite being, whom we call God, or Nature, acts by the same necessity whereby it exists. That the necessity of his nature whereby he acts is the same as that whereby he exists has been demonstrated (Prop.16,I). So the reason or cause why God, or nature, acts, and the reason or cause why he exists, are one and the same. Therefore, just as he does not exist for an end, so he does not act for an end; just as there is no beginning or end to his existing, so there is no beginning or end to his acting. What is termed a 'final cause' is nothing but human appetite in so far as it is considered as the starting-point or primary cause of some thing. For example, when we say that being a place of habitation was the final cause of this or that house, we surely mean no more than this, that a man, from thinking of the advantages of domestic life, had an urge to build a house. Therefore, the need for a habitation in so far as it is considered as a final cause is nothing but this particular urge, which is in reality an efficient cause, and is considered as the prime cause because men are commonly ignorant of the causes of their own urges; for, as I have repeatedly said, they are conscious of their actions and appetites but unaware of the causes by which they are determined to seek something. As to the common saying that Nature sometimes fails or blunders and produces imperfect things, I count this among the fictions with which I dealt in Appendix I.

So perfection and imperfection are in reality only modes of thinking, notions which we are wont to invent from comparing individuals of the same species or kind; and it is for this reason that I previously said (Def.6,II) that by reality and perfection I mean the same thing. For we are wont to classify all the individuals in Nature under one genus which is called the highest genus, namely, the notion of Entity, which pertains to all the individuals in Nature without exception. Therefore in so far as we classify individuals in Nature under this genus and compare them with one another and find that some have more being or reality than others, to that extent we say some are more perfect than others. And in so far as we attribute to them something involving negation, such as limit, end, impotence and so on, to that extent we call them imperfect because they do not affect our minds as much as those we call perfect, and not because they lack something of their own or because Nature has blundered. For nothing belongs to the nature of any thing except that which follows from the necessity of nature of its efficient cause; and whatever follows from the necessity of the nature of its efficient cause must necessarily be so.

As for the terms 'good' and 'bad,' they likewise indicate nothing positive in things considered in themselves, and are nothing but modes of thinking, or notions which we form from comparing things with one another. For one and the same thing can at the same time be good and bad, and also indifferent. For example, music is good for one who is melancholy, bad for one in mourning, and neither good nor bad for the deaf. However, although this is so, these terms ought to be retained. For since we desire to form the idea of a man which we may look to as a model of human nature, we shall find it useful to keep these terms in the sense I have indicated. So in what follows I shall mean by 'good' that which we certainly know to be the means for our approaching nearer to the model of human nature that we set before ourselves, and by 'bad' that which we certainly know prevents us from reproducing the said model. Again, we shall say that men are more perfect or less perfect in so far as they are nearer to or further from this model. For it is important to note that when I say that somebody passes from a state of less perfection to a state of greater perfection, and vice versa, I do not mean that he changes from one essence or form to another (for example, a horse is as completely destroyed if it changes into a man as it would be if it were to change into an insect), but that we conceive his power of activity, in so far as this is understood through his nature, to be increased or diminished.

Finally, by perfection in general I shall understand reality, as I have said; that is, the essence of any thing whatsoever in as far as it exists and acts in a definite manner, without taking duration into account. For no individual thing can be said to be more perfect on the grounds that it has continued in existence over a greater period of time. The duration of things cannot be determined from their essence, for the essence of things involves no fixed and determinate period of time. But any thing whatsoever, whether it be more perfect or less perfect, will always be able to persist in existing with that same force whereby it begins to exist, so that in this respect all things are equal.

DEFINITIONS

1.   By *good* I understand that which we certainly know to be useful to us.

2.   By *bad* I understand that which we certainly know to be an obstacle to our attainment of some good.
    For these, see the foregoing preface, towards the end.

3.   I call individual things *contingent* in so far as, in attending only to their essence, we find nothing that necessarily posits their existence or necessarily excludes it.

4.   I call individual things *possible* in so far as, in attending to the causes by which they should be brought about, we do not know whether these causes are determined to bring them about.
    In Sch.1,Pr.33,I, I did not differentiate between possible and contingent because at that point it was unnecessary to distinguish carefully between them.

5.   In what follows, by *conflicting emotions* I shall understand those that draw a man in different directions, although they belong to the same

genus, such as dissipation and avarice, which are species of love, and contrary not by nature, but indirectly (per accidens).

6. In Schs.1 and 2,Pr.18,III I have explained what I mean by emotion towards a thing future, present, and past.

But it should be further noted that just as we cannot distinctly imagine spatial distance beyond a certain limit, the same is true of time. That is, just as we are wont to imagine that all those objects more than 200 feet away from us, or whose distance from our position exceeds what we can distinctly imagine, are the same distance from us and appear to be in the same plane, so too in the case of objects whose time of existence is further away from the present by a longer distance than we are wont to distinctly imagine, we think of them all as equally far from the present, and we refer them to one point of time, as it were.

7. By the *end* for the sake of which we do something, I mean appetite.

8. By *virtue* and *power* I mean the same thing; that is (Pr.7,III), virtue, in so far as it is related to man, is man's very essence, or nature, in so far as he has power to bring about that which can be understood solely through the laws of his own nature.

AXIOM

There is in Nature no individual thing that is not surpassed in strength and power by some other thing. Whatsoever thing there is, there is another more powerful by which the said thing can be destroyed.

PROPOSITION 1

Nothing positive contained in a false idea can be annulled by the presence of what is true, in so far as it is true.

Proof

Falsity consists solely in the privation of knowledge, a privation which is involved in inadequate ideas (Pr.35,II), and it is not by possessing something positive that they are called false (Pr.33,II). On the contrary, in so far as they are related to God, they are true (Pr.32,II). If therefore what is positive in a false idea were to be annulled by the presence of what is true, in so far as it is true, a true idea would be annulled by itself, which is absurd (Pr.4,III). Therefore . . . etc.

Scholium

This proposition is more clearly understood from Cor.2,Pr.16,II. For imagination (imaginatio) is an idea that indicates the present disposition of the human body more than the nature of an external body, not indeed distinctly, but confusedly, whence it comes about that the mind is said to err. For example, when we gaze at the sun, it seems to us to be about 200 feet away; and in this we are deceived as long as we are unaware of its true distance. With knowledge of its distance the error is

removed, but not the imagining (imaginatio), that is, the idea of the sun
that explicates its nature only in so far as the body is affected by it. Thus
although we know its true distance, we shall nevertheless see it as being
close to us. For as we said in Sch.Pr.35,II, it is not by reason of our ignorance of its true distance that we see it as being so near, but because
the mind conceives the magnitude of the sun in so far as the body is
affected by it. In the same way, when the rays of the sun falling on the
surface of water are reflected back to our eyes, we see it as if it were in
the water although we know its true position. Similarly other imaginings
whereby the mind is deceived, whether they indicate the natural disposition of the body or the increase or diminution of its power of activity, are
not contrary to what is true and do not disappear at the presence of
truth. It does indeed happen that when we mistakenly fear some evil, the
fear disappears when we hear the truth. But the contrary also happens;
when we fear an evil that is assuredly going to overtake us, the fear
likewise disappears on our hearing false tidings. So imaginings do not
disappear at the presence of what is true in so far as it is true, but
because other imaginings that are stronger supervene to exclude the
present existence of the things we imagine, as we demonstrated in Pr.
17,II.

PROPOSITION 2

*We are passive in so far as we are a part of Nature which cannot be
conceived independently of other parts.*

Proof

We are said to be passive when something arises in us of which we
are only the partial cause (Def.2,III); that is (Def.1,III), something that
cannot be deduced solely from the laws of our own nature. So we are
passive in so far as we are a part of Nature which cannot be conceived
independently of other parts.

PROPOSITION 3

*The force (vis) whereby a man persists in existing is limited, and
infinitely surpassed by the power of external causes.*

Proof

This is clear from the Axiom of this Part. In the case of every man
there is something else, say A, more powerful than he, and then there is
another thing, say B, more powerful than A, and so ad infinitum. Therefore the power of a man is limited in comparison with something else,
and is infinitely surpassed by the power of external causes.

PROPOSITION 4

*It is impossible for a man not to be part of Nature and not to
undergo changes other than those which can be understood solely
through his own nature and of which he is the adequate cause.*

Proof

The power whereby each single thing, and consequently man, pre-serves its own being is the very power of God, or Nature (Cor.Pr.24,I), not in so far as it is infinite but in so far as it can be explicated through actual human essence (Pr.7,III). Therefore the power of man in so far as it is explicated through his actual essence is part of the infinite power of God, or Nature, that is, of God's essence (Pr.34,I). This is the first point. Again, if it were possible for man to undergo no changes except those which can be understood solely through his own nature, it would follow (Prs.4 and 6,III) that he cannot perish but would always necessarily exist; and this would have to follow from a cause whose power is either finite or infinite, namely, either from the power of man alone, in that he would be capable of removing from himself all changes which might arise from external causes, or else from the infinite power of Nature, by which all particular things would be so governed that man could undergo no changes other than those that serve for his preservation. But of these al-ternatives the first is absurd (by the preceding proposition, whose proof is universal and can be applied to all particular things). Therefore if it were possible that man could undergo no changes except such as could be understood through man's nature alone, and consequently (as I have already demonstrated) that he should always necessarily exist, this would have to follow from the infinite power of God. Consequently (Pr.16,I), the entire order of Nature as conceived under the attributes of Extension and Thought would have to be deducible from the necessity of the divine nature in so far as it is considered as affected by the idea of some man. And so it would follow (Pr.21,I) that man would be infinite, which is absurd (by the first part of this proof). Therefore it is impossible that man should not undergo any changes except those of which he is the adequate cause.

Corollary

Hence it follows that man is necessarily always subject to pas-sive emotions, and that he follows the common order of Nature, and obeys it, and accommodates himself to it as far as the nature of things demands.

PROPOSITION 5

The force and increase of any passive emotion and its persistence in existing is defined not by the power whereby we ourselves endeavor to persist in existing, but by the power of external causes compared with our own power.

Proof

The essence of a passive emotion cannot be explicated through our own essence alone (Defs.1 and 2,III); that is, (Pr.7,III) the power of a passive emotion cannot be defined by the power whereby we endeavor to persist in our own being, but (as we have demonstrated in Pr.16,II) must necessarily be defined by the power of an external cause compared with our own power.

PROPOSITION 6

The force of any passive emotion can surpass the rest of man's activities or power so that the emotion stays firmly fixed in him.

Proof

The force and increase of any passive emotion and its persistence in existing is defined by the power of an external cause compared with our own power (by the preceding proposition) and so (Pr.3,IV) can surpass man's power.

PROPOSITION 7

An emotion cannot be checked or destroyed except by a contrary emotion which is stronger than the emotion which is to be checked.

Proof

An emotion, in so far as it is related to the mind, is an idea whereby the mind affirms a greater or less force of existence in its body than was previously the case (General Definition of Emotions, near the end of Part III). So when the mind is assailed by an emotion, the body at the same time is affected by an affection whereby its power of acting is increased or diminished. Furthermore, this affection of the body (Pr.5,IV) receives from its own cause its force for persisting in its own being, and therefore this force cannot be checked or destroyed except by a corporeal cause (Pr.6,II) which affects the body with an affection contrary to the other (Pr.5,III) and stronger than it (Ax.IV). So (Pr.12,II) the mind will be affected by the idea of an affection stronger than and contrary to the earlier one; that is (by the General Definition of Emotions), the mind will be affected by an emotion stronger than and contrary to the previous one, an emotion which will exclude or destroy the existence of the previous one. So an emotion cannot be either destroyed or checked except by a contrary and stronger emotion.

Corollary

An emotion, in so far as it is related to the mind, can neither be checked nor destroyed except through the idea of an affection of the body contrary to and stronger than the affection which we are experiencing. For the emotion we are experiencing can neither be checked nor destroyed except by an emotion stronger than and contrary to it (preceding Pr.), that is, except through the idea of an affection of the body stronger than and contrary to the affection we are experiencing (General Definitions of Emotions).

PROPOSITION 8

Knowledge of good and evil is nothing other than the emotion of pleasure or pain in so far as we are conscious of it.

Proof

We call good or bad that which is advantageous, or an obstacle, to the preservation of our being (Defs.1 and 2,IV); that is (Pr.7,III), that which increases or diminishes, helps or checks, our power of activity. Therefore in so far as we perceive some thing to affect us with pleasure or pain (by the definitions of pleasure and pain, q.v., in Sch.Pr.11,III), we call it good or bad; and so knowledge of good and evil is nothing other than the idea of pleasure or pain which necessarily follows from the emotion of pleasure or pain (Pr.22,II). But this idea is united to the emotion in the same way as the mind is united to the body (Pr.21,II); that is (as has been demonstrated in the Scholium to the same Proposition) this idea is not distinct in reality from the emotion, or, in other words (by the General Definition of the Emotions), from the idea of an affection of the body, save only in conception. Therefore this knowledge of good and evil is nothing other than the emotion itself, in so far as we are conscious of it.

PROPOSITION 9

An emotion whose cause we think to be with us in the present is stronger than it would be if we did not think the said cause to be with us.

Proof

An imagining (imaginatio) is an idea whereby the mind regards a thing as present (see its definition in Sch.Pr.17,II), but which indicates the disposition of the human body rather than the nature of the external thing (Cor.2,Pr.16,II). Therefore an emotion (by the General Definition of Emotions) is an imagining in so far as it indicates the disposition of the body. Now an imagining (Pr.17,II) is more intense as long as we think of nothing that excludes the present existence of the external thing. Therefore that emotion, too, whose cause we think to be with us in the present, is more intense or stronger than it would be if we did not think the said cause to be with us.

Scholium

When I asserted above in Proposition 18,III that from the image of a thing future or past we are affected by the same emotion as if the thing we are thinking of were present, I deliberately gave warning that this is true only in so far as we attend to the image of the thing; for an image is of the same nature whether or not we picture things as present. But I did not deny that the image becomes feebler when we regard as present to us other things which exclude the present existence of a future thing. I omitted to emphasise this at the time because I had decided to treat of the strength of the emotions in this Part.

Corollary

The image of a thing future or past, that is, a thing which we regard as related to future or past time to the exclusion of present time, is feebler, other things being equal, than the image of a present thing. Consequently the emotion towards a thing future or past, other things being equal, is weaker than an emotion towards a present thing.

PROPOSITION 10

We are affected towards a future thing which we imagine to be imminent more intensely than if we were to imagine its time of existence to be further away from the present. We are also affected by remembrance of a thing we imagine to belong to the near past more intensely than if we were to imagine it to belong to the distant past.

Proof

In so far as we imagine a thing to be imminent or to belong to the near past, by that very fact we are imagining something that excludes the thing's presence to a less degree than if we were to imagine that its future time of existence was further from the present or that it happened long ago (as is self-evident). So to that extent (preceding proposition) we are more intensely affected towards it.

Scholium

From our note to Definition 6,IV, it follows that with regard to objects that are distant from the present by a longer interval of time than comes within the scope of our imagination, although we know that they are far distant in time from one another, we are affected towards them with the same degree of faintness.

PROPOSITION 11

An emotion towards a thing which we think of as inevitable (necessarius) is more intense, other things being equal, than emotion towards a thing possible, or contingent, that is, not inevitable.

Proof

In so far as we imagine a thing to be inevitable, to that extent we affirm its existence. On the other hand, in so far as we imagine a thing not to be inevitable, we deny its existence (Sch.1,Pr.33,I), and therefore (Pr.9,IV) emotion towards an inevitable thing, other things being equal, is more intense than emotion towards something not inevitable.

PROPOSITION 12

Emotion towards a thing which we know not to exist in the present, and which we imagine to be possible, is, other things being equal, more intense than emotion towards a contingent thing.

Proof

In so far as we imagine a thing to be contingent, we are not affected by any image of another thing that posits the existence of the former

(Def.3,IV). On the contrary, by hypothesis, we are thinking of things that exclude its present existence. But in so far as we think of a thing as possible in the future, we are thinking of things that posit its existence (Def.4,IV); that is (Pr.18,III), things that encourage hope or fear. Therefore emotion towards a possible thing is more intense.

Corollary

Emotion towards a thing which we know not to exist in the present and which we think of as contingent is much feebler than if we were to think of the thing as with us in the present.

Proof

Emotion towards a thing that we imagine to exist in the present is more intense than if we were to imagine it to belong to the future (Cor.Pr.9,IV), and much stronger than it would be if we were to think of that future time as far distant from the present (Pr.10,IV). Therefore emotion towards a thing whose time of existence we imagine to be far distant from the present is much weaker than it would be if we were to imagine the said thing to be present, but is nevertheless (preceding Pr.) more intense than it would be if we were to imagine the said thing to be contingent. So emotion towards a contingent thing is much feebler than it would be if we were to imagine the thing to be with us in the present.

PROPOSITION 13

Emotion towards a contingent thing which we know not to exist in the present is, other things being equal, feebler than emotion towards a thing past.

Proof

In so far as we imagine a thing to be contingent, we are not affected by the image of any other thing that posits the existence of the former (Def.3, IV). On the contrary, by hypothesis, we are imagining things that exclude its present existence. But in so far as we think of the said thing as belonging to the past, to that extent it is assumed that we are thinking of something that brings it back to memory, that is, which activates the image of the thing (Pr.18,II and Sch.), and therefore to that extent causes us to regard the thing as present (Cor.Pr.17,II). So (Pr.9,IV) emotion towards a contingent thing which we know not to exist in the present is, other things being equal, feebler than emotion towards a thing past.

PROPOSITION 14

No emotion can be checked by the true knowledge of good and evil in so far as it is true, but only in so far as it is considered as an emotion.

Proof

An emotion is an idea whereby the mind affirms a greater or less force of existence of its body than was previously the case (by the General Definition of Emotions), and so (Pr.1,IV) it contains nothing positive that can be annulled by the presence of what is true. Consequently, true knowledge of good and evil cannot check an emotion by virtue of being true. But in so far as it is an emotion (Pr.8,IV), if it be stronger than the emotion which is to be checked, to that extent only (Pr.7,IV) it can check an emotion.

PROPOSITION 15

Desire that arises from the true knowledge of good and evil can be extinguished or checked by many other desires that arise from the emotions by which we are assailed.

Proof

From the true knowledge of good and evil, in so far as this is an emotion (Pr.8,IV), there necessarily arises desire (Definition of Emotions,1), whose strength is proportionate to the strength of the emotion from which it arises (Pr.37,III). But since this desire, by hypothesis, arises from our truly understanding something, it therefore follows in us in so far as we are active (Pr.3,III), and so must be understood solely through our essence (Def.2,III). Consequently, (Pr.7,III) its force and increase must be defined solely in terms of human power. Now desires that arise from emotions by which we are assailed are also greater in proportion to the strength of the emotions, and so their force and increase (Pr.5,IV) must be defined in terms of the power of external causes which indefinitely surpasses our power when compared with it (Pr.3, IV). So desires that arise from emotions of this kind may be stronger than that desire which arises from the true knowledge of good and evil, and therefore (Pr.7,IV) are able to check or extinguish it.

PROPOSITION 16

The desire that arises from a knowledge of good and evil in so far as this knowledge has regard to the future can be the more easily checked or extinguished by desire of things that are attractive in the present.

Proof

Emotion towards a thing that we imagine to be future is feebler than emotion towards something present (Cor.Pr.9,IV). But desire that arises from the true knowledge of good and evil, even when this knowledge is concerned with things that are good in the present, can be extinguished or checked by any chance desire (by the preceding proposition, whose proof is universally valid). Therefore desire that arises from the said knowledge in so far as it has regard to the future can be the more easily checked or extinguished . . . etc.

PROPOSITION 17

Desire that arises from the true knowledge of good and evil in so far as this knowledge is concerned with contingent things can be even more easily checked by desire for things which are present.

Proof

This proposition is proved in the same way as the preceding proposition, from Cor.Pr.12,IV.

Scholium

I think I have thus demonstrated why men are motivated by uncritical belief (opinio) more than by true reasoning, and why the true knowledge of good and evil stirs up conflict in the mind and often yields to every kind of passion. Hence the saying of the poet, "I see the better course and approve it, but I pursue the worse course."[2] Ecclesiastes seems to have had the same point in mind when he said: "He who increaseth knowledge increaseth sorrow."[3] My purpose in saying this is not to conclude that ignorance is preferable to knowledge, or that there is no difference between a fool and a wise man in the matter of controlling the emotions. I say this because it is necessary to know both the power of our nature and its lack of power, so that we can determine what reason can and cannot do in controlling the emotions, and in this Part I have said that I shall treat only of human weakness. As for the power of reason over the emotions, it is my intention to treat of that in a separate Part.

PROPOSITION 18

Desire arising from pleasure is, other things being equal, stronger than desire arising from pain.

Proof

Desire is the very essence of man (Definition of Emotions,1); that is, (Pr.7,III) the conatus whereby man endeavors to persist in his own being. Therefore the desire that arises from pleasure is assisted or increased by the very emotion of pleasure (by Definition of Pleasure, q.v., in Sch.Pr.11,III); whereas the desire that arises from pain is diminished or checked by the very emotion of pain (same Sch.). So the force of the desire that arises from pleasure must be defined by human power together with the power of an external cause, whereas the desire that arises from pain must be defined by human power alone. Therefore the former is stronger than the latter.

Scholium

I have thus briefly explained the causes of human weakness and inconstancy, and why men do not abide by the precepts of reason. It now remains for me to demonstrate what it is that reason prescribes for us, and which emotions are in harmony with the rules of human reason, and

2. Ovid, *Metamorphoses* VII, 20

3. *Ecclesiastes* 1:18

which are contrary to them. But before I embark on the task of proving these things in our detailed geometrical order, it would be well first of all to make a brief survey of the dictates of reason, so that my meaning may be more readily grasped by everyone.

Since reason demands nothing contrary to nature, it therefore demands that every man should love himself, should seek his own advantage (I mean his real advantage), should aim at whatever really leads a man towards greater perfection, and, to sum it all up, that each man, as far as in him lies, should endeavor to preserve his own being. This is as necessarily true as that the whole is greater than its part (Pr.4,III).

Again, since virtue (Def.8,IV) is nothing other than to act from the laws of one's own nature, and since nobody endeavors to preserve his own being (Pr.7,III) except from the laws of his own nature, it follows firstly that the basis of virtue is the very conatus to preserve one's own being, and that happiness consists in a man's being able to preserve his own being. Secondly, it follows that virtue should be sought for its own sake, and that there is nothing preferable to it or more to our advantage, for the sake of which it should be sought. Thirdly, it follows that those who commit suicide are of weak spirit and are completely overcome by external causes opposed to their own nature. Further, it follows from Post.4,II that we can never bring it about that we should need nothing outside ourselves to preserve our own being and that we should live a life quite unrelated to things outside ourselves. Besides, if we consider the mind, surely our intellect would be less perfect if the mind were in solitude and understood nothing beyond itself. Therefore there are many things outside ourselves which are advantageous to us and ought therefore to be sought. Of these none more excellent can be discovered than those which are in complete harmony with our own nature. For example, if two individuals of completely the same nature are combined, they compose an individual twice as powerful as each one singly.

Therefore nothing is more advantageous to man than man. Men, I repeat, can wish for nothing more excellent for preserving their own being than that they should all be in such harmony in all respects that their minds and bodies should compose, as it were, one mind and one body, and that all together should endeavor as best they can to preserve their own being, and that all together they should aim at the common advantage of all. From this it follows that men who are governed by reason, that is, men who aim at their own advantage under the guidance of reason, seek nothing for themselves that they would not desire for the rest of mankind; and so are just, faithful and honourable.

These are the dictates of reason, which I have decided to set forth in brief at this point before embarking upon their more detailed demonstration. This I have done so that I may, if possible, gain the attention of those who believe that the principle that every man is bound to seek his own advantage is the basis, not of virtue and piety, but of impiety. Now that I have briefly shown that the contrary is the case, I proceed to its proof, using the same method as hitherto.

PROPOSITION 19

Every man, from the laws of his own nature, necessarily seeks or avoids what he judges to be good or evil.

Proof

Knowledge of good and evil is (Pr.8,IV) the emotion of pleasure or pain in so far as we are conscious of it, and therefore every man (Pr.28,III) necessarily seeks what he judges to be good and avoids what he judges to be evil. But this appetite is nothing other than man's very essence or nature (Definition of Appetites, q.v. in Sch.Pr.9,III and Definition of Emotions,1). Therefore every man, solely from the laws of his own nature, necessarily seeks or avoids . . . etc.

PROPOSITION 20

The more every man endeavors and is able to seek his own advantage, that is, to preserve his own being, the more he is endowed with virtue. On the other hand, in so far as he neglects to preserve what is to his advantage, that is, his own being, to that extent he is weak.

Proof

Virtue is human power, which is defined solely by man's essence (Def.8,IV); that is, it is defined solely by the conatus whereby man endeavors to persist in his own being (Pr.7,III). Therefore the more every man endeavors and is able to preserve his own being, the more he is endowed with virtue, and consequently (Prs.4 and 6,III) in so far as he neglects to preserve his own being, to that extent he is weak.

Scholium

Therefore nobody, unless he is overcome by external causes contrary to his own nature, neglects to seek his own advantage, that is, to preserve his own being. Nobody, I repeat, refuses food or kills himself from the necessity of his own nature, but from the constraint of external causes. This can take place in many ways. A man kills himself when he is compelled by another who twists the hand in which he happens to hold a sword and makes him turn the blade against his heart; or when, in obedience to a tyrant's command, he, like Seneca,[4] is compelled to open his veins, that is, he chooses a lesser evil to avoid a greater. Or it may come about when unobservable external causes condition a man's imagination and affect his body in such a way that the latter assumes a different nature contrary to the previously existing one, a nature whereof there can be no idea in mind (Pr.10,III). But that a man from the necessity of his own nature should endeavor to cease to exist or to be changed into another form, is as impossible as that something should come from nothing, as anyone can see with a little thought.

4. Seneca (4 B.C.–A.D. 66), the Roman writer and statesman, committed suicide under political pressure rather than suffer public disgrace. In many of his essays and letters he praised and justified suicide under certain conditions.

PROPOSITION 21

Nobody can desire to be happy, to do well and to live well without at the same time desiring to be, to do, and to live; that is, actually to exist.

Proof

The proof of this proposition, or rather, the fact itself, is self-evident, and also follows from the definition of desire. For the desire (Definition of Emotions,1) to live happily, to do well and so on is the very essence of man; that is (Pr.7,III), the conatus whereby every man endeavors to preserve his own being. Therefore nobody can desire . . . etc.

PROPOSITION 22

No virtue can be conceived as prior to this one, namely, the conatus to preserve oneself.

Proof

The conatus to preserve itself is the very essence of a thing (Pr.7,III). Thus if any virtue could be conceived as prior to this one—namely, this conatus—then (Def.8,IV) the essence of a thing would be conceived as prior to itself, which is obviously absurd. Therefore no virtue . . . etc.

Corollary

The conatus to preserve oneself is the primary and sole basis of virtue. For no other principle can be conceived as prior to this one (preceding Pr.), and no virtue can be conceived independently of it (Pr.21,IV).

PROPOSITION 23

In so far as a man is determined to some action from the fact that he has inadequate ideas, he cannot be said, without qualification, to be acting from virtue; he can be said to do so only in so far as he is determined from the fact that he understands.

Proof

In so far as a man is determined to action from the fact that he has inadequate ideas, to that extent (Pr.1,III) he is passive; that is (Defs.1 and 2,III), he does something that cannot be perceived solely in terms of his own essence, that is (Def.8,IV), something that does not follow from his own virtue. But in so far as he is determined to an action from the fact that he understands, to that extent he is active (Pr.1,III); that is (Def.2,III), he does something that is perceived solely in terms of his own essence, that is (Def.8,IV), which follows adequately from his own virtue.

PROPOSITION 24

To act in absolute conformity with virtue is nothing else in us but to act, to live, to preserve one's own being (these three mean the same) under the guidance of reason, on the basis of seeking one's own advantage.

Proof

To act in absolute conformity with virtue is nothing else (Def.8,IV) but to act according to the laws of one's own nature. But we are active only in so far as we understand (Pr.3,III). Therefore to act from virtue is nothing else in us but to act, to live, and to preserve one's own being under the guidance of reason, on the basis (Cor.Pr.22,IV) of seeking one's own advantage.

PROPOSITION 25

Nobody endeavors to preserve his being for the sake of some other thing.

Proof

The conatus whereby each thing endeavors to preserve its own being is defined solely by the essence of the thing itself (Pr.7,III); given this essence alone, and not from the essence of any other thing, it necessarily follows (Pr.6,III) that every one endeavors to preserve his own being. Moreover, this proposition is obvious from Cor.Pr.22,IV. For if a man were to endeavor to preserve his own being for the sake of another thing, then that thing would be the primary basis of his virtue (as is self-evident), which is absurd (by the aforementioned corollary). Therefore nobody . . . etc.

PROPOSITION 26

Whatever we endeavor according to reason is nothing else but to understand; and the mind, in so far as it exercises reason, judges nothing else to be to its advantage except what conduces to understanding.

Proof

The conatus to preserve itself is nothing but the essence of a thing (Pr.7,III), which, in so far as it exists as such, is conceived as having a force to persist in existing (Pr.6,III) and to do those things that necessarily follow from its given nature (see Definition of Appetite in Sch. Pr.9,III). But the essence of reason is nothing other than our mind in so far as it clearly and distinctly understands (see its Definition in Sch.2,Pr.40,II). Therefore (Pr.40,II) whatever we endeavor according to reason is nothing else but to understand. Again, since this conatus of the mind wherewith the mind, in so far as it exercises reason, endeavors to preserve its own being is nothing else but a conatus to understand (by the first part of this proof), this conatus to understand (Cor.Pr.22,IV) is therefore the primary and only basis of virtue, and it is not for some further purpose that we endeavor to understand things (Pr.25,IV). On the contrary, the mind, in so far as it exercises reason, cannot conceive any good for itself except what is conducive to understanding (Def.1,IV).

PROPOSITION 27

We know nothing to be certainly good or evil except what is really conducive to understanding or what can hinder understanding.

Proof

The mind, in so far as it exercises reason, seeks nothing else but to understand, and judges nothing else to be to its advantage except what is conducive to understanding (preceding Pr.). But the mind (Prs.41 and 43,II, and Sch.) possesses no certainty save in so far as it has adequate ideas, or (which is the same thing by Sch.Pr.40,II) in so far as it exercises reason. Therefore we do not know anything to be certainly good except what is truly conducive to understanding, or certainly evil except what can hinder understanding.

PROPOSITION 28

The mind's highest good is the knowledge of God, and the mind's highest virtue is to know God.

Proof

The highest object that the mind can understand is God, that is (Def.6,I), an absolutely infinite being, and one without whom (Pr.15,I) nothing can be or be conceived. Thus (Prs.26 and 27,IV) the mind's utmost advantage or (Def.1,IV) its highest good is knowledge of God. Again, the mind is active only to the extent that it understands (Prs.1 and 3,III), and to that extent only (Pr.23,IV) can it be said without qualification to act from virtue. So the absolute virtue of the mind is to understand. But the highest thing the mind can understand is God (as we have just proved). Therefore the highest virtue of the mind is to understand or to know God.

PROPOSITION 29

No individual thing whose nature is quite different from ours can either assist or check our power to act, and nothing whatsoever can be either good or evil for us unless it has something in common with us.

Proof

The power of each individual thing (and consequently of man (Cor.Pr.10,II), whereby he exists and acts is determined only by another particular thing (Pr.28,I) whose nature (Pr.6,II) must be understood through the same attribute as that through which human nature is conceived. So our power to act, in whatever way it be conceived, can be determined, and consequently assisted or checked, by the power of another individual thing which has something in common with us, and not by the power of a thing whose nature is entirely different from our own. And since we call good or evil that which is the cause of pleasure or pain (Pr.8,IV), that is, (Sch.Pr.11,III) which increases or diminishes, assists or checks our power of activity, a thing whose nature is entirely different from our own can be neither good nor evil for us.

PROPOSITION 30

No thing can be evil for us through what it possesses in common with our nature, but in so far as it is evil for us, it is contrary to us.

Proof

We call bad that which is the cause of pain (Pr.8,IV), that is (through Definition of Pain, q.v. in Sch.Pr.11,III), that which diminishes or checks our power of activity. So if something were bad for us through that which it has in common with us, that thing would be able to diminish or check the very thing that it has in common with us, which is absurd (Pr.4,III). So nothing can be bad for us through that which it has in common with us. On the contrary, in so far as it is bad—that is, (as we have just demonstrated) in so far as it can diminish or check our power of activity—to that extent (Pr.5,III) it is contrary to us.

PROPOSITION 31

In so far as a thing is in agreement with our nature, to that extent it is necessarily good.

Proof

In so far as a thing is in agreement with our nature, it cannot be bad (preceding Pr.). Therefore it is necessarily either good or indifferent. If we make the latter assumption, namely, that it is neither good nor bad, then nothing will follow from its nature (Ax3,IV)[5] which serves to preserve our nature; that is, (by hypothesis) which serves to preserve the nature of the thing itself. But this is absurd (Pr.6,III). Therefore, in so far as it is in agreement with our nature, it is necessarily good.

Corollary

Hence it follows that the more a thing is in agreement with our nature, the more advantageous it is to us, that is, the more it is good; and, conversely, the more advantageous a thing is to us, to that extent it is in more agreement with our nature. For in so far as it is not in agreement with our nature, it is necessarily either different from our nature or contrary to it. If it is different (Pr.29,IV), it can be neither good nor bad; but if contrary, it will therefore be contrary also to that which is in agreement with our nature, that is (preceding Pr.), contrary to our good; that

5. The standard Latin text of Gebhardt has a reference to Axiom 3 of Part IV. However, in our current text there is only *one* Axiom for Part IV. Translators have suggested various corrections; but Gebhardt notes in his critical apparatus that in Spinoza's original draft of the *Ethics* there were probably several axioms for Part IV. In the final version all but one of these axioms were deleted, although in Proposition 31 Spinoza still has Axiom 3 in mind.

is, it will be evil. So nothing can be good save in so far as it is in agreement with our nature. So the more a thing is in agreement with our nature, the more advantageous it is to us, and vice versa.

PROPOSITION 32

In so far as men are subject to passive emotions, to that extent they cannot be said to agree in nature.

Proof

Things which are said to agree in nature are understood to agree in respect of their power (Pr.7,III), not in respect of their weakness or negation, and consequently (Sch.Pr.3,III) not in respect of passive emotions. Therefore, men, in so far as they are subject to passive emotions, cannot be said to agree in nature.

Scholium

This is also self-evident. For he who says that white and black agree only in the fact that neither is red is making an absolute assertion that white and black agree in no respect. So, too, if someone says that stone and man agree only in this respect, that they are both finite, or weak, or that they do not exist from the necessity of their own natures, or that they are indefinitely surpassed by the power of external causes, he is making the general assertion that stone and man agree in no respect. For things that agree only negatively, that is, in what they do not possess, in reality agree in nothing.

PROPOSITION 33

Men can differ in nature in so far as they are assailed by emotions that are passive, and to that extent one and the same man, too, is variable and inconstant.

Proof

The nature or essence of emotions cannot be explicated solely through our own essence or nature (Defs.1 and 2,III), but must be defined by the potency, that is, (Pr.7,III) the nature, of external causes as compared with our own power. Hence there are as many kinds of each emotion as there are kinds of objects by which we are affected (Pr.56, III), and men are affected in different ways by one and the same object (Pr.51,III), and to that extent they differ in nature. Finally, one and the same man (Pr.51,III) is affected in different ways towards the same object, and to that extent he is variable . . . etc.

PROPOSITION 34

anger
hatred —
jealousy

In so far as men are assailed by emotions that are passive, they can be contrary to one another.

Proof

A man, Peter, for example, can be the cause of Paul's feeling pain

Reality is one   humans are hostile, violent, aggressive, competitive because Peter has something similar to a thing that Paul hates (Pr.16,III), or because Peter has sole possession of a thing that Paul also loves (Pr.32,III and Sch.), or for other reasons (for the principal reasons, see Sch.Pr.55,III). Thus it will come about (Def. of Emotions,7) that Paul will hate Peter. Consequently it will easily happen (Pr.40,III, and Sch.) that Peter will hate Paul in return; thus (Pr.39,III) they will endeavor to injure each other, that is (Pr.30,IV), they will be contrary to each other. But the emotion of pain is always a passive emotion (Pr.59,III). Therefore men, in so far as they are assailed by passive emotions, can be contrary to one another.

Scholium

I said that Paul hates Peter because he thinks that Peter possesses something that Paul also loves, from which at first sight it seems to follow that these two are injurious to each other as a result of loving the same thing, and consequently of their agreeing in nature. So if this is true, Propositions 30 and 31,IV would be false. But if we examine this question with scrupulous fairness, we find that there is no contradiction at any point. These two do not dislike each other in so far as they agree in nature, that is, in so far as they both love the same thing, but in so far as they differ from each other. For in so far as they both love the same thing, each one's love is thereby fostered (Pr.31,III); that is (Def. of Emotions 6) each one's pleasure is fostered. Therefore it is by no means true that in so far as they both love the same thing and agree in nature, they dislike each other. As I have said, the reason for their dislike is none other than that they are assumed to differ in nature. For we are supposing that Peter has an idea of the loved thing as now in his possession, while Paul has an idea of the loved thing lost to him. Hence the latter is affected with pain, while the former is affected with pleasure, and to that extent they are contrary to each other. In this way we can readily demonstrate that all other causes of hatred depend on men being different in nature, and not on a point wherein they agree.

PROPOSITION 35

In so far as men live under the guidance of reason, to that extent only do they always necessarily agree in nature. realize our similarities

Proof

In so far as men are assailed by passive emotions, they can be different in nature (Pr.33,IV) and contrary to one another (preceding Pr.). But we say that men are active only in so far as they live under the guidance of reason (Pr.3,III). Thus whatever follows from human nature, in so far as it is defined by reason, must be understood (Def.2,III) through human nature alone as its proximate cause. But since everyone, in accordance with the laws of his own nature, aims at what he judges to be good and endeavors to remove what he judges to be evil (Pr.19,IV), and since furthermore what he judges from the dictates of reason to be good or evil is necessarily good or evil (Pr.41,II), it follows that in so far as men live under the guidance of reason, to that extent only do they necessarily do the things which are necessarily good for human nature and consequently for every single man; that is (Cor.Pr.31,IV), which agree with the nature of every single man. So men also are necessarily in agreement in so far as they live under the guidance of reason.

Corollary 1

There is no individual thing in the universe more advantageous to man than a man who lives by the guidance of reason. For the most advantageous thing to man is that which agrees most closely with his nature (Cor.Pr.31,IV); that is (as is self-evident), man. But man acts absolutely according to the laws of his own nature when he lives under the guidance of reason (Def.2,III), and only to that extent is he always necessarily in agreement with the nature of another man (preceding Pr.). Therefore among individual things there is nothing more advantageous to man than a man who . . . etc.

Corollary 2

It is when every man is most devoted to seeking his own advantage that men are of most advantage to one another. For the more every man seeks his own advantage and endeavors to preserve himself, the more he is endowed with virtue (Pr.20,IV), or (and this is the same thing (Def.8,IV)) the greater the power with which he is endowed for acting according to the laws of his own nature; that is (Pr.3,III), for living by the guidance of reason. But it is when men live by the guidance of reason that they agree most in nature (preceding Pr.). Therefore (preceding Cor.) it is when each is most devoted to seeking his own advantage that men are of most advantage to one another.

Scholium

What we have just demonstrated is also confirmed by daily experience with so many convincing examples as to give rise to the common saying: 'Man is a God to man.' Yet it is rarely the case that men live by the guidance of reason; their condition is such that they are generally disposed to envy and mutual dislike. Nevertheless they find solitary life scarcely endurable, so that for most people the definition 'man is a social animal' meets with strong approval. And the fact of the matter is that the social organisation of man shows a balance of much more profit than loss. So let satirists deride as much as they like the doings of mankind, let theologians revile them, and let the misanthropists (melancholici) heap praise on the life of rude rusticity, despising men and admiring beasts. Men will still discover from experience that they can much more easily meet their needs by mutual help and can ward off ever-threatening perils only by joining forces, not to mention that it is a much more excellent thing and worthy of our knowledge to study the deeds of men than the deeds of beasts. But I shall say more on this subject later on.

PROPOSITION 36

The highest good of those who pursue virtue is common to all, and all can equally enjoy it. [handwritten: radical idea, everyone can win, not just one person]

Proof

To act from virtue is to act by the guidance of reason (Pr.24,IV), and whatever we endeavour to do in accordance with reason is to understand (Pr.26,IV). So (Pr.28,IV) the highest good of those who pursue virtue is to know God; that is (Pr.47,II and Sch.) a good that is common to all men and can be possessed equally by all men in so far as they are of the same nature.

Scholium

Somebody may ask: "What if the highest good of those who pursue virtue were not common to all? Would it not then follow, as above (Pr.34,IV), that men who live by the guidance of reason, that is (Pr.35,IV), men in so far as they agree in nature, would be contrary to one another?" Let him take this reply, that it arises not by accident but from the very nature of reason that men's highest good is common to all, because this is deduced from the very essence of man in so far as that is defined by reason, and because man could neither be nor be conceived if he did not have the ability to enjoy this highest good. For it belongs to the essence of the human mind (Pr.47,II) to have an adequate knowledge of the eternal and infinite essence of God.

PROPOSITION 37

The good which every man who pursues virtue aims at for himself he will also desire for the rest of mankind, and all the more as he acquires a greater knowledge of God. [handwritten: = reality] [handwritten: more knowledge = more successful = more knowledge out to all others]

Proof

In so far as men live by the guidance of reason, they are most useful to man (Cor.1,Pr.35,IV), and so (Pr.19,IV) by the guidance of reason we shall necessarily endeavor to bring it about that men should live by the guidance of reason. But the good that every man who lives according to the dictates of reason, that is (Pr.24,IV), who pursues virtue, seeks for himself is to understand (Pr.26,IV). Therefore the good which every man who pursues virtue seeks for himself he will also desire for the rest of mankind. Again, desire, in so far as it is related to mind, is the very essence of mind (Def. of Emotions 1). Now the essence of mind consists in knowledge (Pr.11,II) which involves the knowledge of God (Pr.47,II), without which (Pr.15,I) it can neither be nor be conceived. So the more the essence of the mind involves knowledge of God, the greater the desire with which he who pursues virtue desires for another the good which he seeks for himself.

Another Proof

The good which a man seeks for himself, and loves, he will love with greater constancy if he sees others loving the same thing (Pr.31,III). Thus (Cor.Pr.31,III) he will endeavor that others should love the same thing. And because this good (preceding Pr.) is common to all, and all can enjoy it, he will therefore endeavor (by the same reasoning) that all should enjoy it, and the more so (Pr.37,III) the more he enjoys this good.

Scholium 1

He who from emotion alone endeavors that others love what he himself loves and live according to his way of thinking acts only by impulse, and therefore incurs dislike, especially from those who have different preferences and who therefore strive and endeavor by that same impulse that others should live according to their way of thinking. Again, since the highest good sought by men under the sway of emotion is often such that only one man can possess it, the result is that men who love it are at odds with themselves; and, while they rejoice to sing the praises of the object of their love, they are afraid of being believed. But he who endeavors to guide others by reason acts not from impulse but from kindly concern, and is entirely consistent with himself.

Whatever we desire and do, whereof we are the cause in so far as we have the idea of God, that is, in so far as we know God, I refer to Religion (religio). The desire to do good which derives from our living by the guidance of reason, I call Piety (pietas). Again, the desire to establish friendship with others, a desire that characterizes the man who lives by the guidance of reason, I call Sense of Honour (honestas); and I use the term 'honourable' for what is praised by men who live by the guidance of reason, and 'base' for what is opposed to the establishing of friendship. Moreover, I have demonstrated what are the foundations of the state. Again, the difference between true virtue and weakness can readily be apprehended from what has been said above; namely, true virtue is nothing other than to live by the guidance of reason, and so weakness consists solely in this, that a man suffers himself to be led by things external to himself and is determined by them to act in a way required by the general state of external circumstances, not by his own nature considered only in itself.

These are the proofs which I undertook in Sch.Pr.18,IV to establish. From this it is clear that the requirement to refrain from slaughtering beasts is founded on groundless superstition and womanish compassion rather than on sound reason. The principle of seeking our own advantage teaches us to be in close relationship with men, not with beasts or things whose nature is different from human nature, and that we have the same right over them as they over us. Indeed, since every individual's right is defined by his virtue or power, man's right over beasts is far greater than their rights over man. I do not deny that beasts feel; I am denying that we are on that account debarred from paying heed to our own advantage and from making use of them as we please and dealing with them as best suits us, seeing that they do not agree with us in nature and their emotions are different in nature from human emotions (Sch.Pr.57,III).

It remains for me to explain what is just, what is unjust, what is sin, and what is merit. On these matters, see the following Scholium.

Scholium 2

In Appendix Part I I undertook to explain what is praise, what is blame, what is merit, what is sin, what is just and what is unjust. With regard to praise and blame, I have explained them in Sch.Pr.29,III. The occasion has now arrived for me to speak of the others. But I must first speak briefly of man in a state of nature and of man in society.

Every man exists by the sovereign natural right, and consequently by the sovereign natural right every man does what follows from the necessity of his nature. So it is by the sovereign natural right that every man judges what is good and what is bad, and has regard for his own advantage according to his own way of thinking (Prs.19 and 20,IV), and seeks revenge (Cor.2,Pr.40,III), and endeavors to preserve what he loves and to destroy what he hates (Pr.28,III). Now if men lived by the guidance of reason, every man would possess this right of his (Cor.1,Pr.35,IV) without any harm to another. But since men are subject to emotions (Cor.Pr.4,IV) which far surpass the power or virtue of men (Pr.6,IV), they are therefore often pulled in different directions (Pr.33,IV) and are contrary to one another (Pr.34,IV), while needing each other's help (Sch.Pr.35,IV).

Therefore, in order that men may live in harmony and help one another, it is necessary for them to give up their natural right and to create a feeling of mutual confidence that they will refrain from any action that may be harmful to another. The way to bring this about, (that men who are necessarily subject to passive emotions (Cor.Pr.4,IV) and are inconstant and variable (Pr.33,IV) should establish a mutual confidence and should trust one another) is obvious from Pr.7,IV and Pr.39,III. There it was demonstrated that no emotion can be checked except by a stronger emotion contrary to the emotion which is to be checked, and that every man refrains from inflicting injury through fear of greater injury. On these terms, then, society can be established, provided that it claims for itself the right that every man has of avenging himself and deciding what is good and what is evil; and furthermore if it has the power to prescribe common rules of behaviour and to pass laws to enforce them, not by reason, which is incapable of checking the emotions (Sch.Pr.17,IV), but by threats.

Now such a society, strengthened by law and by the capacity to preserve itself, is called a State (civitas): and those who are protected by its rights are called Citizens (cives). From this it can readily be understood that in a state of nature there is nothing that is universally agreed upon as good or evil, since every man in a state of nature has regard only to his own advantage and decides what is good and what is bad according to his own way of thinking and only in so far as he has regard to his own advantage, and is not bound by any law to obey anyone but himself. Thus in a state of nature wrong-doing cannot be conceived, but it can be in a civil state where good and bad are decided by common agreement and everyone is bound to obey the state. Wrong-doing is therefore nothing other than disobedience, which is therefore punishable only by the right of the State, and on the other hand obedience is held to be merit in a citizen because he is thereby deemed to deserve to enjoy the advantages of the state.

Again, in a state of nature nobody is by common agreement the owner (dominus) of any thing, and in nature there is nothing that can be said to belong to this man rather than that man. Everything belongs to everybody, and accordingly in a state of nature there cannot be conceived any intention to render to each what is his own or to rob someone of what is his. That is, in a state of nature nothing can be said to be just or unjust; this is so only in a civil state, where it is decided by common agreement what belongs to this or that man. From this it is clear that justice and injustice, wrong-doing and merit, are extrinsic notions, not attributes that explicate the nature of the mind. But I have said enough on this subject.

PROPOSITION 38

That which so disposes the human body that it can be affected in more ways, or which renders it capable of affecting external bodies in more ways, is advantageous to man, and proportionately more advantageous as the body is thereby rendered more capable of being affected in more ways and of affecting other bodies in more ways. On the other hand, that which renders the body less capable in these respects is harmful.

Proof

In proportion as the body is rendered more capable in these respects, so is the mind rendered more capable of apprehension (Pr.14,II); so that which disposes the body in this way and renders it more capable in these respects is necessarily good or advantageous (Prs.26 and 27,IV), and the more so as it renders the body more capable in these respects. On the other hand, (by inversion of the same Pr.14,II, and Prs.26 and 27,IV) that which renders it less capable in these respects is harmful.

PROPOSITION 39

Whatever is conducive to the preservation of the proportion of motion-and-rest, which the parts of the human body maintain towards one another, is good; and those things that effect a change in the proportion of motion-and-rest of the parts of the human body to one another are bad.

Proof

The human body needs many other bodies for its preservation (Post.4,II). But that which constitutes the form (forma) of the human body consists in this, that its parts communicate their motions to one another in a certain fixed proportion (Def. before Lemma 4, q.v. after Pr.13,II). Therefore whatever is conducive to the preservation of the proportion of motion-and-rest, which the parts of the human body maintain towards one another, preserves the form of the human body, and consequently (Posts.3 and 6,II), brings it about that the human body can be affected in many ways and can affect external bodies in many ways, and is therefore, (by preceding Pr.) good. Again, whatever effects a change in the proportion of motion-and-rest of the parts of the human body (by the same Def.II) causes the human body to assume a different form; that is (as is self-evident, and as we noted at the end of the Preface to Part IV), it causes it to be destroyed, and consequently quite incapable of being affected in many ways, and is therefore bad (preceding Pr.).

Scholium

In Part V I shall explain to what extent these things can hinder or be of service to the mind. But here it should be noted that I understand a body to die when its parts are so disposed as to maintain a different proportion of motion-and-rest to one another. For I do not venture to deny that the human body, while retaining blood circulation and whatever else is regarded as essential to life, can nevertheless assume another nature quite different from its own. I have no reason to hold that a body does not die unless it turns into a corpse; indeed, experience seems to teach otherwise. It sometimes happens that a man undergoes such changes that I would not be prepared to say that he is the same person. I have heard tell of a certain Spanish poet who was seized with sickness, and although he recovered, he remained so unconscious of his past life that he did not believe that the stories and tragedies he had written were his own. Indeed, he might have been taken for a child in adult form if he had also forgotten his native tongue. And if this seems incredible, what are we to say about babies? A man of advanced years believes their nature to be so different from his own that he could not be persuaded that he had ever been a baby if he did not draw a parallel from other cases. But I prefer to leave these matters unresolved, so as not to afford material for the superstitious to raise new problems.

PROPOSITION 40

Whatever is conducive to man's social organisation, or causes men to live in harmony, is advantageous, while those things that introduce discord into the state are bad.

trying to get out of political separation between good + evil

Proof

Whatever things cause men to live in harmony cause them also to live by the guidance of reason (Pr.35,IV), and so are good (Prs.26 and 27,IV), while those things that introduce discord are bad (by the same reasoning).

PROPOSITION 41

Pleasure is not in itself bad, but good. On the other hand, pain is in itself bad.

Proof

Pleasure (Pr.11,III and Sch.) is an emotion whereby the body's power of activity is increased or assisted. Pain, on the other hand, is an emotion whereby the body's power of activity is diminished or checked. Therefore (Pr.38,IV) pleasure in itself is good . . . etc.

PROPOSITION 42

Cheerfulness (hilaritas) cannot be excessive; it is always good. On the other hand, melancholy is always bad.

Proof

Cheerfulness (see its definition in Sch.Pr.11,III) is pleasure which, in so far as it is related to the body, consists in this, that all parts of the body are affected equally; that is, (Pr.11,III), the body's power of activity is increased or assisted in such a way that all its parts maintain the same proportion of motion-and-rest towards one another. Thus (Pr.39,IV) cheerfulness is always good, and cannot be excessive. But melancholy (see again its definition in same Sch.Pr.11,III) is pain, which, in so far as it is related to the body, consists in this, that the body's power of activity is absolutely diminished or checked, and therefore (Pr.38,IV) it is always bad.

PROPOSITION 43

Titillation (titillatio) can be excessive and bad. But anguish (dolor) can be good to the extent that titillation or pleasure is bad.

Proof

Titillation is pleasure which, in so far as it is related to the body, consists in one or more of the body's parts being affected more than the rest. (See its definition in Sch.Pr.11,III). The power of this emotion can be so great as to surpass the other activities of the body (Pr.6,IV) and to stay firmly fixed therein, and thus hinder the body's ability to be affected in numerous other ways. So (Pr.38,IV) it can be bad. Again, anguish (dolor) on the other hand, which is pain, cannot be good considered solely in itself (Pr.41,IV). However, because its force and increase is defined by the power of an external cause compared with our own power (Pr.5,IV), we can therefore conceive this emotion as having infinite degrees of strength and infinite modes (Pr.3,IV). Thus we can conceive it as being able to check titillation so that it does not become excessive, and to that extent (by the first part of this proposition) it would prevent the body from being rendered less capable. Therefore to that extent it is good.

PROPOSITION 44

Love and desire can be excessive.

Proof

Love is pleasure (Def. of Emotions 6) accompanied by the idea of an external cause. Therefore titillation (Sch.Pr.11,III) accompanied by the idea of an external cause is love, and thus love (by the preceding Pr.) can be excessive. Again, the strength of a desire is in proportion to that of the emotion from which it arises (Pr.37,III). Therefore just as an emotion (Pr.6,IV) can surpass the other activities of man, so too a desire arising from that same emotion can surpass the other desires, and can therefore be excessive in the same way as was the case with titillation in the previous proposition.

Scholium

Cheerfulness, which I have asserted to be good, is more easily conceived than observed. For the emotions by which we are daily assailed are generally related to some part of the body which is affected more than the rest. Therefore emotions are as a general rule excessive, and keep the mind obsessed with one single object to such an extent that it cannot think of anything else. And although men are subject to numerous emotions, and so few are found who are always assailed by one and the same emotion, yet there are some in whom one and the same emotion stays firmly fixed. For sometimes we see men so affected by one object that they think they have it before them even though it is not present. When this happens to a man who is not asleep, we say he is delirious or mad, and no less mad are those thought to be who are fired with love, dreaming night and day only of their sweetheart or mistress, for they usually provoke ridicule. But when the miser thinks of nothing but gain or money, and the ambitious man of honour, they are not reckoned as mad, for they are usually unpopular and arouse disgust. But in reality avarice, ambition, lust, etc. are kinds of madness, although they are not accounted as diseases.

[handwritten: ✱ Remember Reality is one = Universe = God]

PROPOSITION 45

Hatred can never be good.

[handwritten: passive emotion causes discord against people]

Proof

We endeavor to destroy the man we hate (Pr.39,III); that is (Pr.37,IV), we endeavor to do something that is bad. Therefore . . . etc.

Scholium

Note that here and in what follows, by hatred I mean only hatred towards men.

Corollary 1

Envy, derision, contempt, anger, revenge, and the other emotions related to hatred or arising from hatred are bad. This is also clear from Pr.39,III and Pr.37,IV.

Corollary 2

Whatever we desire as a result of being affected by hatred is base, and, in a state, unjust. This is also clear from Pr.39,III and from the definitions of base and unjust, q.v. in Sch.Pr.37,IV.

Scholium

I make a definite distinction between derision (which in Cor.1 I said is bad) and laughter. For laughter, and likewise merriment, are pure pleasure, and so, provided that they are not excessive, they are good in themselves (Pr.41,IV). Certainly nothing but grim and gloomy superstition forbids enjoyment. Why is it less fitting to drive away melancholy than to dispel hunger and thirst? The principle that guides me and shapes my attitude to life is this: no deity, nor anyone else but the envious, takes pleasure in my weakness and my misfortune, nor does he take to be a virtue our tears, sobs, fearfulness and other such things that are a mark of a weak spirit. On the contrary, the more we are affected with pleasure, the more we pass to state of greater perfection; that is, the more we necessarily participate in the divine nature. Therefore it is the part of a wise man to make use of things and to take pleasure in them as far as he can (but not to the point of satiety, for that is not taking pleasure). It is, I repeat, the part of a wise man to refresh and invigorate himself in moderation with good food and drink, as also with perfumes, with the beauty of blossoming plants, with dress, music, sporting activities, theatres and the like, in which every man can indulge without harm to another. For the human body is composed of many parts of various kinds which are continually in need of fresh and varied nourishment so that the entire body may be equally capable of all the functions that follow from its own nature, and consequently that the mind may be equally capable of simultaneously understanding many things. So this manner of life is in closest agreement both with our principles and with common practice. Therefore, of all ways of life, this is the best and is to be commended on all accounts. There is no need for me to deal more clearly or at greater length with this subject.

PROPOSITION 46

He who lives by the guidance of reason endeavors as far as he can to repay with love or nobility another's hatred, anger, contempt, etc. towards himself.

Proof

All emotions of hatred are bad (Cor.1 preceding Pr.), and thus he who lives by the guidance of reason will endeavor as far as he can not to be assailed by emotions of hatred (Pr.19,IV), and consequently (Pr.37, IV) he will also endeavor that another should not suffer these same emotions. But hatred is increased by reciprocal hatred, and can on the other hand be extinguished by love (Pr.43,III), so that hatred is transformed into love (Pr.44,III). Therefore he who lives by the guidance of reason will endeavor to render back love, that is, nobility, (for whose definition see Sch.Pr.59,III), in return for another's hatred, etc.

Scholium

He who wishes to avenge injuries through reciprocal hatred lives a miserable life indeed. But he who strives to overcome hatred with love is surely fighting a happy and carefree battle. He resists several opponents as easily as one, and stands in least need of fortune's help. Those whom he conquers yield gladly, not through failure of strength but through its increase. All this follows so clearly solely from the definitions of love and intellect that there is no need of detailed proof.

PROPOSITION 47

The emotions of hope and fear cannot be good in themselves.

Proof

The emotions of hope and fear cannot be without pain. For fear is pain (Def. of Emotions 13), and there cannot be hope without fear (see Def. of Emotions 12 and 13, Explications). Therefore (Pr.41,IV) these emotions cannot be good in themselves, but only in so far as they can check excessive pleasure (Pr.43,IV).

Scholium

We should add that these emotions indicate a lack of knowledge and a weakness of mind, and for this reason, too, confidence, despair, joy and disappointment are also indications of our weakness. For although confidence and joy are emotions of pleasure, they imply a preceding pain, namely, hope and fear. Therefore the more we endeavor to live by the guidance of reason, the more we endeavor to be independent of hope, to free ourselves from fear, and to command fortune as far as we can, and to direct our actions by the sure counsel of reason.

PROPOSITION 48

The emotions of over-esteem (existimatio) and disparagement (despectus) are always bad.

Proof

These emotions (Def. of Emotions 21 and 22) are opposed to reason, and so (Prs.26 and 27,IV) are bad.

PROPOSITION 49

Over-esteem is apt to render its recipient proud.

Proof

If we see that someone by reason of love has too high an opinion of us, we are inclined to exult (Sch.Pr.41,III), that is, to be affected with pleasure (Def. of Emotions 30), and we readily believe whatever good we hear said of us (Pr.25,III). Thus we shall think too highly of ourselves through self-love; that is, (Def. of Emotions 28), we shall be inclined to pride.

PROPOSITION 50

In the man who lives by the guidance of reason, pity is in itself bad and disadvantageous.

Proof

Pity is pain (Def. of Emotions 18) and therefore in itself it is bad (Pr.41,IV). Now the good that follows from it (that we endeavour to free from distress one whom we pity (Cor.3,Pr.27,III)) we desire to do solely from the dictates of reason (Pr.37,IV), and it is only from the dictates of reason that we desire to do something that we certainly know to be good (Pr.27,IV). So in the man who lives by the guidance of reason pity in itself is bad and disadvantageous.

Corollary

Hence it follows that the man who lives by the dictates of reason endeavors, as far as he can, not to be touched by pity.

Scholium

He who rightly knows that all things follow from the necessity of the divine nature and happen in accordance with the eternal laws and rules of Nature will surely find nothing deserving of hatred, derision or contempt nor will he pity anyone. Rather, as far as the virtue of man extends, he will endeavor to do well, as the saying goes, and be glad. Furthermore, he who is easily touched by the emotion of pity and is moved by another's distress or tears often does something which he later regrets, both because from emotion we do nothing that we certainly know to be good and because we are easily deceived by false tears. Now I emphasise that I am here speaking of the man who lives by the guidance of reason. For he who is moved neither by reason nor by pity to render help to others is rightly called inhuman. For (Pr.27,III) he seems to be unlike a man.

PROPOSITION 51

Approbation (favor) is not opposed to reason; it can agree with reason and arise from it.

Proof

Approbation is love towards one who has benefited another (Def. of Emotions 19); thus it can be related to the mind in so far as the mind is said to be active (Pr.59,III), that is, (Pr.3,III) in so far as it understands. Therefore it is in agreement with reason . . . etc.

Another Proof

He who lives by the guidance of reason desires for another, too, the good that he seeks for himself (Pr.37,IV). Therefore, as a result of seeing someone do good to another, his own conatus to do good is assisted; that is, (Sch.Pr.11,III) he will feel pleasure accompanied (by hypothesis) by the idea of him who has benefited another and so he feels well-disposed towards him (Def. of Emotions 19).

Scholium

Indignation, as we have defined it (Def. of Emotions 20), is necessarily evil (Pr.45,IV). But it should be noted that when the sovereign power, through its duty to safeguard peace, punishes a citizen who has injured another, I am not saying that it is indignant with citizen. It punishes him not because it is stirred by hatred to destroy the citizen, but from a sense of duty (pietate).

PROPOSITION 52

Self-contentment (acquiescentia in se ipso) can arise from reason, and only that self-contentment which arises from reason is the highest there can be.

Proof

Self-contentment is the pleasure arising from a man's contemplation of himself and his power of activity (Def. of Emotions 25). Now man's true power of activity, or his virtue, is reason itself (Pr.3,III), which man regards clearly and distinctly (Prs. 40 and 43,II). Therefore self-contentment arises from reason. Again, in contemplating himself a man perceives clearly and distinctly, that is, adequately, only what follows from his power of activity (Def.2,III), that is (Pr.3,III) what follows from his power of understanding. So the greatest self-contentment there can be arises only from this contemplation.

Scholium

In fact self-contentment is the highest good we can hope for. For (as we proved in Pr.25,IV) nobody endeavors to preserve his own being for the sake of somethng else. And because this self-contentment is increasingly fostered and strengthened by praise (Cor.Pr.53,III), and on the other hand is increasingly disturbed by blame (Cor.Pr.55,III), honour (gloria) is the greatest incentive, and we can scarcely endure life in disgrace.

PROPOSITION 53

Humility is not a virtue; that is, it does not arise from reason.

Proof

Humility is the pain arising from a man's contemplation of his own weakness (Def. of Emotions 26). Now in so far as a man knows himself by true reason, to that extent he is assumed to understand his own essence, that is (Pr.7,III), his own power. Therefore if a man, in contemplating himself, perceives some weakness in himself, this does not arise from his understanding himself but (Pr.55,III) from the checking of his power of activity. Now if we suppose that a man conceives his own weakness from understanding something more powerful than himself, by the knowledge of which he measures his own power of activity, we are conceiving only that the man understands himself distinctly; that is (Pr.26,IV), that his power of activity is assisted. Therefore the humility, or the pain, that arises from a man's contemplation of his own weakness, does not arise from true contemplation or reason, and is not a virtue but a passive emotion.

PROPOSITION 54

Repentance is not a virtue, i.e. it does not arise from reason; he who repents of his action is doubly unhappy or weak.

Proof

The first part of this Proposition is proved in the same way as the preceding proposition. The second part is evident simply from the definition of this emotion (Def. of Emotions 27). For the subject suffers himself to be overcome first by a wicked desire (cupiditas), and then by pain.

Scholium

As men seldom live according to the dictates of reason, these two emotions, humility and repentance, and also hope and fear, bring more advantage than harm; and thus, if sin we must, it is better to sin in their direction. For if men of weak spirit should all equally be subject to pride, and should be ashamed of nothing and afraid of nothing, by what bonds could they be held together and bound? The mob is fearsome, if it does not fear. So it is not surprising that the prophets, who had regard for the good of the whole community, and not of the few, have been so zealous in commending humility, repentance, and reverence. And in fact those who are subject to these emotions can be far more readily induced than others to live by the guidance of reason in the end, that is, to become free men and enjoy the life of the blessed.

PROPOSITION 55

Extreme pride, or self-abasement, is extreme ignorance of oneself.

Proof

This is clear from Definition of Emotions 28 and 29.

PROPOSITION 56

Extreme pride, or self-abasement, indicates extreme weakness of spirit.

Proof

The primary basis of virtue is to preserve one's own being (Cor.Pr.22,IV), and this by the guidance of reason (Pr.24,IV). So he who is ignorant of himself is ignorant of the basis of all the virtues, and consequently of all the virtues. Again, to act from virtue is nothing else but to act from the guidance of reason (Pr.24,IV), and he who acts from the guidance of reason must necessarily know that he acts from the guidance of reason (Pr.43,II). Therefore he whose ignorance of himself, (and consequently as I have just demonstrated, of all the virtues) is extreme, acts least of all from virtue; that is (as is evident from Def.8, IV), he is most impotent in spirit. And so (by the preceding Pr.) extreme pride or self-abasement indicates extreme weakness of spirit.

Corollary

Hence it clearly follows that the proud and the self-abased are most subject to emotions.

Scholium

But self-abasement can be more easily corrected than pride, since the latter is an emotion of pleasure, while the former is an emotion of pain. So the latter is stronger than the former (Pr.18,IV).

PROPOSITION 57

The proud man loves the company of parasites or flatterers, and hates the company of those of noble spirit.

Proof

Pride is the pleasure arising from a man's thinking too highly of himself (Def. of Emotions 28 and 6), a belief which the proud man will endeavor to foster as much as he can (Sch.Pr.13,III). So the proud love the company of parasites and flatterers (I omit their definitions as being too well-known), and shun the company of those of noble spirit, who value them according to their deserts.

Scholium

It would be tedious to recount here all the ills that spring from pride, for the proud are subject to all the emotions, though to love and pity least of all. But I must not omit here to mention that the term 'proud' is also applied to a man who thinks too meanly of others, and so in this sense pride should be defined as the pleasure arising from false belief, in that a man thinks himself above others. And the self-abasement which is the opposite of this pride should be defined as the pain arising from false belief, in that a man thinks himself beneath others. Now on this basis we readily conceive that the proud man is necessarily envious (Sch.Pr.55,III) and hates most those who are praised for their virtues—a hatred that cannot easily be conquered by their love and kindness (Sch.Pr.41,III)—and finds pleasure only in the company of those who humour his weakness of spirit and turn his folly to madness.

Although self-abasement is the opposite of pride, the self-abased man is very close to the proud man. For since his pain arises from judging his own weakness by the power or virtue of others, his pain will be assuaged, that is, he will feel pleasure, if his thoughts are engaged in contemplating other people's faults. This is the origin of the proverb: "The consolation of the wretched is to have fellows in misfortune." On the other hand, he will be more pained in proportion as he thinks himself lower than others. Hence it comes about that the self-abased are more prone to envy than all others, and that they, more than any, endeavor to keep watch on men's deeds with a view to criticising rather than correcting them, and they end up by praising only self-abasement and exulting in it even while still preserving the appearance of self-abasement.

Now these results follow from this emotion with the same necessity as it follows from the nature of a triangle that its angles are equal to two right angles, and I have already stated that it is only in respect of the good of man that I call these and similar emotions evil. But the laws of Nature have regard to the universal order of Nature, of which man is a part. I have thought first to note this in passing lest anyone should think that my intention here has been to recount the faults and absurdities of mankind rather than to demonstrate the nature and properties of things. As I said in the Preface to Part Three, I consider human emotions and their properties on the same footing with other natural phenomena. And surely human emotions indicate, if not human power, at any rate the power and intricacy of Nature to no less a degree than many other things that evoke our wonder and whose contemplation gives pleasure. But I am going on to point out what features in our emotions bring advantage or harm to men.

PROPOSITION 58

Honour is not opposed to reason, but can arise from it.

Proof

This is evident from Def. of Emotions 30, and from the definition of honourable, for which see Sch.1,Pr.37,IV.

Scholium

Vainglory, as it is called, is the self-contentment that is fostered only by popular esteem and ceases with it; that is (Sch.Pr.52,IV), the highest good which everyone loves, ceases. So it happens that he who exults in popular esteem has the daily burden of anxiously striving, acting and contriving to preserve his reputation. For the populace is fickle and inconstant, and unless a reputation is preserved it soon withers away. Indeed, since all are eager to capture the applause of the populace, each is ready to decry another's reputation. As a result, since the prize at stake is what is esteemed the highest good, there arises a fierce desire to put down one's rivals in whatever way one can, and he who finally emerges victorious prides himself more on having hindered another than on having gained an advantage for himself. So this kind of glory, or self-contentment, is really vain because it is nothing.

As to what is to be remarked about Shame (pudor), this can readily be gathered from our account of compassion and repentance. I shall merely add this, that shame, like pity, although not a virtue, can be good in so far as it is an indication that the man who feels ashamed has a desire to live honourably, just as is the case with anguish, which is said to be good in so far as it indicates that the injured part has not yet putrefied. Therefore, although the man who is ashamed of some deed is in fact pained, he is nearer perfection than the shameless man who has no desire to live honourably.

I have now completed my undertaking to deal with the emotions of pleasure and pain. As for desires, they are, of course, good or evil in so far as they arise from good or evil emotions. But in truth all desires in so far as they are engendered in us from passive emotions, are blind (as can easily be gathered from a reading of Sch.Pr.44,IV) and would be ineffective if men could readily be induced to live only according to the dictates of reason, as I shall now demonstrate in brief.

PROPOSITION 59

In the case of all actions to which we are determined by a passive emotion, we can be determined thereto by reason without that emotion.

Proof

To act from reason is nothing else but to do what follows from the necessity of our own nature considered solely in itself (Pr.3 and Def.2,III). Now pain is bad to the extent that it diminishes or checks this power of action (Pr.41,IV). Therefore we cannot be determined from this emotion to any action that we could not do if we were guided by reason. Moreover, pleasure is bad to the extent that it hinders a man's capacity for action (Prs.41 and 43,IV), and to that extent also we cannot be determined to any action that we could not do if we were guided by reason. Finally, in so far as pleasure is good, it is in agreement with reason (for it consists in this, that a man's power of activity is increased or assisted), and it is a passive emotion only in so far as a man's power of activity is not increased to such a degree that he adequately conceives himself and his actions (Pr.3,III and Sch.) Therefore if a man affected with pleasure were brought to such a degree of perfection that he were adequately to conceive himself and his actions, he would be capable, indeed, more capable, of those same actions to which he is now determined by passive emotions. Now all emotions are related to pleasure, pain or desire (see Explication of Def. of Emotions 4), and desire is merely the endeavor to act (Def. of Emotions 1). Therefore in the case of all actions to which we are determined by a passive emotion, we can be guided thereto by reason alone, without the emotion.

Another Proof

Any action is said to be bad in so far as it arises from our having been affected with hatred or some evil emotion (Cor.1,Pr.45,IV). But no action, considered solely in itself, is good or evil (as we demonstrated in the Preface, Part IV), but one and the same action can be now good, now evil. Therefore we can be guided by reason to that same action which is now bad, that is, which arises from an evil emotion (Pr.19,IV).

Scholium

An example will make this clearer. The act of striking a blow, in so far as it is considered physically and in so far as we look only to the fact that a man raises an arm, clenches his fist and violently brings his arm down, is a virtue, conceived as resulting from the structure of the human body. So if a man, stirred by anger or hatred, is determined to clench his fist or move his arm, this happens because (as we demonstrated in Part II), one and the same action can be associated with any images whatsoever. And so we can be determined to one and the same action both from images of things which we conceive confusedly and from those we conceive clearly and distinctly. It is therefore clear that if men could be guided by reason, all desire that arises from passive emotion would be ineffective (nullius esset usus).

Now let us see why desire that arises from an emotion, that is, a passive emotion, is called blind.

PROPOSITION 60

Desire that arises from the pleasure or pain that is related to one or more, but not to all, parts of the body takes no account of the advantage of the whole man.

Proof

Let it be supposed that part A of the body is so strengthened by the force of some external cause that it prevails over the other parts (Pr.6,IV). This part will not endeavor to abate its own strength in order that other parts of the body may perform their function, for then it would have to possess the force or power to abate its own strength, which is absurd (Pr.6,III). Therefore that part of the body, and consequently the mind too (Prs.7 and 12,III), will endeavor to preserve the existing condition. Therefore the desire that arises from such an emotion of pleasure takes no account of the whole. Now if we suppose on the other hand that part A is checked so that the other parts prevail over it, it can be proved in the same way that desire arising from pain likewise takes no account of the whole.

Scholium

Therefore since pleasure is usually related to one part of the body (Sch.Pr.44,IV), we usually desire to preserve our being without taking account of our entire well-being. There is also the fact that the desires by which we are most enslaved (Cor.Pr.9,IV) take into account only the present, not the future.

PROPOSITION 61

Desire that arises from reason cannot be excessive.

Proof

Desire (Def. of Emotions 1), considered absolutely, is man's very essence in so far as he is conceived as determined in any manner to some action. Therefore desire that arises from reason, that is (Pr.3,III), desire that is engendered in us in so far as we are active, is man's very essence or nature in so far as it is conceived as determined to such actions as are adequately conceived through man's essence alone (Def.2,III). So if this desire could be excessive, human nature, considered absolutely, could exceed itself, that is, it could do more than it can do, which is a manifest contradiction. Therefore this desire cannot be excessive.

PROPOSITION 62

In so far as the mind conceives things in accordance with the dictates of reason, it is equally affected whether the idea be of the future, in the past, or the present.

Proof

Whatsoever the mind conceives under the guidance of reason, it conceives under the same form of eternity or necessity (Cor.2,Pr.44,II), and is affected with the same certainty (Pr.43,II and Sch.). Therefore, whether the idea be of the future, the past, or the present, the mind conceives the thing with the same necessity and is affected with the same certainty; and whether the idea be of the future, the past, or the present, it will nevertheless be equally true (Pr.41,II); that is (Def.4,II), it will nevertheless always have the same properties of an adequate idea. Therefore in so far as the mind conceives things according to the dictates of reason, it is affected in the same way, whether the idea be of a thing future, past, or present.

Scholium

If we could have an adequate knowledge of the duration of things and could determine by reason the periods of their existence, we should regard things future with the same emotion as things present, and the mind would seek the good that it conceives as future just as much as present good. Consequently it would necessarily prefer a future greater good to a lesser present good, and would by no means seek that which is good in the present but the cause of future evil, as we shall later demonstrate. But we can have only a very inadequate knowledge of the duration of things (Pr.31,II), and we determine the periods of existence of things by imagination alone (Sch.Pr.44,II), which is more strongly affected by the image of a thing present than of a thing future. Thus it comes about that the true knowledge we have of good and evil is only abstract or universal, and the judgment that we make concerning the order of things and the connection of causes so that we may determine what is good or bad for us in the present pertains more to the imagination than to reality. So it is not surprising that desire that arises from a knowledge of good and evil, in so far as this knowledge has reference to the future, can be more readily checked by desire of things that are attractive in the present. See Pr.16,IV.

PROPOSITION 63

He who is guided by fear, and does good so as to avoid evil, is not guided by reason.

Proof

All emotions that are related to the mind in so far as it is active, that is (Pr.3,III), emotions that are related to reason, are emotions of pleasure and desire only (Pr.59,III). Therefore (Def. of Emotions 13) he who is guided by fear and does good through fear of evil is not guided by reason.

Scholium

The superstitious, who know how to censure vice rather than to teach virtue, and who are eager not to guide men by reason but to restrain them by fear so that they may shun evil rather than love virtue, have no other object than to make others as wretched as themselves. So it is not surprising that they are generally resented and hated.

Corollary

Through the desire that arises from reason we pursue good directly and shun evil indirectly.

Proof

The desire that arises from reason can arise only from an emotion of pleasure that is not passive (Pr.59,III), that is, from a pleasure that cannot be excessive (Pr.61,IV), and not from pain; and therefore this pleasure (Pr.8,IV) arises from knowledge of good, not of evil. So by the guidance of reason we directly aim at the good, and only to that extent do we shun evil.

Scholium

This corollary can be illustrated by the example of the sick man and the healthy man. The sick man eats what he dislikes through fear of death. The healthy man takes pleasure in his food and thus enjoys a better life than if he were to fear death and directly seek to avoid it. Likewise the judge who condemns a man to death not through hatred or anger but solely through love of public welfare is guided only by reason.

PROPOSITION 64

Knowledge of evil is inadequate knowledge.

Proof

Knowledge of evil is pain itself (Pr.8,IV) in so far as we are conscious of it. Now pain is a transition to a state of less perfection (Def. of Emotions 3), which therefore cannot be understood through man's essence itself (Prs.6 and 7,III) and so is a passive emotion (Def.2,III) which depends on inadequate ideas (Pr.3,III). Consequently knowledge of it (Pr.29,II)—that is, knowledge of evil—is inadequate knowledge.

Corollary

Hence it follows that if the human mind had only adequate ideas, it could not form any notion of evil.

[handwritten: If we use reason to make a choice we chose the]

PROPOSITION 65 *[handwritten: right path.]*

By the guidance of reason we pursue the greater of two goods and the lesser of two evils. *[handwritten: Let reason be your guide to make right choice.]*

Proof

The good that prevents us from enjoying a greater good is in reality an evil; for evil and good are terms used (as I have demonstrated in the Preface to Part IV) in so far as we compare things with one another, and by the same reasoning a lesser evil is in reality a good. Therefore (Cor. Pr.63,IV) by the guidance of reason we aim at or pursue only the greater good and the lesser evil.

Corollary

Under the guidance of reason we pursue a lesser evil for a greater good, and we reject a lesser good which is the cause of a greater evil. For what is here called the lesser evil is in reality a good, and the good on the other hand an evil. Therefore we choose the former and reject the latter (Cor.Pr.63,IV).

PROPOSITION 66

Under the guidance of reason we seek a future greater good in preference to a lesser present good, and a lesser present evil in preference to a greater future evil.

Proof

If the mind could have an adequate knowledge of what is to come, it would be affected by the same emotion towards a future thing as towards a present thing (Pr.62,IV). Thus in so far as we have regard to reason itself, as we assume we are doing in this proposition, a thing is the same whether it is supposed to be a greater good or evil in the future or in the present. Therefore (Pr.65,IV) we seek a future greater good in preference to a lesser present good . . . etc.

Corollary

Under the guidance of reason we choose a present lesser evil which is the cause of a future greater good, and we reject a present lesser good which is the cause of a future greater evil. This corollary is related to the preceding proposition, just as Cor.Pr.65 to Pr.65.

Scholium

If these statements be compared with what we have demonstrated in this Part up to Pr.18 with reference to the strength of the emotions, we shall readily see the difference between the man who is guided only by emotion or belief and the man who is guided by reason. The former, whether he will or not, performs actions of which he is completely ignorant. The latter does no one's will but his own, and does only what he knows to be of greatest importance in life, which he therefore desires above all. So I call the former a slave and the latter a free man, of whose character and manner of life I have yet a few things to say.

PROPOSITION 67

A free man thinks of death least of all things, and his wisdom is a meditation of life, not of death.

Proof

A free man, that is, he who lives solely according to the dictates of reason, is not guided by fear of death (Pr.63,IV), but directly desires the good (Cor.Pr.63,IV); that is (Pr.24,IV), to act, to live, to preserve his own being in accordance with the principle of seeking his own advantage. So he thinks of death least of all things, and his wisdom is a meditation upon life.

PROPOSITION 68

If men were born free, they would form no conception of good and evil so long as they were free.

Proof

I have said that a free man is he who is guided solely by reason. Therefore he who is born free and remains free has only adequate ideas and thus has no conception of evil (Cor.64,IV), and consequently no conception of good (for good and evil are correlative).

Scholium

It is clear from Pr.4,IV that the hypothesis in this proposition is false and cannot be conceived except in so far as we have regard solely to the nature of man, or rather, to God not in so far as he is infinite but only in so far as he is the cause of man's existence. This and other truths that we have already demonstrated seem to be what Moses intended by his history of the first man. For in that narrative no other power of God is conceived save that whereby he created man; that is, the power whereby he had regard only for man's advantage. And this is the point of the story that God forbade the free man to eat of the tree of the knowledge of good and evil, saying that as soon as he should eat of it he would straightway fear death instead of desiring to live. Again, the story goes that when man had found woman, who agreed entirely with his own nature, he realised that there could be nothing in Nature more to his advantage than woman. But when he came to believe that the beasts were like himself, he straightway began to imitate their emotions (Pr.27,III) and to lose his freedom, which the Patriarchs later regained under the guidance of the spirit of Christ, that is, the idea of God, on which alone it depends that a man should be free and should desire for mankind the good that he desires for himself, as I have demonstrated above (Pr.37,IV).

PROPOSITION 69

The virtue of a free man is seen to be as great in avoiding dangers as in overcoming them.

Proof

An emotion cannot be checked or removed except by a contrary emotion stronger than the emotion which is to be checked (Pr.7,IV). But blind daring (caeca audacia) and fear are emotions that can be conceived as equally strong (Prs.5 and 3,IV). Therefore the virtue or strength of mind (for its definition see Sch.Pr.59,III) needed to check daring must be equally as great as that needed to check fear; that is (Def. of Emotions 40 and 41), the free man avoids dangers by that same virtue as that whereby he attempts to overcome them.

Corollary

Therefore, for a free man timely retreat is as much a mark of courage as is fighting; that is, the free man chooses flight by the same courage or spiritedness as he chooses battle.

Scholium

I have explained in Sch.Pr.59,III what courage is, or what I understand by it. By danger I mean everything that can be the cause of some evil, such as pain, hatred, discord, etc.

PROPOSITION 70

The free man who lives among ignorant people tries as far as he can to avoid receiving favors from them.

Proof

Every man judges what is good according to his own way of thinking (Sch.Pr.39,III). Thus the ignorant man who has conferred a favour on someone will value it according to his own way of thinking, and if he sees that the recipient values it less, he will feel pain (Pr.42,III). Now the free man tries to establish friendship with others (Pr.37,IV) and not to repay men with favours that are equivalent in their eyes. Rather he tries to guide himself and others by the free judgment of reason and to do only those things that he himself knows to be of primary importance. Therefore, to avoid both the hatred of the ignorant and the need to comply with their expectations, and so as to make reason his sole ruler, he will endeavor as far as he can to avoid their favours.

Scholium

I say, 'as far as he can'; for men, however ignorant, are still men, who in time of need can bring human help, than which nothing is more valuable. So it often happens that it is necessary to accept a favour from them, and consequently to return it so as to give them satisfaction. Furthermore, we should exercise caution even in avoiding their favours so as to avoid appearing to despise them or to be reluctant through avarice to repay them, thus giving offence by the very attempt to escape their hatred. Thus in avoiding favours one should take account of what is advantageous and honourable.

PROPOSITION 71

Only free men are truly grateful to one another.

Proof

Only free men are truly advantageous to one another and united by the closest bond of friendship (Pr.35,IV and Cor.1), and are equally motivated by love in endeavoring to benefit one another (Pr.37,IV). And thus (Def. of Emotions 34) only free men are truly grateful to one another.

Scholium

The gratitude mutually exhibited by men who are governed by blind desire is more in the nature of a bargain or inducement than gratitude. Moreover, ingratitude is not an emotional state. Nevertheless, ingratitude is base, because it generally is a sign that a man is affected with excessive hatred, anger, pride, or avarice, etc. For if out of stupidity a man knows not how to repay benefits, he is not an ungrateful man; and far less so is he who is not won over by the gifts of a loose woman to serve her lust, nor by the gifts of a thief to conceal his thefts, nor by the gifts of anyone of like character. On the contrary, he shows a steadfast spirit, in that he refuses to be corrupted by gifts to his own hurt or that of society.

PROPOSITION 72

The free man never acts deceitfully, but always with good faith.

Proof

If the free man, in so far as he is free, were to act deceitfully, he would be doing so in accordance with the dictates of reason (for it is in this respect only that we term him free), and thus to act deceitfully would be a virtue (Pr.24,IV), and consequently (by the same proposition), in order to preserve his own being, it would be better for every man to act deceitfully, that is (as is self-evident) it would be better for men to agree in words only, but to be contrary to one another in reality, which is absurd (Cor.Pr.31,IV). Therefore the free man . . . etc.

Scholium

The question may be asked: "What if a man could by deception free himself from imminent danger of death? Would not consideration for the preservation of his own being be decisive in persuading him to deceive?" I reply in the same way, that if reason urges this, it does so for all men; and thus reason urges men in general to join forces and to have common laws only with deceitful intention; that is, in effect, to have no laws in common at all, which is absurd.

PROPOSITION 73

The man who is guided by reason is more free in a state where he lives under a system of law than in solitude where obeys only himself.

Proof

The man who is guided by reason is not guided to obey out of fear (Pr.63,IV), but in so far as he endeavors to preserve his own being according to the dictates of reason—that is (Sch.Pr.66,IV), in so far as he endeavors to live freely—he desires to take account of the life and the good of the community (Pr.37,IV), and consequently (as I have pointed out in Sch.2,Pr.37,IV) to live according to the laws of the state. Therefore the man who is guided by reason desires to adhere to the laws of the state so that he may live more freely.

Scholium

These and similar observations that we have made concerning the true freedom of man are related to strength of mind, that is (Pr.59,III), courage and nobility. I do not think it worthwhile at this point to give separate proof of all the properties of strength of mind, and far less to show that the strong-minded man hates nobody, is angry with nobody, envies nobody, is indignant with nobody, despises nobody, and is in no way prone to pride. For these points and all that concern the true way of life and religion are readily proved from Prs. 37 and 46,IV, to wit, that hatred is to be conquered by returning love, and that every man who is guided by reason aims at procuring for others, too, the good that he seeks for himself. Furthermore, as we have noted in Sch.Pr.50,IV and elsewhere, the strong-minded man has this foremost in his mind, that everything follows from the necessity of the divine nature, and therefore whatever he thinks of as injurious or bad, and also whatever seems impious, horrible, unjust and base arises from his conceiving things in a disturbed, fragmented and confused way. For this reason his prime endeavor is to conceive things as they are in themselves and to remove obstacles to true knowledge, such as hatred, anger, envy, derision, pride, and similar emotions that we have noted. And so he endeavors, as far as he can, to do well and to be glad, as we have said.

In the next Part I shall pass on to demonstrate the extent to which human virtue can achieve these objectives, and the nature of its power.

APPENDIX

In this Part my exposition of the right way of living is not arranged so that it can be seen at one view. The proofs are scattered so as to meet the convenience of logical deduction one from another. So I propose to gather them together here, and arrange them under their main headings.

1. All our endeavors or desires follow from the necessity of our nature in such a way that they can be understood either through it alone as their proximate cause, or in so far as we are a part of Nature, a part that can-

not be adequately conceived through itself independently of the other individual parts.

2. Desires that follow from our nature in such a way that they can be understood through it alone are those that are related to the mind in so far as the mind is conceived as consisting of adequate ideas. The other desires are related to the mind only in so far as it conceives things inadequately; and their force and increase must be defined not by human power but by the power of things external to us. So the former are rightly called active emotions, the latter passive emotions. For the former always indicate our power, the latter our weakness and fragmentary knowledge.

3. Our active emotions, that is, those desires that are defined by man's power, that is, by reason, are always good; the other desires can be either good or evil.

4. Therefore it is of the first importance in life to perfect the intellect, or reason, as far as we can, and the highest happiness or blessedness for mankind consists in this alone. For blessedness is nothing other than that self-contentment that arises from the intuitive knowledge of God. Now to perfect the intellect is also nothing other than to understand God and the attributes and actions of God that follow from the necessity of his nature. Therefore for the man who is guided by reason, the final goal, that is, the highest Desire whereby he strives to control all the others, is that by which he is brought to an adequate conception of himself and of all things that can fall within the scope of his understanding.

5. So there is no rational life without understanding, and things are good only in so far as they assist a man to enjoy the life of the mind, which is defined by understanding. Those things only do we call evil which hinder a man's capacity to perfect reason and to enjoy a rational life.

6. But since all those things of which man is the efficient cause are necessarily good, nothing evil can befall a man except from external causes, namely, in so far as he is a part of the whole of Nature, whose laws human nature is constrained to obey, and to which it must conform in almost an infinite number of ways.

7. A man is bound to be a part of Nature and to follow its universal order; but if he dwells among individuals who are in harmony with man's nature, by that very fact his power of activity will be assisted and fostered. But if he be among individuals who are by no means in harmony with his nature, he will scarcely be able to conform to them without a great change in himself.

8. Whatsoever in nature we deem evil, that is, capable of hindering us from being able to exist and to enjoy a rational life, it is permissible for us to remove in whatever seems the safer way. On the other hand, whatever we deem good, that is, advantageous for preserving our being and for enjoying a rational life, it is permissible for us to take for our use and

to use it as we please. And as an absolute rule, it is permissible by the highest natural right for everyone to do what he judges to be to his own advantage.

9.   Nothing can be more in harmony with the nature of any thing than other individuals of the same species, and so (see No. 7) there is nothing more advantageous to man for preserving his own being and enjoying a rational life than a man who is guided by reason. Again, since among particular things we know of nothing more excellent than a man who is guided by reason, nowhere can each individual display the extent of his skill and genius more than in so educating men that they come at last to live under the sway of their own reason.

10.   In so far as men feel envy or some other emotion of hatred towards one another, they are contrary to one another; consequently, the more powerful they are, the more they are to be feared than other individuals of Nature.

11.   Nevertheless men's hearts are conquered not by arms but by love and nobility.

12.   It is of the first importance to men to establish close relationships and to bind themselves together with such ties as may most effectively unite them into one body, and, as an absolute rule, to act in such a way as serves to strengthen friendship.

13.   But to this end skill and watchfulness are needed. For men are changeable (few there are who live under the direction of reason) and yet for the most part envious, and more inclined to revenge than to compassion. So it needs an unusually powerful spirit to bear with each according to his disposition and to restrain oneself from imitating their emotions. On the other hand, those whose skill is to criticise mankind and to censure vice rather than to teach virtue, and to shatter men's spirit rather than strengthen it, are a stumbling-block both to themselves and to others. Hence many men, over-impatient and with false religious zeal, have chosen to live among beasts rather than among men, just as boys or young men, unable patiently to endure the upbraidings of their parents, run away to join the army, and prefer the hardships of war and tyrannical discipline to the comfort of home and parental admonition, and suffer any burdens to be imposed on them so long as they can spite their parents.

14.   So although men for the most part allow lust to govern all their actions, the advantages that follow from living in their society far exceed the disadvantages. Therefore it is better to endure their injuries with patience, and to apply oneself to such measures as promote harmony and friendship.

15.   Conduct that brings about harmony is that which is related to justice, equity, and honourable dealing. For apart from resenting injustice and unfairness, men also resent what is held to be base, or contempt for the accepted customs of the state. But for winning their love

the most important factors are those that are concerned with religion and piety, for which see Schs.1 and 2,Pr.37, and Sch.Pr.46 and Sch.Pr.73,IV.

16.   Harmony is also commonly produced by fear, but then it is untrustworthy. Furthermore, fear arises from weakness of spirit, and therefore does not belong to the use of reason. Neither does pity, although it bears the appearance of piety.

17.   Again, men are won over by generosity, especially those who do not have the wherewithal to produce what is necessary to support life. Yet it is far beyond the power and resources of a private person to come to the assistance of everyone in need. For the wealth of a private person is quite unequal to such a demand. It is also a practical impossibility for one man to establish friendship with all. Therefore the care of the poor devolves upon society as a whole, and looks only to the common good.

18.   The care to be taken in accepting favours and in returning them must be of quite a different kind, for which see Sch.Pr.70 and Sch. Pr.71,IV.

19.   Furthermore, love of a mistress, that is, sexual lust that arises from physical beauty, and in general all love that acknowledges any other cause than freedom of the spirit, easily passes in hatred unless (and this is worse) it be a kind of madness, and then it is fostered by discord rather than harmony.

20.   As for marriage, it is certain that this is in agreement with reason if the desire for intercourse be engendered not simply by physical beauty but also by love of begetting children and rearing them wisely, and if, in addition, the love of both man and woman has for its cause not merely physical beauty but especially freedom of the spirit.

21.   Flattery, too, produces harmony, but at the cost of base servility, or through perfidy. None are more taken in by flattery than the proud, who want to be foremost, but are not.

22.   In self-abasement there is a false appearance of piety and religion. And although self-abasement is opposed to pride, the self-abased man is closest to the proud man. See Sch.Pr.57,IV.

23.   Shame, too, contributes to harmony, but only in matters that cannot be concealed. Again, since shame is species of pain, it does not concern the use of reason.

24.   The other painful emotions towards men are directly opposed to justice, equity, honour, piety and religion; and although indignation seems to bear an outward show of equity, it is a lawless state of society where each is permitted to pass judgment on another's deeds and assert his own or another's right.

25.   Courtesy, that is, the desire to please men as determined by reason, is related to piety (as we have said in Sch.1,Pr.37,IV). But if it arises from emotion, it is ambition, or the desire whereby under a false cover of piety men generally stir up discord and quarrelling. For he who desires to

help others by word or deed to enjoy the highest good along with him, will strive above all to win their love, but not to evoke their admiration so that some system of philosophy may be named after him, nor to afford any cause whatsoever for envy. Again, in ordinary conversation he will beware of talking about the vices of mankind and will take care to speak only sparingly of human weakness, but will dwell on human virtue, or power, and the means to perfect it, so that men may thus endeavor as far as they can to live in accordance with reason's behest, not from fear or dislike, but motivated only by the emotion of pleasure.

26. Except for mankind, we know of no individual thing in Nature in whose mind we can rejoice, and with which we can unite in friendship or some kind of close tie. So whatever there is in Nature external to man, regard for our own advantage does not require us to preserve it, but teaches us to preserve or destroy it according to its varying usefulness, or to adapt it to our own use in whatever way we please.

27. The advantage that we get from things external to us, apart from the experience and knowledge we gain from observing them and changing them from one form to another, is especially the preservation of the body, and in this respect those things above all are advantageous which can so feed and nourish the body that all its parts can efficiently perform their function. For as the body is more capable of being affected in many ways and of affecting external bodies in many ways, so the mind is more capable of thinking (see Prs.38 and 39,IV). But there appear to be few things of this kind in Nature; wherefore to nourish the body as it should be one must use many foods of different kinds. For the human body is composed of numerous parts of different natures, which need a continual supply of food of various sorts so that the whole body is equally capable of all that can follow from its nature, and consequently that the mind too is equally capable of conceiving many things.

28. Now to provide all this the strength of each single person would scarcely suffice if men did not lend mutual aid to one another. However, money has supplied a token for all things, with the result that its image is wont to obsess the minds of the populace, because they can scarcely think of any kind of pleasure that is not accompanied by the idea of money as its cause.

29. But this vice is characteristic only of those who seek money not through poverty nor to meet their necessities, but because they have acquired the art of money-making, whereby they raise themselves to a splendid estate. They feed the body from habit, but thriftily, because they believe that what they spend on preserving the body is lost to their goods. But those who know the true use of money set the limit of their wealth solely according to their needs, and live content with little.

30. Since those things are good which assist the parts of the body to perform their function, and pleasure consists in this, that a man's power is assisted or increased in so far as he is composed of mind and body, all those things that bring pleasure are good. On the other hand, since things

do not act with the object of affecting us with pleasure, and their power of acting is not adjusted to suit our needs, and, lastly, since pleasure is usually related to one part of the body in particular, the emotions of pleasure (unless one exercises reason and care), and consequently the desires that are generated from them, can be excessive. There is this further point, that from emotion we place prime importance on what is attractive in the present, and we cannot feel as strongly about the future. See Sch.Pr.44 and Sch.Pr.60,IV.

31. But superstition on the other hand seems to assert that what brings pain is good and what brings pleasure is bad. But, as we have already said (Sch.Pr.45,IV), nobody but the envious takes pleasure in my weakness and my misfortune. For the more we are affected with pleasure, the more we pass to a state of greater perfection, and consequently the more we participate in the divine nature. Nor can pleasure ever be evil when it is controlled by true regard for our advantage. Now he who on the other hand is guided by fear and does good in order to avoid evil is not guided by reason.

32. But human power is very limited and is infinitely surpassed by the power of external causes, and so we do not have absolute power to adapt to our purposes things external to us. However, we shall patiently bear whatever happens to us that is contrary to what is required by consideration of our own advantage, if we are conscious that we have done our duty and that our power was not extensive enough for us to have avoided the said things, and that we are a part of the whole of Nature whose order we follow. If we clearly and distinctly understand this, that part of us which is defined by the understanding, that is, the better part of us, will be fully resigned and will endeavor to persevere in that resignation. For in so far as we understand, we can desire nothing but that which must be, nor, in an absolute sense, can we find contentment in anything but truth. And so in so far as we rightly understand these matters, the endeavor of the better part of us is in harmony with the order of the whole of Nature.

PART V

OF THE POWER OF THE INTELLECT,
OR OF HUMAN FREEDOM

PREFACE

I pass on finally to that part of the *Ethics* which concerns the method, or way, leading to freedom. In this part, then, I shall be dealing with the power of reason, pointing out the degree of control reason has over the emotions, and then what is freedom of mind, or blessedness, from which we shall see how much to be preferred is the life of the wise man to the life of the ignorant man. Now we are not concerned here with the manner or way in which the intellect should be perfected, nor yet with the science of tending the body so that it may correctly perform its functions. The latter is the province of medicine, the former of logic. Here then, as I have said, I shall be dealing only with the power of the mind or reason. Above all I shall be showing the degree and nature of its command over the emotions in checking and controlling them. For I have already demonstrated that we do not have absolute command over them.

Now the Stoics thought that the emotions depend absolutely on our will, and that we can have absolute command over them. However, with experience crying out against them they were obliged against their principles to admit that no little practice and zeal are required in order to check and control emotions. One of them tried to illustrate this point with the example of two dogs, if I remember correctly, one a house-dog, and the other a hunting-dog; in the end he succeeded in training the house-dog to hunt and the hunting-dog to refrain from chasing hares.

This view is much favoured by Descartes. He maintained that the soul or mind is united in a special way with a certain part of the brain called the pineal gland, by means of which the mind senses all movements that occur in the body, as well as external objects, and by the mere act of willing it can move the gland in various ways. He maintained that this gland is suspended in the middle of the brain in such a way that it can be moved by the slightest motion of the animal spirits. He further maintained that the number of different ways in which the gland can be suspended in the middle of the brain corresponds with the number of different ways in which the animal spirits can impinge upon it, and that, furthermore, as many different marks can be imprinted on the gland as there are external objects impelling the animal spirits towards it. As a result, if by the will of the soul, which can move it in various ways, the gland is later suspended in that particular way in which it had previously been suspended by a particular mode of agitation of the spirits, then the gland will impel and determine the animal spirits in the same way as they had previously been acted upon by a similar mode of suspension of the gland. He furthermore maintained that every single act of willing is by nature united to a particular motion of the gland. For example, if anyone wills to gaze at a distant object, this act of willing will bring about the dilation of the pupil. But if he thinks only of dilating the pupil, it will be useless for him to will this, because the motion of the gland which serves to impel the spirits towards the optic nerve in a manner that will bring about dilation or contraction of the pupil has not been joined by nature to the act of willing its contraction or dilation, but only to the act of willing to gaze at distant or near objects. Finally, he maintained that although each motion of this gland seems to have been connected through nature from the beginning of our lives to particular thoughts, these motions can be joined to other thoughts through training, and this he endeavors to prove in Article 50, Part I of *On the Passions of the Soul.* From this he concludes that there is no soul so weak that it cannot, through good guidance, acquire absolute power over its passions. For these passions are defined by him as "perceptions, or feelings, or disturbances of the soul, which are related to the soul as species, and which are produced (note well!), preserved and strengthened through some motion of the spirits." (See Article 27, Part I, *On the Passions of the Soul.*) But as we are able to join any motion of the gland, and consequently of the spirits, to any act of willing, and as the determination of the will depends only on our own power, if therefore we determine our will by the sure and firm decisions in accordance with which we want to direct the actions of our lives, and if to these decisions we join the movements of the passions which we want to have, we shall acquire absolute command over our passions.

Such is the view of this illustrious person (as far as I can gather from his own words), a view which I could scarcely have believed to have been put forward by such a great man, had it been less ingenious. Indeed, I am lost in wonder that a philosopher who had strictly resolved to deduce nothing except from self-evident bases and to affirm nothing that he did not clearly and distinctly perceive, who had so often censured the Scholastics for seeking to explain obscurities through occult qualities, should adopt a theory more occult than any occult quality. What, I ask, does he understand by the union of mind and body? What clear and distinct conception does he have of thought closely united to a certain particle of matter? I should have liked him, indeed, to explain this union through its proximate cause. But he had conceived mind as so distinct from body that he could assign no one cause either of this union or of mind itself, and found it necessary to have recourse to the cause of the entire universe, that is, God. Again, I should like to know how many degrees of motion mind can impart to that pineal gland of his, and by what force it can hold it suspended. For I know not whether this gland can be moved about more slowly or more quickly by the mind than by animal spirits, and whether the movements of the passions which we have joined in a close union with firm decisions cannot again be separated from those decisions by corporeal causes, from which it would follow that, although the mind firmly decides to face danger and joins to that decision the motions of boldness, when the danger appears, the gland may assume such a form of suspension that the mind can think only of flight. And surely, since will and motion have no common standard, there cannot be any comparison between the power or strength of the mind and body, and consequently the strength of the latter cannot possibly be determined by the strength of the former. There is the additional fact that this gland is not to be found located in the middle of the brain in such a way that it can be driven about so easily and in so many ways, nor do all nerves extend as far as the cavities of the brain.

Finally, I omit all Descartes' assertions about the will and its freedom, since I have already abundantly demonstrated that they are false. Therefore, since the power of the mind is defined solely by the understanding, as I have demonstrated above, we shall determine solely by the knowledge of the mind the remedies for the emotions—remedies which I believe all men experience but do not accurately observe nor distinctly see—and from this knowledge we shall deduce all that concerns the blessedness of the mind.

AXIOMS

1. If two contrary actions are instigated in the same subject, a change must necessarily take place in both or in the one of them until they cease to be contrary.

2. The power of an effect is defined by the power of the cause in so far as its essence is explicated or defined through the essence of its cause. This Axiom is evident from Pr.7,III.

PROPOSITION 1

The affections of the body, that is, the images of things, are arranged and connected in the body in exactly the same way as thoughts and the ideas of things are arranged and connected in the mind.

Proof

The order and connection of ideas is the same (Pr.7,II) as the order and connection of things, and, vice versa, the order and connection of things is the same (Cor.Pr.6 and Pr.7,II) as the order and connection of ideas. Therefore, just as the order and connection of ideas in the mind occurs in accordance with the order and connection of the affections of the body (Pr.18,II), so vice versa (Pr.2,III) the order and connection of the affections of the body occurs in just the way that thoughts and the ideas of things are arranged and connected in the mind.

PROPOSITION 2

If we remove an agitation of the mind, or emotion, from the thought of its external cause, and join it to other thoughts, then love or hatred towards the external cause, and also vacillations, that arise from these emotions will be destroyed.

Proof

That which constitutes the form of love or hatred is pleasure or pain accompanied by the idea of an external cause (Def. of Emotions 6 and 7). So when the latter is removed, the form of love or hatred is removed with it; and thus these emotions, and those that arise from them, are destroyed.

[handwritten: when you understand something is bad you no longer think of it as a passive emotion so you don't do it]

PROPOSITION 3

A passive emotion ceases to be a passive emotion as soon as we form a clear and distinct idea of it.

[handwritten: being control of it. If you understand the anger you can't fully be angry]

Proof *[handwritten: any longer]*

A passive emotion is a confused idea (Gen. Def. of Emotions). So if we form a clear and distinct idea of the emotion, this idea is distinguishable only in concept from the emotion in so far as the latter is related only to mind (Pr.21,II and Sch.); and so the emotion will cease to be passive (Pr.3,III).

Corollary

So the more an emotion is known to us, the more it is within our control, and the mind is the less passive in respect of it.

[handwritten: the way the body = idea = copies of perception]
[handwritten margin: copies of perception]

PROPOSITION 4

There is no (affection) of the body of which we cannot form a clear and distinct conception.

[handwritten: There is nothing that cannot be understood.]

Proof

What is common to all things can only be conceived adequately (Pr.38,II), and thus (Pr.12 and Lemma 2 which comes after Sch.Pr.13, II) there is no affection of the body of which we cannot form a clear and distinct conception.

Corollary

Hence it follows that there is no emotion of which we cannot form a clear and distinct conception. For an emotion is the idea of an affection of the body (Gen. Def. of Emotions), which must therefore involve some clear and distinct conception (preceding Pr.).

Scholium

Since there exists nothing from which some effect does not follow (Pr.36,I), and all that follows from an idea that is adequate in us is understood by us clearly and distinctly (Pr.40,II), it therefore follows that everyone has the power of clearly and distinctly understanding himself and his emotions, if not absolutely, at least in part, and consequently of bringing it about that he should be less passive in respect of them. So we should pay particular attention to getting to know each emotion, as far as possible, clearly and distinctly, so that the mind may thus be determined from the emotion to think those things that it clearly and distinctly perceives, and in which it finds full contentment. Thus the emotion may be detached from the thought of an external cause and joined to true thoughts. The result will be that not only are love, hatred, etc. destroyed (Pr.2,V) but also that the appetites or desires that are wont to arise from such an emotion cannot be excessive (Pr.61,IV). For it is very important to note that it is one and the same appetite through which a man is said both to be active and to be passive. For example, we have shown that human nature is so constituted that everyone wants others to live according to his way of thinking (Cor.Pr.31,III). Now this appetite in a man who is not guided by reason is a passive emotion which is called ambition, and differs to no great extent from pride. But in a man who lives according to the dictates of reason it is an active emotion, or virtue, which is called piety (Sch.1, Pr.37,IV and second proof of that same proposition). In this way all appetites or desires are passive emotions only in so far as they arise from inadequate ideas, and they are accredited to virtue when they are aroused or generated by adequate ideas. For all desires whereby we are determined to some action can arise both from adequate and from inadequate ideas (Pr.59,IV). To return to the point from which I digressed, there is available to us no more excellent remedy for the emotions than that which consists in a true knowledge of them, since there is no other power of the mind than the power of thought and of forming adequate ideas, as I have shown above (Pr.3,III).

PROPOSITION 5

An emotion towards a thing which we imagine merely in itself, and not as necessary, possible or contingent, is the greatest of all emotions, other things being equal.

Proof

An emotion towards a thing that we imagine to be free is greater than an emotion towards a necessary thing (Pr.49,III), and consequently still greater than an emotion towards a thing that we imagine to be possible or contingent (Pr.11,IV). But to imagine some thing as free can be nothing else than to imagine it merely in itself, while we are ignorant of the causes by which it has been determined to act (Sch.Pr.35,II). Therefore, an emotion towards a thing that we imagine merely in itself is greater, other things being equal, than an emotion towards a necessary, possible, or contingent thing, and consequently it is the greatest of all emotions.

PROPOSITION 6

In so far as the mind understands all things as governed by necessity, to that extent it has greater power over emotions, i.e. it is less passive in respect of them.

Proof

The mind understands all things to be governed by necessity

(Pr.29,I) and to be determined to exist and to act by an infinite chain of causes (Pr.28,I). And so (preceding Pr.) to that extent the mind succeeds in becoming less passive to the emotions that arise from things, and (Pr.48,III) less affected towards the things themselves.

Scholium

The more this knowledge (namely, that things are governed by necessity) is applied to particular things which we imagine more distinctly and more vividly, the greater is this power of the mind over the emotions, as is testified by experience. For we see that pain over the loss of some good is assuaged as soon as the man who has lost it realises that that good could not have been saved in any way. Similarly, we see that nobody pities a baby because it cannot talk or walk or reason, and because it spends many years in a kind of ignorance of self. But if most people were born adults and only a few were born babies, then everybody would feel sorry for babies because they would then look on infancy not as a natural and necessary thing but as a fault or flaw in Nature. There are many other examples of this kind that we might note.

PROPOSITION 7

Emotions which arise or originate from reason are, if we take account of time, more powerful than those that are related to particular things which we regard as absent.

Proof

We do not look on a thing as absent by reason of the emotion with which we think of it, but by reason of the body being affected by another emotion which excludes the existence of the said thing (Pr.17,II). Therefore the emotion that is related to a thing that we regard as absent is not of a kind to overcome the rest of man's activities and power (see Pr.6,IV). On the contrary, its nature is such that it can be checked in some way by those affections which exclude the existence of its external cause (Pr.9,IV). But an emotion that arises from reason is necessarily related to the common properties of things (see Def. of Reason in Sch.2,Pr.40,II) which we regard as being always present (for there can be nothing that excludes their present existence) and which we always think of in the same way (Pr.38,II). Therefore such an emotion always remains the same. Consequently (Ax.1,V) emotions which are contrary to it and are not fostered by their external causes must adapt themselves to it more and more until they are no longer contrary; and to that extent an emotion that arises from reason is more powerful.

PROPOSITION 8

The greater the number of causes that simultaneously concur in arousing an emotion, the greater the emotion.

Proof

Several causes acting together are more effective than if they were fewer (Pr.7,III). So (Pr.5,IV) the more simultaneous causes there are in arousing an emotion, the stronger will be the emotion.

Scholium

This Proposition is also obvious from Ax.2,V.

PROPOSITION 9

An emotion that is related to several different causes, which the mind regards together with the emotion itself, is less harmful, and we suffer less from it and are less affected by each individual cause, than if we were affected by another equally great emotion which is related to only one or to a few causes.

Proof

An emotion is bad or harmful only in so far as the mind is thereby hindered from being able to think (Pr.26 and 27,IV). Thus an emotion whereby the mind is determined to regard several objects simultaneously is less harmful than another equally great emotion which so keeps the mind in the contemplation of only one or few objects that it cannot think of anything else. This is the first point. Again, because the essence of the mind, that is (Pr.7,III), its power, consists only in thought (Pr.11,II), it follows that the mind is less passive through an emotion by which it is determined to regard several things all together than through an equally great emotion which keeps the mind engrossed in the contemplation of only one or few objects. This is the second point. Finally, this emotion (Pr.48,III), in so far as it is related to several external causes, is also less towards each cause.

PROPOSITION 10

As long as we are not assailed by emotions that are contrary to our nature, we have the power to arrange and associate affections of the body according to the order of the intellect.

Proof

Emotions that are contrary to our nature, that is (Pr.30,IV), which are bad, are bad to the extent that they hinder the mind from understanding (Pr.27,IV). Therefore as long as we are not assailed by emotions contrary to our nature, the power of the mind whereby it endeavors to understand things (Pr.26,IV) is not hindered, and thus it has the ability to form clear and distinct ideas, deducing them from one another (Sch.2, Pr.40 and Sch.Pr.47,II). Consequently (Pr.1,V) in this case we have the ability to arrange and associate affections of the body according to the order of the intellect.

Scholium

Through the ability to arrange and associate rightly the affections of the body we can bring it about that we are not easily affected by bad emotions. For (Pr.7,V) greater force is required to check emotions arranged and associated according to intellectual order than emotions that are uncertain and random. Therefore the best course we can adopt, as long as we do not have perfect knowledge of our emotions, is to conceive a right method of living, or fixed rules of life, and to commit them to memory and continually apply them to particular situations that are frequently encountered in life, so that our casual thinking is thoroughly permeated by them and they are always ready to hand. For example, among our practical rules, we laid down (Pr.46,IV and Sch.) that hatred should be conquered by love or nobility, and not repaid with reciprocal hatred. Now in order that we may have this precept of reason always ready to hand we should think about and frequently reflect on the wrongs that are commonly committed among mankind, and the best way and method of warding them off by nobility of character. For thus we shall associate the image of a wrong with the presentation of this rule of conduct, and it will always be at hand for us (Pr.18,II) when we suffer a wrong. Again, if we always have in readiness consideration of our true advantage and also of the good that follows from mutual friendship and social relations, and also remember that supreme contentment of spirit follows from the right way of life (Pr.52,IV), and that men, like everything else, act from the necessity of their nature, then the wrong, or the hatred that is wont to arise from it, will occupy just a small part of our imagination and will easily be overcome. Or if the anger that is wont to arise from grievous wrongs be not easily overcome, it will nevertheless be overcome, though not without vacillation, in a far shorter space of time than if we had not previously reflected on these things in the way I have described, as is evident from Prs.6,7, and 8,V. We ought, in the same way, to reflect on courage to banish fear; we should enumerate and often picture the everyday dangers of life, and how they can best be avoided and overcome by resourcefulness and strength of mind.

But it should be noted that in arranging our thoughts and images we should always concentrate on that which is good in every single thing (Cor.Pr.63,IV and Pr.59,III) so that in so doing we may be determined to act always from the emotion of pleasure. For example, if anyone sees that he is devoted overmuch to the pursuit of honour, let him reflect on its proper function, and the purpose for which it ought to be pursued, and the means by which it can be attained, and not on its abuse and hollowness and the fickleness of mankind and the like, on which nobody reflects except from a morbid disposition. It is by thoughts like these that the most ambitious especially torment themselves when they despair of attaining the honour that they covet, and in vomiting forth their anger they try to make some show of wisdom. It is therefore certain that those who raise the loudest outcry about the abuse of honour and about worldly vanity are most eager for honour. Nor is this trait confined to the ambitious: it is shared by all who meet with adverse fortune and are weak in spirit. For the miser, too, who is in poverty, does not cease to talk of the abuse of money and the vices of the rich, with the result that he merely torments himself and makes it clear that he resents not only his own poverty but also the wealth of others. So, too, those who have been ill-received by a sweetheart are obsessed by thoughts of the fickleness and deceitfulness of women and the other faults commonly attributed to them, but immediately forget about all this as soon as they again find favour with their sweetheart. Therefore he who aims solely from love of freedom to control his emotions and appetites will strive his best to familiarise himself with virtues and their causes and to fill his mind with the joy that arises from the true knowledge of them, while refraining from dwelling on men's faults and abusing mankind and deriving pleasure from a false show of freedom. He who diligently follows these precepts and practises them (for they are not difficult) will surely within a short space of time be able to direct his actions for the most part according to reason's behest.

PROPOSITION 11

In proportion as a mental image is related to more things, the more frequently does it occur—i.e. the more often it springs to life—and the more it engages the mind.

Proof

In proportion as an image or emotion is related to more things, the more causes there are by which it can be aroused and fostered, all of which the mind, by hypothesis, regards simultaneously as a result of the emotion. And so the emotion thereby occurs more frequently —i.e. springs to life more often—and engages the mind the more (Pr. 8,V).

PROPOSITION 12

Images are more readily associated with those images that are related to things which we clearly and distinctly understand than they are to others.

Proof

Things that are clearly and distinctly understood are either the common properties of things or deductions made from them (see Def. of Reason in Sch.2,Pr.40,II) and consequently they are more often before the mind (preceding Pr.). So it is more likely that we should regard other things in conjunction with these than in conjunction with different things, and consequently (Pr.18,II) that they should more readily be associated with these than with others.

PROPOSITION 13

The greater the number of other images with which an image is associated, the more often it springs to life.

Proof

The greater the number of images with which an image is associated, the more causes there are by which it can be aroused (Pr.18,II).

we see how everything fits in to reality.

PROPOSITION 14

The mind can bring it about that all the affections of the body—i.e. images of things—be related to the idea of God. = all of universe.

Proof

There is no affection of the body of which the mind cannot form a clear and distinct conception (Pr.4,V), and so the mind can bring it about (Pr.15,I) that they should all be related to the idea of God.

PROPOSITION 15

He who clearly and distinctly understands himself and his emotions loves God, and the more so the more he understands himself and his emotions.

Proof

He who clearly and distinctly understands himself and his emotions feels pleasure (Pr.53,III) accompanied by the idea of God (preceding Pr.). So (Def. of Emotions 6) he loves God, and, by the same reasoning, the more so the more he understands himself and his emotions.

PROPOSITION 16

This love towards God is bound to hold chief place in the mind.

Proof

This love is associated with all the affections of the body (Pr.14,V), and is fostered by them all (Pr.15,V), and so (Pr.11,V) it is bound to hold chief place in the mind.

PROPOSITION 17

God is without passive emotions, and he is not affected with any emotion of pleasure or pain.

Proof

All ideas, in so far as they are related to God, are true (Pr.32,III), that is (Def.4,II), they are adequate. Thus (Gen. Def. of Emotions) God is without passive emotions. Again, God cannot pass to a state of greater or less perfection (Cor.2,Pr.20,I), and so (Def. of Emotions 2 and 3) he is not affected with any emotion of pleasure or pain.

Corollary

Strictly speaking, God does not love or hate anyone. For God (preceding Pr.) is not affected with any emotion of pleasure or pain, and consequently (Def. of Emotions 6 and 7) he neither loves nor hates anyone.

PROPOSITION 18

Nobody can hate God.

Proof

The idea of God which is in us is adequate and perfect (Prs.46 and 47,II). Therefore in so far as we contemplate God, we are active (Pr.3,III). Consequently (Pr.59,III) there can be no pain accompanied by the idea of God; that is (Def. of Emotions 7), nobody can hate God.

Corollary

Love towards God cannot turn to hatred.

Scholium

It may be objected that in understanding God to be the cause of all things we thereby consider God to be the cause of pain. To this I reply that in so far as we understand the causes of pain, it ceases to be a passive emotion (Pr.3,V); that is (Pr.59,III), to that extent it ceases to be pain. So in so far as we understand God to be the cause of pain, to that extent we feel pleasure.

PROPOSITION 19

He who loves God cannot endeavor that God should love him in return.

Proof

If a man were so to endeavor, he would therefore desire (Cor.Pr.17,V) that God whom he loves should not be God, and consequently (Pr.19,III) he would desire to feel pain, which is absurd (Pr.28,III). Therefore he who loves God . . . etc.

PROPOSITION 20

This love towards God cannot be tainted with emotions of envy or jealousy, but is the more fostered as we think more men to be joined to God by this same bond of love.

Proof

This love towards God is the highest good that we can aim at according to the dictates of reason (Pr.28,IV) and is available to all men (Pr.36,IV), and we desire that all men should enjoy it (Pr.37,IV). Therefore (Def. of Emotions 23) it cannot be stained by the emotion of envy, nor again by the emotion of jealousy (Pr.18,V and Def. of Jealousy, q.v. in Sch.Pr.36,III). On the contrary (Pr.31,III), it is the more fostered as we think more men to be enjoying it.

Scholium

We can in the same way demonstrate that there is no emotion directly contrary to this love by which this love can be destroyed; and so we may conclude that this love towards God is the most constant of all emotions, and in so far as it is related to the body it cannot be destroyed except together with the body. As to its nature in so far as it is related solely to the mind, this we shall examine later on.

With this I have completed the account of all the remedies for the emotions: that is, all that the mind, considered solely in itself, can do against the emotions. From this it is clear that the power of the mind over the emotions consists:

1. In the very knowledge of the emotions (Sch.Pr.4,V).

2. In detaching the emotions from the thought of their external cause, which we imagine confusedly. (See Pr.2 together with Sch.Pr.4,V).

3. In the matter of time, in respect of which the affections that are related to things we understand are superior to those which are related to things that we conceive in a confused or fragmentary way (Pr.7,V).

4. In the number of causes whereby those affections are fostered which are related to the common properties of things, or to God (Prs.9 and 11,V).

5. Lastly, in the order wherein the mind can arrange its emotions and associate them one with another. (Sch.Pr.10 and also Prs. 12,13,14,V).

But in order that this power of the mind over the emotions may be better understood, it is important to note that we call emotions strong when we compare the emotion of one man with that of another, and when we see one man more than another assailed by the same emotion, or when we compare with one another the emotions of the same man and find that the same man is affected or moved by one emotion more than by another. For (Pr.5,IV) the strength of every emotion is defined by the power of an external cause as compared with our own power. Now the power of the mind is defined solely by knowledge, its weakness or passivity solely by the privation of knowledge; that is, it is measured by the extent to which its ideas are said to be inadequate. Hence it follows that that mind is most passive whose greatest part is constituted by inadequate ideas, so that it is characterised more by passivity than by activity. On the other hand, that mind is most active whose greatest part is constituted by adequate ideas, so that even if the latter mind contains as many inadequate ideas as the former, it is characterised by those ideas which are attributed to human virtue rather than by those that point to human weakness.

Again, it should be noted that emotional distress and unhappiness have their origin especially in excessive love towards a thing subject to considerable instability, a thing which we can never completely possess. For nobody is disturbed or anxious about any thing unless he loves it, nor do wrongs, suspicions, enmities, etc. arise except from love towards things which nobody can truly possess.

So from this we readily conceive how effective against the emotions is clear and distinct knowledge, and especially the third kind of knowledge (for which see Sch.Pr.47,II) whose basis is the knowledge of God. In so far as they are passive emotions, if it does not completely destroy them (Pr.3, and Sch.Pr.4,V), at least it brings it about that they constitute the least part of the mind (Pr.14,V). Again, it begets love towards something immutable and eternal (Pr.15,V) which we can truly possess (Pr.45,II), and which therefore cannot be defiled by any of the faults that are to be found in the common sort of love, but can continue to grow more and more (Pr.15,V) and engage the greatest part of the mind (Pr.16,V) and pervade it.

And now I have completed all that concerns this present life; for, as I said at the beginning of this Scholium, in this brief account I have covered all the remedies against the emotions. This everyone can see who gives his mind to the contents of this Scholium, and likewise to the definitions of the mind and its emotions, and lastly to Props. 1 and 3,III. So it is now time to pass on to those matters that concern the duration of the mind without respect to the body.

PROPOSITION 21

The mind can exercise neither imagination nor memory save while the body endures.

Proof

It is only while the body endures that the mind expresses the actual existence of its body and conceives the affections of the body as actual (Cor.Pr.8,II). Consequently (Pr.26,II) it does not conceive any body as actually existing save while its own body endures. Therefore (see Def. of Imagination in Sch.Pr.17,II) it cannot exercise either imagination or memory save while the body endures (See Def. of Memory in Sch.Pr. 18,II).

PROPOSITION 22

Nevertheless there is necessarily in God an idea which expresses the essence of this or that human body under a form of eternity (sub specie aeternitatis).

Proof

God is the cause not only of the existence of this or that human body but also of its essence (Pr.25,I), which must therefore necessarily be conceived through God's essence (Ax.4,I) by a certain eternal necessity (Pr.16,I), and this conception must necessarily be in God (Pr.3,II).

PROPOSITION 23

The human mind cannot be absolutely destroyed along with the body, but something of it remains, which is eternal.

Proof

In God there is necessarily a conception, or idea, which expresses the essence of the human body (preceding Pr.) and which therefore is necessarily something that pertains to the essence of the human mind (Pr.13, II). But we assign to the human mind the kind of duration that can be defined by time only in so far as the mind expresses the actual existence of the body, an existence that is explicated through duration and can be defined by time. That is, we do not assign duration to the mind except while the body endures (Cor.Pr.8,II). However, since that which is conceived by a certain eternal necessity through God's essence is nevertheless a something (preceding Pr.), this something, which pertains to the essence of mind, will necessarily be eternal.

Scholium

As we have said, this idea, which expresses the essence of the body under a form of eternity, is a definite mode of thinking which pertains to the essence of mind, and which is necessarily eternal. Yet it is impossible that we should remember that we existed before the body, since neither can there be any traces of this in the body nor can eternity be defined by time, or be in any way related to time. Nevertheless, we feel and experience that we are eternal. For the mind senses those things that it conceives by its understanding just as much as those which it has in its memory. Logical proofs are the eyes of the mind, whereby it sees and observes things. So although we have no recollection of having existed before the body, we nevertheless sense that our mind, in so far as it involves the essence of the body under a form of eternity, is eternal, and that this aspect of its existence cannot be defined by time, that is, cannot be explicated through duration. Therefore our mind can be said to endure, and its existence to be defined by a definite period of time, only to the extent that it involves the actual existence of the body, and it is only to that extent that it has the power to determine the existence of things by time and to conceive them from the point of view of duration.

PROPOSITION 24

The more we understand particular things, the more we understand God.

Proof

This is evident from Cor.Pr.25,I.

PROPOSITION 25

The highest conatus of the mind and its highest virtue is to understand things by the third kind of knowledge.

Proof

The third kind of knowledge proceeds from the adequate idea of certain of God's attributes to the adequate knowledge of the essence of things (see its definition in Sch.2,Pr.40,II), and the more we understand things in this way, the more we understand God (preceding Pr.). Therefore (Pr.28,IV) the highest virtue of the mind, that is (Def.8,IV), its power or nature, or its highest conatus (Pr.7,III) is to understand things by this third kind of knowledge.

Hobbes is more simplistic and optimistic
Spinoza - pestimiste - better

PROPOSITION 26

The more capable the mind is of understanding things by the third kind of knowledge, the more it desires to understand things by this same kind of knowledge.

Proof

This is evident; for in so far as we conceive the mind to be capable of understanding things by the third kind of knowledge, to that extent we conceive it as determined to understand things by that same kind of knowledge. Consequently (Def. of Emotions 1), the more the mind is capable of this, the more it desires it.

The more you learn about individual things the more you'll learn about the Universe

PROPOSITION 27

From this third kind of knowledge there arises the highest possible contentment of mind.

feels pleased / applausable — When we acheive to see reality gives us highest possible contentment

Proof

The highest virtue of the mind is to know God (Pr.28,IV), that is, to understand things by the third kind of knowledge (Pr.25,V), and this virtue is all the greater the more the mind knows things by the third kind of knowledge (Pr.24,V). So he who knows things by this third kind of knowledge passes to the highest state of human perfection, and consequently (Def. of Emotions 2) is affected by the highest pleasure, this pleasure being accompanied (Pr.43,II) by the idea of himself and his own virtue. Therefore (Def. of Emotions 25) from this kind of knowledge there arises the highest possible contentment.

PROPOSITION 28

The conatus, or desire, to know things by the third kind of knowledge, cannot arise from the first kind of knowledge, but from the second.

Proof

This proposition is self-evident. For whatever we understand clearly and distinctly, we understand either through itself or through something else which is conceived through itself. That is, ideas which are clear and distinct in us or which are related to the third kind of knowledge (Sch.2,Pr.40,II) cannot follow from fragmentary or confused ideas which (same Sch.) are related to the first kind of knowledge, but from adequate ideas, that is, (same Sch.) from the second or third kind of knowledge. Therefore (Def. of Emotions 1) the desire to know things by the third kind of knowledge cannot arise from the first kind of knowledge, but from the second.

PROPOSITION 29

Whatever the mind understands under a form of eternity it does not

More you understand reality the more you become one of the Universe

*understand from the fact that it conceives the present actual existence of
the body, but from the fact that it conceives the essence of the body
under a form of eternity.*

Proof

In so far as the mind conceives the present existence of its body, to
that extent it conceives a duration that can be determined by time, and
only to that extent does it have the power to conceive things in relation to
time (Pr.21,V and Pr.26,II). But eternity cannot be explicated through
duration (Def.8,I and its explication). Therefore to that extent the mind
does not have the power to conceive things under a form of eternity. But
since it is the nature of reason to conceive things under a form of eternity
(Cor.2,Pr.44,II), and since it belongs to the nature of mind, too, to conceive the essence of the body under a form of eternity (Pr.23,V), and
since there belongs to the essence of mind nothing but these two ways of
conceiving (Pr.13,II), it follows that this power to conceive things under
a form of eternity pertains to the mind only in so far as it conceives the
essence of the body under a form of eternity.

Scholium

We conceive things as actual in two ways: either in so far as we conceive them as related to a fixed time and place, or in so far as we conceive
them to be contained in God and to follow from the necessity of the
divine nature. Now the things that are conceived as true or real in this
second way, we conceive under a form of eternity, and their ideas involve
the eternal and infinite essence of God, as we demonstrated in Pr.45,II.
See also its Scholium.

PROPOSITION 30

*Our mind, in so far as it knows both itself and the body under a
form of eternity, necessarily has a knowledge of God, and knows that it
is in God and is conceived through God.*

Proof

Eternity is the very essence of God in so far as this essence involves
necessary existence (Def.8,I). Therefore to conceive things under a form
of eternity is to conceive things in so far as they are conceived through
God's essence as real entities; that is, in so far as they involve existence
through God's essence. Therefore our mind, in so far as it conceives
itself and the body under a form of eternity, necessarily has knowledge
of God, and knows . . . etc.

PROPOSITION 31

*The third kind of knowledge depends on the mind as its formal
cause in so far as the mind is eternal.*

Proof

The mind conceives nothing under a form of eternity except in so far as it conceives the essence of its body under a form of eternity (Pr.29,V), that is (Prs.21 and 23,V), except in so far as the mind is eternal. Therefore (preceding Pr.) in so far as it is eternal, it has knowledge of God, knowledge which is necessarily adequate (Pr.46,II). Therefore the mind, in so far as it is eternal, is capable of knowing all the things that can follow from this given knowledge of God (Pr.40,II): that is, of knowing things by the third kind of knowledge (see its definition in Sch.2,Pr.40, II), of which the mind is therefore (Def.1,III) the adequate or formal cause in so far as it is eternal.

Scholium

So the more each man is advanced in this kind of knowledge, the more clearly conscious he is of himself and of God, that is, the more perfect and blessed he is, as will become even more evident from what is to follow. But here it should be noted that although we are at this point certain that the mind is eternal in so far as it conceives things under a form of eternity, yet, to facilitate the explanation and render more readily intelligible what I intend to demonstrate, we shall consider the mind as if it were now beginning to be and were now beginning to understand things under a form of eternity, as we have been doing hitherto. This we may do without any danger of error, provided we are careful to reach no conclusion except from premisses that are quite clear.

PROPOSITION 32

We take pleasure in whatever we understand by the third kind of knowledge, and this is accompanied by the idea of God as cause.

Proof

From this kind of knowledge there arises the highest possible contentment of mind (Pr.27,V), that is (Def. of Emotions 25), the highest possible pleasure, and this is accompanied by the idea of oneself, and consequently (Pr.30,V) also by the idea of God, as cause.

Corollary

From the third kind of knowledge there necessarily arises the intellectual love of God (amor Dei intellectualis). For from this kind of knowledge there arises (preceding Pr.) pleasure accompanied by the idea of God as cause, that is (Def. of Emotions 6), the love of God not in so far as we imagine him as present (Pr.29,V) but in so far as we understand God to be eternal. And this is what I call the intellectual love of God.

PROPOSITION 33

The intellectual love of God which arises from the third kind of knowledge is eternal.

Proof

The third kind of knowledge is eternal (Pr.31,V and Ax.3,I), and therefore (by the same Ax.3,I) the love that arises from it is also necessarily eternal.

Scholium

Although this love towards God has had no beginning (preceding Pr.), it yet has all the perfections of love just as if it had originated in the manner we supposed in the corollary to the preceding proposition. There is no difference, except that the mind has possessed from eternity those perfections which we then supposed to be accruing to it, accompanied by the idea of God as eternal cause. If pleasure consists in the transition to a state of greater perfection, blessedness must surely consist in this, that the mind is endowed with perfection itself.

PROPOSITION 34

It is only while the body endures that the mind is subject to passive emotions.

Proof

Imagining is the idea whereby the mind regards some thing as present (see its definition in Sch.Pr.17,II), an idea which, however, indicates the present state of the body rather than the nature of an external thing (Cor.2,Pr.16,II). Therefore an emotion (Gen. Def. of Emotions) is an imagining in so far as it indicates the present state of the body. So (Pr.21,V) it is only while the body endures that the mind is subject to passive emotions.

Corollary

Hence it follows that no love is eternal except for intellectual love (amor intellectualis).

Scholium

If we turn our attention to the common belief entertained by men, we shall see that they are indeed conscious of the eternity of the mind, but they confuse it with duration and assign it to imagination or to memory, which they believe to continue after death.

PROPOSITION 35

God loves himself with an infinite intellectual love.

Proof

God is absolutely infinite (Def.6,I), that is (Def.6,II), God's nature enjoys infinite perfection, accompanied (Pr.3,II) by the idea of itself, that is (Pr.11 and Def.1,I), by the idea of its own cause; and that is what, in Cor.Pr.32,V, we declared to be intellectual love.

PROPOSITION 36

The mind's intellectual love towards God is the love of God wherewith God loves himself not in so far as he is infinite, but in so far as he can be explicated through the essence of the human mind considered under a form of eternity. That is, the mind's intellectual love towards God is part of the infinite love wherewith God loves himself.

Proof

This, the mind's love, must be related to the active nature of the mind (Cor.Pr.32,V and Pr.3,III), and is therefore an activity whereby the mind regards itself, accompanied by the idea of God as cause (Pr.32,V and Cor.); that is (Cor.Pr.25,I and Cor.Pr.11,II), an activity whereby God, in so far as he can be explicated through the human mind, regards himself, accompanied by the idea of himself. And therefore (preceding Pr.) this, the mind's love, is part of the infinite love wherewith God loves himself.

Corollary

Hence it follows that God, in so far as he loves himself, loves mankind, and, consequently, that the love of God towards men and the mind's intellectual love towards God are one and the same.

Scholium

From this we clearly understand in what our salvation or blessedness or freedom consists, namely, in the constant and eternal love towards God, that is, in God's love towards men. This love or blessedness is called glory in the Holy Scriptures, and rightly so. For whether this love be related to God or to the mind, it can properly be called spiritual contentment, which in reality cannot be distinguished from glory (Def. of Emotions, 25 and 30). For in so far as it is related to God, it is (Pr.35,V) pleasure (if we may still use this term) accompanied by the idea of himself, and this is also the case in so far as it is related to the mind (Pr.27,V). Again, since the essence of our mind consists solely in knowledge, whose principle and basis is God (Pr.15,I and Sch.Pr.47,II), it follows that we see quite clearly how and in what way our mind, in respect of essence and existence, follows from the divine nature and is continuously dependent on God.

I have thought this worth noting here in order to show by this example the superiority of that knowledge of particular things which I have called 'intuitive' or 'of the third kind,' and its preferability to that abstract knowledge which I have called 'knowledge of the second kind.' For although I demonstrated in a general way in Part I that everything (and consequently the human mind, too) is dependent on God in respect of its essence and of its existence, that proof, although legitimate and exempt from any shadow of doubt, does not so strike the mind as when it is inferred from the essence of each particular thing which we assert to be dependent on God.

PROPOSITION 37

There is nothing in Nature which is contrary to this intellectual love, or which can destroy it.

Proof

This intellectual love follows necessarily from the nature of the mind in so far as that is considered as an eternal truth through God's nature (Prs.33 and 29,V). Therefore if there were anything that was contrary to this love, it would be contrary to truth, and consequently that which could destroy this love could cause truth to be false, which, as is self-evident, is absurd. Therefore there is nothing in Nature . . . etc.

Scholium

The Axiom in Part IV is concerned with particular things in so far as they are considered in relation to a definite time and place, of which I think no one can be in doubt.

PROPOSITION 38

The greater the number of things the mind understands by the second and third kinds of knowledge, the less subject it is to emotions that are bad, and the less it fears death.

Proof

The essence of the mind consists in knowledge (Pr.11,II). Therefore the greater the number of things the mind knows by the second and third kinds of knowledge, the greater is the part of it that survives (Prs.23 and 29,V), and consequently (preceding Pr.) the greater is that part of it that is not touched by emotions contrary to our nature; that is (Pr.30,IV) by emotions that are bad. Therefore the greater the number of things the mind understands by the second and third kinds of knowledge, the greater is that part of it that remains unimpaired, and consequently the less subject it is to emotions . . . etc.

Scholium

Hence we understand that point which I touched upon in Sch.Pr.39,IV and which I promised to explain in this part, namely that death is less hurtful in proportion as the mind's clear and distinct knowledge is greater, and consequently the more the mind loves God. Again, since (Pr.27,V) from the third kind of knowledge there arises the highest possible contentment, hence it follows that the human mind can be of such a nature that that part of it that we have shown to perish with the body (Pr.21,V) is of no account compared with that part of it that survives. But I shall be dealing with this at greater length in due course.

PROPOSITION 39

He whose body is capable of the greatest amount of activity has a mind whose greatest part is eternal.

Proof

He whose body is capable of the greatest amount of activity is least assailed by emotions that are evil (Pr.38,IV), that is (Pr.30,IV), by emotions that are contrary to our nature. Thus (Pr.10,V) he has the capacity to arrange and associate the affections of the body according to intellectual order and consequently to bring it about (Pr.14,V) that all the affections of the body are related to God. This will result (Pr.15,V) in his being affected with love towards God, a love (Pr.16,V) that must occupy or constitute the greatest part of the mind. Therefore (Pr.33,V) he has a mind whose greatest part is eternal.

Scholium

Since human bodies are capable of a great many activities, there is no doubt that they can be of such a nature as to be related to minds which have great knowledge of themselves and of God, and whose greatest or chiefest part is eternal, with the result that they scarcely fear death. But in order that this may be more clearly understood, it should here be remarked that our lives are subject to continual variation, and as the change is for the better or worse, so we are said to be fortunate or unfortunate. For he who passes from being a baby or child into being a corpse is said to be unfortunate; while, on the other hand, to have been able to pass the whole of one's life with a healthy mind in a healthy body is regarded as a mark of good fortune. And in fact he who, like a baby or a child, has a body capable of very little activity and is most dependent on external causes, has a mind which, considered solely in itself, has practically no consciousness of itself, of God, or of things, while he whose body is capable of very considerable activity has a mind which, considered solely in itself, is highly conscious of itself and of God and of things. In this life, therefore, we mainly endeavor that the body of childhood, as far as its nature allows and is conducive thereto, should develop into a body that is capable of a great many activities and is related to a mind that is highly conscious of itself, of God, and of things, and in such a way that everything relating to its memory or imagination should be of scarcely any importance in comparison with its intellect, as I have already stated in the scholium to the preceding proposition.

PROPOSITION 40

The more perfection a thing has, the more active and the less passive it is. Conversely, the more active it is, the more perfect it is.

Proof

The more perfect a thing is, the more reality it has (Def.6,II); consequently (Pr.3,III and Sch.), the more active it is and the less passive. This proof proceeds in the same manner in inverse order, from which it follows that a thing is the more perfect as it is more active.

Corollary

Hence it follows that the part of the mind that survives, of whatever extent it may be, is more perfect than the rest. For the eternal part of the mind (Prs.23 and 29,V) is the intellect, through which alone we are said to be active (Pr.3,III), whereas that part which we have shown to perish is the imagination (Pr.21,V), through which alone we are said to be passive (Pr.3,III and Gen. Def. of Emotions). Therefore the former (preceding Pr.), of whatever extent it be, is more perfect than the latter.

Scholium

This is what I had resolved to demonstrate concerning the mind in so far as it is considered without reference to the existence of the body. It is clear from this, and also from Pr.21,I and other propositions, that our mind, in so far as it understands, is an eternal mode of thinking which is determined by another eternal mode of thinking, and this again by another, and so on ad infinitum, with the result that they all together constitute the eternal and infinite intellect of God.

PROPOSITION 41

Even if we did not know that our mind is eternal, we should still regard as being of prime importance piety and religion and, to sum up completely, everything which in Part IV we showed to be related to courage and nobility.

Proof

The first and only basis of virtue, that is, of the right way of life (Cor.Pr.22 and Pr.24,IV), is to seek one's own advantage. Now in order to determine what reason prescribes as advantageous we took no account of the mind's eternity, a topic which we did not consider until Part V. So although at that point we were unaware that the mind is eternal, we regarded as being of prime importance whatever is related to courage and nobleness. So even if now we were unaware of the mind's eternity, we should still regard the said precepts of reason as being of prime importance.

Scholium

The common belief of the multitude seems to be quite different. For the majority appear to think that they are free to the extent that they can indulge their lusts, and that they are giving up their rights to the extent that they are required to live under the commandments of the divine law. So they believe that piety and religion, in fact everything related to strength of mind, are burdens which they hope to lay aside after death, when they will receive the reward of their servitude, that is, of piety and religion. And it is not by this hope alone, but also and especially by fear of incurring dreadful punishment after death, that they are induced to live according to the commandments of the divine law as far as their feebleness and impotent spirit allows. And if men did not have this hope and this fear, and if they believed on the contrary that minds perish with bodies and that they, miserable creatures, worn out by the burden of piety, had no prospect of further existence, they would return to their own inclinations and decide to shape their lives according to their lusts, and to be ruled by fortune rather than by themselves. This seems to me no less absurd than if a man, not believing that he can sustain his body on good food forever, were to decide to glut himself on poisons and deadly fare; or, on realising that the mind is not eternal or immortal, he preferred to be mad and to live without reason. Such attitudes are so absurd that they are scarcely worth recounting.

PROPOSITION 42

Blessedness is not the reward of virtue, but virtue itself. We do not enjoy blessedness because we keep our lusts in check. On the contrary, it is because we enjoy blessedness that we are able to keep our lusts in check.

Proof

Blessedness consists in love towards God (Pr.36,V and Sch.), a love that arises from the third kind of knowledge (Cor.Pr.32,V), and so this love (Prs.59 and 3,III) must be related to the mind in so far as the mind is active; and therefore it is virtue itself (Def.8,IV). That is the first point. Again, the more the mind enjoys this divine love or blessedness, the more it understands (Pr.32,V); that is (Cor.Pr.3,V), the more power it has over the emotions and (Pr.38,V) the less subject it is to emotions that are bad. So the mind's enjoyment of this divine love or blessedness gives it the power to check lusts. And since human power to keep lusts in check consists solely in the intellect, nobody enjoys blessedness because he has kept his emotions in check. On the contrary, the power to keep lusts in check arises from blessedness itself.

Scholium

I have now completed all that I intended to demonstrate concerning the power of the mind over the emotions and concerning the freedom of the mind. This makes clear how strong the wise man is and how much he surpasses the ignorant man whose motive force is only lust. The ignorant man, besides being driven hither and thither by external causes, never possessing true contentment of spirit, lives as if he were unconscious of himself, God, and things, and as soon as he ceases to be passive, he at once ceases to be at all. On the other hand, the wise man, in so far as he is considered as such, suffers scarcely any disturbance of spirit, but being conscious, by virtue of a certain eternal necessity, of himself, of God and of things, never ceases to be, but always possesses true spiritual contentment.

If the road I have pointed out as leading to this goal seems very difficult, yet it can be found. Indeed, what is so rarely discovered is bound to be hard. For if salvation were ready to hand and could be discovered without great toil, how could it be that it is almost universally neglected? All things excellent are as difficult as they are rare.

END

INTRODUCTION

This brief essay is both early and unfinished. In recent years several scholars have claimed that this treatise (henceforth "TIE," for "Tractatus de Intellectus Emendatione") was Spinoza's first philosophical effort. In a letter written in April of 1662 Spinoza reports that he has written a treatise that contains a part devoted to the topic of "the emendation of the intellect" (Letter 6). It has been suggested that at this early phase in Spinoza's philosophical career he had been engaged in writing a comprehensive philosophical work, a part of which concerned a theme that was of major interest to Spinoza's contemporaries—methodology. In the TIE Spinoza refers to such a larger work as "My Philosophy." Most likely this is his *Short Treatise on God, Man and His Well-being.* The editors of Spinoza's posthumous works claimed that Spinoza had intended to finish the TIE but was "snatched away by death." Modern scholars have maintained, however, that Spinoza left the essay in its incomplete form because either he got into philosophical knots from which he was unable to extricate himself or he "outgrew" some of its ideas by the time he started to work on the *Ethics,* which was only a few years later. Whatever the reason, Spinoza's treatise contains several important elements of his theory of knowledge that remained constant throughout his thinking and writing. It is therefore an expression not only of his early epistemological views but of a persistent philosophical orientation, from whose main lines he never deviated.

The title of the essay deserves some comment. The term 'emendation' connotes in English correction or improvement. But since Spinoza believes, as we shall see, that the human intellect is in some sense perfect, or at least competent to reach the important truths, it really doesn't need to be improved or corrected. In the essay itself he speaks of the need to "purge the mind" or "to heal the mind." The intellect seems to be one of several faculties, or parts, of the mind, which can be contaminated by the other parts, especially the imagination, hence, the need to purify or purge the intellect from these "foreign" elements. In this respect the TIE bears comparison with Descartes' early essay *Rules for the Direction of the Mind* or his *Discourse on Method.* These treatises, as well as many other philosophical works of the pe-

riod, are intended to set the philosophical novice on the right road to
and in philosophy by advising how to cleanse the mind of unnecessary
dross and how to avoid error. Thus, Spinoza frequently refers to the
main theme of the TIE as "Method," whose meaning is 'the right
road.'

Before Spinoza begins on this path, however, he motivates the
reader by showing that intellectual purification is an important, perhaps the most important, goal in the pursuit of human happiness. The
opening paragraphs of the essay sound the theme of the ancient Greek
philosophers: What kind of life should a person pursue? Like Aristotle, Spinoza quickly realizes that worldly goods in and of themselves
are not sufficient and satisfying: They depend entirely on external factors; even to acquire them, we need something else, namely, the intellect. What is truly ours and independent of anything else is the
intellect. Thus, for Spinoza the life of intellectual perfection and activity is the only one worth pursuing and living. Not that he despises the
nonintellectual goods: They have their place, but it is clearly subordinate to what Spinoza calls later in the treatise "the union of the mind
with the totality of Nature." It is clear then that the methodological
focus of the TIE is essentially practical: The purification of the mind
has as its goal the liberation of intellect, so that it can pursue what is
truly human. Virtually every one of Spinoza's philosophical works has
a practical thrust; his major philosophical book has, of course, the title
Ethics. Even when the topic is methodological, the goal is moral.

The first step in this process of healing the intellect is to take a survey of all the various types of human cognition or, better, what we
take to be cognition. Quite early in the treatise Spinoza introduces us
to a classification schema that recurs in both the *Short Treatise* and the
Ethics, although with modifications. Here in the TIE he distinguishes
four different modes of perception, or cognition: 1) indirect information or hearsay; 2) random or vague sense experience; 3) causal inferences; and, finally, 4) the kind of perception in which we know a thing
through its essence or proximate cause. Levels 1 and 2 are so defective
that for Spinoza they are not genuine cases of knowledge. Reports are
simply secondhand beliefs, which we all know are frequently distor-
tions, if not utterly false. Random sensory experience is just that;
since we don't know the underlying causes, it really is superficial and
unstructured. The third type of perception is an improvement, since
here we form causal generalizations on the basis of our experience or
infer some properties of things from more general, empirically
grounded propositions. Spinoza regards this kind of perception as inadequate, however, because it proceeds merely from effect to cause
and does so in a general or abstract way, without getting at the essence
of the cause. Only the fourth type of perception is adequate cognition,
for now the mind apprehends the thing directly through its proximate
cause or its essence. Later in the essay Spinoza will identify this essence with the proper definition of the thing (Paragraphs 94–98). Here
Spinoza calls this kind of perception "intuitive," suggesting that it is a

noninferential kind of cognition (Paragraph 24). The term 'intuitive' plays an important role in the *Ethics,* where intuitive science is explicitly asserted to be the knowledge of God that we should strive to attain in order to achieve blessedness (*Ethics* V:Prs. 24–33). In the *Ethics,* however, it is not altogether clear whether intuition is still noninferential, since Spinoza characterizes it as an adequate knowledge of God's Attributes by means of which we proceed to have adequate knowledge of the essences of particular things (*Ethics* II:Pr.40, Sch.2 and V:Pr.25). There is more than just a suggestion here that this highest level of cognition is deductive and comprehensive, as well as specific. Having distinguished the various types of perception and after specifying the type that is uniquely adequate, Spinoza now takes upon himself the task of indicating the proper method for attaining this kind of perception.

But it is also at this point that someone might object: How can we look for the right method to acquire knowledge, when to find this method we need to know whether we have indeed found the right one? Spinoza seems to be caught in the same circle or vicious regress that Plato in the *Meno* and Descartes in the *Third Meditation* were faced with. Spinoza doesn't think so. We are not trapped in a circle or a vicious regress, because we have at the outset "innate intellectual instruments," or "true ideas," that are specimens of what we are looking for. In some important sense, the "truth is within us." Possessing these true ideas, we can readily use them for gaining new ideas. Each such idea shows itself to be true: "The truth is its own sign," as Spinoza likes to say. Of such ideas we are certain that they are true. The method consists in a knowledge of the true idea, or a "reflection on truth." In methodology we examine the true ideas we already possess to determine their internal marks, or signs. One such sign is self-evidence: All true ideas are either self-evident or reducible to self-evident ideas. Once these ideas are recognized, we need only to proceed carefully and orderly, i.e., "methodically," and we will be on the "right road."

Spinoza's appeal to these innate instruments of the intellect, by means of which it forges its own cognitive material for further intellectual work, is reminiscent of Plato and Descartes, who also made use of the notion of "innatism." Whatever the exact lines of intellectual affiliation, Spinoza's use of this metaphor has its own flavor. Later in the essay he introduces another metaphor that is quite interesting on its own account: The intellect is, he says, a "spiritual automaton" that operates according to its own laws, independent of external stimuli and inputs (Paragraphs 85–86). By this metaphor Spinoza suggests that the intellect is a kind of "computing system" that generates by its own rules the basic sources of its cognitive capital. Since for Spinoza ideas are essentially propositional, virtually equivalent to judgments, a true idea is a true proposition that the intellect forms and assents to on its own. On the basis of these initial truths, the intellect proceeds "methodically" to derive other truths and eventually attains its ultimate goal of constructing an adequate and relatively complete picture of the structure of Nature; just as the earliest artisans began with very primitive tools (their hands) and went on to make more sophisticated tools for the manufacture of even more complicated devices and machines.

Even at this early stage in his discussion, Spinoza introduces another important concept that will play a significant role in his philosophy—the true idea of God. Although we have many true ideas and several that can be considered as basic, one stands out as "privileged" for Spinoza. He tells us that we must quickly recognize or perceive the idea of the most perfect being, or the First Cause, the "origin and source of the whole of Nature" (Paragraphs 38 and 42). Two points in connexion with this concept should be noted. First, the true idea of God is the source of many other ideas. Once we adequately apprehend this idea, we are able to deduce other true ideas, especially those relevant to the study of nature. Second, the phrase "the origin and source of the whole of Nature" is ambiguous, since it can connote the biblical idea of divine creation or the philosophical concept of God as the transcendent First Cause of the world. Spinoza's position differs from both these traditional theses. As Part I of the *Ethics* shows, Spinoza's God is in some sense identical with nature. This is also suggested in paragraphs 75–76 of the TIE, where Spinoza introduces the notion of the "primary elements of Nature as a whole" and equates these primary elements with God, the "origin and source of Nature." These "primary elements" are the divine attributes, the substantial and constitutive factors of and in nature, which Spinoza entitles "Natura naturans" in the *Ethics* and *Short Treatise*. The rest of nature consists of that which is caused eternally and necessarily by God: Natura naturata, or the modes, in the language of the *Ethics* (*Ethics* I:Pr.29 Scholium. See Introduction under "God and Nature.").

Since the major and first theme of the TIE is the purging of the intellect, Spinoza devotes considerable space to an analysis of those mental contents that must be eliminated or diminished in order to liberate the intellect. As we all know, we are often plagued by doubt, fantasy, and error. Spinoza proceeds to offer a philosophical therapy for the cure and purgation of these "mental diseases." Referring anonymously to Descartes, Spinoza boldly claims that skepticism is really not a genuine problem. No one can really doubt a true idea or not know that a true idea is true (paragraph 47). Spinoza, unlike Descartes, has no patience with the skeptic: The skeptic is for him either not conscious of what he is saying, insincere, or just plain stupid. This does not mean that Spinoza doesn't recognize that we are all subject to doubt. But doubting occurs when we have a conflict of ideas no one of which is sufficiently "clear and distinct." This occurs because of the fragmentary or disorderly character of our information. A clear and distinct, or true, idea is indubitable (Paragraph 80). The contaminating ideas that have to be eliminated are fictions and falsehoods. By the former Spinoza means suppositions: We imagine life on Mars, or we imagine a being whose essence is both human and feline.

The first thing to note is that in supposing such an existent state of affairs or essence, we are using our imagination, a faculty that is virtually unlimited in its power to present us with ideas of the most extraordinary kind. The more we exercise our intellect, however, the more restrained our imagination becomes, i.e., ideas are now regulated by the rules of logic and the laws of science. Indeed, the more we know Nature, the more we recognize that many of these suppositions are truly impossible; e.g., there cannot be a being that is both human and feline. Or, the more we know Nature, the more we recognize that some of our suppositions are necessarily true; e.g., motion is a necessary fact of Nature. The intellect can demonstrate that an existent state of affairs is necessary or that a nonexistent state of affairs is impossible. There is no genuine contingency (Paragraph 53; Ethics I:Pr.33,Sch.1). Our original suppositions were just reflections of our ignorance or confusion.

On the other hand, these fictions are less worrisome than false ideas. For in a false idea there is an affirmation or denial: We no longer merely suppose some state of affairs but assert its existence. In such a case, Spinoza claims, we have an idea A but no other idea B or C from which we can see that A is false, so we affirm A. As in the case of fictitious ideas, false ideas result from fragmentary information. For example, not having too much mathematical knowledge, a person believes that one infinite magnitude cannot be larger than another (See Letter 12). In general, falsity occurs when we assign a property to something that doesn't belong to its proper concept; e.g., I affirm of the deity that it can be divided. The true idea of God is such that divisibility cannot be one of its properties (Paragraph 72.*Ethics* I:Prs.12–13). In sum, the more we use the intellect, the less subject we are to the snares of the imagination. It is the intellect that furnishes us with ideas whose truth is immediately recognizable. Why settle for anything else?

The second part of the TIE is concerned with the proper order in our inquiries. Already Spinoza has hinted at the notion of beginning with an idea that is not only basic but so fertile that we can deduce from it many other, perhaps all, the true ideas. At this juncture in the treatise, this notion becomes increasingly important and serves to introduce into this essay on method several metaphysical themes. As we have seen, this "privileged" idea is the idea of a First Cause. To make this idea the basis of our thinking, we have to have a correct definition of this being. But before we can formulate such a definition, we need to have a clear understanding of the nature of definition. This is now the main theme of the remainder of the treatise.

Spinoza immediately lays down two rules: 1) Definitions ought to be as "particular" as possible: Instead of beginning with definitions of the more abstract genera and species, we should start with the "physical" particular thing, which is for Spinoza "Real" (Paragraphs 95 and 99). 2) The definition ought to formulate the essence of a particular thing, not its derivative properties. Although reminiscent of Aris-

totle's distinction between essential properties and accidental properties, Spinoza's distinction should not be identified with it, since
Spinoza was critical of Aristotle's theory of definition, which he believed was too abstract and presupposed an incorrect metaphysical
foundation (*Ethics* II: Pr.40,Sch.1). However, in the TIE, Spinoza's
distinction between the essence of a thing and its properties is not
adequately developed, and we have to turn to the later works for a
fuller treatment of this subject.

After these rules have been stated, Spinoza proceeds to make a fundamental distinction between definitions of created things and definitions of uncreated things. Again we can see the metaphysical
overtones of his theory of definitions. Since there is for Spinoza a very
important distinction between God, or Substance, and modes, the
corresponding definitions have a different logic. (Note that for Spinoza God can be defined, contrary to the common view of the medieval philosophers and theologians that God is indefinable.) A created
thing should be defined in terms of its proximate cause, such that from
this cause all the properties of this thing can be deduced. In other
words, the definition "generates" the thing. Spinoza gives this example: The definition of a circle as a figure that is described by any line of
which one end is fixed and the other movable literally generates the
circle by providing a procedure whereby we "make" the thing to be
defined. Since the uncreated thing is not made, its logic of definition
will differ: To define an uncreated thing, we need to show that such a
thing cannot have a cause for its existence; i.e., it is its own cause.
Such a definition makes the question "Does such an entity exist?"
pointless. Again, Spinoza reminds us, the definition should be fertile:
From it we should be able to deduce all the other properties of this
uncreated thing.

In the course of this discussion, Spinoza introduces into his story a
new character that has occasioned considerable controversy concerning its identity. Insisting that our definitions should be of real, physical things, Spinoza tells us that these things are not identical with the
"fixed and eternal things," which constitute their essences. Spinoza
characterizes these fixed and eternal things as the laws according to
which the particular things come into existence and are ordered; indeed, they are the proximate causes of these things (Paragraphs 99–
101). Some scholars have suggested that these fixed things are the divine attributes; others have claimed that they are the infinite modes
that follow directly from God, of which these particular things are
parts or exemplifications. Saturn, for example, is a particular moving
body (i.e., finite mode) whose behavior is to be understood through
the attribute of Extension; but it is also a specific exemplification of
the infinite mode that follows from Extension, motion, and rest (*Ethics* II:Pr.13, axioms 1–2, lemmas 1–2; Letters 64 and 81). Both the
attribute and the infinite mode are eternal (*Ethics* I:Pr.10, Sch. and
Prs.21–23).

The concluding paragraphs of the TIE take us back to our original theme: the human intellect. Spinoza asks whether we can acquire knowledge of the intellect's powers. We can if we attend to the properties of the intellect that are clearly and distinctly understood. In addition to those features that have already been noted—certainty, truth, "innateness," among others—Spinoza mentions a characteristic that will play a very important role in his *Ethics*: the intellect has the power to consider things "under some form of eternity" (paragraph 108). Since both the First Cause and the laws in accordance with which particular, changeable things are generated and ordered are eternal, the highest form of knowledge is to apprehend even mutable things as in some sense eternal. Time and duration are for Spinoza modes of the imagination, which, we have seen, needs to be separated from the intellect and eliminated as much as possible from our intellectual operations. To perceive particular mutable things under an aspect of eternity is to recognize their fixed place within a comprehensive, indeed infinite scheme whose ultimate ground is God, an eternal, immutable being. Such an insight is the true good that we sought at the outset of our inquiry and the ultimate purpose for purifying the intellect.

Seymour Feldman
Rutgers University

TRANSLATOR'S PREFACE

The text adopted is that of Gebhardt (1925), with a few changes proposed by Mignini. These changes are marked by translator's footnotes.

The paragraph numbers introduced by Bruder, and now generally accepted, are included for ease of reference. But my paragraphing is not consistently either Gebhardt's or Bruder's.

Footnotes are of two kinds. Spinoza's own, of which there are many, are indicated by letters, as in Gebhardt; mine, usually referring to textual matters, are indicated by asterisks.

This work, probably the earliest of Spinoza's Latin writings, presents special difficulties to the translator, partly because it was never adequately revised, and partly because Spinoza had not yet attained such facility in Latin as appears in his later works. This latter point is attested by the comment of his friends the editors of the *Opera Posthuma*—'adhuc rudia et impolita.'

I am, of course, indebted to all previous translators of this work. But I hope that this new translation will be considered as justified.

NOTICE TO THE READER

(by the editors of the *Opera Posthuma*)

This "Treatise on the Emendation of the Intellect, etc.," which in its unfinished state we here present to you, dear reader, was written by our author many years ago. He always intended to finish it, but, distracted by his other occupations and taken from us by death, he did not succeed in bringing it to the desired conclusion. But since it contains many excellent and useful things which we are convinced will be of considerable interest to an earnest seeker after truth, we did not wish to deprive you of them. That you may the more readily excuse occasional obscurities and lack of polish that appear in places in the text, we have thought it proper that you, too, should be made aware of these circumstances.

TREATISE ON THE EMENDATION
OF THE INTELLECT

and on the way by which it is best directed to the true
knowledge of things

After experience had taught me the hollowness and futility of every- 1
thing that is ordinarily encountered in daily life, and I realised that all
the things which were the source and object of my anxiety held nothing of good or evil in themselves save in so far as the mind was influenced by them, I resolved at length to enquire whether there existed a
true good, one which was capable of communicating itself and could
alone affect the mind to the exclusion of all else, whether, in fact, there
was something whose discovery and acquisition would afford me a
continuous and supreme joy to all eternity.

I say 'I resolved at length,' for at first sight it seemed ill-advised to 2
risk the loss of what was certain in the hope of something at that time
uncertain. I could well see the advantages that derive from honour
and wealth, and that I would be forced to abandon their quest if I were
to devote myself to some new and different objective. And if in fact
supreme happiness were to be found in the former, I must inevitably
fail to attain it, whereas if it did not lie in these objectives and I devoted myself entirely to them, then once again I would lose that highest happiness.

I therefore debated whether it might be possible to arrive at a new 3
guiding principle—or at least the sure hope of its attainment—without changing the manner and normal routine of my life. This I frequently attempted, but in vain. For the things which for the most part
offer themselves in life, and which, to judge from their actions, men
regard as the highest good, can be reduced to these three headings:
riches, honour, and sensual pleasure. With these three the mind is so
distracted that it is quite incapable of thinking of any other good.
With regard to sensual pleasure, the mind is so utterly obsessed by it 4
that it seems as if it were absorbed in some good, and so is quite pre-
vented from thinking of anything else. But after the enjoyment of this
pleasure there ensues a profound depression which, if it does not completely inhibit the mind, leads to its confusion and enervation. The
pursuit of honour and wealth, too, engrosses the mind to no small
degree, especially when the latter is sought exclusively for its own

5   sake,[a] for it is then regarded as the highest good. Even more so is the
       mind obsessed with honour, for this is always regarded as a good in
       itself and the ultimate end to which everything is directed. Then
       again, in both these cases, there is no repentance as in the case of
       sensual pleasure. The more each of them is possessed, the more our
       joy is enhanced, and we are therefore more and more induced to in-
       crease them both. But if it should come about that our hopes are dis-
       appointed, there ensues a profound depression. And finally, honour
       has this great drawback, that to attain it we must conduct our lives to
       suit other men, avoiding what the masses avoid and seeking what the
       masses seek.

6   So when I saw that all these things stood in the way of my embark-
       ing on a new course, and were indeed so opposed to it that I must
       necessarily choose between the one alternative and the other, I was
       forced to ask what was to my greater advantage; for, as I have said, I
       seemed set on losing a certain good for the sake of an uncertain good.
       But after a little reflection, I first of all realised that if I abandoned the
       old ways and embarked on a new way of life, I should be abandoning a
       good that was by its very nature uncertain—as we can clearly gather
       from what has been said—in favour of one that was uncertain not of
       its own nature (for I was seeking a permanent good) but only in re-
7   spect of its attainment. Then persistent meditation enabled me to see
       that, if only I could be thoroughly resolute, I should be abandoning
       certain evils for the sake of a certain good. For I saw that my situation
       was one of great peril and that I was obliged to seek a remedy with all
       my might, however uncertain it might be, like a sick man suffering
       from a fatal malady who, foreseeing certain death unless a remedy is
       forthcoming, is forced to seek it, however uncertain it be, with all his
       might, for therein lies all his hope. Now all those objectives that are
       commonly pursued not only contribute nothing to the preservation of
       our being but even hinder it, being frequently the cause of the destruc-
       tion of those who gain possession of them, and invariably
8   the cause of the destruction of those who are possessed by them.[b] For
       there are numerous examples of men who have suffered persecution
       unto death because of their wealth, and also of men who have exposed
       themselves to so many dangers to acquire riches that they have finally
       paid for their folly with their lives. Nor are there less numerous exam-
       ples of men who, to gain or preserve honour, have suffered a most
       wretched fate. Finally, there are innumerable examples of men who
       have hastened their death by reason of excessive sensual pleasure.

9   These evils, moreover, seemed to arise from this, that all happiness
       or unhappiness depends solely on the quality of the object to which we

---

[a] This could be explained more fully and clearly by making a distinction between
wealth that is sought for its own sake, for the sake of honour, for sensual pleasure, for
health, or for the advancement of the sciences and the arts. But this is reserved for its
proper place, such a detailed investigation being inappropriate here.

[b] This is to be demonstrated at greater length.

are bound by love. For strife will never arise on account of that which is not loved; there will be no sorrow if it is lost, no envy if it is possessed by another, no fear, no hatred—in a word, no emotional agitation, all of which, however, occur in the case of the love of perishable things, such as all those of which we have been speaking. But love   10 towards a thing eternal and infinite feeds the mind with joy alone, unmixed with any sadness. This is greatly to be desired, and to be sought with all our might. However, it was not without reason that I used these words, 'If only I could be earnestly resolute,' for although I perceived these things quite clearly in my mind, I could not on that account put aside all greed, sensual pleasure, and desire for esteem.

This one thing I could see, that as long as my mind was occupied   11 with these thoughts, it turned away from those other objectives and earnestly applied itself to the quest for a new guiding principle. This was a great comfort to me, for I saw that those evils were not so persistent as to refuse to yield to remedies. And although at first these intermissions were rare and of very brief duration, nevertheless, as the true good became more and more discernible to me, these intermissions became more frequent and longer, especially when I realised that the acquisition of money, sensual pleasure, and esteem is a hindrance only as long as they are sought on their own account, and not as a means to other things. If they are sought as means, they will then be under some restriction, and far from being hindrances, they will do much to further the end for which they are sought, as I shall demonstrate in its proper place.

At this point I shall only state briefly what I understand by the true   12 good, and at the same time what is the supreme good. In order that this may be rightly understood, it must be borne in mind that good and bad are only relative terms, so that one and the same thing may be said to be good or bad in different respects, just like the terms perfect and imperfect. Nothing, when regarded in its own nature, can be called perfect or imperfect, especially when we realise that all things that come into being do so in accordance with an eternal order and Nature's fixed laws.

But human weakness fails to comprehend that order in its thought,   13 and meanwhile man conceives a human nature much stronger than his own, and sees no reason why he cannot acquire such a nature. Thus he is urged to seek the means that will bring him to such a perfection, and all that can be the means of his attaining this objective is called a true good, while the supreme good is to arrive at the enjoyment of such a nature, together with other individuals, if possible. What that nature is we shall show in its proper place; namely, the knowledge of the union which the mind has with the whole of Nature.[c]

This, then, is the end for which I strive, to acquire the nature I have   14 described and to endeavour that many should acquire it along with me. That is to say, my own happiness involves my making an effort to

[c] This is explained more fully in its proper place.

persuade many others to think as I do, so that their understanding and their desire should entirely accord with my understanding and my desire. To bring this about, it is necessary[d] (1) to understand as much about Nature as suffices for acquiring such a nature, and (2) to establish such a social order as will enable as many as possible to reach this
15   goal with the greatest possible ease and assurance. Furthermore, (3) attention must be paid to moral philosophy and likewise the theory of the education of children; and since health is of no little importance in attaining this end, (4) the whole science of medicine must be elaborated. And since many difficult tasks are rendered easy by contrivance, and we can thereby gain much time and convenience in our daily lives, (5) the science of mechanics is in no way to be despised.
16   But our first consideration must be to devise a method of emending the intellect and of purifying it, as far as is feasible at the outset, so that it may succeed in understanding things without error and as well as possible. So now it will be evident to everyone that my purpose is to direct all the sciences to one end and goal,[e] to wit (as we have said), the achievement of the highest human perfection. Thus everything in the sciences which does nothing to advance us towards our goal must be rejected as pointless—in short, all our activities and likewise our thoughts must be directed to this end.
17   But since we have to continue with our lives while pursuing this end and endeavouring to bring the intellect into the right path, our first priority must be to lay down certain rules for living, as being good rules. They are as follows:

1. To speak to the understanding of the multitude and to engage in all those activities that do not hinder the attainment of our aim. For we can gain no little advantage from the multitude, provided that we accommodate ourselves as far as possible to their level of understanding. Furthermore, in this way they will give a more favourable hearing to the truth.

2. To enjoy pleasures just so far as suffices to preserve health.

3. Finally, to seek as much money or any other goods as are sufficient for sustaining life and health and for conforming with those social customs that do not conflict with our aim.

18   Having laid down these rules, I shall embark upon the first and most important task, emending the intellect and rendering it apt for the understanding of things in a manner appropriate to the achievement of our purpose. To this end our natural order of exposition requires that I should here recapitulate all the modes of perceiving which I

---

[d] Note that here I am only concerned to enumerate the sciences necessary to our purpose, without regard to their order.

[e] In the sciences there is only one end, to which all must be directed.

have hitherto employed in confidently affirming or denying something, so that I may select the best of all, and at the same time begin to know my powers and the nature which I desire to perfect.

If I examine them carefully, they can all be classified under four headings. **19**

1. There is the perception we have from hearsay, or from some sign conventionally agreed upon.

2. There is the perception we have from casual experience; that is, experience that is not determined by intellect, but is so called because it chances thus to occur, and we have experienced nothing else that contradicts it, so that it remains in our minds unchallenged.

3. There is the perception we have when the essence of a thing is inferred from another thing, but not adequately. This happens either when we infer a cause from some effect[f] or when an inference is made from some universal which is always accompanied by some property.

4. Finally, there is the perception we have when a thing is perceived through its essence alone, or through knowledge of its proximate cause.

All these I shall illustrate with examples. By hearsay alone I know **20** the date of my birth, who my parents were, and things of that sort, which I have never doubted. By casual experience I know that I shall die; this I affirm because I have seen that others like me have died, although they have not all lived to the same age nor have they died from the same disease. Again, by casual experience I know that oil has the property of feeding fire, and water of extinguishing it. I know too that a dog is a barking animal and man a rational animal. And it is in this way that I know almost everything that is of practical use in life.

We deduce one thing from another as follows. When we clearly per- **21** ceive that we sense such-and-such a body and no other, then from this, I say, we clearly infer that the soul is united to the body,[g] a union

---

[f] In such a case, we understand nothing about the cause except what we consider in the effect. This is sufficiently evident from the fact that the cause is then explained only in very general terms: e.g., 'Therefore there is something; therefore there is some power,' etc. Or again from the fact that the cause is expressed negatively: 'Therefore there is not this, or that,' etc. In the second case something clearly conceived is ascribed to the cause by reason of the effect, as we shall show by an example. But it is only the properties, not the particular essence of the thing.

[g] From this example one can clearly see what I have just noted. For by this union we understand nothing beyond the sensation itself; that is, the effect* from which we inferred a cause of which we have no understanding.

*With Mignini, I here read *effectus,* not Gebhardt's *effectūs.*

which is the cause of such-and-such a sensation. But from this[h] we cannot positively understand what is that sensation and union. Or, after I have come to know the nature of vision and realise that it has the property of making us see one and the same thing as smaller at a distance than if we were to see it near at hand, we infer that the sun is bigger than it appears, and other similar instances.

22   Finally, a thing is perceived through its essence alone when, from the fact that I know something, I know what it is to know something; or, from the fact that I know the essence of the soul, I know that it is united to the body. By the same kind of knowledge we know that two and three are five, and that if two lines are parallel to a third line, they are parallel to one another, and so on. But the things that I have hitherto been able to know by this kind of knowledge have been very few.

23   For the better understanding of all this, I shall make use of a single example, as follows. Three numbers are given; a fourth number is required, which is to the third as the second to the first. Here tradesmen generally tell us that they know what to do to find the fourth number, for they have not forgotten the procedure which they merely learned without proof from their teachers. Others formulate a universal axiom from their experience with simple numbers when the fourth number is self-evident, as in the case of the numbers 2, 4, 3, 6. Here they find that when the second is multiplied by the third and the product is divided by the first, the answer is 6. Seeing that the same number is produced which they knew to be the proportional number without going through the procedure, they conclude that this procedure is al-

24 ways a good way to find the fourth proportional. But mathematicians, because of the force of the demonstration of Proposition 19 of Book 7 of Euclid, know what numbers are proportional to one another from the nature and property of proportion, which tells us that the product of the first and fourth numbers is equal to the product of the second and third. However, they do not see the adequate proportionality of the given numbers, and if they do see it, they see it not by the force of that proposition but intuitively, without going through any procedure.

25   To choose from these the best mode of perceiving, we should briefly enumerate the means necessary to attain our end, as follows:

    1. To have an exact knowledge of our nature which we wish to perfect, and at the same time to know as much of the nature of things as is necessary.

---

[h] Such a conclusion, although it be certain, is not to be relied on without great caution; for unless we take great care, we shall immediately fall into error. When things are conceived in this abstract way and not through their true essence, they are at once confused by the imagination. For to the things that they conceive abstractly, separately, and confusedly, men apply terms which they use to signify other more familiar things. Consequently, they imagine the former things in the same way as they are wont to imagine the things to which they originally applied these terms.

2. Therefrom to infer correctly the differences, agreements and oppositions of things.

3. To conceive aright the extent to which things can, and cannot, be acted upon.

4. To compare this result with the nature and power of man.

From this the highest degree of perfection that man can attain will readily be made manifest.

With these considerations in mind, let us see which mode of perceiving we ought to choose.   26

As to the first mode, it is self-evident that from hearsay, besides the considerable degree of uncertainty therein, we perceive nothing of the essence of the thing, as our example makes clear. And since a thing's individual existence is not known unless its essence is known (as will later be seen), we can clearly infer from this that any degree of certainty that we have from hearsay must be excluded from the sciences. For no one can ever be affected by mere hearsay unless his own understanding has already preceded it.

As to the second mode, again[i] it cannot be said to contain the idea of   27
the proportion which it seeks. Besides its considerable uncertainty and indefiniteness, no one will in this way perceive anything in natural things except their accidents, which are never clearly understood unless their essences are first known. Hence this mode, too, must be excluded.

As for the third mode, we can in some sense say that we have the   28
idea of the thing, and also that we can make inferences without danger of error. Yet it is not in itself the means of our acquiring our perfection.

Only the fourth mode comprehends the adequate essence of the   29
thing, and is without danger of error. So this is the one we must chiefly adopt. Therefore we shall proceed to explain how it is to be employed, so that we may understand by this kind of knowledge what is unknown, and also may do this as directly as possible. That is, now that   30
we know what kind of knowledge is necessary for us, we must describe the way and method by which we may come to know by this kind of knowledge the things that are needful to be known.

To this end, the first point to consider is that this is not a case of an enquiry extending to infinity. That is, to find the best method of seeking the truth, there is no need of another method for seeking the method of seeking the truth, and there is no need of a third method to seek the second method, and so on to infinity. For in that way we should never arrive at knowledge of the truth, or indeed at any knowledge. The case is analogous to that of material tools, where the same kind of argument could be employed. To work iron, a hammer is

---

[i] Here I shall discuss experience at some greater length, and examine the method of proceeding of Empiricists and the new philosophers.

needed, and to have a hammer, it must be made. For this purpose there is need of another hammer and other tools, and again to get these there is need of other tools, and so on to infinity. In this way one might try to prove, in vain, that men have no power to work iron.

31   But the fact is that at first, with the tools they were born with, men succeeded, however laboriously and imperfectly, in making some very simple things; and when these were made they made other more complex things with less labour and greater perfection; and thus advancing gradually from the simplest works to the making of tools, and from tools to other works and other tools, they have reached a point where they can make very many complex things with little labour. In just the same way the intellect by its inborn power[k] makes intellectual tools for itself by which it acquires other powers for other intellectual works,[l] and from these works still other tools—or capacity for further investigation—and thus makes steady progress until it reaches the summit of wisdom.

32   That this is the case with the intellect will readily be seen, provided we understand what is the method of seeking truth, and what are those innate tools which are all the intellect needs for making other tools from them so as to progress further. To demonstrate this I proceed as follows.

33   A true idea[m] (for we do have a true idea) is something different from its object (ideatum). A circle is one thing, the idea of a circle another. For the idea of a circle is not something having a circumference and a centre, as is a circle, nor is the idea of a body itself a body. And since it is something different from its object, it will also be something intelligible through itself. That is, in respect of its formal essence the idea can be the object of another objective essence,* which in turn, regarded in itself, will also be something real and intelligible, and so on indefinitely.

34   For example, Peter is something real. Now the true idea of Peter is the objective essence of Peter and is in itself something real, something entirely different from Peter. So since the idea of Peter is some-

---

[k] By inborn power I mean that which is not caused in us by external causes, as I shall later explain in my Philosophy.

[l] Here they are called works. In my Philosophy, I shall explain what they are.

[m] Note that here we shall endeavour to demonstrate not only what has just been said, but also the correctness of our procedure so far, and likewise other points of primary importance.

* The Latin 'objectivus' is used by Spinoza and his contemporaries in a way quite opposed to the modern usage where 'objective' is the opposite of 'subjective.' An 'essentia objectiva' is an idea, a mental action, whose object is an 'essentia formalis.' The Latin adverbs 'objectivè' and 'formaliter' are the adverbial counterparts. In the face of this difficulty, the translator can do no better than to translate as 'objective essence' and 'formal essence,' having warned the reader that these terms are used in Spinoza in this special sense.

thing real, having its own individual essence, it will also be something intelligible, that is, the object of another idea which has in itself objectively everything that the idea of Peter has formally. And in turn the idea of the idea of Peter again has its own essence, which can also be the object of another idea, and so on without end. This anyone can experience for himself when he realises that he knows what Peter is, and also that he knows that he knows, and again that he knows that he knows that he knows, and so on. From this it is evident that, to understand the essence of Peter, it is not necessary to understand the idea of Peter, and far less the idea of the idea of Peter. This is no more than to say that, in order to know, I need not know that I know, and far less do I need to know that I know that I know. It is no more necessary than, in order to understand the essence of a triangle, one needs to understand the essence[n] of a circle. Indeed, in the case of these ideas it is the other way round; for in order to know that I know, it is necessary that I must first know.

Hence it is evident that certainty is nothing else than the objective   35
essence itself; that is to say, the way in which we become aware of the formal essence is certainty itself. And from this again it is evident that for the certainty of truth no other sign is needed but to have a true idea. For, as we have shown, in order to know, there is no need for me to know that I know. From this, again, it is clear that no one can know what the highest certainty is unless he has an adequate idea or the objective essence of some thing. For certainty and objective essence are the same.

Since truth, then, needs no sign, and to have the objective essences   36
of things, or—which is the same thing—their ideas, is enough to remove all doubt, it follows that the true method does not consist in seeking a sign of truth after acquiring ideas; the true method is the path whereby truth itself, or the objective essences of things, or ideas (all these mean the same) is to be sought[o] in proper order.

Again, method must necessarily be discourse about reasoning or in-   37
tellection. That is, method is not reasoning itself which leads to the understanding of the causes of things, and far less is it the understanding of the causes of things. It is the understanding of what is a true idea, distinguishing it from other kinds of perception and examining its nature, so that we may thereby come to know our power of understanding and may so train the mind that it will understand according to that standard all that needs to be understood, laying down definite rules as aids, and also ensuring that the mind does not waste its energy on useless pursuits.

From this we may conclude that method is nothing but reflexive   38

[n] Note that we are not here inquiring as to how the first objective essence is innate in us. For that topic belongs to the investigation of Nature, where these matters are dealt with more fully and where we also demonstrate that there is no affirmation or negation or act of will apart from the idea.

[o] The nature of this seeking in the soul is explained in my Philosophy.

knowledge, or the idea of an idea; and because there is no idea of an idea unless there is first an idea, there will be no method unless there is first an idea. So a good method will be one which shows how the mind is to be directed according to the standard of a given true idea. Again, since the relation between two ideas is the same as the relation between the formal essences of those ideas, it follows that the reflexive knowledge of the idea of the most perfect Being will be more excellent than the reflexive knowledge of other ideas. That is, the most perfect method will be one which shows how the mind should be directed according to the standard of a given idea of the most perfect Being.

39   From this one can readily understand how the mind, as it understands more things, at the same time acquires other tools which facilitate its further understanding. For, as may be gathered from what has been said, there must first of all exist in us a true idea as an innate tool, and together with the understanding of this idea there would likewise be an understanding of the difference between this perception and all other perceptions. Herein consists one part of our method. And since it is self-evident that the more the mind understands of Nature, the better it understands itself, it clearly follows that this part of our method will become that much more perfect as the mind understands more things, and will become then most perfect when the mind attends to, or reflects upon, the knowledge of the most perfect Being.

40   Then again, the more things the mind knows, the better it understands both its own powers and the order of Nature. Now the better it understands its own powers, the more easily it can direct itself and lay down rules for its own guidance; and the better it understands the order of Nature, the more easily it can restrain itself from useless pursuits. And it is in this, as we have said, that the whole of our method consists.

41   Moreover, an idea is situated in the context of thought exactly as is its object in the context of reality. Therefore, if there were something in Nature having no interrelation with other things, and if there were also granted its objective essence (which must agree entirely with its formal essence), then this idea likewise would have no interrelation[p] with other ideas; that is, we could make no inference regarding it. On the other hand, those things that do have interrelation with other things—as is the case with everything that exists in Nature—will be intelligible, and their objective essences will also have that same interrelation; that is, other ideas will be deduced from them, and these in turn will be interrelated with other ideas, and so the tools for further progress will increase. This is what we were endeavouring to demonstrate.

42   Furthermore, from the point just mentioned—that the idea must entirely agree with its formal essence—it is again evident that, for the human mind to reproduce a faithful image of Nature, it must draw all its ideas from that idea which represents the source and origin of the

---

[p] To be interrelated with other things is to produce, or be produced by, other things.

whole of Nature, so that this may likewise become the source of other ideas.

Here it may seem surprising that, having said that the good method   43
is one which demonstrates how the mind is to be directed according to the standard of a given true idea, I resort to reasoning to prove this point, which appears to indicate that it is not self-evident. So the question can be raised as to whether our reasoning is sound. If our reasoning is sound, we have to begin from a given idea, and since to begin from a given idea is something that needs proving, we ought again to prove the validity of our reasoning, and then again the validity of that reasoning, and so on ad infinitum.

To this I reply that if anyone in his investigation of Nature had by   44
some chance advanced in this way—that is, by acquiring other ideas in proper order according to the standard of a given true idea—he would never have doubted[q] his own truth (inasmuch as truth, as we have said, reveals its own self), and all would have progressed smoothly for him. But since this rarely or never happens, I have been constrained to posit those guide-lines, so that what we cannot acquire by chance, we may yet acquire by deliberate planning, and also in order to make it clear that, for the validation of truth and sound reasoning, we need no other instruments than truth and sound reasoning. For it is by sound reasoning that I have validated sound reasoning, and still continue so to do. Furthermore, it is this way of thinking that   45
men usually adopt in their own internal meditations.

That the proper order is rarely employed in the investigation of Nature is due to prejudices whose causes I shall later explain in my Philosophy. A further reason, as I shall later show, is the need for a considerable capacity to make accurate distinctions, a very laborious task. And finally, there is the matter of the human condition, which, as has already been shown, is highly unstable. There are yet other reasons, which we shall not pursue.

If anyone perchance should ask why at the very outset I adopted   46
that arrangement in demonstrating the truths of Nature—for does not truth reveal its own self?—I reply by urging him not to reject these things as false because of paradoxes which will occasionally occur here and there. Let him first please to consider the arrangement of our demonstration, and he will then be convinced that we have arrived at the truth. This explains the reason why I began as I did.

But if after this there is some sceptic who still entertains doubt both   47
as to the first truth itself and all the deductions we shall make according to the standard of the first truth, then surely either he is speaking contrary to his own consciousness or else we shall have to declare that there are men whose minds are also blinded either from birth or by reason of their prejudices, that is, through some accident that has befallen them. For they are not even aware of their own selves. If they affirm or doubt something, they do not know that they are doubting or

[q] Just as here, too, we do not doubt our truth.

affirming. They say that they know nothing, and they say that they are ignorant of this very fact of knowing nothing. And they do not even say this without qualification; for they are afraid that, in saying they know nothing, they are declaring that they exist, so that in the end they have to maintain silence lest they should perchance say something that has the savour of truth.

48   Finally, although in matters relating to the usages of life and society necessity has compelled them to suppose their existence, to seek their own good and frequently to affirm and deny things on oath, it is quite impossible to discuss the sciences with them. If a proof is presented to them, they do not know whether the argumentation is valid or not. If they deny, grant or oppose, they do not know that they deny, grant or oppose. So they must be regarded as automata, completely lacking in mind.

49   Let us now return to our theme. Up to the present, we have in the first place established the end to which we strive to direct all our thoughts. Second, we have learned which is the best mode of perception that will help us to attain our perfection. Third, we have learned which is the path our mind should first take in order to make a good beginning, and that is, to proceed to its enquiry by fixed rules, taking as its standard some given true idea. To do this correctly, our method must enable us, first, to distinguish a true idea from all other perceptions and to restrain the mind from those other perceptions; second, to lay down rules for perceiving things unknown according to the aforementioned standard; third, to establish an orderly procedure which will enable us to avoid useless toil. Having discovered this method, we realised, fourthly, that this method would be most perfect when we possessed the idea of a most perfect Being. So at the outset this must be our chief objective, to arrive at the knowledge of such a Being as speedily as possible.

50   Let us then make a beginning with the first part of the method, which is, as we have said, to distinguish and separate the true idea from other perceptions, and to keep the mind from confusing false, fictitious, and doubtful ideas with true ideas. Here I intend to dwell on this subject at some length so as to engage my readers in the study of so important a topic, and also because there are many who, failing to attend to the distinction between a true perception and all other perceptions, have come to doubt even their true perceptions. Their condition is like that of men who, when they were awake, did not doubt that they were awake, but having once in their dreams—as is often the case—felt certain that they were wide awake and later found this to be untrue, doubted even their waking experiences. This comes about because they have never distinguished between dreaming and being awake.

51   But I must first warn the reader that I shall not here be discussing the essence of every perception, explaining it through its proximate cause, for this pertains to Philosophy. I shall confine myself to discussing what the method demands; that is, what are the circumstances

with which the fictitious, the false, and the doubtful perception are concerned, and how we may be delivered from each of them. Let our first inquiry, then, deal with the fictitious idea.*

Every perception has for its object either a thing considered as existing or solely the essence of a thing. Now since in most cases fictions are concerned with things considered as existing, I shall deal first with that situation—that is, where the existence of some action is the sole object of the fiction, and the thing which is supposed to be so acting is comprehensible by intellect, or is posited as such. For example, I make up the idea that Peter, whom I well know, is on his way home, is coming to visit me, or the like.[r] Here I ask, with what is such an idea concerned? I see that it is concerned only with what is possible, not with what is necessary, nor with what is impossible. 52

I call a thing impossible if its nature implies that it would be a contradiction for it to exist; necessary, if its nature implies that it would be a contradiction for it not to exist; and possible, if, by its very nature, neither its existence nor its non-existence implies a contradiction, the necessity or impossibility of its existence being dependent on causes which are unknown to us while we are assuming its existence. So if its necessity or impossibility, which are dependent on external causes, were known to us, it could not then be for us the subject of any fiction. 53

Hence it follows that if there is a God, or some omniscient being, such a being cannot engage in any fiction. For in our own case, knowing as I do that I exist,[s] my existence or non-existence cannot be a matter of fiction for me; nor again can I engage in the fiction of an elephant that can pass through the eye of a needle; nor, knowing the nature of God,[t] can his existence or non-existence be a matter of fiction for me. The same applies to the Chimera, whose nature implies 54

---

* Fiction and fictitious idea. The reader needs to be warned that these terms are not really adequate to Spinoza's meaning, but I can devise no better. The Latin verb 'fingo' and its derivatives, which Spinoza here uses so frequently, means basically 'to make up, to fashion.' I have avoided translating it by 'to feign' because of the latter's suggestion of deliberate deceit. But 'fiction' is not free from this association, and it must be emphasized that in Spinoza a fictitious idea may turn out to be true or false (see paragraph 61). As Spinoza says, it is concerned with the possible, but is not warranted by evidence. It is not deceit or falsity that 'fictio' mainly conveys, but the lack of basis for a supposition.

[r] See later on what we shall have to say about hypotheses. These are clearly understood by us, but the fiction consists in our saying that the hypotheses are actually true of the heavenly bodies.

[s] Since a thing, when once it is understood, manifests itself, we need only an example without further proof. The same is true of its contradictory, which needs only to be examined to expose its falsity, as will later become clear when we shall be discussing the fiction that concerns essence.

[t] Note that, although many may say that they doubt the existence of God, they have in mind nothing but a word, or some fictitious idea they call God. This does not accord with the nature of God, as I shall later demonstrate in its proper place.

its non-existence. From this it is evident, as I have said, that eternal truths do not allow of the fiction of which we are here speaking.[u]

55   But before proceeding further, I must first observe in passing that the difference between the essence of one thing and the essence of another thing is the same as that which holds between the actuality or existence of the one thing and the actuality or existence of the other. So if we were to conceive the existence of Adam, for example, under the general category of existence, this would be the same as if, to conceive his essence, we were to focus our attention on the nature of being, so that we end up by defining Adam as a being. Thus the more generally existence is conceived, the more confusedly it is conceived and the more readily it can be ascribed to any one thing. Conversely, the more singularly existence is conceived, the more clearly it is then understood, and the less likely we are to ascribe it (when we are not attending to the order of Nature) to anything other than the thing itself. This is worth noting.

56   We must now proceed to consider those cases which are loosely called fictions in common parlance even though we clearly understand that the reality is not as we feign it to be. For example, although I know that the earth is round, nothing prevents my saying to somebody that the earth is a hemisphere, like half an orange on a plate, or saying that the sun moves round the earth, and the like. If we consider these cases, we shall find nothing that is not consistent with what we have already said, provided that we note that, first, we have occasionally fallen into errors of which we are now conscious; and second, that we can entertain the fictitious idea, or at least the thought, that others have fallen into the same error, or may so do, as we once did. This fiction, I say, is feasible for us as long as we see no impossibility and no necessity therein. So when I say to somebody that the earth is not round, and the like, I do no more than to recall to mind an error which I perchance have made, or into which I might have fallen, and thereafter I feign, or think, that the person to whom I tell this is as yet a victim of this same error or is capable of falling into it. As I have said, I can engage in this fiction only as long as I see that no impossibility and no necessity lies therein. For had I understood this to be so, there would have been no room whatsoever for fiction, and it would have to be said that I had done no more than utter words.

57   It remains for us now furthermore to consider the kind of suppositions that are made in connection with problems: for these, too, not infrequently involve impossibilities. For example, we may say, "Let us suppose that this burning candle is not now burning," or "Let us

---

[u] I shall also presently demonstrate that eternal truths do not admit of fiction of any kind.* By an eternal truth I mean one which, if it is affirmative, will never be able to be negative. Thus it is a first and eternal truth that 'God is,' but that 'Adam thinks' is not an eternal truth. That 'there is no Chimera' is an eternal truth, but not that 'Adam does not think.'

*In placing this first sentence at the beginning of Note *u* and not in the text, I am following Mignini.

suppose that it is burning in some imaginary space where there are no bodies." Such suppositions are quite commonly made, although the latter example is obviously understood to be impossible. But in such cases there is no question of fiction. In the first case I have done no more than recall to memory[x] another candle which was not burning (or I have conceived this candle without a flame), and my thoughts of the latter candle I now transfer to the former, dismissing the flame from my mind. In the second case I merely withdraw my thoughts from the surrounding bodies so that the mind concentrates its attention on the candle alone, regarded in itself. This leads to the conclusion that the candle contains in itself no cause for its own destruction, so that, if there were no surrounding bodies, this candle and likewise its flame would remain immutable, or some such conclusion. Here, then, there is no question of fiction; there are really mere assertions,[y] and no more.

Let us now pass on to those fictions which are concerned either with essences alone or with essences combined with some actuality or existence. With regard to these it must especially be noted that, the less the mind understands while yet perceiving more things, the greater its capacity to form fictions; and the more it understands, the less its capacity to form fictions. For example, just as we saw above that while we are actually thinking, it cannot be for us a fictional idea that we are thinking or not thinking, so too, when we have come to know the nature of body, we cannot entertain the idea of an infinite fly; or when we have come to know the nature of the soul,[z] we cannot entertain the idea that it is square—though anything can be put into words. But as we have said, the less men know of Nature, the more easily they can fashion numerous fictitious ideas, as that trees speak, that men can change instantaneously into stones or springs, that ghosts appear in

58

---

[x] Later, when we shall be speaking of fictions concerning essences, it will be manifest that fiction never invents or presents to the mind anything new; it recalls to mind only things that are in the brain or the imagination, and the mind attends to all these together in a confused way. For example, the uttering of words and a tree are recalled to memory, and when the mind attends to them in a confused way without distinction, it forms the notion of a tree speaking. The same applies to existence, especially when, as we have said, it is conceived in a very general way as entity, for it is then liable to be attached to all things that occur together in memory. This is a very important point.

[y] This is also the case with hypotheses which are formed to explain the regular movements which accord with celestial phenomena, except that, if the hypotheses are actually applied to the celestial movements, an inference is drawn as to the nature of the heavens, which may nevertheless be quite different. For one may conceive many other causes to explain these movements.

[z] It often happens that a man recalls to mind this term 'soul' and at the same time forms some material image. Now when these two things are presented together in his mind, he is prone to think that he imagines and forms the idea of a material soul, failing to distinguish between word and reality. Here I ask my readers not to be too hasty to refute what I have said, which I hope they will refrain from doing provided that they pay close attention to the examples, and also to what follows.

mirrors, that something can come from nothing, even that gods can change into beasts or men, and any number of such fantasies.

59   Someone may perhaps think that the limits of fiction are set by fiction, not by intellection. That is, when I have formed a fictitious idea and then, by some sort of freedom, assented to its existence in reality, this has the consequence that I cannot thereafter think it in any other way. For instance, when I have engaged in the fiction (to speak as they do) that body has a certain nature, and of my own freewill I convince myself that this is so in reality, I can no longer entertain the idea, say, of an infinite fly; and when I have formed an idea of the essence of the soul, I can no longer conceive it as square, and so forth.

60   But this view must be examined. First, either they deny or they grant that we have the capacity to understand something. If they grant this, then it must follow that what they say about fiction also applies to intellection. If they deny it, then let us, who know that we know something, consider what they are saying. They are in fact saying that the soul can be conscious of and perceive, in a variety of ways, not its own self nor things that exist, but only things that are neither in themselves nor anywhere at all; that is, the soul can by its unaided power create sensations or ideas which are not ideas of things. So to some extent they are likening the soul to God. Further, they are saying that we, or our soul, possess a freedom of such a kind that it can constrain our own selves, or the soul's self—nay, it can constrain its own freedom. For after it has formed some fictitious idea and given assent thereto, it cannot think it or fashion it in any other way, and is even compelled by that fictitious idea to form all its other thoughts so as not to conflict with the original fiction—just as here, too, their own fictitious idea compels them to allow the absurdities which I am here reviewing. We shall waste no time on demonstrations to refute this nonsense.

61   But leaving them to their delusions, we shall endeavour to draw from our discussion with them something true and to our purpose, namely, that when the mind attends to a thing that is both fictitious and false by its very nature, so as to ponder over it and achieve understanding, and then deduces from it in proper order what is to be deduced, it will easily detect its falsity;[a] and if the fictitious idea is by its own nature true, when the mind attends to it so as to understand it, and begins to deduce from it in proper order the conclusions that follow from it, it will proceed smoothly without any interruption—just as we have seen that, in the case of the false fiction just mentioned, the intellect immediately applied itself to exposing its absurdity and the absurdities that follow from it.

62   We need therefore be in no way apprehensive about engaging in

---

[a] Although I seem to infer this from experience, and someone may deny its cogency because no proof is attached, he may take this if he wants one. Since there can be nothing in Nature contrary to her laws and all things happen in accordance with her fixed laws, so that definite effects are produced by definite laws in unalterable sequence, it follows that when the soul conceives a thing truly, it will proceed to produce in thought those same effects. See below, where I discuss the false idea.

fiction provided that we clearly and distinctly perceive what is really the case. If we were perchance to say that men are suddenly changed into beasts, this is a statement of a very general kind, such that there would be in the mind no conception, that is, no idea or connection of subject with predicate. For if there were such, the mind would at that time see the means and causes, the 'how' and the 'why' such a thing took place. Then again, no attention is given to the nature of the subject and predicate.

Furthermore, provided that the first idea is not fictitious and all the   63 other ideas are deduced from it, the hasty tendency to form fictitious ideas will gradually disappear. Then again, since a fictitious idea cannot be clear and distinct but only confused, and since all confusion arises from mind's having only partial knowledge of a complete whole or a unity composed of many constituents—failing to distinguish between the known and the unknown, and also attending at the same time without any distinction to the many constituents contained in a single thing—it follows, first, that if the idea is of a thing completely simple, it can only be clear and distinct. For such a thing would have to be known not in part, but either wholly or not at all. Secondly, it   64 follows that if a thing composed of many constituents is divided in thought into all its simplest parts, and attention is given to each part separately, then all confusion will disappear. Thirdly, it follows that a fictitious idea cannot be simple, but is formed by the blending of various confused ideas of various things and actions existing in Nature; or, as better expressed, fiction results from attending at the same time, without assent, to various ideas of this kind.[b] For if fiction were simple, it would be clear and distinct, and consequently true. And if it were formed from the blending of distinct ideas, their composition would also be clear and distinct, and therefore true. For example, once we know the nature of a circle and also that of a square, we cannot compound the two and make a square circle, or a square soul and the like.

Let us then once more sum up briefly and see why we need in no   65 way fear that fiction may be confused with true ideas. For as to the first case we mentioned earlier, i.e., when a thing is clearly conceived, we saw that if the thing which is clearly conceived, and also its existence, is in itself an eternal truth, we cannot engage in any fiction regarding such a thing. But if the existence of the thing conceived is not an eternal truth, we need only to ensure that the existence of the thing is compared with its essence, while at the same time attending to the order of Nature. As to the second case of fiction, which we said to consist in attending simultaneously, without assenting, to various

---

[b] Fiction, considered in itself, does not much differ from dreaming, except that those causes which their senses present to the waking, from which they infer that those presentations are not presented at that time by things external to them, are not presented in dreaming. Now error, as will soon be manifest, is dreaming while awake, and if it reaches a certain pitch, it is called madness.

confused ideas of various things and actions existing in Nature, we again saw that a completely simple thing cannot be the object of fiction, but only of intellect. And the same is true of a composite thing provided we attend to its simplest component parts. Indeed, these things cannot be the subject of fiction involving any actions that are not true, for at the same time we shall be compelled to consider how and why such a thing came about.

66   With these matters thus understood, let us now pass on to the investigation of the false idea so as to see with what it is concerned, and how we may guard ourselves against falling into false perceptions. Neither of these objectives will now afford us any difficulty after our investigation of the fictitious idea. For between these ideas there is no difference except that the false idea implies assent; that is (as we have already noted), while the ideas are presented to the mind, there are no causes presented from which it can infer (as in the case of fiction) that they do not arise from things extraneous. It is practically the same as dreaming with one's eyes open or while wide awake. Therefore the false idea is like the fictitious idea in that it is concerned with, or (as better expressed) has reference to, the existence of a thing whose essence is known, or it is concerned with an essence.

67   The false idea that has reference to existence is emended in the same way as the fictitious idea. For if the nature of the known thing implies necessary existence, we cannot possibly be deceived regarding the existence of that thing. If the existence of the thing is not an eternal truth (as is its essence) and the necessity or impossibility of its existence depends on external causes, then follow the same course which we indicated in our discussion of fiction, for it can be emended in the same way.

68   As for the kind of false idea that is related to essences, and also to actions, such perceptions are necessarily always confused, being compounded of various confused perceptions of things existing in Nature, as when men are convinced that divinities are present in woods, in images, in animals and other things, that there are bodies whose mere composition gives rise to intelligence, that corpses can reason, walk and speak, that God can be deceived, and the like. But ideas which are clear and distinct can never be false; for ideas of things which are clearly and distinctly conceived either are absolutely simple or are compounded of absolutely simple ideas—that is, deduced from absolutely simple ideas. But that an absolutely simple idea cannot be false is obvious to everyone, provided that he knows what is truth or understanding, and likewise what is falsity.

69   As to what constitutes the specific character of truth, it is certain that a true thought is distinguishable from a false thought not merely by its extrinsic relation but more particularly by an intrinsic characteristic. If an architect conceives a building in proper fashion, although such a building has never existed nor is ever likely to exist, his thought is nevertheless a true thought, and the thought is the same whether the building exists or not. On the other hand, if someone says,

for example, that Peter exists, while yet not knowing that Peter exists, that thought in respect to the speaker is false, or, if you prefer, not true, although Peter really exists. The statement 'Peter exists' is true only in respect of one who knows for certain that Peter exists.

Hence it follows that there is something real in ideas through which 70
the true are distinguished from the false, and this must now be the subject of our inquiry so that we may possess the best standard of truth (for we have said that we ought to determine our thoughts according to the standard of a given* true idea, and method consists in reflexive knowledge) and may get to know the properties of the intellect. Nor must we say that the difference between true and false ideas derives from the fact that a true thought is to know things through their first causes—wherein it would indeed be very different from a false thought as we have explained it above. For a thought is also said to be true when it involves as its object the essence of some basic principle which is uncaused and is known through itself and in itself.

Therefore the specific character of a true thought must be intrinsic 71
to the thought itself without reference to other thoughts. Nor does it acknowledge its object as cause, but must depend on the very power and nature of the intellect. For let us suppose that the intellect has perceived some new entity which has never existed, as some conceive the intellect of God before he created things (a perception which obviously could not have arisen from any object), and that from such a perception it deduces other perceptions in logical order. All those thoughts would be true and would not be determined by any external object, but would depend entirely on the power and nature of the intellect. Therefore that which constitutes the specific character of a true thought must be sought in that very same thought and deduced from the nature of intellect.

So to investigate this question, let us set before us a true idea whose 72
object we are absolutely certain depends on our power of thought, there being no object to it in Nature; for such an idea, as is clear from what has been said, will more easily enable us to pursue the enquiry we have in view. For example, to form the concept of a sphere, I invent a cause at will, namely, that a semicircle rotates about its centre, and a sphere, as it were, is produced by this rotation. Now this is, of course, a true idea, and although we know that in Nature no sphere has ever been produced in this way, this is nevertheless a true perception and a very convenient way of forming the concept of a sphere. Now, we should observe that this perception affirms that a semicircle rotates, an affirmation that would be false were it not conjoined with the concept of a sphere, or else with a cause determining such motion; that is, in short, if this were a completely isolated affirmation. For in that case the mind would not be extending its affirmation to anything beyond the motion of the semicircle, and neither is this contained in the concept of a semicircle nor does it originate from the conception

* I here adopt Mignini's emendation of *datā* to *datae*.

of a cause determining the motion. Therefore the falsity consists solely in this, that something is affirmed of a thing when it is not contained in the conception we have formed of the thing, as in this case motion or rest is affirmed of the semicircle. Hence it follows that simple thoughts are bound to be true, such as the simple idea of a semicircle, of motion, of quantity, and so on. Whatever of affirmation is contained in these thoughts is co-extensive with their concept, and extends no further. Therefore we may form simple ideas at will without any danger of error.

73   It remains, then, only to inquire by what power the mind can form these simple ideas, and what is the extent of this power; for once this is discovered we shall easily see what is the highest knowledge we can attain. It is certain that this power of the mind does not extend to infinity; for when we affirm of a thing something that is not contained in the concept we form of the thing, this indicates that our perception is defective, or in other words that we have thoughts or ideas that are, as it were, mutilated and fragmentary. For we saw that the motion of the semicircle is false when taken in isolation, but true if it is conjoined with the concept of a sphere, or the concept of some cause determining such motion. Now if it is in the nature of a thinking being, as seems apparently to be the case, to form true or adequate thoughts, it is certain that inadequate ideas arise in us from this, that we are part of some thinking being, some of whose thoughts constitute our mind in their entirety, and some only in part.

74   But we have yet to consider another case, which was not worth raising when dealing with fiction, and wherein one can go far astray. This happens when certain things presented in the imagination are also in the intellect; that is, are clearly and distinctly conceived. For then, when the distinct is not differentiated from the confused, the result is that certainty, i.e., a true idea, is mixed up with the non-distinct. For example, certain Stoics perhaps heard the word 'soul,' and also that it is immortal, which things they imagined only confusedly. They also imagined, and at the same time understood, that the most subtle bodies penetrate all other bodies and are penetrated by none. Since all these things were presented together in the imagination and were accompanied by the certainty of this axiom, they forthwith became convinced that the mind consists of those most subtle bodies, that those most subtle bodies cannot be divided, and so on.

75   But we are delivered from this error, too, as long as we make an effort to examine all our perceptions according to the standard of a given true idea, being on our guard, as we initially said, against those perceptions that we have from hearsay or from casual experience. In addition, this kind of mistake arises from their conceiving things in too abstract a way; for it is sufficiently clear in itself that what I conceive in its true object I cannot apply to any other object. Finally, this mistake also arises from their failure to understand the primary elements of Nature as a whole, so that, proceeding without due order and confusing Nature with abstractions (although these are true axioms),

they fall into confusion and distort the order of Nature. However, if we proceed with the least possible abstraction and begin at the earliest stage from the primary elements—that is, from the source and origin of Nature—we need in no way fear this kind of mistake.

As for our knowledge of the origin of Nature, we need have no fear   76
of confusing it with abstractions. For when things are conceived in an abstract way (as is the case with all universals), they always have a wider extension in the intellect than is really possessed by their particular exemplifications existing in Nature. Again, since there are many things in Nature whose difference is so slight as to be hardly perceptible to the intellect, it can easily come about that they are confused if they are conceived in an abstract way. But since, as we shall later see, the origin of Nature can neither be conceived in an abstract or universal way, nor can it have a wider extension in the intellect than in reality, nor has it any resemblance to things mutable, we need fear no confusion as to its idea, provided we possess the standard of truth as before shown. For this entity is unique and infinite;[z] that is, it is total being, beyond which there is no being.[a]

So much for the false idea. It remains for us to enquire into the   77
doubtful idea, that is, to consider what are the things that can lead us to doubt, and also how that doubt may be removed. I am speaking of genuine doubt in the mind, not the sort of doubt that we frequently encounter when somebody verbally asserts that he doubts, although he mentally does not doubt. The correction of the latter is not the province of our method; rather does it pertain to an enquiry into obstinacy and its emendation.

Doubt, then, never arises in the soul through the thing itself which is   78
the object of doubt. That is, if there should be only one idea in our consciousness, whether true or false, there will be neither doubt nor certainty, but only a certain kind of awareness. For an idea in itself is nothing but a certain awareness. Doubt arises through another idea, which is not so clear and distinct that we can infer from it any certainty as to the thing which is doubted. That is, the idea which causes us to doubt is not clear and distinct. For example, if someone has never been led, whether by experience or in any other way, to reflect upon the deceptiveness of the senses, he will never entertain doubt as to whether the sun is greater or smaller than it appears. Hence countryfolk are frequently surprised when they hear that the sun is much greater than the earth's sphere. But reflection on the deceptiveness of the senses induces doubt.[b] If, after being in doubt, a man acquires true

[z] These are not attributes of God, displaying his essence, as I shall make clear in my Philosophy.

[a] This has already been demonstrated above. For if such a being did not exist, it could never be produced, and so the mind could understand more than Nature could furnish, which has been shown above to be false.

[b] That is to say, a man knows that the senses have sometimes deceived him, but he

knowledge of the senses and of the manner whereby through their means distant things are represented, then the doubt is in turn removed.

79   Hence it follows that it is only when we do not have a clear and distinct idea of God that we can cast doubt on our true ideas on the grounds of the possible existence of some deceiving God who misleads us even in things most certain. That is, this can happen only if, attending to the knowledge we have of the origin of all things, we find nothing there to convince us that he is not a deceiver, with the same conviction that we have when, attending to the nature of a triangle, we find that its three angles are equal to two right angles. But if we do possess such knowledge of God as we have of a triangle, all doubt is removed. And just as we can attain such knowledge of a triangle although not knowing for sure whether some arch-deceiver is misleading us, so too can we attain such knowledge of God although not knowing for sure whether there is some arch-deceiver. Provided we have that knowledge, it will suffice, as I have said, to remove all doubt that we may have concerning clear and distinct ideas.

80   Furthermore, if anyone follows the correct procedure, investigating first what should be first investigated without any interruption in the interconnection of things, and if he knows how to define problems precisely before seeking to solve them, he will never have anything but the most certain ideas, that is, clear and distinct ideas. For doubt is nothing but the suspension of judgment in respect of some affirmation or denial which would be made but that something comes to mind which, being outside our understanding, must render imperfect our knowledge of the thing in question. We may therefore conclude that doubt always arises from want of order in the investigation.

81   These are the matters which I promised to set forth in this first part of our Method. But to omit nothing that can advance our knowledge of the intellect and its powers, I shall add a few words on memory and forgetting. Here the most important point to be considered is that memory is strengthened both by the aid of the intellect and also without its aid. As to the first case, the more intelligible a thing is, the more easily it is retained; the less intelligible, the more easily it is forgotten. For example, if I give someone a list of unconnected words, he will find it much more difficult to retain them than if I were to give him the same words in the form of a story.

82   It is also strengthened without the aid of the intellect, namely, through the force wherewith the imagination, or what is termed the common sense, is affected by some singular corporeal thing. I say 'singular,' for the imagination is affected by singular things only. For example, if someone reads just one love story, he will retain it very well as long as he does not read many others of the same kind, for then it

knows this only confusedly, for he does not know in what way the senses deceive him.*
    *With Mignini, I take this to be a footnote, not as Gebhardt.

flourishes alone in his imagination. But if he reads several of the same kind, he will imagine them all together, and they will easily be confused. I say 'corporeal,' for the imagination is affected only by bodies. Since, then, the memory is strengthened not only by the intellect but also independently of the intellect, we may conclude that it is something different from the intellect, and that the intellect considered in itself does not involve either memory or forgetting.

What, then, is memory? It is nothing but the sensation of impressions in the brain together with the thought of the determinate duration[c] of the sensation. This is further demonstrated by recollection, for in this the soul thinks of that sensation, but without the notion of a continuous duration; and thus the idea of that sensation is not identical with the duration of the sensation, that is, with memory itself. The question as to whether the ideas themselves undergo some corruption will be discussed in my Philosophy.

If this seems quite absurd to anyone, it will be enough for our purpose that he should reflect that, the more singular a thing is, the more easily it is retained, as is evident from the example of the comedy just mentioned. And again, the more intelligible a thing is, the more easily it is retained. Hence we cannot fail to retain a thing that is most singular and sufficiently intelligible.

Thus we have distinguished between the true idea and other perceptions, and we have established that the fictitious, the false, and other ideas have their origin in the imagination, that is, in certain sensations that are (so to speak)* fortuitous and unconnected, arising not from the power of the mind but from external causes, in accordance as the body, dreaming or waking, receives various motions. Or if you wish, you may here understand by imagination whatever you please, as long as it is something different from the intellect, and the soul has a passive relation to it. It matters not how you understand it, now that we know that it is something random, and that the soul is passive to it, while we also know how we may be delivered from it with the aid of the intellect. And so let no one be surprised that, without as yet having proved that there is such a thing as body and other important matters, I speak of the imagination, the body, and its constitution. For, as I have said, it matters not how I understand it, now that I know that it is something random, and so on.

But we have demonstrated that a true idea is simple or compounded of simple ideas, and that it shows how and why something is the case,

83

84

85

---

[c] But if the duration is indeterminate, the memory of the thing is imperfect, as each of us seems also to have learned naturally. For it often happens that, to confirm our belief in what someone is telling us, we ask when and where it occurred. And although ideas, too, have their own duration in the mind, since we are accustomed to determine duration with the help of some measure of motion which also involves the imagination, we still do not see in memory anything which appertains solely to the mind.

* I here follow Mignini's reading of (*ut sic loquar*) in its original place in the text, not as Gebhardt.

or has been so, and that its ideal effects in the soul correspond to the specific reality of its object. This is identical with the saying of the ancients that true science proceeds from cause to effect, except that, as far as I know, they never conceived the soul, as we are here doing, as acting according to fixed laws, a sort of spiritual automaton.

86   From these demonstrations, as far as was possible in the initial stages of our enquiry, we have acquired knowledge of our intellect, and such a standard of the true idea that we no longer fear we may confuse true ideas with false or fictitious ideas. Nor again will we wonder why we understand some things that do not in any way fall within the scope of the imagination, and why there are in the imagination some things that are completely opposed to the intellect, while there are other things which agree with the intellect. For we know that the operations by which imaginings are produced are subject to other laws which are quite different from the laws of the intellect, and that in relation to imagining, the soul has only a passive rôle.

87   From this we may also see how easily those who have not made a careful distinction between imagination and intellection may fall into grave errors, such as, for instance, that extension must be localised, that it must be finite, that its parts are really distinct from one another, that it is the first and only foundation of all things, that it occupies more space at one time than at another, and many other beliefs of this kind, all of which are completely opposed to truth, as we shall demonstrate in its proper place.

88   Then again, since words are a part of the imagination—that is, since many of our concepts are formed according to the haphazard composition of words in memory from some disposition of the body—there can be no doubt that words no less than imagination can bring about many grave errors unless we exercise great caution in that respect.

89   Add to this that words owe their formation to the whim and understanding of the common people, so that they are merely symbols of things as they are in the imagination, not in the intellect. This is evident from the fact that men have often devised negative terms for all those things that are only in the intellect and not in the imagination (e.g., incorporeal, infinite, etc.), and they also express negatively many things that are really affirmative, and conversely (e.g., uncreated, independent, infinite, immortal, etc.).[d] The reason for this is that the contraries of these words are much more easily imagined, and so they occurred first to the early generations, and they used them as positive terms.

90   Furthermore, we avoid another frequent cause of confusion, one that prevents the intellect from reflecting on itself; viz., by failing to distinguish between imagination and intellection, we think that the

[d] We affirm and deny many things because the nature of words, not the nature of things, suffers us to do so; and in our ignorance of the latter, we may easily take the false to be true.*
*With Mignini, I take this to be a footnote, not text.

things we more easily imagine are clearer to us, and we think that we understand what we imagine. Thus we put first what should be put later, and so the true order of procedure is reversed and there can be no legitimate conclusion drawn.

To move on in turn to the second part^e of this Method, I shall first   91
set forth our aim in this Method, and then the means of attaining it. Our aim, then, is to have clear and distinct ideas, that is, such as originate from pure mind and not from fortuitous motions of the body. Next, so that all ideas may be subsumed under one, we shall endeavour to connect and arrange them in such a manner that our mind, as far as possible, may reproduce in thought the reality of Nature, both as to the whole and as to its parts.

As to the first point, our ultimate aim, as we have already said,   92
requires that a thing be conceived either through its essence alone or through its proximate cause. That is, if the thing is in itself, or, as is commonly said, self-caused, then it will have to be understood solely through its essence; if the thing is not in itself and needs a cause for its existence, then it must be understood through its proximate cause. For in fact knowledge of the effect is nothing other than to acquire a more perfect knowledge of the cause.^{f}

Therefore, as long as we are engaged in an enquiry into real things,   93
it will never be permissible for us to draw a conclusion from what is abstract, and we shall take great care not to mix the things that are merely in the intellect with those things that are in reality. The most secure conclusion is to be drawn from some particular affirmative essence, i.e., from a true and legitimate definition. For, starting from universal axioms alone, the intellect cannot descend to particulars, since axioms are of infinite extension and do not determine the intellect to contemplate one particular thing rather than another. So the   94
correct path to discovery is to develop our thinking from the basis of some given definition, and progress will be more successful and easier as a thing is better defined. Therefore the whole of this second part of our method hinges on this alone: getting to know the conditions of a good definition, and then devising a way to discover them. I shall therefore first discuss the conditions of definition.

For a definition to be regarded as complete, it must explain the in-   95
most essence of the thing, and must take care not to substitute for this any of its properties. To explicate this, passing over other examples so as not to appear bent on exposing the errors of others, I shall choose only the example of an abstract thing where the manner of definition is unimportant, a circle, say. If this is defined as a figure in which the

---

^{e} The principal rule of this part, as follows from the first part, is to review all the ideas which we discover in us as originating from pure intellect, so that they may be distinguished from those we imagine. This distinction will have to be elicited from the properties of each, that is, imagination and intellection.

^{f} Note that this leads to the conclusion that we cannot properly understand anything of Nature without at the same time extending our knowledge of the first cause, or God.

lines drawn from the centre to the circumference are equal, it is obvious that such a definition by no means explains the essence of a circle, but only one of its properties. And although, as I have said, this is a matter of little importance when it is a question of figures and other mental constructs, it is nevertheless a matter of prime importance when it is a question of physical and real beings. For the properties of things are not understood as long as their essences are not known; and if the latter are neglected, this is bound to distort the interconnections made by our intellect which ought to reproduce the interconnections of Nature, and we shall go far astray from our goal.

96   So if we are to be delivered from this fault, the following requirements must be satisfied in definition.

1. If the thing be a created thing, the definition, as we have said, must include its proximate cause. For example, according to this rule a circle would have to be defined as follows: a figure described by any line of which one end is fixed and the other movable. This definition clearly includes the proximate cause.

2. The conception or definition of the thing must be such that all the properties of the thing, when regarded by itself and not in conjunction with other things, can be deduced from it, as can be seen in the case of this definition of a circle. For from it we clearly deduce that all the lines drawn from the centre to the circumference are equal.

That this is a necessary requirement of a definition is so self-evident to one who pays attention that it does not seem worth while spending time in demonstrating it, nor again in showing that according to this second requirement every definition must be affirmative. I am speaking of intellectual affirmation, disregarding verbal affirmation, which, because of poverty of language, may sometimes be expressed negatively, although understood affirmatively.

97   The requirements for the definition of an uncreated thing are as follows:

1. That it should exclude every cause; that is, that the thing should need nothing else for its explanation besides its own being.

2. That, given the definition of the thing, there should remain no room for the question: Does it exist?

3. That, as far as the mind is concerned, it should contain no substantives that can be put in adjectival form; that is, it should not be explicated through any abstractions.

4. And finally (although it is not really necessary to make this observation), it is required that all its properties can be deduced from its definition.

All these points are evident if careful attention is paid.

I have also stated that the best basis for drawing a conclusion will be   98
a particular affirmative essence. For the more individualised an idea
is, the more distinct it is, and therefore the clearer it is. Hence our
most important task is to seek knowledge of particular things.

As to the ordering of all our perceptions and their proper arrange-   99
ment and unification, it is required that, as soon as is possible and
reason demands, we should ask whether there is a being—and also
what kind of being—which is the cause of all things so that its essence
represented in thought is also the cause of all our ideas. Then our
mind, as we have said, will reproduce Nature as closely as possible; for
it will possess in the form of thought the essence, order, and unity of
Nature. Hence we can see that it is above all necessary for us always to
deduce our ideas from physical things, i.e., from real beings, advancing, as far as we can, in accordance with the chain of causes from one
real being to another real being, and in such a manner as never to get
involved with abstractions and universals, neither inferring something real from them nor inferring them from something real. For in
either case the true progress of the intellect is interrupted.

But it should be noted that by the series of causes and real beings I   100
do not here mean the series of mutable particular things, but only the
series of fixed and eternal things. It would be impossible for human
limitation to grasp the series of mutable particular things, not only
because they are innumerable but also because of the infinite number
of factors affecting one and the same thing, each of which can be the
cause of the existence or non-existence of the thing. For the existence
of mutable particular things has no connection with their essence; that
is (as we have said), their existence is not an eternal truth.

But neither is there any need for us to understand their series. For   101
the essences of particular mutable things are not to be elicited from
their series or order of existing, which would furnish us with nothing
but their extrinsic characteristics, their relations, or, at the most, their
circumstances. All these are far from the inmost essence of things.
This essence is to be sought only from the fixed and eternal things, and
at the same time from the laws inscribed in these things as in their true
codes, which govern the coming into existence and the ordering of all
particular things. Indeed, these mutable particular things depend so
intimately and essentially (so to phrase it) on the fixed things that they
can neither be nor be conceived without them. Hence, although these
fixed and eternal things are singular, by reason of their omnipresence
and wide-ranging power they will be to us like universals, i.e., the genera of the definitions of particular mutable things, and the proximate
causes of all things.

But this being so, there appears to be no small difficulty to surmount   102
before we can arrive at the knowledge of these particular things. For to
conceive them all at once is a task far beyond the powers of the human
intellect. And, as we have said, the order wherein one thing may be
understood before another is not to be sought from their position in

the series of existing, nor again from eternal things. For in the latter case all these things are by nature simultaneous. Therefore we must resort to other aids apart from those employed in understanding the eternal things and their laws. However, this is not the appropriate place to give an account of those aids, nor do we need to do so until we have acquired a sufficient knowledge of the eternal things and their infallible laws, and have gained an understanding of the nature of our senses.

103   Before we embark upon an enquiry into our knowledge of particular things, it will be timely for us to treat of those aids, all of which will serve to assist us in knowing how to use our senses and to conduct experiments under fixed rules and proper arrangement, such as will suffice to determine the thing which is the object of our enquiry. From these we may finally infer what are the laws of eternal things that govern the thing's production, and may gain an insight into its inmost nature, as I shall duly show. Here, to return to our theme, I shall confine my efforts to setting forth what seems necessary to enable us to attain to knowledge of eternal things, and to frame their definitions on the terms previously explained.

104   To achieve this, we must recall what we said earlier, namely, that when the mind attends to some thought so as to examine it and to deduce from it in proper order what can legitimately be deduced, if it is false, the mind will detect its falsity; but if it is true, the mind will proceed fruitfully without interruption to deduce truths from it. This, I say, is what our purpose requires. For our thoughts cannot be determined on any other foundation.

105   If, therefore, we wish to investigate the first of all things, there has to be some foundation which may direct our thoughts there. Next, since method is reflexive knowledge itself, the foundation which is to give direction to our thoughts can be nothing other than knowledge of what constitutes the specific reality of truth, and knowledge of the intellect, its properties and powers. For when this is acquired, we shall have a foundation from which we shall deduce our thoughts, and a path by which the intellect, according to its capacity, may attain knowledge of eternal things, taking into account, of course, the powers of the intellect.

106   But if, as has been demonstrated in the first part, it pertains to the nature of thought to form true ideas, we must here enquire what we understand by the faculties and power of the intellect. Now since the chief part of our Method is to achieve a good understanding of the powers of the intellect and its nature, we are necessarily constrained (through considerations set out in this second part of our Method) to

107   deduce these simply from the definition of thought and intellect. But so far we have not had any rules for finding definitions; and since we cannot treat of these rules without knowing the nature or definition of the intellect and its power, it follows that either the definition of the intellect must be self-evident or we cannot understand anything. But that definition is not absolutely self-evident. Nevertheless, since its

properties—like everything we have from the intellect—can be clearly and distinctly perceived only if their nature is known, the definition of intellect will become self-evident if we attend to its properties that we do understand clearly and distinctly. So let us here enumerate the properties of the intellect, consider them, and begin a discussion of our innate tools.[g]

The properties of the intellect which I have chiefly noted and clearly   108
understand are as follows:

1. That it involves certainty; that is, it knows that things are in reality as they are contained in the intellect in the form of thought.

2. That it perceives some things, or forms some ideas, independently, and some ideas it forms from other ideas. To wit, it forms the idea of quantity independently without attending to other thoughts, but it forms ideas of motion only by attending to the idea of quantity.

3. The ideas that it forms independently express infinity, but determinate ideas are formed from other ideas.* For if it perceives the idea of a quantity through a cause, then it determines that idea through the idea of a quantity, as when it perceives that a body is formed from the motion of a plane, a plane from the motion of a line, and a line from the motion of a point. These perceptions do not serve for the understanding of quantity, but only to determine it. This is evident from the fact that we conceive these quantities as formed, as it were, from motion, whereas motion is not perceived unless quantity is perceived; and again we can prolong the motion to form a line of infinite extent, which we could not do if we did not possess the idea of infinite quantity.

4. It forms positive ideas before negative ones.

5. It perceives things not so much under duration as under some form of eternity, and as being of infinite number. Or rather, in its perception of things, it attends neither to number nor duration. But when it imagines things, it perceives them as being of fixed number, with determinate duration and quantity.

6. The clear and distinct ideas that we form seem to follow solely from the necessity of our nature in such a way as to seem to depend absolutely on our power alone. But with confused ideas the contrary is the case; they are often formed without our consent.

7. There are many ways in which the mind can determine the ideas

[g] See above, section 31.

* The text here being corrupt, in this sentence I follow the translation proposed by Curley.

that the intellect forms from other ideas. For example, to determine the plane of an ellipse, the mind supposes that a pencil attached to a string moves about two centres, or alternatively it conceives an infinite number of points always maintaining the same fixed relation to a given straight line, or a cone cut in an oblique plane so that the angle of inclination is greater than the angle at the vertex of the cone. There are innumerable other ways.

8. Ideas are the more perfect as they express a greater degree of perfection of an object. For we do not admire the architect who has designed a chapel as much as one who has designed a splendid temple.

109   Other things that are referred to thought, such as love, joy, and so on, I shall not pause to consider; for they are neither relevant to our purpose, nor again can they be conceived unless the intellect is perceived. For if perception is entirely removed, all these are removed.

110   False and fictitious ideas have nothing positive (as we have abundantly shown) through which they are called false or fictitious; they are considered as such only from the defectiveness of our knowledge. Therefore false and fictitious ideas, as such, can teach us nothing concerning the essence of thought; this is to be sought from those positive properties just reviewed. That is, we must now establish some common basis from which these properties necessarily follow; a basis which, when given, necessarily entails these properties, and which, when removed, removes them all.

The rest is lacking.

SELECTED LETTERS

Letter 2

To the most honourable and learned Henry Oldenburg[1] from Benedict de Spinoza.

Illustrious Sir,

You yourself could judge what pleasure your friendship affords me, if only your modesty would allow you to consider the estimable qualities with which you are so richly endowed. With these qualities in mind, I feel it not a little presumptuous on my part to enter into a bond of friendship with you, the more so when I reflect that between friends all things, and particularly things of the spirit, should be shared. Nevertheless, this is to be attributed to both your modesty and your kindness, rather than to me. Your modesty in so condescending, and the abundant kindness that you have bestowed on me have banished any uncertainty I may have had in accepting the hand of friendship which you firmly hold out to me and deign to ask of me in return, a friendship which it shall be my earnest endeavour diligently to foster.

As for my mental endowments, such as they are, I would most willingly have you claim them for your own even if I knew that this would be to my great detriment. However, it is not my intention in this way to deny you what you ask by right of friendship, and so I shall attempt to explain my views on the subjects we spoke of, although I can scarcely believe that this will be the means of strengthening our friendship, if your kind indulgence does not intervene.

I shall therefore begin with a discussion of God, whom I define as a Being consisting of infinite attributes, each of which is infinite or supremely perfect in its own kind. Here it should be observed that by attribute I mean every thing that is conceived through itself and in itself, so that its conception does not involve the conception of anything else. For example, extension is conceived through itself and in itself, but not motion; for the latter is conceived in something else, and its conception involves extension.

That this is the true definition of God is evident from the fact that by God we understand a supremely perfect and absolutely infinite Being. The existence of such a Being is easily proved from the definition; but as this is not the place for such a proof, I shall pass it over. The points I need to prove here in order to satisfy your first enquiry, illustrious Sir,

1. Henry Oldenburg (d.1677) was a German theologian with a scientific bent. He eventually became secretary of the London Royal Society. He met Spinoza in 1661, and when he went to London, he continued to correspond with Spinoza for many years. It was through Oldenburg that Spinoza learned of Robert Boyle's work in chemistry.

are as follows: —first, that in the universe there cannot exist two sub-stances without their differing entirely in essence; secondly, a substance cannot be produced, since to exist is of its essence; thirdly, every sub-stance must be infinite, or supremely perfect in its kind.

With these points established, illustrious Sir, provided that at the same time you attend to the definition of God, you will readily perceive the direction of my thought, so that I need not be more explicit on this subject. However, in order to provide a clear, concise proof, I can think of no better expedient than to arrange them in geometrical style and to submit them to the bar of your judgment. I therefore enclose them separately herewith[2] and await your judgment.

Secondly, you ask me what errors I see in the philosophy of Descartes and Bacon. In this request, too, I shall try to oblige you, although it is not my custom to expose the errors of others. The first and most important error is this, that they have gone far astray from knowl-edge of the first cause and origin of all things. Secondly, they have failed to achieve understanding of the true nature of the human mind. Thirdly, they have never grasped the true cause of error. Only those who are com-pletely destitute of all learning and scholarship can fail to see the critical importance of true knowledge of these three points.

How far astray they have wandered from true knowledge of the first cause and of the human mind can readily be gathered from the truth of the three propositions to which I have already referred. So I confine myself to pointing out the third error. Of Bacon I shall say little; he speaks very confusedly on this point, and simply makes assertions while proving hardly anything.[3] In the first place, he takes for granted that the human intellect, apart from the fallibility of the senses, is by its very nature liable to error, framing its assumptions on the analogy of its own nature, and not on the analogy of the universe, so that it is like a mirror of irregular surface receiving rays, mingling its own nature with the nature of reality, and so forth. Secondly, he holds that the human in-tellect, by reason of its own nature, is prone to abstractions, and im-agines that things that are in flux are stable, and so on. Thirdly, he holds that the human intellect is continually increasing and cannot come to a halt or rest. Whatever other causes he assigns can readily be reduced to the one Cartesian principle, that the human will is free and more exten-sive than the intellect, or, as Verulam himself more confusedly puts it (Aph.49) the intellect is not characterised by a dry light, but receives in-fusion from the will. (We should here observe that Verulam takes 'in-tellect' for 'mind', therein differing with Descartes.) This cause, then, disregarding the others as being of little importance, I shall show to be false. Indeed, they would easily have seen this for themselves, had they but given consideration to the fact that the will differs from this or that

2. See *Ethics,* Part I, from the beginning to Proposition 4.

3. Francis Bacon, *Novum Organum* I: 41-51. Bacon was also called 'Verulam.'

volition in the same way as whiteness differs from this or that white object, or as humanity differs from this or that human being. So to conceive the will to be the cause of this or that volition is as impossible as to conceive humanity to be the cause of Peter or Paul.

Since, then, the will is nothing more than a mental construct (*ens rationis*), it can in no way be said to be the cause of this or that volition. Particular volitions, since they need a cause in order to exist, cannot be said to be free; rather they are necessarily determined to be such as they are by their own causes. Lastly, according to Descartes, errors are themselves particular volitions, from which it necessarily follows that errors—that is, particular volitions—are not free, but are determined by external causes and in no way by the will. This is what I undertook to prove.

September 1661

Letter 9 (in part)

To the learned young man, Simon de Vries[4] from Benedict de Spinoza.

My Worthy Friend,

. . . As to the questions which you raise,[5] I see that your difficulty arises because you do not differentiate between the various kinds of definition. There is the definition that serves to explicate a thing whose essence alone is the subject of enquiry and doubt. Then there is the definition that is put forward simply for consideration. The former, since it has a determinate object, must be a true definition, while this need not be so in the latter case. For example, if someone were to ask me for a description of Solomon's temple, I ought to give him a true description of the temple, unless I propose to talk nonsense with him. But if I have in my own mind formed the design of a temple that I want to build, and have concluded therefrom that I will have to purchase such-and-such a site and so many thousands of stones and other materials, will any sane person tell me that I have reached a wrong conclusion because my definition may be incorrect? Will anyone demand that I prove my definition? Such a person would be telling me that I had not conceived that which in fact I had conceived, or would be requiring me to prove that I had conceived that which I had con-

4. Simon de Vries, an Amsterdam merchant who studied under Spinoza and left the philosopher a pension when he died in 1667. Spinoza accepted less than the original amount.

5. In Letter 8, de Vries had asked Spinoza several questions pertaining to the nature of definition and the distinction between a definition and an axiom.

ceived, which is utter nonsense. Therefore, a definition either explicates a thing as it exists outside the intellect—and then it should be a true definition, differing from a proposition or axiom only in having reference to either the essences of things or the essences of the affections of things, whereas the latter has a wider scope, extending also to eternal truths—or it explicates a thing as we conceive it, or can conceive it. This again differs from an axiom or proposition for it requires merely that it be conceived without respect to the truth with which an axiom is concerned. In this case, a bad definition is one which is not conceived.

To make my meaning clearer, I will take Borellus'[6] example of a man who declares that two straight lines enclosing an area shall be called figurals. If he means by a straight line what everybody else means by a curved line, his definition is quite sound (for the figure intended by the definition would be $\bigcirc a$ or some such figure), provided that he does not at a later stage mean a square or any other such figure. But if by a straight line he means what we all mean, the thing is plainly inconceivable, and so there is no definition. All these considerations are obviously confused by Borellus, whose view you are too much inclined to embrace.

Here is another example, the one that you adduce towards the end of your letter. If I say that each substance has only one attribute, this is a mere assertion unsupported by proof. But if I say that by substance I mean that which consists of only one attribute, the definition is sound provided that entities consisting of more than one attribute are given a name other than substance.

In saying that I do not prove that a substance (or an entity) can have more than one attribute, it may be that you have not given sufficient attention to the proofs. I advanced two proofs, the first of which is as follows. It is clear beyond all doubt that every entity is conceived by us under some attribute, and the more reality or being an entity has, the more attributes are to be attributed to it. Hence an absolutely infinite entity must be defined . . . and so on. A second proof—and this proof I take to be decisive—states that the more attributes I attribute to any entity, the more existence I am bound to attribute to it, that is, the more do I conceive it as true. The exact contrary would be the case if I had imagined a chimera or something of the sort.

But when you say that you do not conceive thought otherwise than under ideas because thought vanishes with the removal of ideas, I believe that you experience this because when you, as thinking things, do as you say, you are banishing all your thoughts and conceptions. So it is not surprising that when you have banished all your thoughts, there is nothing left for you to think.

To return to the main point, I think I have demonstrated with sufficient clarity and evidence that the intellect, although infinite, belongs to Natura naturata, not to Natura naturans.[7]

6. Giovanni Borelli (1608–1679), Italian mathematician.

7. See Introduction, p. 11.

Furthermore, I fail to see what this has to do with understanding the Third Definition, or why this definition causes you difficulty. The definition as I gave it to you runs, if I am not mistaken, "By substance I understand that which is in itself and is conceived through itself; that is, that whose conception does not involve the conception of another thing. I understand the same by attribute, except that attribute is so called in respect to the intellect, which attributes to substance a certain specific kind of nature." This definition, I repeat, explains clearly what I mean by substance or attribute. However, you want me to explain by example— though it is not at all necessary—how one and the same thing can be signified by two names. Not to appear ungenerous, I will give you two examples. First, by "Israel" is meant the third patriarch; by "Jacob" is meant that same person, the latter name given to him because he seized his brother's heel. Secondly, by a "plane surface" I mean one that reflects all rays of light without any change. I mean the same by "white surface," except that it is called "white" in respect of a man looking at it.

March 1663

Letter 12

To the learned and wise Ludwig Meyer,[8] *Doctor in Philosophy and in Medicine, from Benedict de Spinoza.*

(On the Nature of the Infinite)

Dearest friend,

I have received two letters from you, one dated January 11 and delivered to me by our friend N.N.,[9] the other dated March 26 and sent to me by an unknown friend from Leyden. They were both very welcome, especially as I gathered from them that all is well with you and that I am often in your thoughts. My most cordial thanks are due to you for the kindness and esteem you have always shown me. At the same time I beseech you to believe that I am in no less a degree your devoted friend, and this I shall endeavour to prove whenever the occasion arises, as far as my slender abilities allow. As a first offering, I will try to answer the request made in your letters to me, in which you ask me to let you have my considered views on the question of the infinite. I am glad to oblige.

The question of the infinite has universally been found to be very

---

8. Ludwig Meyer, physician and philosopher, was a close friend of Spinoza. He participated in preparing Spinoza's writings for posthumous publication.

9. Most likely Peter Balling, another of Spinoza's close friends.

difficult, indeed, insoluble, through failure to distinguish between that which must be infinite by its very nature or by virtue of its definition, and that which is unlimited not by virtue of its essence but by virtue of its cause. Then again, there is the failure to distinguish between that which is called infinite because it is unlimited, and that whose parts cannot be equated or explicated by any number, although we may know its maximum and minimum. Lastly, there is the failure to distinguish between that which we can apprehend only by intellect and not by imagination, and that which can also be apprehended by imagination. I repeat, if men had paid careful attention to these distinctions, they would never have found themselves overwhelmed by such a mountain of difficulties. They would clearly have understood what kind of infinite cannot be divided into, or possess any, parts, and what kind can be so divided without contradiction. They would also have understood what kind of infinite can be considered, without contradiction, as greater than another infinite, and what kind cannot be so conceived. This will become clear from what I am about to say. However, I shall first briefly explain these four terms: Substance, Mode, Eternity, Duration.

The points to be noted about Substance are as follows. First, existence pertains to its essence; that is, solely from its essence and definition it follows that Substance exists. This point, if my memory does not deceive me, I have proved to you in an earlier conversation without the help of any other propositions. Second, following from the first point, substance is not many; rather, there exists only one substance of the same nature. Thirdly, all Substance can be understood only as infinite.

The affections of Substance I call Modes. The definition of Modes, in so far as it is not a definition of Substance, cannot involve existence. Therefore, even when they exist, we can conceive them as not existing. It therefore follows that when we have regard only to the essence of Modes and not to the order of Nature as a whole, we cannot deduce from their present existence that they will or will not exist in the future, or that they did or did not exist in the past. Hence it is clear that we conceive the existence of Substance as of an entirely different kind from the existence of Modes. This is the source of the difference between Eternity and Duration. It is to the existence of Modes only that we can apply the term Duration; the corresponding term for the existence of Substance is Eternity, that is, the infinite enjoyment of existence or—pardon the Latin—of being (essendi).

What I have said makes it quite clear that when we have regard only to the essence of Modes and not to Nature's order, as is most frequently the case, we can arbitrarily limit the existence and duration of Modes (without thereby impairing to any degree our conception of them); and we can conceive this duration as greater or less, and divisible into parts. But Eternity and Substance, being conceivable only as infinite, cannot be thus treated without annulling our concept of them. So it is nonsense, bordering on insanity, to hold that extended Substance is composed of parts or bodies really distinct from one another. It is as if, by adding circle to circle and piling one on top of another, one were to attempt to construct a square or a triangle or any other figure of a completely different nature. Therefore the whole heap of arguments whereby the common run of philosophers strive to prove that extended Substance is finite collapses of its own accord. All such arguments assume that corporeal Substance is composed of parts. A parallel case is presented by those who, having convinced themselves that a line is made up of points, have devised many arguments to prove that a line is not infinitely divisible.

However, if you ask why we have such a strong natural tendency to divide extended Substance, I answer that we conceive quantity in two ways: abstractly, or superficially, as we have it in the imagination with the help of the senses; or as substance apprehended solely by means of the intellect. If we have regard to quantity as it exists in the imagination (and this is what we most frequently and readily do), it is found to be divisible, finite, composed of parts, and multiplex. But if we have regard to it as it is in the intellect and apprehend the thing as it is in itself (and this is very difficult), then it is found to be infinite, indivisible, and one alone, as I have already sufficiently proved.

Further, from the fact that we are able to limit Duration and Quantity as we please, conceiving Quantity in abstraction from Substance and ignoring the efflux of Duration from things eternal, there arise Time and Measure: Time to limit Duration, and Measure to limit Quantity in such wise that we are thereby enabled to form images of them as best we may. Again, from the fact that we separate the Affections of Substance from Substance itself, and arrange them in classes so that we can form images of them as best we may, there arises Number, whereby we limit them. Hence it can clearly be seen that Measure, Time and Number are nothing other than modes of thinking, or rather, modes of the imagination. It is therefore not surprising that all who have attempted to understand the workings of Nature by such concepts, and without really understanding these concepts, have tied themselves into such extraordinary knots that in the end they have been unable to extricate themselves except by breaking all laws and perpetrating the grossest absurdities. For there are many things that can in no way be apprehended by the imagination but only by the intellect, such as Substance, Eternity, and the like. If anyone tries to explicate such things by notions of this kind, which are nothing more than aids to the imagination, he will meet with no more success than if he were deliberately to encourage his imagination to run mad. The Modes of Substance, too, can never be correctly understood if they are confused with such mental constructs (entia rationis) or aids to the imagination. For by so doing we are abstracting them from Substance and from the manner of their efflux from Eternity, and in such isolation they can never be correctly understood.

To make the matter still clearer, take the following example. If someone conceives Duration in this abstracted way and, confusing it with Time, begins dividing it into parts, he can never understand how, for instance, an hour can pass by. For in order that an hour should pass by, a half-hour must first have passed by, and then half of the remainder, and then half of what is left of the remainder; and if you go on subtracting half of the remainder to infinity, you can never reach the end of the hour. Therefore, many who are not used to distinguishing mental constructs from reality have ventured to assert that Duration is composed of moments, thus falling into the clutches of Scylla in their eagerness to avoid Charybdis. To say that Duration is made up of moments is the same as to say that Number is made up by adding noughts together.

Further, it is obvious from the above that Number, Time and Measure, being merely aids to the imagination, cannot be infinite, for in that case Number would not be number, nor Measure measure, nor Time time. Hence one can easily see why many people, confusing these three concepts with reality because of their ignorance of the true nature of reality, have denied the actual existence of the Infinite. But let their deplorable reasoning be judged by mathematicians who, in matters that they clearly and distinctly perceive, are not to be delayed by arguments of that sort. For they not only have come upon many things inexpressible by any number, which clearly reveals the inadequacy of number to determine all things; in addition they have encountered many things that cannot be equalled by any number, and exceed any possible number. Now they do not draw the conclusion that it is because of the multitude of parts that such things exceed all number; rather, it is because the nature of the thing is such that number is inapplicable to it without manifest contradiction.

For example, all the inequalities of the space lying between the two circles ABCD in the diagram exceed any number, as do all the variations of speed of matter moving through that area. Now this conclusion is not reached because of the excessive magnitude of the intervening space; for however small a portion of it we take, the inequalities of this small portion will still be beyond any numerical expression. Nor, again, is this conclusion reached, as happens in other cases, because we do not know the maximum and minimum; in our example we know them both, the maximum being AB and the minimum CD. Our conclusion is reached because number is not applicable to the nature of the space between the two non-concentric circles. Therefore, if anyone sought to express by number all those inequalities, he would have to bring it about that a circle should not be a circle.

Similarly, to return to our main topic of discussion, if anyone were to attempt to determine all the motions of matter that have ever been, by reducing them and their duration to a certain number and time, he would be attempting to deprive corporeal Substance, which we cannot conceive as other than existing, of its Affections, and bring it about that Substance should not possess the nature which it does possess. I could here clearly demonstrate this and many other points touched on in this letter, did I not consider it unnecessary.

From all that I have said one can clearly see that certain things are infinite by their own nature and cannot in any way be conceived as finite, while other things are infinite by virtue of the cause in which they have their being, and when the latter are conceived in abstraction, they can be divided into parts and be regarded as finite. Lastly, there are things that are called infinite, or if you prefer, indefinite, because they cannot be accurately expressed by any number, while yet being conceivable as greater or less. For it does not follow that things that cannot be accurately expressed by any number must necessarily be equal, as is evident from the given example and from many others.

To sum up, I have here briefly set before you the causes of error and of the confusions that have arisen regarding the question of the Infinite, explaining them all, unless I am mistaken, in such a way that I do not believe there is any question regarding the Infinite on which I have not touched, or which cannot be readily solved from what I have said. Therefore, I think it is pointless to detain you any longer on this matter.

However, in passing, I should like it here to be observed that in my opinion our modern Peripatetics have quite misunderstood the proof whereby scholars of old sought to prove the existence of God. According to a certain Jew named Rabbi Chasdai,[10] this proof runs as follows: —"If there is granted an infinite series of causes, all things which are, are also caused. But nothing that is caused can exist necessarily by virtue of its own nature. Therefore, there is nothing in Nature to whose essence existence necessarily pertains. But this is absurd. Therefore the premise is absurd." So the force of the argument lies not in the impossibility of an actual infinite, or an infinite series of causes, but in the assumption that things which by their own nature do not necessarily exist are not determined by a thing that necessarily exists by its own nature.

I would now pass on—for I am pressed for time—to your second question, but I shall be able more conveniently to reply to the points contained therein when you kindly pay me a visit. So do please try to come as soon as you can. For the time for my departure is rapidly approaching. Enough, farewell, and keep me ever in your thoughts. Yours, etc.

April 20, 1663

Letter 19

To the learned and wise William de Blyenbergh[11] from Benedict de Spinoza.

10. Hasdai Crescas (1340–1410), a Spanish-Jewish theologian, whose *The Light of the Lord* subjects Aristotle's physics to a 'radical' critique.

11. William Blyenbergh, a Dutch businessman with interests in theology. He was vigorously opposed to Spinoza's philosophy, which he regarded as tantamount to atheism.

My unknown friend,

I received at Schiedam on the 26th of December your letter of the 12th of December enclosed in another dated the 21st of the same month. I gather from it that you are deeply devoted to truth, which you make the sole aim of your studies. Since I have exactly the same objective, I am resolved not only to grant without stint your request to answer to the best of my ability the questions which you are now sending me and may send me in the future, but also to do everything in my power conducive to further acquaintance and sincere friendship. For my part, of all the things that are not under my control, what I value most is to enter into a bond of friendship with sincere lovers of truth. For I believe that such a loving relationship affords us a serenity surpassing any other boon in the whole wide world. The love that such men bear to one another, grounded as it is in the love that each has for knowledge of truth, is as unshakeable as the acceptance of truth once it has been perceived. It is, moreover, the highest source of happiness to be found in things not under our command, for truth more than anything else has the power to effect a close union between various sentiments and dispositions. I say nothing of the considerable advantages that derive therefrom, not wishing to detain you any longer on a matter on which you need no instruction. This much I have said so that you may better understand how pleased I am, and shall continue to be, to have the opportunity of serving you.

To avail myself of the present opportunity, I shall now go on to answer your question.[12] This seems to hinge on the following point, that it seems clearly to follow, both from God's Providence, which is identical with his will, and from God's concurrence and the continuous creation of things, either that there is no such thing as sin or evil, or that God brings about sin and evil. Now you do not explain what you mean by evil, and as far as one can gather from the example of Adam's determinate will, by evil you seem to mean the will itself in so far as it is conceived as determined in a particular way, or in so far as it is in opposition to God's command. So you say that it is quite absurd (and I would agree, if the case were as you say) to maintain either of the following alternatives, that God himself brings to pass what is contrary to his will, or else that what is opposed to God's will can be good. For my own part, I cannot concede that sin and evil are anything positive, much less that anything can be or come to pass against God's will. On the contrary, I not only assert that sin is not anything positive; I maintain that it is only by speaking improperly or in merely human fashion that we can say that we sin against God, as in the expression that men offend against God.

Now as to the first point, we know that whatever is, when considered in itself without regard to anything else, possesses a perfection

---

12. Blyenbergh had asked whether, on Spinoza's doctrine of God and divine causality, it would not follow that either there was no such thing as evil or God Himself produces evil.

co-extensive in every case with the thing's essence, for essence is the same as perfection. I take as an example Adam's resolve or determinate will to eat of the forbidden fruit. This resolve, or determinate will, considered solely in itself, contains in itself perfection to the degree that it expresses reality. This can be inferred from the fact that we cannot conceive imperfection in things except by having regard to other things possessing more reality. For this reason, when we consider Adam's decision in itself without comparing it with other things more perfect or displaying a more perfect status, we cannot find any imperfection in it. Indeed, we may compare it with many other things much more lacking in perfection in comparison with it, such as stones, logs, and so forth. In actual practice, too, this is universally conceded. For everybody admires in animals what he dislikes and regards with aversion in men, like the warring of bees, the jealousy of doves, and so on. In men such things are despised, yet we esteem animals as more perfect because of them. This being the case, it clearly follows that sin, since it indicates only imperfection, cannot consist in anything that expresses reality, such as Adam's decision and its execution.

Furthermore, we cannot say that Adam's will was at variance with God's law and was evil because it was displeasing to God. It would argue great imperfection in God if anything happened against his will, or if he wanted something he did not possess, or if his nature were determined in such a manner that just like his creatures, he felt sympathy with some and antipathy to others. Furthermore, this would be in complete contradiction to the nature of God's will; for since his will is identical with his intellect, it would be no less impossible for anything to take place in opposition to his will than in opposition to his intellect. That is to say, anything that would take place against his will would have to be of such a nature as likewise to be in opposition to his intellect, as, for example, a round square. Therefore, since Adam's will or decision, regarded in itself, was neither evil nor yet, properly speaking, against God's will, it follows that God can be—or rather, according to the reasoning which you advance, must be—the cause of it. But not in so far as it was evil, for the evil that was in it was simply the privation of a more perfect state which Adam was bound to lose because of his action.

Now it is certain that privation is not something positive, and is so termed in respect of our intellect, not God's intellect. It arises from the fact that we express by one and the same definition all the individual instances of the same genus—for instance, all that have the outward appearance of men—and we therefore deem them all equally capable of the highest degree of perfection that can be inferred from that particular definition. Now when we find one thing whose actions are at variance with that perfection, we consider that it is deprived of that perfection and is astray from its own nature. This we would not do if we had not referred the individual to that particular definition and ascribed to it such a nature. Now God does not know things in abstraction, nor does he formulate general definitions of that kind, and things possess no more reality than God's intellect and potency have implanted in them and assigned to them in actual fact. From this clearly follows that the privation in question is a term applicable in respect of our intellect only, and not of God.

This, I believe, is a complete answer to the question. However, to make the path smoother and remove every trace of doubt, I think it necessary to answer the two following questions: —First, why does Holy Scripture say that God requires the wicked to turn from their evil ways, and why did he forbid Adam to eat of the fruit of the tree when he had ordained the contrary? Secondly, it seems to follow from what I have said that the wicked serve God by their pride, greed, and desperate deeds no less than the good by their nobleness, patience, love, etc. For they both carry out God's will.

In reply to the first question, I say that Scripture, being particularly adapted to the service of the common people, invariably speaks in merely human fashion, for the common people are incapable of understanding higher things. It is for this reason, I am convinced, that all that God has revealed to the Prophets as necessary for salvation is set down in the form of law, and in this way the Prophets made up entire parables depicting God as a king and lawgiver, because he had revealed the means that lead to salvation and perdition, and was the cause thereof. These means, which are simply causes, they called laws, and wrote them down in the form of laws; salvation and perdition, which are simply effects necessarily resulting from these means, they represented as reward and punishment. All that they wrote was adjusted to the framework of this parable rather than to truth. They constantly depicted God in human form, sometimes angry, sometimes merciful, now looking to what is to come, now jealous and suspicious, and even deceived by the Devil. So philosophers and all who have risen to a level beyond law, that is, all who pursue virtue not as a law but because they love it as something very precious, should not find such writing a stumbling-block.

Therefore the command given to Adam consisted solely in this, that God revealed to Adam that eating of that tree brought about death, in the same way that he also reveals to us through our natural understanding that poison is deadly. If you ask to what end he made this revelation, I answer that his purpose was to make Adam that much more perfect in knowledge. So to ask God why he did not give Adam a more perfect will is no less absurd than to ask why he has not bestowed on a circle all the properties of a sphere, as clearly follows from what I have said above, and as I have demonstrated in the Scholium to Proposition 15 of my "Principles of Cartesian Philosophy Demonstrated In Geometrical Form," Part I.

As to your second difficulty, it is indeed true that the wicked express God's will in their own way, but they are not for that reason at all comparable with the good; for the more perfection a thing has, the more it participates in Deity, and the more it expresses God's perfection. Since, then, the good have incomparably more perfection than the wicked, their virtue cannot be compared with the virtue of the wicked, because the wicked lack the love of God that flows from the knowledge of God by which alone, within the limits of our human intellect, we are said to be servants of God. Indeed, the wicked, not knowing God, are but an instrument in the hands of the Master, serving unconsciously and being used up in that service, whereas the good serve consciously, and in serving become more perfect.

January 1665

Letter 21 (in part)

To the learned and accomplished William de Blyenberg from Benedict de Spinoza.

Sir and Friend,

When I read your first letter, I had the impression that our views were almost the same. From your second letter, however, which I received on the 21st of this month, I realise that this is far from being so, and I see that we disagree not only in what inferences are to be drawn by a chain of reasoning from first principles, but in those very same first principles. So it is hardly likely that our correspondence can afford us mutual instruction. I see that no proof, however firmly established by the rules of logic, has any validity with you unless it agrees with the explanation which you, or other theologians of your acquaintance, assign to Holy Scripture. However, if it is your conviction that God speaks more clearly and effectually through Holy Scripture than through the natural light of the intellect, which he has also granted to us and constantly maintains strong and uncorrupted through his Divine wisdom, you have good reason to subordinate your intellect to the opinions which you attribute to Holy Scripture. Indeed, I myself could do no other. For my part, I plainly and unambiguously avow that I do not understand Holy Scripture, although I have devoted quite a number of years to its study. And since I am conscious that when an indisputable proof is presented to me I find it impossible to entertain thoughts that cast doubt upon it, I entirely acquiesce in what my intellect shows me, without any suspicion that I am deceived therein, or that Scripture, even though I am not examining it, can contradict it. For truth is not at odds with the truth, as I have made clear in my Appendix. . . .

To return to your letter, I owe you many and sincere thanks for having confided in me in time your method of philosophy, but I do not thank you for attributing to me the sort of opinions you try to read into my letter. What grounds did my letter give you for attributing to me these opinions: that men are like beasts, that men die and perish after the manner of beasts, that our actions are displeasing to God, and so forth? (It is in this last point that our disagreement is most striking, for I take your meaning to be that God is pleased with our actions like someone who has attained his end when things fall out as he wished.) As for me, surely I have clearly stated that the good worship God, and by their constancy in worship they become more perfect, and that they love God. Is this to liken them to beasts, or to say that they perish in the manner of beasts, or that their actions are not pleasing to God? If you had read my letter with more care, it would have been obvious to you that our point of disagreement lies in this alone: are the perfections received by the good imparted to them by God in his capacity as God, that is, by God taken absolutely without ascribing any human attributes to him—this is the view I hold—or by God in his capacity as judge? The latter is what you maintain, and for this reason you support the wicked because whatever they do is done according to God's decree, and so they serve God no less than the good serve him. But this in no way follows from what I say. I do not bring in the notion of God as judge, and so my evaluation of actions turns on the quality of the actions, not on the potency of the doer, and the reward that follows from the action does so by the same necessity as it follows from the nature of a triangle that its three angles have to be equal to two right angles. This will be obvious to everyone who attends simply to the following point, that our supreme blessedness consists in love towards God, and that this love flows necessarily from that knowledge of God that is so heartily urged on us. This can be readily demonstrated in a general way if only one has regard to the nature of God's decree, as I have explained in my Appendix.[13] I admit, however, that all those who confuse God's nature with the nature of man are quite unqualified to understand this.

    . . . I will now pass on to an explanation of the words 'negation' and 'privation,' and attempt briefly to throw some light on any obscurities in my previous letter.

    First, then, I say that privation (privatio) is not the act of depriving: it is nothing more than simply a state of want, which in itself is nothing. It is only a construct of the mind (ens rationis) or a mode of thinking which we form from comparing things with one another. For instance, we say that a blind man is deprived of sight because we readily imagine him as seeing. This imagining may arise from our comparing him with those who can see, or from comparing his present state with a past state when he could see. When we consider the man in this perspective, comparing his nature with that of others or with his own past nature, we assert that sight pertains to his nature, and so we say that he is deprived of it. But when we consider God's nature and God's decree, we can no more assert of that man that he is deprived of sight than we can assert it

13. Spinoza alludes here to his *Metaphysical Thoughts,* Part II, chapters 7-9, a work that is the appendix to his *Principles of Cartesian Philosophy.*

of a stone, for to say that sight belongs to that man at that time is quite as illogical as to say that it belongs to a stone, since nothing more pertains to that man, and is his, than that which God's intellect and will has assigned to him. Therefore God is no more the cause of his not seeing than of a stone's not seeing, this latter being pure negation. So, too, when we consider the nature of a man who is governed by a lustful desire and we compare his present desire with the desire of a good man, or with the desire that he once had, we assert that this man is deprived of the better desire, judging that a virtuous desire belonged to him at that point of time. This we cannot do if we have regard to the nature of the decree and intellect of God. For in that perspective the better desire pertains to that man's nature at that point of time no more than to the nature of the Devil or a stone. Therefore in that perspective the better desire is not a privation but a negation. So privation is to deny of a thing something that we judge pertains to its nature, and negation is to deny something of a thing because it does not pertain to its nature.

From this it is clear why Adam's desire for earthly things was evil only in respect of our intellect, not God's intellect. For granted that God knew the past and present state of Adam, this does not mean that he understood Adam as deprived of a past state, that is, that the past state pertained to his nature. If that were so, God would be understanding something that was contrary to his will, that is, he would be understanding something that was contrary to his understanding. Had you grasped this point, and also that I do not concede the sort of freedom that Descartes ascribes to the mind—as Ludwig Meyer bears witness on my behalf in his Preface[14]—you would have found no trace of contradiction in what I said. But I see now that it would have been far better if in my first letter I had adhered to Descartes' line, that we cannot know in what way our freedom, and whatever stems from it, can be reconciled with the providence and freedom of God. (see my Appendix, various passages). As a result, we cannot find any contradiction between God's creation and our freedom because it is beyond us to understand how God created the world and—which is the same thing—how he preserves it. I thought you had read the Preface, and that I would be failing in the duty of friendship, which I sincerely offered, if I did not give you my genuine opinion. But no matter.

However, as I see that you have not yet thoroughly understood Descartes' meaning, I ask you to consider carefully the following two points. First, neither Descartes nor I have ever said that it pertains to our nature to confine our will within the limits of the intellect but only that God has given us a determinate intellect and an indeterminate will, without our knowing to what end he created us. Further, an indeterminate or perfect will of that kind not only renders us more perfect, but

---

14. Ludwig Meyer had written a preface to Spinoza's *Principles of Cartesian Philosophy*, in which he warned the reader that Spinoza differed from Descartes on some important issues, especially on the topic of freedom.

is also very necessary for us, as I shall point out in due course.

Secondly, our freedom lies not in a kind of contingency nor in a kind of indifference, but in the mode of affirmation and denial, so that the less indifference there is in our affirmation and denial, the more we are free. For instance, if God's nature is known to us, the affirmation of God's existence follows from our nature with the same necessity as it results from the nature of a triangle that its three angles are equal to two right angles. Yet we are never more free than when we make an affirmation in this way. Now since this necessity is nothing other than God's decree, as I have clearly pointed out in my Appendix, hence we may understand after a fashion how we act freely and are the cause of our action notwithstanding that we act necessarily and from God's decree. This, I repeat, we can understand in a way when we affirm something that we clearly and distinctly perceive. But when we assert something that we do not clearly and distinctly perceive—that is, when we suffer our will to exceed the bounds of our intellect,—then we are not able in this way to perceive that necessity and God's decrees; however, we do perceive that freedom of ours that is always involved in the will (in which respect alone our actions are termed good and bad). If we then attempt to reconcile our freedom with God's decree and with continuous creation, we confuse that which we clearly and distinctly understand with that which we do not perceive, and so our effort is in vain. It is therefore sufficient for us to know that we are free, and that we can be so notwithstanding God's decree, and that we are the cause of evil; for nothing can be called evil except in respect of our freedom. I have said so much concerning Descartes in order that I might show that in this matter his philosophy is perfectly consistent.

Turning now to my own philosophy, I shall first briefly draw attention to an advantage that accrues from my opinion, an advantage that lies chiefly in this, that by this view of things our intellect puts our mind and body in God's hands free from all superstition. Nor do I deny the utility of prayer, for my intellect is not extensive enough to embrace all the means that God possesses for bringing men to the love of himself, that is, to salvation. So far is my opinion from being pernicious that, on the contrary, for those who are not hampered by prejudices and childish superstition, it is the one means of attaining the highest degree of blessedness.

When you say that by making men so dependent on God I reduce them to the level of elementary things, plants and stones, you clearly reveal that you have completely misunderstood my views and are confusing the field of intellect with the field of imagination. If you had apprehended by pure intellect the meaning of dependence on God, you would certainly not think that things, in so far as they depend on God, are dead, corporeal and imperfect. (Who has ever dared to speak so basely of the supremely perfect Being?) On the contrary, you would realise that it is in so far as they depend on God that they are perfect. So this dependence on God and necessity of action can be best understood through God's decree when we have regard, not to logs and plants, but to created things of the highest degree of intelligibility and perfection. This is quite clear from my second observation on the meaning of Descartes, which you should have considered carefully.

I am bound to express astonishment at your saying that if God does not punish wrongdoing (that is, in the way a judge inflicts a punishment that is not entailed by the wrongdoing itself, for this alone is the point at issue), what consideration hinders me from plunging headlong into all sorts of crime? Surely, he who refrains from so doing by fear of punishment—which I do not impute to you—in no way acts from love and by no means embraces virtue. For my own part I refrain, or try to refrain, from such behaviour because it is in direct opposition to my own nature, and would cause me to stray from the love and knowledge of God.

Again, if you had given a little thought to the nature of man and had understood the nature of God's decree as explained in my Appendix, and had come to know how inference should be made before a conclusion is reached, you would not have so rashly asserted that my view puts us on a level with logs and the like, nor would you have saddled me with all the absurdities you can imagine.

. . . I pass on now to your second rule, and I assert that for my part, while I do not ascribe to Scripture the sort of truth that you believe to be contained in it, yet I think that I ascribe to it as much authority, if not more, and that I am far more cautious than others in not assigning to it certain childish and absurd doctrines, for which one must needs be supported either by a thorough knowledge of philosophy or by divine revelation. So I am quite unmoved by the explanations of Scripture advanced by the common run of theologians especially if they are of the kind that take Scripture literally by its outward meaning. Apart from the Socinians,[15] I have never found any theologian so stupid as not to see that Holy Scripture speaks of God in merely human style and expresses its meaning in parables. As for the contradiction which you vainly, in my opinion, try to prove, I think that by parable you understand something quite different from what is generally accepted. Who has ever heard that a man who expresses his concepts in parables goes astray from his intended meaning? When Michaiah told King Ahab that he had seen God sitting on his throne and the celestial hosts standing on his right hand and on his left, and that God asked them who would deceive Ahab, that was surely a parable wherein the Prophet on that occasion (which was not one for teaching the high doctrines of theology) sufficiently expressed the main purport of the message he was charged to deliver in God's name. So in no way did he stray from his intended meaning. Likewise the other Prophets by God's command made manifest to the people the Word of God in this way, as being the best means—though not means enjoined by God—of leading the people to the primary objective of Scripture, which according to Christ himself consists in loving God above all things and

15. The Socinians were an extreme Protestant sect that denied the divinity of Jesus and anticipated some of the ideas of modern Unitarianism.

your neighbour as yourself. Deep speculative thought, in my view, has nothing to do with Scripture. For my part I have never learned, or been able to learn, any of God's eternal attributes from Holy Scripture.

As to your fifth argument (that the Prophets in that way made manifest the word of God, since truth is not contrary to truth), it amounts to no more than asking me to prove (as anyone will agree, who understands the methodology of proof) that Scripture, as it stands, is the true revealed Word of God. A mathematically exact proof of this proposition can be attained only by divine revelation. I therefore said, "I believe, but do not know with mathematical accuracy, that all things revealed by God to the Prophets . . ." and so on. For I firmly believe, but do not know with mathematical accuracy, that the Prophets were the trusted counsellors and faithful messengers of God. So there is no contradiction whatsoever in what I have affirmed, whereas many contradictions can be found in my opponents. . . .

January 28, 1665

Letter 32 (in part)

*To the most honourable and learned Henry
Oldenburg from Benedict de Spinoza.*

Most honourable Sir,

Please accept my most grateful thanks for the kind encouragement which you and the most honourable Master Boyle have given me in the pursuit of philosophy. As far as my poor abilities will allow, I shall continue in this way, with the assurance of your assistance and goodwill.

When you ask for my views on "how we know the way in which each part of Nature agrees with the whole, and the manner of its coherence with the other parts," I presume you are asking for the grounds of our belief that each part of Nature agrees with the whole and coheres with the other parts. As to knowing the actual manner of this coherence and the agreement of each part with the whole, I made it clear in my previous letter that this is beyond my knowledge. To know this it would be necessary to know the whole of Nature and all its parts. So I shall attempt to give the reasoning that compels me to this belief. But I would first ask you to note that I do not attribute to Nature beauty, ugliness, order or confusion. It is only with respect to our imagination that things can be said to be beautiful, ugly, well-ordered or confused.

By "coherence of parts" I mean simply this, that the laws or nature of one part adapts itself to the laws or nature of another part in such wise that there is the least possible opposition between them. On the question of whole and parts, I consider things as parts of a whole to the extent that their natures adapt themselves to one another so that they are in the closest possible agreement. In so far as they are different from one another, to that extent each one forms in our mind a separate idea and is therefore considered as a whole, not a part. For example, when the motions of particles of lymph, chyle, etc. adapt themselves to one another in accordance with size and shape so as to be fully in agreement with one another and to form all together one single fluid, to that extent only are the chyle, lymph, etc. regarded as parts of the blood. But in so far as we conceive the particles of lymph as different from the particles of chyle in respect of shape and motion, to that extent we regard them each as a whole, not a part.

Now let us imagine, if you please, a tiny worm living in the blood, capable of distinguishing by sight the particles of the blood—lymph, etc.—and of intelligently observing how each particle, on colliding with another, either rebounds or communicates some degree of its motion, and so forth. That worm would be living in the blood as we are living in our part of the universe, and it would regard each individual particle as a whole, not a part, and it would have no idea as to how all the parts are modified by the overall nature of the blood and compelled to mutual adaptation as the overall nature of the blood requires, so as to agree with one another in a definite relation. For if we imagine that there are no causes external to the blood which would communicate new motions to the blood, nor any space external to the blood, nor any other bodies to which the particles of the blood could transfer their motions, it is beyond doubt that the blood will remain indefinitely in its present state and that its particles will undergo no changes other than those which can be conceived as resulting from the existing relation between the motion of the blood and that of the lymph, chyle, etc. Thus the blood would always have to be regarded as a whole, not a part. But since there are many other causes which do in fact modify the laws of the nature of the blood and are reciprocally modified by the blood, it follows that there occur in the blood other motions and other changes, resulting not solely from the reciprocal relation of its particles but from the relation between the motion of the blood on the one hand and external causes on the other. In this perspective the blood is accounted as a part, not as a whole. So much, then, for the question of whole and part.

Now all the bodies in Nature can and should be conceived in the same way as we have here conceived the blood; for all bodies are surrounded by others and are reciprocally determined to exist and to act in a fixed and determinate way, the same ratio of motion to rest being preserved in them taken all together, that is, in the universe as a whole. Hence it follows that every body, in so far as it exists as modified in a definite way, must be considered as a part of the whole universe and must agree with the whole and cohere with the other parts. Now since the nature of the universe, unlike the nature of the blood, is not limited, but is absolutely infinite, its parts are modified by the nature of this infinite potency in infinite ways and are compelled to undergo infinite variations. But I conceive that, in respect to substance, each individual part has a more intimate union with the whole. For, as I endeavoured to prove in my first letter written some time ago, while I was living at Rhijnsburg,[16] since it is of the nature of substance to be infinite, it follows that each part pertains to the nature of corporeal substance, and can neither be nor be conceived without it.

So you see how and why I hold that the human body is a part of Nature. As regards the human mind, I maintain that it also is a part of Nature, for I hold that in Nature there also exists an infinite power of thinking which, in so far as it is infinite, contains within itself the whole of Nature as an object of thought, and whose thoughts proceed in the same manner as does Nature, which is clearly its object of thought.[17]

Further, I maintain that the human mind is that same power of thinking, not in so far as that power is infinite and apprehends the whole of Nature, but in so far as it is finite, apprehending the human body only. The human mind, I maintain, is in this way part of an infinite intellect. . . .

November 20, 1665

Letter 56

To the highly respected and wise Hugh
Boxel[18] from Benedict de Spinoza.

Respected Sir,

I hasten to reply to your letter received yesterday, for if I delay any further I shall have to postpone my reply longer than I could wish. I should have been anxious about your health, had I not learned that you are better. I hope that you are by now completely recovered.

When two people follow different first principles, the difficulty they experience in coming together and reaching agreement in a matter that involves many other questions might be shown simply from this discussion of ours, even if it were not confirmed by rational considerations.

16. This is an allusion to Letter 2.

17. See Translator's Foreword, items 13 and 17.

18. Not all of Spinoza's correspondents were worthy of this honor, and Boxel was no exception. He was for some time active in political affairs in the Netherlands, but he wasn't much of a philosopher. In his letters to Spinoza he asked the philosopher some silly questions about ghosts and made a legitimate query about free-will.

Tell me, pray, whether you have seen or read any philosophers who have maintained that the world was made by chance, taking chance in the sense you give it, that God had a set aim in creating the world and yet departed from his resolve. I am unaware that any such idea has ever entered the thoughts of any man. I am similarly at a loss to understand the reasoning whereby you try to convince me that chance and necessity are not contraries. As soon as I perceive that the three angles of a triangle are necessarily equal to two right angles, I thereby deny that this is the result of chance, likewise, as soon as I perceive that heat is the necessary effect of fire, I thereby deny that this is the result of chance. That 'necessary' and 'free' are contraries seems no less absurd and opposed to reason. Nobody can deny that God freely knows himself and all other things, and yet all are unanimous in granting that God knows himself necessarily. Thus you fail, I think, to make any distinction between Constraint (coactio) or force, and Necessity. That a man wills to live, to love, etc. does not proceed from constraint, but is nevertheless necessary, and far more so is God's will to be, to know and to act. If, in addition to these points, you will reflect that a state of indifference is nothing but ignorance or a condition of doubt, and that a will that is always constant and determined in all things is a virtue and a necessary property of the intellect, you will see that my view is in complete accord with the truth. If we maintain that God was able not to have willed what he willed, but that he was bound to understand what he willed, we are attributing to God two different kinds of freedom, the freedom of necessity, and the freedom of indifference. Consequently, we shall conceive God's will as different from his essence and his intellect, and in this way we shall fall into one absurdity after another.

The attention which I requested in my former letter you have not deemed necessary, and it is for this reason that you have failed to direct your thoughts to the main point at issue, and have disregarded what was most relevant.

Further, when you say that you do not see what sort of God I have if I deny in him the actions of seeing, hearing, attending, willing, etc., and that he possesses these faculties in an eminent degree, I suspect that you believe that there is no greater perfection than can be explicated by the aforementioned attributes. I am not surprised, for I believe that a triangle, if it could speak, would likewise say that God is eminently triangular, and a circle that God's nature is eminently circular. In this way each would ascribe to God its own attributes, assuming itself to be like God, and regarding all else as ill-formed.

The briefness of a letter and the pressure of time do not permit me to deal with my view of the divine nature and with the questions you have propounded; anyway, to bring up difficulties is not to put forward constructive reasoning. It is true that in this world we often act from conjecture, but it is not true that speculative thought proceeds from conjecture. In the common round of life we follow what is probable, but in speculative thought we have to follow what is true. A man would perish of hunger and thirst if he refused to eat and drink until he had obtained a perfect proof that food and drink would be good for him, but this does not hold in the field of contemplation. On the contrary, we should take care not to admit as true anything that is merely probable. When one false proposition is allowed entry, innumerable others follow.

Again, because the sciences of things divine and human are full of quarrels and controversies, it cannot be concluded therefrom that the whole of the subject-matter with which they deal is uncertain. There have been many whose zeal for controversy was such that they even scoffed at geometrical proof. Sextus Empiricus[19] and other Sceptics whom you quote say that it is false that the whole is greater than its part, and they pass similar judgment on other axioms.

However, allowing and granting that in default of proof we must be content with the probable, I say that a probable proof must be such that, although it is open to doubt, it cannot be contradicted; for that which can be contradicted is akin not to truth, but to falsehood. If, for example, I say that Peter is alive, because I saw him yesterday in good health, this is indeed probable in so far as nobody is able to contradict me. But if somebody else says that yesterday he saw Peter unconscious, and that he believes that since then Peter has died, he makes my statement seem false. That your conjecture regarding spectres and ghosts is false and has not even a show of truth, I have demonstrated so clearly that I find nothing in your reply worth taking up.

To your question as to whether I have as clear an idea of God as of a triangle, I reply in the affirmative. But if you ask me whether I have as clear an image of God as of a triangle, I reply in the negative. We cannot imagine God, but we can apprehend him by the intellect. Here it should be observed that I do not claim to have complete knowledge of God, but I do understand some of his attributes—not indeed all of them, or the greater part—and it is certain that my ignorance of very many attributes does not prevent me from having knowledge of some of them. When I was studying Euclid's *Elements*, I understood early on that the three angles of a triangle are equal to two right angles, and I clearly perceived this property of a triangle although I was ignorant of many others.

As regards spectres and ghosts, I have hitherto not heard of any intelligible property of theirs; I have heard only of fantasies beyond anyone's understanding. In saying that spectres and ghosts here below (I follow your usage of words, though I do not know why matter here below should be inferior to matter above) are made of very tenuous, rarified and subtle substance, you seem to be speaking of spiders' webs, air, or mist. To say that they are invisible is, in my view, tantamount to saying not what they are, but what they are not. But perhaps you wish to indicate that they render themselves visible or invisible as and when they please, and that the imagination will find no more difficulty in this than in other impossibilities.

19. Third-century Greek sceptical philosopher. His writings were influential among Renaissance sceptical writers.

The authority of Plato, Aristotle and Socrates carries little weight with me. I should have been surprised if you had produced Epicurus, Democritus, Lucretius, or one of the Atomists or defenders of the atomic theory. It is not surprising that those who have thought up occult qualities, intentional species, substantial forms and a thousand more bits of nonsense should have devised spectres and ghosts and given credence to old wives' tales with a view to disparaging the authority of Democritus, whose high reputation they so envied that they burned all the books that he had published with much acclaim. If you are minded to put your trust in such people, what reason have you to deny the miracles of the Holy Virgin and all the saints? These have been reported by so many renowned philosophers, theologians and historians that I could produce at least a hundred of the latter to scarcely one of the former.

In conclusion, my dear Sir, I find I have gone further than I intended, and I will trouble you no longer with matters which I know you will not concede, your first principles being far different from my own.

October 1674

Letter 58 (in part)

To the learned and wise G. H.
Schuller[20] from Benedict de Spinoza.

Dear Sir,

Our friend J.R.[21] has sent me the letter which you were kind enough to write to me, together with your friend's estimation of the views expressed by Descartes and myself on the question of free will. I was very glad to have them. Although I am at present fully occupied with other matters and my health is causing me some concern, I feel impelled by your singular courtesy and by your devotion to truth, which I particularly esteem, to satisfy your wish as far as my slender abilities allow. . . .

I now pass on to that definition of freedom which he ascribes to me, but I do not know whence he obtained it. I say that that thing is free which exists and acts solely from the necessity of its own nature, and I say that that thing is constrained (coactus) which is determined by

---

20. G. H. Schuller, a physician with philosophical leanings, served as Spinoza's doctor and was the only person present when Spinoza died. Shortly before the writing of this letter, Schuller had received a letter from the German philosopher and mathematician E. W. Tschirnhaus, who had raised several questions about Spinoza's views on free-will. Schuller gave the letter to Spinoza who in turn replied to Schuller.

21. Jan Rieuwertsz was Spinoza's publisher.

another to exist and to act in a fixed and determinate way. For example, although God exists necessarily, he nevertheless exists freely because he exists from the sole necessity of his own nature. Similarly, too, God freely understands himself and all things absolutely, because it follows from the sole necessity of his nature that he should understand all things. So you see that I place freedom, not in free decision, but in free necessity.

However, let us move down to created things, which are all determined by external causes to exist and to act in a fixed and determinate way. To understand this clearly, let us take a very simple example. A stone receives from the impulsion of an external cause a fixed quantity of motion whereby it will continue necessarily to move when the impulsion of the external cause has ceased. The stone's continuance in motion is constrained, not because it is necessary, but because it must be defined by the impulsion received from the external cause. What here applies to the stone must be understood of every individual thing, however complex its structure and varied its functions. For every single thing is necessarily determined by an external cause to exist and to act in a fixed and determinate way.

Furthermore, conceive, if you please, that while continuing in motion the stone thinks, and knows that it is endeavouring, as far as in it lies, to continue in motion. Now this stone, since it is conscious only of its endeavour and is not at all indifferent, will think it is completely free, and that it continues in motion for no other reason than that it so wishes. This, then, is that human freedom which all men boast of possessing, and which consists solely in this, that men are conscious of their desire and unaware of the causes by which they are determined. In the same way a baby thinks that it freely desires milk, an angry child revenge, and a coward flight. Again, a drunken man believes that it is from free decision that he says what he later, when sober, would wish to have concealed. So, too, the delirious, the loquacious, and many others of this kind believe that they act from free decision, and are not carried away by impulse. Since this prejudice is innate in all men, they cannot easily be rid of it. For although experience teaches us again and again that nothing is less within men's power than to moderate their appetites, and that frequently, when subject to conflicting emotions, they see the better course and pursue the worse, they nevertheless believe themselves to be free, a belief which stems from the fact that in some cases our desire has no great force and can easily be checked by the recurrence to mind of some other thing which is frequently in our thoughts.

I have now, if I am not mistaken, sufficiently set forth my views on free and constrained necessity and on the alleged human freedom, and with this your friend's objections are readily answered. For when he says, along with Descartes, that the free man is he who is not constrained by any external cause, if by constrained he means acting against one's will, I agree that in some instances we are in no way constrained and that in this sense we have free will. But if by constrained he means acting necessarily, although not against one's will, I deny that in any instance we are free, as I have explained above.

But your friend, on the contrary, asserts that "we can employ our rational faculty in complete freedom, that is, absolutely," in which assertion he is somewhat overconfident. "For who," he goes on to say, "could deny, without contradicting his own consciousness, that with my thoughts I can think that I want to write, or do not want to write?" I should very much like to know what consciousness he is talking about, apart from that which I illustrated above with the example of a stone. For my part, not to contradict my own consciousness—that is, my reason and experience—and not to encourage prejudice and ignorance, I deny that, by any absolute power of thought, I can think that I wish, or do not wish, to write. But I appeal to the consciousness of the man himself, who has doubtless experienced in dreams that he has not the power to think that he wishes, or does not wish, to write; and that, when he dreams that he wishes to write, he does not have the power not to dream that he wishes to write. I think that he must likewise have experienced that the mind is not at all times equally fitted to thinking of the same object; but that as the body is more fitted to have the image of this or that object aroused in it, so the mind is more apt to regard this or that object.

When he further adds that the causes of his resolving to write have indeed impelled him to write, but have not constrained him, if you will weigh the matter impartially he means no more than this, that his mind was at the time in such a state that causes which might not have swayed him at other times—as when he is assailed by some strong emotion— were at this time able to sway him. That is, causes which might not have constrained him at other times did in fact constrain him then, not to write against his will, but necessarily to wish to write.

When he goes on to say that "if we were constrained by external causes, nobody could acquire the habit of virtue," I do not know who told him that we cannot be of strong and constant mind from the necessity of fate, but only from free will.

As to his final remark, that "on this basis all wickedness would be excusable," what of it? Wicked men are no less to be feared and no less dangerous when they are necessarily wicked. But on this point please see my Appendix to Books 1 and 2 of *Principia Cartesiana* demonstrated in geometric form, Part II, Chapter 8.

Finally, I should like your friend who raises these objections to tell me how he reconciles the human virtue that springs from free will with God's pre-ordainment. If he admits with Descartes that he does not know how to affect this reconciliation, then he is trying to hurl against me the weapon by which he himself is transfixed. But to no purpose. If you will examine my opinions attentively, you will see that they are quite consistent.

October 1674

Letter 64

Translator's Note:

In Letter 63, Schuller had written to Spinoza conveying as an intermediary some additional difficulties raised by Tschirnhaus. These can be summarised in the following four problems.

1. "Can it be proved positively, not by *reductio ad absurdum*, that we cannot know any more attributes of God than Thought and Extension? Further, does it therefore follow that on their side creatures consisting of other attributes cannot conceive Extension, and that therefore there must be as many worlds as there are attributes of God? . . .

2. Since God's intellect differs from ours both in essence and in existence, it will have nothing in common with our intellect, and therefore God's intellect cannot be the cause of our intellect.

3. In the Scholium to Proposition 10,I, you say that nothing in Nature is clearer than that every entity must be conceived under some attribute, and that the more it has of reality and being, the more attributes belong to it. It would seem to follow that there are entities having three, four, or more attributes; yet one might have gathered from your proofs that every single entity consists of only two attributes, a certain attribute of God, and the idea of that attribute.

4. I should like to have examples of those things that are directly produced by God and those that are produced through the medium of some infinite modification. Of the first kind there are, I think, Thought and Extension; of the latter, intellect in Thought, motion in Extension, etc."[22]

To the learned and wise G. H.
Schuller. From Benedict de Spinoza

My dear Sir,

I am glad that you have at last found opportunity to favour me with one of your letters, always most welcome to me. I earnestly beg you to do so regularly . . . etc.

And now to the questions you raise. To the first I say that the human mind can acquire knowledge only of those things which the idea of the actually existing body involves, or which can be inferred from this idea. For the potency of a thing is defined solely by its essence (Prop.7, Part III, Ethics); however, the essence of mind (Prop.13,II) consists sole-

22. An allusion to Spinoza's doctrine of immediate and mediate infinite modes (*Ethics* I, Props. 21-23)

ly in its being the idea of an actually existing body, and therefore the mind's potency of understanding extends only as far as that which this idea of the body contains within itself, or which follows therefrom. Now this idea of the body involves and expresses no other attributes of God than Extension and Thought. For its ideate (ideatum), to wit, body (Prop.6,II), has God for its cause in so far as he is considered under the attribute of Extension, and not under any other attribute. So (Ax.6,I) this idea of the body involves knowledge of God only in so far as he is considered under the attribute of Extension. Again, this idea, in so far as it is a mode of thinking, also has God for its cause (same Prop.) in so far as he is a thinking thing, and not in so far as he is considered under any other attribute. Therefore (same Axiom) the idea of this idea involves knowledge of God in so far as he is considered under the attribute of Thought, and not under any other attribute. It is therefore clear that the human mind, —i.e. the idea of the human body—involves and expresses no other attributes of God except these two. Now (by Prop.10,I) no other attribute of God can be inferred or conceived from these two attributes, or from their affections. So I conclude that the human mind can attain knowledge of no other attribute of God than these two, which was the point at issue. With regard to your further question as to whether there must be as many worlds as there are attributes, I refer you to the Scholium on Prop.7,II, of the *Ethics*.

Apart from this proof, the proposition could be more readily demonstrated by reductio ad absurdum, a style of proof I usually prefer to the other in the case of a negative proposition, as being more appropriate in character. But you ask for a positive proof only, and so I pass on to the second question, which asks whether, when both essence and existence are different, one thing can be produced by another, seeing that things that differ thus from one another appear to have nothing in common. I reply that since all particular things, except those that are produced by like things, differ from their causes both in essence and existence, I see no difficulty here. As to the sense in which I understand God to be the efficient cause both of the essence and existence of things, I think I have made this quite clear in the Scholium and Corollary to Prop.25,I, of the *Ethics*.

The axiom in the Scholium to Prop.10,I, as I indicated at the end of the said Scholium, derives from the idea we have of an absolutely infinite Entity, and not from the fact that there are, or may be, entities having three, four, or more attributes.

Lastly, the examples you ask for of the first kind are: in the case of Thought, absolutely infinite intellect; in the case of Extension, motion and rest. An example of the second kind is the face[23] of the whole

23. The Latin word 'facies' is difficult to translate in this context. Most likely the whole phrase 'the face of the universe' is metaphorical. (A similar expression occurs in Seneca's *Moral Letters*, Number 33.) By this phrase Spinoza seems to be referring to the general form, or complexion, of the universe, which remains constant throughout change. It should be noted that Spinoza scholars have given a variety of interpretations to this expression.

universe, which, although varying in infinite ways, yet remains the same. See Scholium to Lemma 7 preceding Prop.14,II.

Thus, most excellent Sir, I think I have answered your objections and those of your friend. If you think there still remains any difficulty, I hope you will not hesitate to tell me, so that I may remove it if I can.

July 29, 1675

Letter 78

To the distinguished and learned Henry Oldenburg from Benedict de Spinoza.

Distinguished Sir,

When I said in my previous letter that the reason why we are without excuse is that we are in God's power as clay in the hands of the potter, I meant to be understood in this sense, that no one can accuse God for having given him a weak nature or a feeble character. For just as it would be absurd for a circle to complain that God has not given it the properties of a sphere, or a child suffering from kidney-stone that God has not given it a healthy body, it would be equally absurd for a man of feeble character to complain that God has denied him strength of spirit and true knowledge and love of God, and has given him so weak a nature that he cannot contain or control his desires. In the case of each thing, it is only that which follows necessarily from its given cause that is within its competence. That it is not within the competence of any man's nature that he should be of strong character, and that it is no more within our power to have a healthy body than to have a healthy mind, nobody can deny without flying in the face of both experience and reason.

"But," you urge, "if men sin from the necessity of their nature, they are therefore excusable." You do not explain what conclusion you wish to draw from this. Is it that God cannot be angry with them, or that they are worthy of blessedness, that is, the knowledge and love of God? If the former, I entirely agree that God is not angry, and that all things happen in accordance with his will. But I deny that on that account all men ought to be blessed; for men may be excusable, but nevertheless be without blessedness, and afflicted in many ways. A horse is excusable for being a horse, and not a man; nevertheless he needs must be a horse, and not a man. He who goes mad from the bite of a dog is to be excused; still, it is right that he should die of suffocation. Finally, he who cannot control his desires and keep them in check through fear of the law, although he also is to be excused for his weakness, nevertheless cannot enjoy tranquillity of mind and the knowledge and love of God, but of necessity he is lost. I do not think I need here to remind you that Scripture, when it says that God is angry with sinners, that he is a judge who takes cognisance of the actions of men, decides, and passes sentence, is speaking in merely human terms according to the accepted beliefs of the multitude; for its aim is not to teach philosophy, nor to make men learned, but to make them obedient.

I fail to see how you come to think that, by equating miracles with ignorance, I am circumscribing God's power and man's knowledge within the same bounds.

The passion, death, and burial of Christ I accept literally, as you do, but His resurrection I understand in an allegorical sense. I do indeed admit that this is narrated by the Evangelists with such detail that we cannot deny that the Evangelists themselves believed that the body of Christ rose again and ascended to heaven to sit at God's right hand, and that they believed that this could also have been seen by unbelievers, if they had been present at the place where Christ appeared to the disciples. Nevertheless, without impairing the doctrine of the Gospels, i.e. its moral training, they could have been deceived, as was the case with other Prophets, examples of which I gave in my last letter. Paul, to whom Christ also appeared later, rejoices that he knew Christ not after the flesh, but after the spirit. Farewell, honourable Sir, and believe me yours in all zeal and affection.

February 7, 1676

Letter 81

Translator's Note:

In Letter 80 Tschirnhaus has raised two questions. First, how can the existence of bodies, with their particular motion and figure, be deduced a priori from a consideration of Extension as such? Secondly, he quotes from Spinoza's Letter 12 on the Infinite (addressed to Ludwig Meyer), "Now they do not draw the conclusion that it is because of the multitude of parts that such things exceed all number," and asks for further elucidation. To understand the point at issue, Letter 12 should be consulted with its diagram of two non-concentric circles.

To the most noble and learned Ehrenfried
Walter von Tchirnhaus

Most Noble Sir,

As to what I stated in my letter regarding the infinite, that it is not from the multitude of parts that their infinity is inferred, this is evident from the fact that if infinity were inferred from the multitude of parts, it would be impossible for us to conceive a greater multitude of parts, but this multitude of parts ought to be greater than any given number. This is untrue, for in the total space intervening between the two non-concentric circles, we conceive twice as many parts as in half that space, and yet the number of parts in both the half-space and the whole space exceeds any assignable number.

On the other point, from Extension as Decartes conceives it—that is, as an inert mass—it is not merely difficult, as you say, to prove the existence of bodies, but quite impossible. For inert matter, regarded simply in itself, will continue in a state of rest, and will not be set in motion unless by a more powerful external cause. For this reason I have not hesitated to say on a former occasion that Descartes' principles of natural things are without value, not to say absurd.

                                                                    May 5, 1676

Letter 83

Translator's Note:

In Letter 82 Tschirnhaus repeats his request for an explanation as to how 'the varity of things' can be deduced a priori from the conception of Extension. He mentions Descartes' view which equates Extension with inert matter, motion being introduced externally by some mysterious action of God, and asks for Spinoza's view. He observes that in mathematics he finds that from the definition of a thing only one property can be deduced, and that further properties can be obtained only by relating the thing to other things.

To the most noble and learned Ehrenfried
Walter von Tschirnhaus

Most Noble Sir,

With regard to your question as to whether the variety of things can be demonstrated a priori solely from the conception of Extension, I believe I have already shown sufficiently clearly that this is impossible, and that therefore Descartes is wrong in defining matter through Extension; it must be explicated through an attribute that expresses eternal and infinite essence. But perhaps I shall discuss this more clearly with you some other time, if I live that long. For hitherto there has been no opportunity for me to arrange these matters in proper order.

As to your further point, that from the definition of each thing considered in itself we can deduce no more than one property, this may be the case with the most simple things, or with constructs of reason (entia rationis), under which I classify figures, but not with real things. For from the mere fact that I define God as a Being to whose essence belongs existence, I infer several properties of him, namely, that he exists necessarily, that he is unique, immutable, infinite, etc. I could adduce several more examples of this kind, which I omit for the present.

Finally, will you please let me know whether Mr. Huet's Treatise (the one he wrote against my Tractatus Theologico-Politicus), which you have previously mentioned, has now been published, and whether you can send me a copy, and also whether you now know what are the new discoveries about refraction.

And so farewell, most Noble Sir, and continue to love, etc.

July 15, 1676

SELECTED BIBLIOGRAPHY

I. BIBLIOGRAPHIES

Curley, Edwin M. Bibliography on recent work in Spinoza, included in *Spinoza: Essays in Interpretation,* ed. E. Freeman & M. Mandelbaum. La Salle, Illinois: Open Court Press, 1973, 267–316.

Oko, Adolph S. *The Spinoza Bibliography.* Boston: G.K. Hall, 1964.

Preposiet, Jean. *Bibliographie Spinoziste.* Besançon: Université de Besançon, 1974.

Wetlesen, Jon. *A Spinoza Bibliography,* 1940–1970. Oslo: Universitets-forlaget, 1971.

II. BIOGRAPHICAL MATERIAL

Dunin-Borkowski, S. *Spinoza.* Munster: Aschendorff, 1910. 4 vols.

Freudenthal, J. *Die Lebensgeschichte Spinozas in Quellenschriften, Urkunden und nichtamtlichen Nachrichten.* Leipzig: Verlag von Veit, 1899.

————. *Spinoza, sein Leben und seine Lehre.* Stuttgart: Frommanns Verlag, 1904. 2 vols.

Meinsma, K. O. *Spinoza et son cercle.* Trans. S. Roosenburg. Paris: Vrin, 1983.

Popkin, Richard. "Spinoza's Earliest Philosophical Years", *Studia Spinozana* 4 (1988).

Revah, I.S. *Spinoza et Juan de Prado.* Paris, 1959.

Vaz Dias, A.M., and W.F. Van der Tak. "Spinoza: Merchant and Autodidact", *Studia Rosenthalia* 16 (1982).

III. SPINOZA'S WORKS

Original Latin

Opera, ed. Carl Gebhardt. Heidelberg: C. Winter, 1972. Reprint of 1925 edition. 4 vols.

English Translations

The Collected Works of Spinoza. Trans. and edited by Edwin Curley. Princeton: Princeton University Press, 1985. Vol. 1. Contains all the early works of Spinoza including the *Ethics.*

The Correspondence of Spinoza. Trans. and edited by Abraham Wolf. New York: Russell & Russell. 1966.

IV. GENERAL STUDIES OF SPINOZA'S PHILOSOPHY

Allison, Henry. *Benedictus de Spinoza: An Introduction.* New Haven, Conn.: Yale University Press, 1987.

Delahunty, R.J. *Spinoza.* London: Routledge and Kegan Paul, 1985.

Deleuze, Gilles. *Expressionism in Philosophy: Spinoza.* Trans. by M. Joughin. New York: Zone Books, 1990.

Donagan, Alan. *Spinoza.* Chicago: University of Chicago Press, 1988.

Hallett, H. Foster. *Benedict de Spinoza. The Elements of his Philosophy.* London: Athlone Press, 1957.

Hampshire, Stuart. *Spinoza.* 3rd ed. Baltimore: Penguin, 1962.

Harris, E. *Salvation from Despair.* The Hague: M. Nijhoff, 1973.

McKeon, Richard Peter. *The Philosophy of Spinoza. The Unity of his Thought.* New York: Longmans, Green & Co., 1928.

Roth, Leon. *Spinoza.* London: Allen & Unwin, 1954.

V. COMMENTARIES ON THE *ETHICS*

Bennett, Jonathan. *A Study of Spinoza's Ethics.* Indianapolis: Hackett, 1984.

Curley, E. *Behind the Geometrical Method.* Princeton: Princeton University Press, 1988.

Gueroult, Martial. *Spinoza, Tome I: Dieu (Ethique I).* Paris: Aubier Montaigne, 1968.

———. *Tome II: L'Ame.* Paris: Aubier Montaigne, 1974.

Joachim, Harold Henry. *A Study of the Ethics of Spinoza (Ethica ordine geometrica demonstrata).* New York: Russell & Russell, 1964. Reprint of 1901 edition.

Wolfson, Harry Austryn. *The Philosophy of Spinoza,* 2 vols. New York: Schocken, 1969. Reprint of 1934 edition.

VI. COMMENTARIES AND STUDIES ON THE *TREATISE ON THE EMENDATION OF THE INTELLECT*

Eisenberg, Paul. "How to Understand *De Intellectus Emendatione*", *Journal of the History of Philosophy* 9 (1971), pp. 171–91.

Joachim, Harold. *Spinoza's Tractatus de Intellectus Emendatione.* London: Oxford University Press, 1940.

VII. STUDIES ON SPECIAL TOPICS IN THE *ETHICS*

A. *Metaphysics*

Charlton, William. "Spinoza's Monism", *Philosophical Review* 90 (1981), pp. 503–29.

Curley, E.M. *Spinoza's Metaphysics: An Essay in Interpretation.* Cambridge: Harvard University Press, 1969.

Friedman, Joel. "How the Finite Follows from the Infinite in Spinoza's Metaphysical System", *Synthese* 69 (1986), pp. 371–407.

Haserot, F.S. "Spinoza's Definitions of Attribute", *Philosophical Review,* vol. 62 (1953), pp. 499–513.

Jarret, Charles. "The Concept of Substance and Mode in Spinoza", *Philosophia* (Israel) 7 (1977), pp. 83–105.

———. "Some Remarks on the 'Objective' and 'Subjective' Interpretation of the Attribute", *Inquiry* 20 (1977), pp. 447–56.

B. *Theory of Mind and Epistemology*

Bend, J.G. van der (ed.). *Spinoza on Knowing, Being and Freedom; Proceedings of the Spinoza Symposium at the International School of Philosophy in the Netherlands, Leiden, September 1973.* Assen, Netherlands: Van Gorcum, 1974.

Doney, Willis. "Spinoza on Philosophical Skepticism", *Monist* 55 (1971), pp. 617–35.

Frank, Isaac. "Spinoza's Logic of Inquiry: Rationalist or Experientalist?" in Kennington, R. (ed.) *The Philosophy of Baruch Spinoza.* Washington, D.C.: Catholic University of America, 1980, pp. 247–272.

Hubberling, H.G. *Spinoza's Methodology.* Assen, Netherlands: Van Gorcum, 1964.

Mark, T.C. *Spinoza's Theory of Truth.* New York: Columbia University Press, 1972.

Matson, W.I. "Spinoza's Theory of Mind", *Monist,* 55 (1971), pp. 567–78.

Odegard, Douglas. "The Body Identical with the Human Mind: A Problem in Spinoza's Philosophy", *Monist* 55 (1971), pp. 579–601.

Parkinson, G.H.P. *Spinoza's Theory of Knowledge.* Oxford: Clarendon Press, 1954.

Studia Spinozana 2 (1986).

C. *Moral Philosophy*

Bidney, David. *The Psychology and Ethics of Spinoza: A Study in the History and Logic of Ideas.* 2nd ed. New York: Russell & Russell, 1962.

Broad, C.D. *Five Types of Ethical Theory.* Paterson, N.J.: Littlefield and Adams, 1954. Chapter 2.

Hampshire, Stuart. "Spinoza and the Idea of Freedom", *Proceedings of the British Academy* 46 (1960), pp. 195–215.

————. "Spinoza's Theory of Human Freedom", *Monist* 55 (1971), pp. 554–66.

Wetlesen, J. *The Sage & The Way.* Assen, Netherlands: Van Gorcum, 1979.

————. ed. *Spinoza's Philosophy of Man.* Assen, Netherlands: Van Gorcum, 1978.

VIII. ANTHOLOGIES OF CRITICAL STUDIES OF SPINOZA

Grene, M. (ed.). *Spinoza: A Collection of Critical Essays.* Garden City, N.Y.: Anchor Books, 1973.

Grene, Marjorie, and Debra Nails. *Spinoza and the Sciences.* Boston Studies in the Philosophy of Science vol. 90 (1986).

Inquiry XII #1 (Spring, 1969).

Kashap, S.P. (ed.). *Studies in Spinoza, Critical and Interpretive Essays.* Berkeley, California: University of Calif. Press, 1972.

Kennington, R. (ed.). *The Philosophy of Baruch Spinoza.* Washington, D.C.: Catholic University of America, 1980.

Freeman, E. and Mandelbaum, M., (eds.). *Spinoza: Essays in Interpretation.* La Salle, Illinois: Open Court Press, 1973.

Shahan, R. and Biro, J. (eds.). *Spinoza: New Perspectives.* Norman, Oklahoma: University of Oklahoma Press, 1978.

Studia Spinozana 1–6.

Wilbur, J.B., (ed.). *Spinoza's Metaphysics: Essays in Critical Appreciation.* Assen, Netherlands: Van Gorcum, 1976.